The EVERYTHING
Baby Names Book
2nd Edition

Dear Reader,

Congratulations! Expecting a new baby is an exciting time. While there's a lot to prepare for, it is a journey filled with hopeful anticipation and fun. Selecting your baby's name should be a joyful and fascinating process, though not always an easy one. With so many factors and choices to consider, it might seem overwhelming at times. But with *The Everything® Baby Names Book* at hand, you are now well equipped to navigate the vast sea of names so you can hone in on just the right one for your new bundle of joy.

Uma? River? Oprah? Tiger? What about a simple Susan or Jack? Whether trendy, one of a kind, or old fashioned, your child's name will likely be a reflection of the times as well as your own personal tastes and values. One thing that all parents have in common is wanting the best for their child, so the best choice you can make when selecting your baby's name will be the one that, ultimately, feels right in your heart.

So grab a pad and a pen, start skimming through the book's name dictionary and sidebars, select your favorite choices, and, most of all, enjoy the process. Your new little star is waiting to be named!

June Rifkin

The EVERYTHING® Series

Editorial

Publishing Director	Gary M. Krebs
Associate Managing Editor	Laura M. Daly
Associate Copy Chief	Brett Palana-Shanahan
Acquisitions Editor	Kate Burgo
Development Editor	Katie McDonough
Associate Production Editor	Casey Ebert

Production

Director of Manufacturing	Susan Beale
Associate Director of Production	Michelle Roy Kelly
Cover Design	Paul Beatrice Matt LeBlanc Erick DaCosta
Design and Layout	Colleen Cunningham Holly Curtis Sorae Lee
Series Cover Artist	Barry Littmann
Interior illustrations	Michelle Dorenkamp

THE

EVERYTHING®

BABY NAMES
BOOK

2ND EDITION

Pick the perfect name for your baby

June Rifkin

Adams Media
Avon, Massachusetts

For all you parents-to-be.
May the process of selecting a name for your baby be fun and enlightening!
. . . .

An Everything® Series Book.
Everything® and everything.com® are registered trademarks of F+W Publications, Inc.

Published by Adams Media, an F+W Publications Company
57 Littlefield Street, Avon, MA 02322 U.S.A.
www.adamsmedia.com

ISBN: 1-59337-578-6

Printed in the United States of America.

J I H G F E D C B A

Library of Congress Cataloging-in-Publication Data
Rifkin, June.
The everything baby names book : pick the
perfect name for your baby.—2nd ed. / June Rifkin.
p. cm.—(An everything series book)
Rev. ed. of: The everything baby names book / Lisa Shaw. ©1997.
ISBN 1-59337-578-6
1. Names, Personal—Dictionaries. I. Rogak, Lisa, Everything baby
names book. II. Title. III. Series: Everything series.
CS2377.S43 2006
929.4'4—dc22
2005026080

This publication is designed to provide accurate and authoritative information with regard to the subject matter covered. It is sold with the understanding that the publisher is not engaged in rendering legal, accounting, or other professional advice. If legal advice or other expert assistance is required, the services of a competent professional person should be sought.

   —From a *Declaration of Principles* jointly adopted by a Committee of the American Bar Association and a Committee of Publishers and Associations

Many of the designations used by manufacturers and sellers to distinguish their products are claimed as trademarks. Where those designations appear in this book and Adams Media was aware of a trademark claim, the designations have been printed with initial capital letters.

This book is available at quantity discounts for bulk purchases.
For information, please call 1-800-872-5627.

contents

>

acknowledgments

Many thanks to Everything® Series editor Kate Burgo for her ever-cheerful and accommodating assistance and input.

Special thanks to the following for their suggestions and name lists: Judy Frohman, Brenda Knight, Eve Marx, Leon Lewandowski, and Constance Stellas.

A nod to my son, Colin Spencer Clark (whose name I'm still happy with after seventeen years), who never failed to amuse me during the writing process with his continual queries of "What are you doing?"

Last, but not least, a big hug to Stuart H. for his support and "computer neck" relief.

Top Ten Things to Consider
When Choosing a Name for Your Baby

1. How popular is the name? In a school full of Jacobs and Emilys, your son or daughter might become Jacob P. or Emily W. or, even worse, "little Jacob" or "chubby Emily."

2. Avoid odd spellings when possible. Others will almost always spell "Soozyn" as the more conventional "Susan."

3. Be mindful of nicknames. Your daughter Isabella might wind up becoming "Izzy" and your son Leonardo, "Nardo."

4. Beware of names that rhyme with something strange (for example, a pretty name like "June" rhymes with "goon" and "baboon") or that rhyme with your last name, like "Mark Clark" or "Toni Baroni."

5. Pair it up with your last name and see how it sounds. "Chantal Levesque" rolls off the tongue a lot more smoothly than "Chantal Berkowitz."

6. Avoid names that might prompt teasing from other kids. "Luna" (meaning "moon") is lovely, but can sound like "Looney" to a bully.

7. Honor your heritage but also honor your child. While you're proud of your cultural and ethnic roots, an American-born child named Ionut Pupazon may be chuckled at among peers.

8. Note those initials. Samantha Emily Xavier and Patrick Ian Granville will become S.E.X. and P.I.G. on a monogrammed sweater.

9. It's okay to ask for opinions from family and friends, but remember that the ultimate choice is the one you (and your partner) like best.

10. A name is for life. Choose well and wisely.

introduction

YOU'RE ABOUT TO WELCOME a new baby into your life, and this bundle of joy needs a name. Seems easy to figure out, right? Think back to your teens when you scribbled down dozens of great names and kept them on file for when you had a baby. If you've found your old list and still love those names, you've got a head start. If not, the search is on.

To get started, create a list of all the important factors you want to consider in choosing a name for your baby. Ask yourself the following questions:

- Is there someone you care about or admire—living or deceased—whom you want your baby to be named after?
- Are you only considering using names that begin with a particular letter of the alphabet?
- Is there a special place that you might consider using as a name?
- Is there something you're passionate about that would make a great name?
- If you're spiritual, would your prefer a name that reflects your religious heritage?
- Do you feel a strong enough affinity to your (or your partner's) family heritage to consider a more ethnic or culturally influenced name?
- How crucial is the meaning of a name to you?

Thinking about your priorities and making note of these criteria will help you narrow your focus considerably.

Do your tastes run traditional or trendy? Traditional names remain popular among the trendy choices, like Ethan, Madison, and Ashley. But trendy has its place, too. Sawyer, Lexi, Ryder, and Destiny seem more common than ever among the tried and true. If you want to be traditional *and* trendy, creative spellings or hybrid names might be an option: Michael becomes "Mykal" and Emily becomes "Emalee"; David and Shawn merge into "Dashawn;" and Jessica and Lynn combine to form "Jessalyn."

Something else to consider is how your child might connect with his or her name. Frank Zappa, the late rock music legend, had four children, whom he named Moon Unit, Dweezil, Ahmet Emuukah Rodan, and Diva Muffin. The kids actually thrived well through the years—Moon had a hit record and Dweezil had a cooking show on television. The uniqueness of their names built character. But if Dad had simply been a hardworking insurance broker in Cincinnati, the kids would likely have had quite a different destiny and maybe a few identity issues to boot.

Names are our identities. Even if we don't love our names, most of us learn to live with them and form our personas around them. So, as you search for the right name for your baby, keep in mind how your own name may have shaped your life. Finally, use the name dictionary to learn the origins and meanings of different names. Check out the sidebars of name lists and tips, too. Make note of the names you like and have your partner do the same—or do it together! Have a discussion and narrow your choices. Then, get ready for the big birthday!

boys'
names

AADI (Hindu) Beginning.

AALAM (Arabic) Great spirit.

AARON (Hebrew) Exalted; enlightened. *Notables:* U.S. Vice-President Aaron Burr; American composer Aaron Copland; singer Aaron Neville; producer Aaron Spelling. *Variations:* Aahron, Aaran, Aaren, Aarao, Aarin, Aeron, Aharon, Ahran, Ahren, Arek, Aran, Aren, Aron, Aronek, Aronne, Aronos, Arran, Arren, Arrin, Arron.

AASIM (Hindu) God's grace.

ABADDON (Hebrew) Knows God.

ABBA (Hebrew) Father. *Notables:* Israeli statesman Abba Eban. *Variations:* Abbas.

ABBEY (Hebrew) A form of Abe or Abraham. *Notables:* activist Abbie Hoffman. *Variations:* Abbe, Abbie, Abby.

ABBOTT (Hebrew) Father. *Variations:* Abbitt, Abbot, Abott.

ABDUL (Arabic) Servant of God. *Variations:* Abdal, Abdel, Abdell, Abdoul.

ABDULAZIZ (Arabic) Servant of friend. *Variations:* Abdalazim, Abdalaziz.

ABDULLAH (Arabic) Servant of Allah. *Variations:* Abdalah, Abdalla, Abdulahi, Abdulla, Abdullah, Abdulaziz.

ABE Variation of Abraham. *Notables:* Actor Abe Vigoda. *Variations:* Abey, Abie.

ABEL (Hebrew) Breathing spirit or breath. *Variations:* Abell, Able, Avel.

ABELARD (Old German) Highborn and steadfast. *Variations:* Ab, Abalard, Abelardo, Abilard.

ABERDEEN (Scottish) Place name in Scotland.

ABERLIN (German) Having ambition.

ABIAH (Hebrew) Child of God. *Variations:* Abia, Aviya.

ABIEL (Hebrew) God is my father. *Variations:* Abyel, Ahbiel, Aviel.

ABIR (Hebrew) Strong.

ABNER (Hebrew) Father of light. Biblical. *Variations:* Ab, Aviner, Avner.

ABRAHAM (Hebrew) Father of many. *Notables:* Biblical patriarch Abraham; U.S. President Abraham Lincoln. *Variations:* Abe, Abrahamo, Abrahan, Abram, Abramo,

Abran, Abrao, Avraham, Avram, Avrum, Ibrahim.

ABRAM (Hebrew) Form of Abraham. *Variations:* Abrams, Avram, Avrom.

ABSALOM (Hebrew) Father of peace. *Variations:* Absalaam, Absalon.

ACACIUS (Latin) Blameless.

ACE (Latin) Unity. Nickname given to one who excels. *Notables:* Kiss lead guitarist Ace Frehley. *Variations:* Acer, Acey, Acie.

ACESTES (Greek) Mythological Trojan king.

ACHAIUS (Irish) Horseman.

ACHILLES (Greek) Unknown meaning. *Notables:* Achilles, hero of Homer's *Iliad*. *Variations:* Achille, Achillios, Achillius, Akil, Akilles, Aquilles.

ACHIYA (Hebrew) God is my brother. *Variations:* Achiyahu, Ahia, Ahiah.

ACKERLEY (Old English) Oak meadow. *Variations:* Ackerlea, Ackerleigh, Ackleigh, Ackley.

ACTAEON (Greek) Ancient mythological figure.

ACTON (English) Town in Great Britain.

ADAIAH (Hebrew) Witness of God. *Variations:* Adaia, Adaya.

ADAIR (Scottish) Of the oak tree. *Variations:* Adaire, Adare.

top ten names of the 1880s

Boys	Girls
John	Mary
William	Anna
Charles	Elizabeth
George	Margaret
James	Minnie
Joseph	Emma
Frank	Martha
Henry	Alice
Thomas	Marie
Harry	Annie, Sarah (tie)

hawaiian names

Boys	Girls
Aikane	Akela
Ailani	Alani
Kahoku	Aloha
Kai	Iolana
Kale	Keilana
Kane	Kiana
Keona	Leilani
Makani	Noelani
Meka	Oliana
Palani	Roselani

ADAM (Hebrew) Man of the red earth. *Notables:* Comedian Adam Sandler; the Batman of television and movie fame, Adam West. *Variations:* Adamec, Adamek, Adamh, Adamik, Adamka, Adamko, Adamo, Adams, Adamson, Adamsson, Adan, Adao, Addam, Addams, Addamson, Addie, Addis, Addy, Adhamh, Adnet, Adnot.

ADAMNAN (Irish) Little Adam. *Variations:* Adhamhnan.

ADAR (Syrian) Ruler or prince; (Hebrew) Noble; fiery.

ADDISON (English) Son of Adam. *Variations:* Addis, Addy, Adison.

ADE (Nigerian) Royal.

ADEBEN (Ghanaian) Twelfth-born son.

ADELL (German) Noble. *Variations:* Adal, Adel.

ADELPHI (Greek) Brother.

ADIKA (Ghanaian) First child from second husband.

ADIL (Arabic) Fair.

ADIR (Hindu) Lightning.

ADITYA (Hindu) The sun. *Variations:* Aaditva.

ADIV (Hebrew) Gentle.

ADLAI (Hebrew) My witness. *Notables:* Politician Adlai Stevenson. *Variations:* Adalia, Adlay, Adley.

ADLER (English) Eagle. *Variations:* Addler, Adlar.

ADMON (Hebrew) Red peony.

ADNAN (Arabic) Settled. *Notables:* Arms dealer Adnan Khashoggi.

ADOLPH (German) Noble wolf. *Notables:* Adolph Hitler; beer maker Adolph Coors. *Variations:* Adolf, Adolfe, Adolfo, Adolfus, Adolphe, Adolphus, Dolph.

ADONIAH (Hebrew) The Lord is my God. *Variations:* Adon, Adonia, Adonijah, Adoniya, Adoniyah.

ADONIS (Greek) Handsome. *Variations:* Addonis, Adonnis.

ADRIAN (Latin) Dark. *Notables:* Actor Adrien Brody. *Variations:* Adrain, Adrean, Adren, Adriane, Adrien, Adrin, Adrion, Hadrian.

ADRIEL (Hebrew) God's flock. *Variations:* Adrial.

AENEAS (Greek) One who is praised. *Variations:* Aineas, Aineis, Eneas, Enneas.

AEOLUS (Greek) The changeable one. *Variations:* Aeolos, Aiolos, Aiolus.

AESON (Greek) Ancient mythological figure.

AFTON (English) From Afton, England. *Variations:* Aften.

AGAMEMNON (Greek) Working slowly.

AGOSTINO (Italian) Respected. Form of August.

AHAB (Hebrew) Father's brother.

AHEARN (Irish) Horse lord. *Variations:* Ahearne, Ahern.

AHMAD (Arabic) More deserving. *Variations:* Achmad, Achmed, Ahamad, Ahmed, Amad, Amed.

AIDAN (Irish) Fiery. *Notables:* Actor Aidan Quinn. *Variations:* Adan, Aden, Adin, Aiden, Aydan, Ayden, Aydn, Eden.

AIKEN (Old English) Made of oak. *Variations:* Aicken, Aikin, Aykin.

AILESH (Hindu) King of all.

AILILL (Irish) Sprite.

AINMIRE (Irish) Great lord.

AINSLEY (Scottish) His very own meadow. *Variations:* Ainsleigh, Ansley, Aynsley.

AISEA (Polynesian) God saves.

AJANI (Nigerian) He fights for possession.

AJAX (Greek) Warrior.

AKBAR (Arabic) Great.

AKE (Scandinavian) Ancestor. *Variations:* Age.

AKEEM (Arabic) Judging thoughtfully. *Variations:* Akim, Hakeem, Hakim.

AKELA (Hawaiian) Noble. *Variations:* Asera.

AKIHITO (Japanese) Bright.

AKIRA (Japanese) Intelligent. *Notables:* Japanese film director Akira Kurosawa.

AKIVA (Hebrew) Heel. *Variations:* Akavia, Akaviah, Akavya, Akiba, Kiba, Kiva.

AKONIIA (Hawaiian) The Lord is my God. *Variations:* Adoniia.

AL (Irish) Short for Alexander or Alan. *Notables:* Reverend Al Sharpton; parody singer/songwriter "Weird Al" Yankovic.

ALADDIN (Arabic) Very faithful. *Notables:* Aladdin is the hero of a story in the *Arabian Nights* popularized in the Walt Disney film *Aladdin.*

ALAN (Irish) Fair; handsome; rock. *Notables:* Composer Alan Jay Lerner; actor Alan Alda; hoopster Alan Iverson. *Variations:* Ailean, Ailin, Al, Alain, Aland, Alano, Alao, Alen, Alin, Allan, Allayne, Allen, Alleyn, Alleyne, Allin, Allon, Allyn, Alon, Alun.

ALANSON (Irish) Son of Alan. *Variations:* Allanson, Allenson.

ALARIC (German) Noble ruler. *Variations:* Alarick, Aleric, Alleric, Alric, Alrick.

ALASTAIR (Scottish) Derivative of Alexander. *Notables: Masterpiece Theatre*'s Alistair Cooke. *Variations:* Alasdair, Alasdaire, Alastaire, Alastare, Alester, Alistair, Alister, Allister.

ALBAN (Latin) From Alba. *Variations:* Albain, Albany, Albean, Albein, Alben.

ALBERT (Old English) Bright; brilliant. *Notables:* Physicist Albert Einstein; actors Albert Finney and Albert Brooks. *Variations:* Alberto, Albie, Albin, Albrecht.

ALBIN (Latin) Pale-skinned. *Variations:* Alben, Albino, Alby.

ALBION (Latin) White mountain.

ALCOTT (English) Old cottage. *Variations:* Alcot.

ALDEN (English) Old. *Variations:* Aldin, Aldon, Elden.

ALDO (Italian) Old. Italian form of Aldous.

ALDOUS (German) Old and wealthy. *Notables:* Writer Aldous Huxley. *Variations:* Aldos, Aldus.

ALDRED (English) Advisor. *Variations:* Aldrid, Eldred.

ALDRICH (English) An old and wise leader. *Variations:* Aldric, Aldridge, Eldridge.

ALDWIN (English) Old friend. *Variations:* Aldren, Aldryn, Aldwyn.

ALEC (Greek) Variation of Alexander. *Notables:* Actors Alec Guinness and Alec Baldwin. *Variations:* Aleck, Alek, Alic.

ALEX (Greek) Short form of Alexander. *Notables: Jeopardy* host Alex Trebek. *Variations:* Alix, Allex.

ALEXANDER (Greek) Protector; helper and defender of mankind. *Notables:* Greek ruler Alexander the Great; U.S. President Alexander Hamilton. *Variations:* Alasdair, Alastair, Alaster, Alec, Alejandro, Alejo, Alek, Alekos, Aleksander, Aleksandr, Alesandro, Alessandre, Alessandri, Alessandro, Alex, Alexandre, Alexandro, Alexandros, Alexei, Alexi, Alexio, Alik, Alisander, Alissander, Alissandre, Alistair, Alister, Alistir, Allistair, Allister, Allistir, Alsandair, Alsandare, Sacha, Sande, Sander, Sanders, Sanderson, Sandey, Sandie, Sandor, Sandy, Sascha, Sasha, Sashenka, Sashka, Saunders, Saunderson.

ALFIE (English) Short form of Alfred. *Variations:* Alfy.

ALFONSO (Spanish/Italian) Noble and ready. *Variations:* Alfons, Alfonsin, Alfonsus, Alfonz, Alfonzo, Alphonso, Alphonsus, Fonzie.

ALFORD (English) The old river ford.

ALFRED (English) Wise listener, counselor. *Notables:* Director Alfred Hitchcock; *Mad Magazine*'s Alfred E. Neuman; Nobel Prize originator Alfred Nobel. *Variations:* Alf, Alfie, Alfredo, Fred, Freddy, Fredo.

ALGERNON (Old French) Having a mustache. *Variations:* Algenon, Alger, Algie, Algin.

ALI (Arabic) Exalted. *Variations:* Aly.

occupations by name

Archer *archer*	Porter *gatekeeper*
Bailey *bailiff*	Sawyer *carpenter*
Barry *marksman*	Squire *landowner*
Baxter *baker*	Tanner *leather worker*
Brewster *beer maker*	Thatcher *roofer*
Chandler *candle maker*	Tucker *cloth cleaner*
Cooper *barrel maker*	Wainwright *wagon maker*
Faulkner *falcon trainer*	Waite *watchman*
Fletcher *bow and arrow maker*	Zeeman *sailor*
Mason *stoneworker*	

palindromes

These palindrome names are spelled the same forwards and backwards.

Boys	Girls
Abba	Anna
Asa	Ava
Bob	Elle
Gig	Eve
Otto	Nan
Pip	Viv

ALISON (English) Son of the highborn.

ALITZ (Hebrew) Happy. *Variations:* Aliz.

ALLAN (Irish) Handsome. Form of Alan.

ALLARD (English/French) Brave; noble one. *Variations:* Alard, Ellard.

ALLEN (Irish) Handsome. Form of Alan.

ALLON (Hebrew) Oak tree. *Variations:* Alon.

ALOIKI (Hawaiian) Famous war. *Variations:* Aloisi.

ALONZO (Spanish) Form of Alphonse. *Notables:* NBA's Alonzo Mourning. *Variations:* Alanzo, Alonso, Alonze, Elonso, Elonzo.

ALOYSIUS (German) Warrior. Form of Louis. *Variations:* Aloisius.

ALPHEUS (Greek) God of the river.

ALPHONSE (German) One who is ready to fight; noble. *Notables:* U.S. Senator Alphonse D'Amato; crime czar Alphonse "Al" Capone. *Variations:* Alfonse, Alfonso, Alfonze, Alfonzo, Alonzo, Alphonso.

ALSTON (English) Manor; settlement. *Variations:* Alstin, Allston.

ALSWORTH (English) From the estate.

ALTAIR (Greek) Bird; bright star.

ALTMAN (German) Old man. *Variations:* Altmann.

ALTON (English) One who lives in an old town. *Variations:* Aldon.

ALVARO (Spanish) Cautious. *Variations:* Alvarado, Alvarro.

ALVIN (German) Friend. *Notables:* Choreographer Alvin Ailey; writer Alvin Toffler. *Variations:* Ailwyn, Alion, Aluin, Aluino, Alva, Alvan, Alven, Alvie, Alvino, Alvy, Alvyn, Alwin, Alwyn, Alwynn, Aylwin.

AMADEUS (Latin) Beloved of God. *Notables:* Composer Wolfgang Amadeus Mozart. *Variations:* Amadeo, Amadio, Amado, Amedeo.

AMADO (Spanish) Loved. *Variations:* Amando, Amandus, Amato.

AMAHL (Hebrew) Hard worker. *Variations:* Amal, Amali.

AMARIAH (Hebrew) God has spoken. *Variations:* Amaria, Amariahu, Amarya, Amaryahu.

AMARILLO (Spanish) Yellow. *Variations:* Amarille, Amarilo.

AMASA (Hebrew) Hardship. *Variations:* Amasai, Amasia, Amasiah, Amasya, Amazu.

AMBROSE (Greek) Immortal being. *Notables:* Writer/journalist Ambrose Bierce. *Variations:* Ambroce, Ambrus.

AMERIGO (Italian) Ruler. *Notables:* Explorer Amerigo Vespucci. *Variations:* America, Americo, Americus, Ameriko.

AMES (French) Friend.

AMIEL (Hebrew) Lord of the people. *Variations:* Ammiel.

AMIN (Arabic) Trustworthy.

AMIR (Arabic) Prince. *Variations:* Ameer.

AMMAR (Arabic) Long life. *Variations:* Amar, Amari, Amario.

AMORY (German) Leader. *Variations:* Amery.

AMOS (Hebrew) Strong one. *Notables:* Amos the Biblical prophet; radio character Amos Jones. *Variations:* Amotz, Amoz, Amus.

ANAD (Hindu) God. *Variations:* Anaadi.

ANAEL (Greek) Guardian for Librans.

ANANYA (Hindu) Unique.

ANASTASIO (Italian) Resurrection. *Variations:* Anas, Anastagio, Anastas, Anastasi, Anastasios, Anastasius, Anastice.

ANATOLE (Greek) From the east. *Variations:* Anatoli, Anatoly.

ANDERS (Swedish) Brave and manly. Form of Andrew. *Variations:* Ander.

ANDERSON (Swedish) Son of Andrew. *Variations:* Andersen.

ANDRÉ (French) Manly. French version of Andrew. *Notables:* Tennis champ Andre Agassi; conductor Andre Previn. *Variations:* Ahndray, Andrae, Andray, Aundray, Aundre, Ondre.

ANDREW (English) Brave and manly. *Notables:* U.S. Presidents Andrew Johnson and Andrew Jackson; artists Andy Warhol and Andrew Wyeth. *Variations:* Aindrea, Aindreas, Anders, Andi, Andonis, Andor, Andre, Andreas, Andrei, Andres, Andrey, Andros, Andrzej.

ANDROCLES (Greek) Glory of man.

ANDY (Greek) Short form of Andrew. *Notables:* Actors Andy Garcia and Andy Griffith; TV commentator Andy Rooney. *Variations:* Andey, Andie.

ANFERNY (American) Praiseworthy. Form of Anthony. *Variations:* Anfernee, Anferney, Anfernie.

ANGEL (Latin) Messenger. *Variations:* Angele, Angell.

ANGELO (Italian/Greek/Portuguese/Spanish) Angelic. *Notables:* Boxing trainer Angelo Dundee. *Variations:* Agnelito, Angeles, Angelos, Anjelo.

ANGUS (Scottish) Only or unique choice. *Variations:* Aengus, Angos, Aonghas.

ANJAY (Hindu) Unconquerable.

ANSEL (French) One who follows a nobleman. *Notables:* Photographer Ansel Adams. *Variations:* Ancel, Anselm.

ANSELM (German) Protector. *Variations:* Anselmo, Anzelmo.

ANSON (English) Son of Ann. *Notables:* Actor Anson Williams (Potsy on *Happy Days*). *Variations:* Annson, Ansson, Ansun.

ANTAEUS (Greek) Enemy. *Variations:* Antaios, Anteus.

ANTHONY (Latin) Praiseworthy; valuable. *Notables:* Actors Anthony Quinn, Anthony Hopkins, and Anthony Perkins. *Variations:* Andonios, Andonis, Anntoin, Antin, Antoine, Anton, Antone, Antonello, Antoney, Antoni, Antonin, Antonino, Antonio, Antonius, Antons, Antony, Antos, Tony.

ANTOINE (French) Form of Anthony. *Notables:* *The Little Prince* writer Antoine de Saint-Exupery. *Variations:* Antwan, Antwon, Antwone.

ANTON (Slavic) Form of Anthony. *Notables:* Playwright Anton Chekhov.

ANTONIO (Spanish) Form of Anthony. *Notables:* Actor Antonio Banderas; composers Antonio Vivaldi and Antonio Salieri.

ANWAR (Arabic) Shafts of light. *Notables:* Egyptian President Anwar Sadat.

APIA (Hawaiian) God is my father. *Variations:* Abia.

APOLLO (Greek) Manly; destroyer. *Variations:* Apollon, Apollos, Apolo.

AQUILO (Greek) The north wind. *Variations:* Aquillo.

ARAM (Syrian) Noble. *Variations:* Aramia.

ARAMIS (French) Clever. *Variations:* Arames, Aramith, Aramys.

ARCAS (Greek) In myth, the son of Jupiter and Callisto.

ARCHER (English) Bowman; archer.

ARCHIBALD (German) Bold. *Notables:* Writer/poet Archibald MacLeish. *Variations:* Archibold.

ARCHIE (English) Short for Archer or Archibald. *Notables:* Comic book character Archie Andrews; TV's Archie Bunker.

ARCHIMEDES (Greek) To first think about.

ARDAL (Irish) Valor. *Variations:* Ardghal.

ARDEN (Celtic) Eager. *Variations:* Ardin, Ardon.

ARES (Greek) The god of war.

ARGUS (Greek) Bright. *Variations:* Argos.

ARI (Hebrew) Lion. Short for Aristotle. *Variations:* Arie, Arye.

ARIEL (Hebrew) Lion of God. *Notables:* Israeli Prime Minister Ariel Sharon. *Variations:* Arel, Ariell, Aryell.

ARIES (Latin) Sign of the ram in astrology. *Variations:* Ares.

ARISTIDES (Greek) The best. *Variations:* Aristidis.

ARISTOTLE (Greek) Superior. *Notables:* Greek philosopher Aristotle; shipping

top ten names of the 1890s

Boys	Girls
John	Mary
William	Anna
James	Elizabeth
George	Emma
Charles	Margaret
Joseph	Rose
Frank	Ethel
Harry	Florence
Henry	Ida
Edward	Bertha, Helen (tie)

popular names in russia

Boys	Girls
Aleksei	Dasha
Arkadiy	Galina
Feodor	Irina
Ilya	Lara
Kolya	Marina
Misha	Natalia
Nikolai	Natasha
Pavel	Oksana
Sacha	Olga
Sergei	Sofia
Vladilen	Tatiana
Yakov	Yelena

tycoon Aristotle Onassis. *Variations:* Ari, Aris, Aristo, Aristokles, Aristotelis.

ARLEDGE (English) By the lake. *Variations:* Arlidge.

ARLEN (Irish) Pledge. *Variations:* Arlan, Arland, Arle, Arlin, Arlyn.

ARLES (Hebrew) Promise. *Variations:* Arlee, Arleigh, Arley, Arlie, Arlis, Arliss, Arly.

ARLO (Spanish) Bayberry tree. *Notables:* Singer/songwriter Arlo Guthrie. *Variations:* Arlow.

ARMAND (German) Man of the army. *Notables:* Actor Armand Assante; business-man Armand Hammer. *Variations:* Arman, Armande, Armando, Armin, Armon, Armond, Armonde, Armondo, Ormand, Ormond.

ARMON (Hebrew) High place. *Variations:* Arman, Armen, Armin.

ARMSTRONG (English) One who has a strong arm.

ARNIE (German) Short form of Arnold. *Variations:* Arne, Arney, Arny.

ARNOLD (German) Strong as an eagle. *Notables:* Golfer Arnold Palmer; "Gover-nator" Arnold Schwarzenegger. *Variations:* Arnald, Arnaldo, Arnaud, Arndt, Arno, Arnolde, Arnoldo, Arnot, Arnst.

ARNOST (Czech) Determined.

ARPAD (Hungarian) Prince.

ARRIO (Spanish) Fierce; warlike. *Variations:* Ario, Arryo, Aryo.

ARSENIO (Greek) Virile; masculine. *Notables:* Comedian Arsenio Hall. *Variations:* Arcenio, Arsanio, Arsinio, Arsonio.

ART (English) Short form of Arthur.

ARTEMUS (Greek) One who follows Artemis, the Greek goddess of the hunt. *Variations:* Artemas, Artemis, Artimas, Artimis, Artimus.

ARTHUR (Celtic) Bear; rock. *Notables:* King Arthur; tennis legend Arthur Ashe; TV host Art Linkletter; writer Arthur C. Clarke; playwright Arthur Miller. *Variations:* Artair, Artek, Arther, Arthor, Arthuro, Artie, Artis, Arto, Artor, Artur, Arturo, Atur.

ARTIE (English) Short form of Arthur. *Variations:* Arte, Arty.

ARUN (Hindu) Reddish-brown sky.

ARUNDEL (English) Valley of the eagle. *Variations:* Arondel, Arundale, Arundell.

ARVIN (German) Friend of the people. *Variations:* Arv, Arven, Arvid, Arvie, Arvon, Arvy.

ASA (Hebrew) Doctor. *Variations:* Ase, Aza.

ASAD (Arabic) More fortunate. *Variations:* Asid, Assad, Azad.

ASCOT (English) Eastern cottage. *Variations:* Ascott.

ASHBY (English) Ash tree farm. *Variations:* Ash, Ashbey, Ashbie, Ashburn.

ASHER (Hebrew) Happy. *Variations:* Ashur.

ASHFORD (English) Place to cross a river near ash trees.

ASHLEY (English) Meadow of ash trees. *Variations:* Ashlea, Ashlee, Ashleigh.

ASHLIN (English) Ash trees that encircle a pond. *Variations:* Ashlen.

ASHTON (English) Town with ash trees. *Notables:* Actor Ashton Kutcher. *Variations:* Ashten, Ashtin.

ASRIEL (Hebrew) Prince of God. *Variations:* Azriel.

ASTON (English) Eastern town. *Variations:* Asten, Astin.

ATHERTON (English) Town by the spring.

ATID (Thai) Sun.

ATLAS (Greek) To carry.

ATLEY (English) Meadow. *Variations:* Atlea, Atlee, Atleigh, Attlee, Attleigh, Attley.

ATTICUS (Latin) From Athens. *Notables:* Atticus Finch, character in *To Kill a Mockingbird*.

ATTILA (Old German) Little father. *Notables:* King and general Attila the Hun. *Variations:* Atilio, Attilio.

ATWATER (English) By the water.

ATWELL (English) At the well.

ATWOOD (English) At the woods.

ATWORTH (English) At the farm.

AUBREY (English) Power. *Variations:* Auben, Aubery, Aubin, Aubry, Aubury.

AUBURN (English) Reddish-brown. *Variations:* Aubern, Auburne.

AUDEN (English) Old friend.

AUDIE (German) Strong. *Notables:* Actor and war hero Audie Murphy. *Variations:* Audi, Audley.

AUGIE (Latin) Short for August or Augustus. *Variations:* Auggie, Augy.

AUGUST (Latin) Worthy of respect. *Notables:* Playwright August Wilson. *Variations:* Agostino, Agosto, Aguistin, Agustin, Agustino, Augie, Augustin, Augustine, Augustino, Augusto, Augustus, Augy.

AUGUSTUS (Latin) Venerable. *Notables:* Roman emperor Augustus Caesar.

AULAY (Scottish) Forefather.

AURELIUS (Latin) Golden. *Variations:* Areliano, Aurelio, Aurelo, Auriel.

AUSTIN (Latin) Form of Augustine or Augustus. *Notables:* Film spy Austin Powers. *Variations:* Astin, Austen, Auston, Austyn.

AVERILL (English) Fighting boar. *Notables:* U.S. diplomat Averell Harriman. *Variations:* Ave, Averel, Averell, Averil, Averyl, Averyll, Avrel, Avrell, Avrill, Avryll.

AVERY (English) Counselor. *Notables:* Philanthropist Avery Fisher.

AVI (Hebrew) My God.

AVIDOR (Hebrew) Father of a people.

AVIRAM (Hebrew) My father is strong. *Variations:* Abiram, Avram, Avrom, Avrum.

AVIV (Hebrew) Spring.

AVNIEL (Hebrew) My God is my strength.

AXEL (Scandinavian) Father of peace; reward from God. *Notables:* Musician Axl Rose of Guns 'N Roses. *Variations:* Aksel, Ax, Axe, Axell, Axil, Axill, Axl.

AXELROD (German) Shoulder; wheel.

AYLMER (English) Noble. *Variations:* Elmer.

AZAD (Turkish) Free.

AZIM (Arabic) Defender. *Variations:* Aseem, Asim, Azeem.

AZIZ (Arabic) Powerful.

AZRIEL (Hebrew) Help from God. *Variations:* Azrael.

BABAR (Hindu) Lion. *Notables:* Babar the Elephant (not lion!) from children's literature. *Variations:* Baber.

BACCHUS (Latin) God of wine.

BACHIR (Hebrew) Oldest son.

BADAR (Arabic) Full moon.

BADEN (German) Bather. *Variations:* Baeden, Bayden.

BAHIR (Arabic) Dazzling.

BAILEY (French) Steward or bailiff. *Variations:* Bailee, Bailie, Baillie, Baily, Baylee, Bayley, Bayly.

BAINBRIDGE (Irish) Pale bridge. *Variations:* Bain, Baynbridge, Bayne, Baynebridge.

BAIRD (Irish) A traveling singer. *Variations:* Bard, Barde, Barr, Bayerd, Bayrd.

BAKER (English) One who bakes. *Variations:* Bax, Baxter.

BALDEMAR (German) Bold. *Variations:* Baldemer, Baldemero.

BALDER (English) Brave warrior. *Variations:* Baldur, Baudier.

BALDRIC (German) Brave ruler. *Variations:* Baldrick, Baudric.

BALDWIN (German) Brave friend. *Variations:* Bald, Baldovino, Balduin, Baldwinn, Baldwyn, Baldwynn, Balldwin, Baudoin.

BALFOUR (Gaelic) Grazing land. *Variations:* Balfor, Balfore.

BALIN (Hindu) Soldier. *Variations:* Bali, Baylin, Baylon.

BALLARD (German) Mighty. *Variations:* Ballerd.

BALTHASAR (Greek) One of the Three Wise Men of Christmas. *Notables:* Actor Balthazar Getty. *Variations:* Balta, Baltazar, Balthazar.

BANAN (Irish) White.

BANCROFT (English) Field.

what celebrities are naming their babies

Since celebrities are newswor-thy, the public is interested in the names they choose for their newborns. Here's what some notables have selected:

Amandine and Lowey
John Malkovich

Apple Blythe Alison
Gwyneth Paltrow and Chris Martin

Ava and Deacon
Reese Witherspoon and Ryan Philippe

Banjo
Rachel Griffiths

Beatrice Milly
Paul McCartney and Heather Mills

Brooklyn, Romeo, and Cruz
David and Victoria Beckham

Caspar and Clementine
Claudia Schiffer

Charles Spencer
Russell Crowe and Danielle Spencer

BANNER (English) Bearing a flag. *Variations:* Bannor.

BANNING (Irish) Small and fair.

BAO (Chinese) Treasure.

BARAK (Hebrew) Lightning. *Variations:* Barrak.

BARAM (Hebrew) Son of the people.

BARCLAY (English) Valley of the birches. *Variations:* Barcley, Barklay, Barkley, Barklie, Berkeley.

BARD (Irish) Poet. Form of Baird. *Variations:* Barde, Barr.

BARDOLF (German) Wolf that wields an ax. *Variations:* Bardolph, Bardou, Bardoul, Bardulf, Bardulph.

BARDRICK (German) Soldier with an ax. *Variations:* Bardric.

BAREND (Scandinavian) Firm bear.

BARIS (Turkish) Peaceful.

BARKER (English) Lumberjack.

BARLOW (English) Bare hillside. *Variations:* Barlowe.

BARNABAS (Hebrew) Comfort. *Notables:* Vampire Barnabas Collins from classic TV soap *Dark Shadows*. *Variations:* Barnabie, Barnabus, Barnaby, Barnebas, Barney, Barnie, Burnaby.

BARNABY (English) A form of Barnabas. *Variations:* Barnabey, Barnabie, Burnaby.

BARNES (English) Barn.

BARNETT (English) Baronet. *Variations:* Barnet.

BARNUM (English) A baron's home. *Variations:* Barnham.

BARON (English) Nobleman. *Variations:* Barron.

BARRETT (German) Strong as a bear. *Variations:* Baret, Barett, Barret.

BARRINGTON (English) Enclosed town.

BARRY (Irish) Marksman. *Notables:* R&B singer Barry White; baseball player Barry Bonds. *Variations:* Barrymore.

BART (English) Short form of Bartholomew or Barton. *Notables:* Bart Simpson from the cartoon *The Simpsons*.

BARTHOLOMEW (Hebrew) Farmer's son. *Variations:* Bart, Bartek, Bartel, Barth, Barthel, Barthelemy, Barthelmy, Barthlomeo, Bartholome, Bartholomieu, Bartoli, Bartolo, Bartolomeo, Bartram.

BARTLET (English) Form of Bartholomew. *Variations:* Bartlett, Bartley.

BARTON (English) Field of barley.

BARUCH (Hebrew) Blessed.

BASANT (Hindu) Spring.

BASIL (Greek) Royal. *Notables:* Actor Basil Rathbone; Basil Fawlty from TV's *Fawlty Towers*. *Variations:* Basile, Basilio, Basilios, Basilius, Bazil, Bazyl.

BASIM (Arabic) To smile. *Variations:* Baseem.

BASIR (Turkish) Intelligent. *Variations:* Bashir.

BASSETT (English) Short person. *Variations:* Basset.

BASTIAN (English) Short form of Sebastian.

BAXTER (English) Form of Baker.

BAYARD (English) Reddish-brown hair.

BEACAN (Irish) Small. *Variations:* Beag, Bec, Becan, Beagan.

BEACHER (English) Near beech trees. *Variations:* Beach, Beachy, Beecher, Beechy.

BEALE (French) Handsome. *Variations:* Beal, Beall, Beals.

BEAMAN (English) Beekeeper. *Variations:* Beman, Beeman.

BEAMER (English) Horn player.

BEANON (Irish) Good. *Variations:* Beinean, Beineon, Binean.

BEASLEY (English) Pea field.

BEAU (French) Handsome. *Notables:* Actor Beau Bridges; English dandy and wit Beau Brummel. *Variations:* Beaux, Bo.

BEAUFORT (French) A beautiful fort. *Variations:* Beauford.

BEAUMONT (French) Beautiful mountain. *Variations:* Bowmont.

BEAUREGARD (French) Beautiful gaze.

BECK (English) Brook. *Variations:* Bec.

BECKER (English) By the brook. *Variations:* Beckett.

BEDE (English) Prayer.

BEDFORD (English) Place name.

BELA (Czech) White. *Notables:* Actor Bela Lugosi.

BELDEN (English) Beautiful valley. *Variations:* Beldin, Beldon, Bellden, Belldon.

BELLAMY (French) Handsome companion. *Variations:* Belamy, Bell, Bellamey, Bellamie.

BEN (Hebrew) Short for Benjamin. *Notables:* Ice cream entrepreneur Ben Cohen; actors Ben Affleck and Ben Stiller.

BENAIAH (Hebrew) God builds. *Variations:* Benaya, Benayahu.

BENEDICT (Latin) Blessed. *Notables:* Revolutionary general and traitor Benedict Arnold; Pope Benedict XVI. *Variations:* Bence, Benci, Bendek, Bendict, Bendix, Benedek, Benedetto, Benedick, Benedicto, Benedictus, Benedik, Benedikt.

BENITO (Italian) Italian form of Benedict. *Notables:* Fascist dictator of Italy Benito Mussolini. *Variations:* Benedo, Benino, Benno.

BENJAMIN (Hebrew) Son of my right hand. *Notables:* Statesman Benjamin Franklin; British Prime Minister Benjamin Disraeli; Dr. Benjamin Spock. *Variations:* Benejamen, Beniamino, Benjaman, Benjamen, Benjamino, Benjamon, Benji, Benjie, Benjiman, Benjimen, Benjy, Bennie, Benny, Minyamin, Minyomei, Minyomi.

BENNETT (English) Formal version of Benedict. *Notables:* Publisher and editor Bennett Cerf. *Variations:* Benet, Benett, Bennet.

BENNY (English) Short form of Benjamin. *Notables:* British comedian Benny Hill; band leader Benny Goodman. *Variations:* Bennie.

BENOIT (French) Form of Benedict.

BENSON (English) Son of Ben. *Variations:* Bensen, Benssen, Bensson.

BENTLEY (English) Meadow of coarse grass. *Variations:* Bentlea, Bentlee, Bentlie.

BENTON (English) Ben's town.

BERG (German) Mountain. *Variations:* Burg.

BERGEN (Scandinavian) Hill dweller. *Variations:* Bergin, Birgin.

BERGER (French) Shepherd.

BERKELEY (English) Town where birches grow. *Variations:* Barcley, Barklay, Barkley, Barklie, Berkley.

BERNAL (German) Bearlike. *Variations:* Bernald, Bernel.

BERNARD (German) Brave as a bear. *Notables:* Statesman Bernard Baruch. *Variations:* Barnard, Barnardo, Barney, Barnhard, Barnhardo, Barnie, Barny, Bernardas, Bernardel, Bernardin, Bernardino, Bernardo, Bernardyn, Bernhard, Bernhardo, Bernie, Berny, Burnard.

BERNIE (German) Short form of Bernard. *Variations:* Berney, Berny, Birney, Birnie, Burney.

BERT (English) Bright and shining. *Notables:* Actors Burt Reynolds and Burt Lancaster; composer Burt Bacharach; *Sesame Street's* Bert—the best friend of Ernie. *Variations:* Berthold, Bertie, Bertold, Bertolde, Berty, Burt, Burtt, Burty.

BERTHOLD (German) Bright. *Variations:* Bertolde.

BERTIE (English) Short form of Bert.

BERTIN (Spanish) Good friend. *Variations:* Berton.

BERTRAM (German) Brightly colored raven. *Variations:* Bert, Bertrand, Bertraum.

boys 19

trendy names from tv

Many popular names are derived from characters in television shows. These recently popular shows, as you can see, have turned a few uncommon boys' names into everyday monikers.

Aidan
Sex and the City

Angel
Angel

Boone
Lost

Caleb
The O.C.

Carter
The O.C.

Chandler
Friends

Locke
Lost

Nate
Six Feet Under

Sandy
The O.C.

Sawyer
Lost

Smith
Sex and the City

Stanford
Sex and the City

Trey
Sex and the City

Xander
Buffy the Vampire Slayer

most popular names for twin boys

According to the Social Security Administration's data for 2005, these are the top names Americans are giving to their twin boys:

Alexander and Andrew

Andrew and Matthew

Christian and Christopher

Daniel and David

Ethan and Evan

Jacob and Joshua

Joseph and Joshua

Matthew and Michael

Nathan and Nicholas

Taylor and Tyler

BERWIN (English) Friend at harvest time. *Variations:* Berwyn, Berwynn, Berwynne.

BEVAN (Welsh) Son of Evan. *Variations:* Beavan, Beaven, Beven, Bevin, Bevon.

BEVERLY (English) Meadow of beavers. *Variations:* Beverlee, Beverleigh, Beverley.

BEVIS (French) From Beauvais, a town in France. *Variations:* Beauvais, Beavis.

BIALAS (Polish) White. *Variations:* Bialy.

BICKFORD (English) Ax-wielding.

BIJAN (Persian) Ancient hero. *Variations:* Bihjan, Bijon, Binjhan.

BILL (German) Short form of William. *Notables:* U.S. President Bill Clinton; comedians Bill Cosby, Bill Murray, and Bill Maher; Buffalo Bill Cody. *Variations:* Billy, Byll.

BING (German) A pot-shaped hollow; a type of cherry. *Notables:* Crooner Bing Crosby.

BIRCH (English) A birch tree. *Notables:* Senator Birch Bayh. *Variations:* Birk, Burch.

BIRKETT (English) Area with birch trees. *Variations:* Birket, Birkit, Birkitt, Burket, Burkett, Burkitt.

BIRNEY (English) Brook with an island. *Variations:* Birnie, Birny, Burney, Burnie.

BISHOP (English) Bishop. *Variations:* Bishup.

BJORN (Scandinavian) Bear. Form of Bernard.

BLACKBURN (Scottish) By the dark brook.

BLADE (English) Sword. *Variations:* Bladen, Blaid.

BLAINE (Irish) Thin. *Variations:* Blain, Blane, Blayne.

BLAIR (English) Flat piece of land. *Notables:* Actor Blair Underwood. *Variations:* Blaire, Blayr, Blayre.

BLAISE (Latin) Stutterer. *Variations:* Blaize, Blase, Blayse, Blayze, Blaze.

BLAKE (English) Attractive. *Notables:* Blake Carrington from TV's *Dynasty*; director Blake Edwards. *Variations:* Blaike, Blayke.

BLAKELY (English) Dark meadow. *Variations:* Blakelee, Blakeley, Blakelie.

BLISS (English) Joy.

BLYTHE (English) Merry and carefree. *Variations:* Blithe.

BOAZ (Hebrew) Quick. *Variations:* Bo, Boas, Boase.

BOB (English) Short form of Robert. *Notables:* Singers Bob Dylan, Bob Seeger, and Bob Marley; comedians Bob Hope and Bob Newhart; home improvement guru Bob Vila; choreographer Bob Fosse.

BOBBY (English) Short form of Robert. *Variations:* Bobbey, Bobbie, Bobby.

BODEN (French) Messenger of news. *Variations:* Bodin, Bowden, Bowdoin.

BOGART (French) Strength of a bow. *Variations:* Bogey, Bogie.

BOLTON (English) Town in Britain.

BONAVENTURE (Latin) Blessed adventure.

BOND (English) Man of the land. *Variations:* Bonde, Bondon, Bonds.

BONIFACE (Latin) Fortunate. *Variations:* Bonifacio, Bonifacius.

BOOKER (English) Bible or book lover; one who places bets. *Notables:* Educator Booker T. Washington.

BOONE (French) Good. *Variations:* Boon.

BOOTH (English) House. *Variations:* Boothe.

BORDEN (English) Boar's house. *Variations:* Bordan, Bordin, Bordon.

BORG (Scandinavian) Castle. *Variations:* Borge.

BORIS (Slavic) Warrior. *Notables:* Actor Boris Karloff; writer Boris Pasternak; Russian President Boris Yeltsin; tennis player Boris Becker. *Variations:* Boriss, Borris, Borys.

BOSLEY (English) Of or near the woods. *Variations:* Boslee, Boslie.

BOSTON (English) Named for the capital city of Massachusetts.

BOURNE (French) Boundary. *Variations:* Bourn, Bourney.

BOWIE (Irish) Blond. *Notables:* Former baseball commissioner Bowie Kuhn.

BOYCE (French) Forest. *Variations:* Boice, Boise.

BOYD (Irish) Blond. *Variations:* Boid, Boyde.

BOYNE (Irish) White cow. *Variations:* Boine, Boyn.

BRAD (English) Short form of Bradford or Bradley. *Notables:* Actors Brad Pitt and Brad Garrett. *Variations:* Bradd, Brade.

BRADEN (English) Broad meadow. *Variations:* Bradon, Braeden, Brayden, Braydon.

BRADFORD (English) A wide stream. *Variations:* Brad, Bradburn, Braddford, Bradfurd.

BRADLEY (English) A wide meadow. *Variations:* Brad, Bradlea, Bradlee, Bradleigh, Bradlie, Bradly.

BRADSHAW (English) Wide forest.

BRADY (English) Broad island. *Variations:* Bradey, Bradie, Braidy.

BRAHMA (Hindu) Prayer.

BRAINARD (English) Princely. *Variations:* Brainerd.

BRAM (Scottish) Bramble. *Notables: Dracula* writer Bram Stoker. *Variations:* Bramm.

BRANCH (Latin) Branch from a tree.

BRAND (English) Short form of Brandon.

BRANDEIS (German) One who dwells in a land burned by fire. *Variations:* Brandis.

BRANDON (English) Sword; hill afire. *Notables:* TV executives Brandon Tartikoff and Brandon Stoddard. *Variations:* Bran, Brandan, Branden, Brandin, Brandyn.

BRANSON (English) Son of Brandon. *Variations:* Bransen, Brantson.

BRANT (English) Proud. *Variations:* Brand, Brandt, Brandy.

BRANTLEY (English) Form of Brant. *Variations:* Brantly, Brentley.

BRASIL (Irish) War. *Variations:* Brazil, Breasal, Bresal, Bressal.

BRATISLAV (Czech) Glorious brother.

BRAWLEY (English) Meadow on a hill. *Variations:* Brawly.

BRAXTON (English) Brock's town. *Variations:* Brackston.

BRAYDEN (English) Form of Braden. *Variations:* Braydon.

BRECK (Irish) Freckled. *Variations:* Brecken.

BREDE (Scandinavian) Iceberg.

BRENDAN (Irish) Little raven. *Notables:* Writer/preservationist Brendan Gill; actor Brendan Fraser. *Variations:* Brenden, Brendin, Brendon.

BRENNAN (Irish) Raven. *Variations:* Brenan, Brennen, Brenner, Brennon.

BRENT (English) Mountaintop. *Variations:* Brentan, Brentin, Brenton, Brentyn.

BRETT (English) From Britain. *Notables:* Writers Bret Harte and Bret Easton Ellis; Green Bay Packers quarterback Brett Favre. *Variations:* Bret, Brette, Bretton, Brit, Britt.

BREWSTER (English) Brewer. *Variations:* Brew, Brewer.

BRIAN (Irish) Strong. *Notables:* Beach Boy Brian Wilson; skater Brian Boitano; singer Bryan Ferry; director Brian De Palma; actor Brian Dennehy. *Variations:* Briano, Brien, Brion, Bryan, Bryon.

BRICE (Welch) Ambitious. Form of Bryce.

BRICK (English) Bridge. *Variations:* Bricker.

BRIDGELY (English) From the bridge. *Variations:* Bridge, Bridgeley.

BRIGHAM (English) Village near a bridge. *Notables:* Brigham Young, founder of Church of Jesus Christ of Latter Day Saints. *Variations:* Brigg, Briggs.

BRIGHTON (English) Bright town. *Variations:* Breighton, Bright, Bryton.

BRITTON (English) From Britain. *Variations:* Brit, Britain, Briton, Britt, Brittan, Britten, Brittin.

BROCK (English) Badger. *Variations:* Broc, Brockley.

BROCKTON (English) Badger town.

---

automobile names

Today, more and more parents are inspired to name their babies after cars!

Boys	Girls
Acura	Altima
Amanti	Camry
Bentley	Celica
Chevy	Corvette
Durango	Elantra
Ferrari	Jetta
Forester	Kia
Jaguar	Lexus
Maxima	Mazda
Montero	Mercedes
Rio	Porsche

BRODERICK (Scottish) Brother. *Notables:* Actor Broderick Crawford. *Variations:* Brod, Broddy, Broderic, Brodric, Brodrick.

BRODY (Irish) Ditch. *Variations:* Brodee, Brodey, Brodi, Brodie.

BROGAN (Irish) Work shoe.

BROMLEY (English) Meadow of brushwood.

BRONISLAW (Polish) Glorious weapon. *Variations:* Bronislav.

BRONSON (English) Dark man's son. *Notables:* Actor Bronson Pinchot. *Variations:* Bron, Bronnson, Bronsen, Bronsin, Bronsonn, Bronsson.

BROOK (English) Stream or brook. *Variations:* Brooks.

BROWN (English) Brown. *Variations:* Browne.

BRUCE (French) Thick brush. *Notables:* Singer Bruce Springsteen; actors Bruce Willis, Bruce Lee, and Bruce Dern. *Variations:* Brucey, Brucie.

BRUNO (German) Dark-skinned. *Variations:* Bruns.

BRUNSWICK (German) Bruno's village.

BRUTUS (Latin) Heavy.

BRYAN (Irish) Variation of Brian.

BRYANT (Irish) A form of Brian. *Notables:* Sportscaster Bryant Gumbel.

BRYCE (Celtic) Swift moving; ambitious; go-getter. *Variations:* Brice.

BRYDEN (English) Town in Britain.

BRYNMOR (Welsh) Great hill. *Variations:* Bryn.

BRYSON (English) Nobleman's son.

BUBBA (German) Boy.

BUCK (English) Male deer. *Notables:* Country/Western singer Buck Owens; comedy writer Buck Henry. *Variations:* Buckey, Buckie, Bucky.

BUCKLEY (English) Meadow where deer graze. *Variations:* Bucklie, Buckly.

BUCKMINSTER (English) Preacher. *Notables:* Buckminster Fuller.

BUD (English) Brother or friend. *Notables:* Comedian Bud Abbott. *Variations:* Budd.

BUDDY (English) Friend. *Notables:* Actor Buddy Ebsen; rock-and-roller Buddy Holly. *Variations:* Bud, Budd, Buddey, Buddie.

BUELL (German) Hill.

BUFORD (English) Ford near a castle.

BURGESS (English) Citizen. *Notables:* Actor Burgess Meredith. *Variations:* Burges, Burgiss.

BURKE (French) Fortress. *Variations:* Berk, Berke, Birk, Birke, Bourke, Burk.

BURL (English) Knotty tree trunk. *Notables:* Folk singer Burl Ives. *Variations:* Berl, Byrle.

BURLEIGH (English) Meadow with knotted trees. *Variations:* Burley, Burlie, Byrleigh, Byrley.

BURNABY (Norse) Warrior's land.

BURNE (English) Brook. *Variations:* Bourn, Bourne, Burn, Byrn, Byrne, Byrnes.

BURNELL (French) Small child with brown hair. *Variations:* Burnel.

BURTON (English) Fort. *Variations:* Bert, Burt.

BUSBY (Scottish) Village in the forest. *Notables:* Choreographer Busby Berkeley.

BUSTER (American) To hit. *Notables:* Comedic actor Buster Keaton; *Flash Gordon*'s Buster Crabbe; cartoon character Buster Brown.

BUTCH (English) Short for Butcher. *Notables:* Western outlaw Butch Cassidy.

BUTCHER (English) A butcher.

BUZZ Short form of Busby. *Notables:* Astronaut Buzz Aldrin. *Variations:* Buzzy.

BYRAM (English) Cattle field.

BYRON (English) Barn. *Variations:* Beyren, Beyron, Biren, Biron, Byram, Byran.

CAB (American) Short for Cabot.

CABOT (English) English family name.

CADE (Welsh) Short form of Cadell.

CADELL (Welsh) Small battle. *Variations:* Caddell, Cadel, Cedell.

CADMAN (Welsh) Soldier.

CAELAN (Irish) Powerful warrior. *Variations:* Caelin, Caelon, Cailean, Calen, Caln, Caulan.

CAESAR (Latin) Hairy. *Variations:* Caezar, Ceasar, Cesar, Cesare, Cesareo, Cesario, Cesaro, Cezar, Cezary, Cezek.

CAFFAR (Irish) Helmet.

CAIN (Hebrew) Spear. *Variations:* Cainan, Caine, Cayne.

CAIRN (Welsh) A mound of stones. *Variations:* Cairne, Carne.

CAL (Latin) Short form of Calvert, Calvin.

CALDER (English) Brook.

names for any season

Whether your baby arrives when it's snowing or when flowers are blooming, the day or time when the birth occurs might inspire you to consider these names!

Boys	Girls
August	April
Christmas	Autumn
Easter	July
February	June
Friday	May
January	November
March	October
Monday	September
Saturday	Spring
Sunday	Summer
Thursday	Tuesday
Winter	Wednesday

CALDWELL (English) Cold well.

CALE (Hebrew) A form of Caleb. *Variations:* Cael, Kale.

CALEB (Hebrew) Brave or dog. *Variations:* Calib, Callob, Kaleb.

CALEY (Irish) Slender. *Variations:* Cailey.

CALHOUN (Irish) Small forest. *Variations:* Colhoun.

CALLAHAN (Irish) An Irish saint. *Variations:* Callaghan.

CALLUM (Irish) Dove. *Variations:* Callam, Calum.

CALVERT (English) Calf herder. *Variations:* Calbert.

CALVIN (English) Bald. *Notables:* U.S. President Calvin Coolidge; designer Calvin Klein; baseball player Cal Ripken. *Variations:* Calvino, Calvon, Kalvin.

CAM (Scottish) Short for Cameron. *Variations:* Cammy.

CAMDEN (English) Twisting valley. *Variations:* Camdon.

CAMERON (Scottish) Crooked nose or river. *Notables:* Writer Cameron Crowe. *Variations:* Camaron, Cameran, Camron.

CAMPBELL (Scottish) Crooked mouth. *Notables:* Actor Campbell Scott. *Variations:* Cam, Camp.

CANICE (Irish) Handsome. *Variations:* Coinneach.

CANNON (French) Church official. *Variations:* Canon, Kanon.

CANUTE (Scandinavian) Knot. *Variations:* Knute.

CAPPY (English) Lucky.

CAREY (Welsh) Near a castle. *Variations:* Cary.

CARL (English) Man. Form of Charles. *Notables:* Astronomer Carl Sagan; poet Carl Sandburg; psychologist Carl Jung; Watergate journalist Carl Bernstein. *Variations:* Karl.

CARLETON (English) Farmer's land. *Variations:* Carlton, Charleton.

CARLIN (Gaelic) Little champion. *Variations:* Carlan, Carlen, Carling.

CARLISLE (English) Fortified tower. *Variations:* Carlyle, Carlysle.

CARLO (Italian) Form of Charles. *Notables:* Director Carlo Ponti. *Variations:* Carolo.

CARLOS (Spanish) Form of Charles. *Notables:* Musician Carlos Santana. *Variations:* Carlino, Carlito.

CARMICHAEL (Scottish) One who follows Michael.

CARMINE (Latin) Song. *Variations:* Carmel, Carmelo.

CARNEY (Irish) Champion. *Variations:* Carny, Karney, Kearney.

CARR (Scandinavian) Marsh. *Variations:* Karr, Kerr.

CARRICK (Irish) Rock.

CARRINGTON (Welsh) Rocky town.

CARROLL (English) Manly. Form of Charles. *Notables:* Actor Carroll O'Connor. *Variations:* Carol, Caroll, Carolus, Carrol, Caryl.

CARSON (English) Son who lives in a marsh. *Notables:* TV host Carson Daly. *Variations:* Carsen, Karsen.

CARSTEN (German) Form of Christian. *Variations:* Carston.

CARTER (English) Cart driver.

CARTWRIGHT (English) One who builds carts.

CARVELL (French) One who lives in a marsh. *Variations:* Carvel.

CARVER (English) Wood-carver.

CARY (English) Stream. *Notables:* Actor Cary Grant.

CASEY (Irish) Observant. *Notables:* Baseball player/manager Casey Stengel; DJ Casey Kasem; train engineer Casey Jones. *Variations:* Cacey, Cayce, Caycey, Kasey.

CASH (Latin) Vain.

CASIMIR (Slavic) He brings peace. *Variations:* Casimire, Casimiro, Castimer, Kazimir.

CASPAR (English) Guardian of the treasure. *Notables:* U.S. Secretary of Defense Caspar Weinberger; cartoon character, Casper the Friendly Ghost. *Variations:* Casper.

CASSIDY (Irish) Clever. *Variations:* Cassady.

CASSIUS (Latin) Narcissistic. *Notables:* Boxing legend Cassius Clay (Muhammad Ali's real name). *Variations:* Casseus, Cassio.

CASTOR (Greek) Beaver. *Variations:* Caster.

CATO (Latin) Wise. *Variations:* Caton, Kato.

CAVAN (Irish) Handsome. *Variations:* Caven, Cavin.

CECIL (English) Blind. *Notables:* Director Cecil B. DeMille; jazz musician Cecil Taylor. *Variations:* Cecile, Cecilio, Cecillo, Cecillus, Celio.

CEDRIC (Welsh) Leader of war. *Notables:* Actor Sir Cedric Hardwicke; comedian Cedric the Entertainer. *Variations:* Cederic, Cedrec, Cedrick.

CHAD (English) Protector. *Notables:* Actor Chad Everett. *Variations:* Chaad, Chaddy.

CHADWICK (English) Warrior's town. *Variations:* Chadwyck.

CHAIM (Hebrew) Life. *Notables:* Zionist/scientist Chaim Weizmann; writer Chaim Potok. *Variations:* Chayim, Haim, Hayim.

CHAL (Gypsy) Boy.

CHALIL (Hebrew) Flute. *Variations:* Halil.

CHANCE (English) Good fortune.

CHAND (Hindu) Shining moon. *Variations:* Chanda, Chandak, Chander, Chandra, Chandrabha, Chandrak, Chandrakant.

CHANDLER (French) Candle maker. *Notables:* Chandler Bing, a character on TV's *Friends*.

CHANNING (English) Church official.

CHAPMAN (English) Merchant. *Variations:* Chap.

CHARLES (English) Man. *Notables:* Actor Charles Bronson; evolutionist Charles Darwin; writer Charles Dickens; hoops star Charles Barkley. *Variations:* Chas, Chaz, Chick.

CHARLIE (English) Short form of Charles. *Notables:* Jazz musician Charlie Parker; comedic actors Charlie Chaplin and Charlie Sheen; cartoon character Charlie Brown. *Variations:* Charley.

CHARLTON (English) Town where Charles lives. *Notables:* Actor Charlton Heston. *Variations:* Carleton, Carlton.

CHASE (French) Hunter. *Variations:* Chace, Chaise, Chasen, Chason.

CHAUNCEY (English) Chancellor. *Variations:* Chance, Chancey, Chaunce, Chauncy.

CHE (Spanish) Nickname for Joseph. *Notables:* Cuban revolutionary Che Guevara.

CHEN (Chinese) Great.

CHESTER (English) Campsite. *Variations:* Cheston.

CHET (English) Short form of Chester. *Notables:* TV news anchor Chet Huntley; Country/Western musician Chet Atkins.

CHEUNG (Chinese) Luck.

CHEVALIER (French) Knight. *Variations:* Chev, Chevi.

CHEVY (French) Short for Chevalier. *Notables:* Actor/comedian Chevy Chase. *Variations:* Chevey.

CHEYENNE (Native American) A city in Wyoming.

CHI (Nigerian) Guardian angel.

CHICK (English) Short form of Charles. *Variations:* Chic.

CHICO (Spanish) Boy.

CHIP (English) Nickname for Charles. *Variations:* Chipper.

CHIRAM (Hebrew) Exalted. *Variations:* Hiram.

CHRIS (Greek) Short form of Christopher and Christian. *Notables:* Comedian Chris Rock; actor Chris Noth.

CHRISTIAN (Greek) Follower of Christ. *Notables:* Actors Christian Slater and Christian Bale; designer Christian Dior.

like father like son?

Former boxing champ and noted grill master George Foreman, in an act of paternal pride (or, perhaps, hubris), named all of his five sons George. There's:

George Jr.

George III

George IV

George V

George VI

It's interesting to wonder who comes when the name "George" is called in the Foreman household.

international location names

Boys	Girls
Chad	China
Cuba	Florence
Donegal	Geneva
Israel	India
Jordan	Ireland
London	Jamaica
Melbourne	Kenya
Oman	Paris
Troy	Sydney
Wellington	Victoria

Variations: Chresta, Chris, Christiaan, Christianos, Chrystian, Cris, Kris, Kriss, Kristian.

CHRISTOPHER (Greek) Christ bearer. *Notables:* Explorer Christopher Columbus; actors Christopher Plummer and Chris Noth; comedians/actors Chris Rock and Chris Tucker; singer/actor Kris Kristofferson. *Variations:* Chris, Christof, Christofer, Christoff, Christoffer, Christoforus, Christoph, Christophe, Christophoros, Christos, Cris, Cristobal, Cristoforo, Kit, Kitt, Kristofer, Kristofor.

CHUCK (American) Nickname for Charles. *Notables:* Jazz musician Chuck Mangione; actors Chuck Connors and Chuck Norris. *Variations:* Chuckie, Chucky.

CHUNG (Chinese) Intelligent.

CHURCHILL (English) Church on the hill.

CIAN (Irish) Ancient; old. *Variations:* Cianan.

CIARAN (Irish) Black; black hair. *Variations:* Ciardha, Ciarrai.

CICERO (Latin) Chickpea. *Variations:* Ciceron.

CISCO (Spanish) Short form of Francisco.

CLANCY (Irish) Red-headed soldier. *Variations:* Clancey.

CLARENCE (English) Clear. *Notables:* U.S. Supreme Court Justice Clarence Thomas. *Variations:* Clair, Clarance, Clare, Clarey.

CLARK (English) Scholar. *Notables:* Actor Clark Gable; *Superman*'s Clark Kent. *Variations:* Clarke, Clerc, Clerk.

CLAUDE (Latin) With a limp. *Notables:* Composers Claude Debussy and Claude Monteverdi; artist Claude Monet. *Variations:* Claud, Claudio, Claudius, Klaudio.

CLAUS (German) Short form of Nicholas. *Variations:* Claus.

CLAY (English) Maker of clay. *Notables:* Singer Clay Aiken.

CLAYBORNE (English) Of the clay. *Variations:* Claiborne, Clayburn.

CLAYTON (English) Town of clay. *Variations:* Clayten, Claytin.

CLEARY (Irish) Learned.

CLEAVON (English) Cliff. *Notables:* Actor Cleavon Little.

CLEMENT (Latin) Merciful. *Variations:* Clem, Cleme, Clemen, Clemens, Clemente, Clementius, Clemento, Clemmie, Clemmons, Clemmy.

CLEON (Greek) Famous.

CLETUS (Greek) Illustrious.

CLEVELAND (English) Land of the cliffs. *Notables:* Writer/animal rights activist Cleveland Amory.

CLIFF (English) Short form of Clifford or Clifton.

CLIFFORD (English) Ford near a cliff. *Notables:* Singer Cliff Richard; writer Clifford Irving; actor Cliff Robertson; mailman Cliff Claven from TV's *Cheers*; children's book character Clifford the Big Red Dog. *Variations:* Cliff, Clyff, Clyfford.

CLIFTON (English) Town near a cliff. *Variations:* Clift, Clyfton.

CLINT (English) Short for Clinton. *Notables:* Actor/director Clint Eastwood; singer Clint Black.

CLINTON (English) Town on a hill.

CLIVE (English) Cliff. *Notables:* Writers Clive Barker and Clive Cussler; music mogul Clive Davis. *Variations:* Clyve.

CLOVIS (German) Famous soldier.

CLUNY (Irish) Meadow.

CLYDE (Scottish) River in Scotland.

COBY Form of Jacob. *Notables:* Soccer player Cobi Jones; basketball player Kobe Bryant. *Variations:* Cob, Cobby, Cobey, Cobi, Cobie, Kobe.

CODY (English) Cushion. *Variations:* Codey, Codie, Coty, Kodey, Kodie, Kody.

COLBERT (English) Mariner. *Variations:* Colvert, Culbert.

COLBY (English) Dark farm. *Variations:* Colbie.

COLE (English) Short form of Coleman. *Notables:* Composer Cole Porter.

COLEMAN (English) Coal miner. *Variations:* Cole, Colman.

COLIN (Irish) A young boy. *Notables:* U.S. Secretary of State Colin Powell; actor Colin Farrell; comedian Colin Quinn. *Variations:* Colan, Cole, Collin, Collins, Colyn.

COLLEY (English) Dark. *Variations:* Collis.

COLLIER (English) Coal miner.

COLM (Irish) Dove. *Variations:* Colum, Columba.

COLSON (English) Son of Nicholas.

COLTON (English) Coal town. *Variations:* Colten.

COLWYN (Welsh) River in Wales.

CONAN (Irish) Exalted. *Notables:* TV host Conan O'Brien. *Variations:* Conant.

CONLAN (Irish) Hero. *Variations:* Conlen, Conley, Conlin, Conlon.

CONNOR (Irish) Longing. *Variations:* Conner, Connie, Conor.

CONRAD (German) Courageous adviser. *Variations:* Conn, Connie, Conny, Conrade, Conrado, Konrad.

CONROY (Irish) Wise man.

CONSTANTINE (Latin) Stable, steady. *Variations:* Constant, Constantin, Constantino, Constantinos, Costa, Konstantin, Konstanz.

CONWAY (Irish) Hound of the plain. *Notables:* Conway Twitty.

COOK (English) Cook. *Variations:* Cooke.

COOPER (English) Barrel maker.

CORBETT (Latin) Black-haired. *Variations:* Corbitt, Corbet, Corbit.

CORBIN (Latin) Raven. *Notables:* Actor Corbin Bernsen. *Variations:* Corban, Corben, Corby.

CORCORAN (Irish) Ruddy.

CORDELL (English) Rope maker.

CORDERO (Spanish) Little lamb.

COREY (Irish) The hollow. *Notables:* Actors Corey Feldman and Corey Haim; singer Corey Hart. *Variations:* Corin, Correy, Cory, Korey.

CORMAC (Irish) Raven's son.

CORNELIUS (Greek) Cornell tree. *Variations:* Cornell, Corney.

CORNWALLIS (English) From Cornwall.

CORRADO (Italian) A form of Conrad. *Variations:* Carrado.

CORRIGAN (Irish) Spearman. *Variations:* Carrigan, Korrigan.

CORRIN (Latin) Carries a spear. *Variations:* Corin, Corion.

CORT (German) Courageous. *Variations:* Corte, Kort.

CORWIN (English) Friend of the heart. *Variations:* Corwyn, Corwynn.

COSGROVE (Irish) Champion. *Variations:* Cosgrave.

COSMO (Greek) Orderly. *Variations:* Cos, Cosimo, Cosme.

COSTA (Greek) Stable, steady. *Variations:* Kostas.

COTY (French) Slope. *Variations:* Cote, Cotey, Cotie, Koty.

COURTLAND (English) Court land. *Variations:* Cortland, Cortlandt, Courtlandt.

COURTNEY (English) One who lives in the court. *Variations:* Cortney, Courtenay, Courtnay.

COWAN (Irish) Hillside. *Variations:* Cowen, Cowyn.

COYLE (Irish) Battle leader.

CRADDOCK (Welsh) Love. *Variations:* Caradoc.

CRAIG (Gaelic) Rock. *Notables:* Actor Craig T. Nelson. *Variations:* Kraig.

CRANDALL (English) Valley of cranes. *Variations:* Crandal, Crandell.

unisex names

These names are popular ones to give to either boys or girls.

Avery	Jordan
Bailey	Kyle
Blake	Lindsay
Brett	Logan
Cameron	Michael
Corey	Morgan
Devin	Quinn
Drew	Riley
Harley	Ryan
Harper	Shawn
Hunter	Spencer
Jamie	Taylor

CRAWFORD (English) Ford of crows.

CREIGHTON (English) Town near a crag. *Variations:* Crayton, Crichton.

CRISPIN (Latin) Curly hair. *Notables:* Actor Crispin Glover. *Variations:* Crepin, Crispen, Crispian, Crispino, Crispo, Crispus.

CROFTON (Irish) Town with cottages.

CROSBY (Scandinavian) By the cross. *Variations:* Crosbey, Crosbie.

CULLEN (Irish) Handsome. *Variations:* Cullan, Cullin.

CULVER (English) Dove. *Variations:* Colver.

CUNNINGHAM (Irish) Village with a milk pail.

CURRAN (Irish) Hero. *Variations:* Curan, Curren, Currin.

CURT Short form of Curtis. *Variations:* Kurt.

CURTIS (French) Courteous. *Variations:* Curtiss, Kurtis.

CUTHBERT (English) Brilliant.

CUTLER (English) Maker of knives. *Variations:* Cutty.

CY Short form of Cyrus. *Notables:* Songwriter Cy Coleman; baseball player/manager Dentron True "Cy" Young. *Variations:* Sy.

CYNAN (Welsh) Chief. *Variations:* Kynan.

CYRANO (Greek) From Cyrene. *Notables:* Literature's Cyrano de Bergerac.

CYRIL (Greek) Lordly. *Notables:* Actors Cyril Cusack and Cyril Ritchard. *Variations:* Cirilio, Cirillo, Cirilo, Cyrill, Cyrille, Cyrillus.

CYRUS (Persian) Sun. *Notables:* Inventor Cyrus McCormick; former U.S. Secretary of State Cyrus Vance. *Variations:* Ciro, Cyris, Syris, Syrus.

DACEY (Gaelic) A man from the south. *Variations:* Dace, Dacia, Dacian, Dacy.

DACIAN (Latin) One from Dacia in Rome.

DAG (Scandinavian) Day. *Notables:* Nobel Peace Prize recipient Dag Hammarskjold. *Variations:* Daeg, Dagen, Dagny.

DAGAN (Hebrew) Earth. *Variations:* Dagon.

DAGWOOD (English) Bright forest. *Notables:* Dagwood Bumpstead, character in comic strip *Blondie*.

DAKOTA (Native American) Friend.

DALAL (Hindu) Salesman.

DALBERT (English) Bright one. *Variations:* Delbert.

DALE (English) One who lives in a dale. *Notables:* Self-improvement motivator Dale Carnegie; race-car driver Dale Earnhardt. *Variations:* Dal, Daley, Daly, Dayle.

DALLAS (Scottish) Town in Scotland. *Variations:* Dalles, Dallis, Dalys.

DALLIN (English) Proud. *Variations:* Dalan, Dallan, Dallen, Dallon, Dalon.

DALTON (English) A town in a valley. *Variations:* Dallton, Dalten.

DALY (Irish) To gather together. *Variations:* Dailey, Daley.

DAMARCUS (African-American) Combination of prefix "Da" and first name "Marcus."

DAMIAN (Greek) Tame. *Variations:* Dameon, Damiano, Damien, Damion, Damyan, Damyen, Damyon.

DAMON (Greek) Loyal one. *Notables:* Damon Runyon. *Variations:* Daemon, Daimen, Daimon, Daman, Damen, Damone, Daymon.

DANA (English) From Denmark. *Notables:* Comedian Dana Carvey; actor Dana Andrews.

DANE (English) Brook. *Notables:* Actor Dane Clark. *Variations:* Dain, Dayne.

DANFORTH (English) Town in Britain.

DANIEL (Hebrew) God is my judge. *Notables:* American frontiersman Daniel Boone; writer Daniel Defoe; actor Daniel Day-Lewis. *Variations:* Dan, Danakas, Danek, Dani, Daniele, Daniels, Danil, Danila, Danilkar, Danilo, Danko, Dannie, Danniel, Danny, Dano, Danya, Danylets, Danylo, Dasco, Donois, Dusan.

DANNY (Hebrew) Short form of Daniel. *Notables:* Comedians Danny DeVito, Danny Kaye, and Danny Thomas.

DANTE (Latin) Everlasting. *Notables:* Poet Dante Alighieri; artist Dante Gabriel Rossetti. *Variations:* Dontae, Donte.

DARBY (English) Area where deer graze. *Variations:* Dar, Darb, Derby.

DARCY (Irish) Dark one. *Variations:* D'Arcy, Darce, Darcey, Darsey, Darsy.

DARIUS (Greek) Wealthy. *Notables:* Singer Darius Rucker from Hootie and the Blowfish. *Variations:* Dario, Darrius.

DARNELL (English) Hidden area. *Variations:* Darnal, Darnall, Darnel.

u.s. president and first lady names

Presidents	First Ladies
Abraham	Abigail
Dwight	Barbara
Franklin	Bess
George	Betty
Gerald	Dolly
Harry	Eleanor
James	Hillary
John	Jacqueline
Lyndon	Laura
Richard	Mamie
Ronald	Martha
Theodore	Nancy
Thomas	Pat
Ulysses	Rosalynn

DARREN (Gaelic) Great. *Notables:* Actor Darren McGavin; Darren Stephens, husband on TV's *Bewitched. Variations:* Daran, Daren, Darin, Darran, Darrin, Darron, Darryn, Daryn.

DARRIE (Irish) Red hair. *Variations:* Darry.

DARRYL (English) An English last name. *Notables:* Baseball player Darryl Strawberry; singer Darryl Hall. *Variations:* Darrel, Darrell, Darrill, Darrol, Darryll, Daryl, Daryll.

DARTON (English) Place where deer graze.

DARWIN (English) Friend. *Variations:* Danvin, Derwin, Derwynn.

DASAN (Native American) Chief. *Variations:* Dassan.

DASHAWN (African-American) Combination of prefix "Da" and first name "Shawn."

DASHIELL (French) Page boy. *Notables:* Writer Dashiell Hammett. *Variations:* Dash.

DAVID (Hebrew) Cherished. *Notables:* Singers David Bowie, David Cassidy, and Davy Jones; TV host David Letterman; Dave Thomas, founder of Wendy's Hamburgers; baseball player Dave Winfield. *Variations:* Dave, Daveed, Davi, Davidek, Davie, Davy, Dewey, Dodya.

DAVIN (Scandinavian) Shining.

DAVIS (English) Son of David. *Variations:* Davison, Dawson.

DAWSON (English) Son of David. *Variations:* Dawsen.

DAYTON (English) Illuminated town.

DEACON (Greek) Servant. *Variations:* Deke, Dekel, Dekle.

DEAGAN (English) Able. *Variations:* Deegan.

DEAN (English) Valley. *Notables:* Singer Dean Martin; actor Dean Cain. *Variations:* Deane, Dene.

DECLAN (Irish) Irish saint. *Variations:* Deaclan.

DEDRICK (German) Ruler of the people.

DEJUAN (African-American) Combination of prefix "De" and first name "John." *Variations:* D'Juan, D'Won, DaJuan, Dawon, Dewaun, Dewon, Dujuan.

DEKER (Hebrew) To pierce.

DELANEY (Irish) Child of a competitor. *Variations:* Delaine, Delainey, Delainy, Delane, Delany.

DELBERT (English) Sunny day. *Notables:* Singer Delbert McClinton.

DELL (English) Valley. *Notables:* Baseball player Del Unser; rock-and-roll singer Del Shannon. *Variations:* Del.

DELMAR (Spanish) Oceanside. *Variations:* Delmer, Delmor, Delmore.

DELON (African-American) Unknown definition. *Variations:* Deelon, DeLon, DeLonn, Delonn, Dlon, DLonn.

DELROY (French) Of the king.

DEMETRIUS (Greek) Lover of the earth. *Variations:* Demeter, Demetre, Demetri, Demetrio, Demetris, Demetrois, Dimetre, Dimitri, Dimitry, Dmitri, Dmitrios, Dmitry.

DEMPSEY (Irish) Proud.

DENBY (Scandinavian) Denmark village. *Variations:* Danby, Denbey.

DENHAM (English) Town in a dell.

DENHOLM (Scottish) Village in Scotland. *Notables:* Actor Denholm Elliott.

DENNIS (Greek) *Notables:* Actors Dennis Weaver and Dennis Quaid, comedian/TV host Dennis Miller. *Variations:* Denies, Denis, Denka, Dennes, Denney, Denny, Dennys, Denys.

DENNISON (English) Son of Dennis. *Variations:* Denison, Dennyson, Dyson.

DENNY Short form of Dennis. *Notables:* Singer Denny Doherty of The Mamas and the Papas.

DENTON (English) Valley town. *Variations:* Dent, Denten, Dentin.

DENVER (English) Green valley.

DENZEL (English) From a town in Cornwall, England. *Notables:* Actor Denzel Washington. *Variations:* Denzell, Denziel, Denzil, Denzill, Denzyl.

DEONTAE (American) Newly created. *Variations:* D'Ante, Deante, Deonte, Diante, Diontay, Dionte, Donte.

DERBY (English) Village with deer.

DEREK (English) Leader. *Notables:* Baseball player Derek Jeter; actor Derek Jacobi. *Variations:* Dereck, Derick, Derik, Derreck, Derrek, Derrick, Derrik, Deryck, Deryk.

DERMOT (Irish) Free of jealousy. *Notables:* Actor Dermot Mulroney. *Variations:* Dermod, Dermott.

DERRY (Irish) Redheaded.

DESHAWN (African-American) Combination of prefix "De" and first name "Shawn." *Variations:* D'chaun, DaShaun, Dashawn, DeSean, DeShaun, Deshaun.

DESMOND (Irish) From South Munster, a region of Ireland. *Notables:* South African archbishop Desmond Tutu; writer Desmond Morris. *Variations:* Desi, Desmund, Dezmond.

DESTIN (French) Fate. *Variations:* Deston.

DEVAL (Hindu) Divine.

DEVEN (Hindu) God.

DEVERALL (English) Riverbank.

DEVIN (Irish) Poet. *Variations:* Dev, Devan, Deven, Devon, Devonn, Devyn.

DEVINE (Irish) Ox.

DEVLIN (Irish) Courageous. *Variations:* Devland, Devlen, Devlyn.

DEWAYNE (African-American) Combination of prefix "De" and first name "Wayne." *Variations:* D'Wayne, DeWayne.

DEWEY (English).

DEWITT (Flemish) Blond. *Notables:* Politician DeWitt Clinton.

DEXTER (Latin) Right-handed. *Variations:* Dex.

DIALLO (African) Bold.

DIAMOND (English) Jewel.

DICK (German) Short form of Richard or Frederick. *Notables:* TV hosts Dick Cavett and Dick Clark; U.S. Vice President Dick Cheney; comedian Dick Martin.

DICKENS (English) Last name. *Variations:* Dickon, Dickons.

DIDIER (French) Desired.

DIEDERIK (Scandinavian) Ruler of the people. *Variations:* Diderik, Didrik, Dierk.

DIEGO (Spanish) Form of James. *Notables:* Artist Diego Rivera.

DIETER (German) People's army.

DIETRICH (German) Leader of the people.

DIGBY (Irish) Village by a ditch.

DILLON (Irish) Loyal. *Variations:* Dillan, Dilon, Dilyn.

DIMA (Russian) Powerful warrior.

DIMITRI (Russian) Lover of the earth. *Variations:* Dimitr, Dimitre, Dimitrios, Dimitry, Dmitri.

DINO (Italian) Small sword. Nickname for Dean. *Variations:* Deno.

DINSMORE (Irish) Fort on the hill.

DION (Greek) Short form of Dionysus. *Notables:* Football player Deion Sanders. *Variations:* Deion, DeOn, Deon.

DIONYSUS (Latin) God of wine. *Variations:* Dionis, Dionusios, Dionysius.

DIPAK (Hindu) Lamp. *Notables:* Motivational speaker/writer Deepak Chopra. *Variations:* Deepak.

DIRK (German) Dagger. *Notables:* Actor Dirk Bogart.

DIXON (English) Son of Dick.

DOANE (English) Hilly area.

DOBRY (Polish) Good.

DOHERTY (Irish) Wicked. *Variations:* Dougherty.

DOLAN (Irish) Dark hair.

DOLPH (German) Short form of Adolph. *Notables:* Dolph Lundgren.

---

last names as first names

Boys	Girls
Campbell	Arden
Carter	Bailey
Cooper	Emerson
Dawson	Flynn
Hamilton	Harper
Hudson	Logan
Kennedy	Mackenzie
Mason	Macy
Parker	Mallory
Payton	Murphy
Porter	Piper
Sawyer	Quinn
Truman	Schuyler
Tucker	Tierney
Walker	Waverly

Boys	Girls
Axl	Alanis
Beck	Aretha
Bono	Avril
Elton	Beyonce
Elvis	Bjork
Eminem	Britney
Garth	Cher
Iggy	Gwen
Kayne	Jewel
Mick	Madonna
Moby	Mariah
P. Diddy	Shania
Prince	Sinead
Usher	Whitney

DOMINICK (Latin) Lord. *Notables:* Actor Dominic Chianese (Uncle Junior on TV's *Sopranos*); comedian Dom DeLuise; writer Dominick Dunne. *Variations:* Dom, Dome, Domek, Domenic, Domenico, Domicio, Domingo, Domingos, Dominic, Dominik, Dominique, Domo, Domokos, Nic, Nick, Nik.

DONAGH (Irish) Brown warrior. *Variations:* Donaghy, Donnchadh, Donogh, Donough.

DONAHUE (Irish) Dark fighter. *Variations:* Donahoe, Donohue.

DONAL (Irish) Form of Donald.

DONALD (Scottish) Mighty. *Notables:* Real estate mogul Donald Trump; actors Donald Sutherland and Donald O'Connor; singers Donny Osmond and Donnie Wahlberg. *Variations:* Don, Donal, Donaldo, Donalt, Donnie, Donny.

DONATO (Italian) Present. *Variations:* Don, Donat, Donatello, Donati, Donatien, Donatus.

DONNAN (Irish) Brown. *Variations:* Donn.

DONNELL (Irish) Brave.

DONNELLY (Irish) Dark-skinned man. *Variations:* Don, Donnell.

DONOVAN (Irish) Dark. *Notables:* Singer Donovan Leach. *Variations:* Don, Donavan, Donavon, Donoven, Donovon.

DOOLEY (Irish) Dark-skinned hero.

DORAN (Irish) Stranger. *Variations:* Doron, Dorran, Dorren.

DORIAN (Greek) A region in Greece. *Notables:* Dorian Gray, character in Oscar Wilde novel. *Variations:* Dorean, Dorien, Dorion, Dorrian, Dorryen.

DOUGAL (Scottish) Dark-skinned stranger. *Variations:* Dougald, Dougall, Dugal, Dugald, Dugall.

DOUGLAS (English) Dark water. *Notables:* General Douglas MacArthur; actor Douglas Fairbanks. *Variations:* Doug, Douglass.

DOV (Hebrew) Bear.

DOWAN (Irish) Black.

DOYLE (Irish) Dark stranger.

DRAKE (English) Dragon.

DREW (English) Wise. Form of Andrew. *Notables:* Comedian Drew Carey. *Variations:* Drewe, Dru.

DRUMMOND (Scottish) Druid's mountain.

DUANE (Irish) Dark-skinned. *Variations:* Duwayne, Dwain, Dwaine, Dwane, Dwayne.

DUDLEY (English) Field where people gather. *Notables:* Comedian Dudley Moore. *Variations:* Dudly.

DUFF (Celtic) Dark-skinned. *Variations:* Duffey, Duffy.

DUGAN (Irish) Swarthy. *Variations:* Doogan, Dougan, Douggan, Duggan.

DUKE (English) Leader. Short form of Marmaduke.

DUNCAN (Scottish) Brown-skinned soldier. *Variations:* Dun, Dune, Dunn.

DUNHAM (Celtic) Dark-skinned man.

DUNLEY (Celtic) Meadow on a hill.

DUNLOP (Scottish) Muddy hill.

DUNMORE (Scottish) Fort on a hill.

DUNN (Scottish) Brown. *Variations:* Dunne.

DUNSTAN (English) Rocky hill.

DUSAN (Czech) Spirit. *Variations:* Dusa, Dusanek, Duysek.

DUSTIN (English) Dusty place. *Notables:* Actor Dustin Hoffman. *Variations:* Dust, Dustan, Duston, Dusty, Dustyn.

DWIGHT (Flemish) Blond. *Notables:* U.S. President Dwight D. Eisenhower.

DWYER (Irish) Dark and wise.

DYER (English) One who dyes clothing for a living.

DYLAN (Welsh) Son of the ocean. *Notables:* Poet/writer Dylan Thomas. *Variations:* Dillan, Dillon, Dylon.

DYSON (English) Short form of Dennison.

EAMON (Irish) Rich protector. *Variations:* Amon, Eamonn.

EARL (English) Leader; nobleman. *Notables:* Writer Erle Stanley Gardner; basketball player Earl Monroe; musician Earl Scruggs. *Variations:* Earle, Earlie, Early, Erl, Erle.

EASTMAN (English) From the east.

EASTON (English) Eastern town.

EATON (English) Town on a river. *Variations:* Eatton, Eton, Eyton.

EBENEZER (Hebrew) Rock foundation. *Notables: A Christmas Carol's* Ebenezer Scrooge. *Variations:* Ebbaneza, Eben, Ebeneezer, Ebeneser, Ebenezar.

EBERHARD (German) Courageous. *Variations:* Eberhardt, Everhardt, Everhart.

ECKHARD (German) Brave.

ED (English) Short form of Edgar or Edward. *Notables:* Actors Ed Begley Jr. and "Kookie" Edd Byrnes. *Variations:* Edd.

EDDIE (English) Short form of Edward. *Notables:* Singers Eddie Van Halen, Eddie Vedder, and Eddy Arnold; actor Eddie Albert; comedian Eddie Murphy. *Variations:* Eddy.

EDEL (German) Noble. *Variations:* Edell.

EDEN (Hebrew) Delight. *Variations:* Eaden, Eadin, Edan, Edin.

EDGAR (English) Wealthy man who holds a spear. *Notables:* "Sleeping Prophet" Edgar Cayce; musician Edgar Winter; writer/poet Edgar Allan Poe. *Variations:* Edgard, Edgardo.

EDISON (English) Edward's son. *Variations:* Eddison, Edson.

EDMUND (English) Wealthy guardian. *Notables:* Explorer Sir Edmund Hillary. *Variations:* Edmand, Edmon, Edmunds, Esmond.

EDSEL (English) Home of a rich man. *Variations:* Edsell.

EDWARD (English) Guardian of property. *Notables:* Playwright Edward Albee; actors Edward Norton and Edward Burns; artist Edouard Manet. Some of the more exotic spellings only help to enhance the image of Edward. *Variations:* Edouard, Eduard, Edvard.

EDWIN (English) Rich friend. *Notables:* Singer Edwin McCain. *Variations:* Edwan, Edwen, Edwyn.

EFRAIN (Hebrew) Fruitful. *Variations:* Efran, Efrane, Efren.

EGAN (Irish) Fiery.

EGBERT (English) Bright sword.

EGINHARD (German) Power of the sword. *Variations:* Eginhardt, Einhard, Einhardt.

EGON (German) Formidable.

EGOR (Russian) Form of George. *Variations:* Igor.

EITAN (Hebrew) Form of Ethan. *Variations:* Eithan, Eiton.

ELAM (Hebrew) Highland.

ELAN (Hebrew) Tree. *Variations:* Ilan.

ELDON (English) Consecrated hill.

ELDRIDGE (English) Wise leader. *Notables:* Black Panther Eldridge Cleaver.

ELEAZAR (Hebrew) God helps. *Variations:* Eliazar, Eliezer.

ELEBERT (English) Noble; shining.

ELGIN (English) White.

ELI (Hebrew) God is great. *Notables:* Actor Eli Wallach; writer/activist Elie Wiesel. *Variations:* Elie, Ely.

ELIAN (English) Form of Elijah. *Variations:* Elion, Ellian, Ellion.

names for redheads

Boys	Girls
Clancy	Auburn
Corcoran	Derry
Flynn	Flannery
Reed	Omaira
Rooney	Pyrrha
Rory	Ruby
Rufus	Ruffina
Russell	Scarlett

school daze: names from teachers (part i)

Teachers often have the best access to up-and-coming, diverse names. This selection comes from a second-grade class in Livingston, New Jersey.

Allix	Kimia
Ariella	Maanas
Bar	Mallika
Bari	Mayer
Beagy	Nadav
Beau	Orentino
Cataldo	Payton
Clement	Reed
Eeshin	Remi
Gavriel	Sage
Giacomo	Sahar
Gianna	Sohan
Hasan	Tali
Hoihim	Thalia
Karmyn	Yuval
Kashimire	Zain
Kayla	Zigie

ELIAZ (Hebrew) My God is powerful. *Variations:* Elias.

ELIJAH (Hebrew) The Lord is my God. *Notables:* Actor Elijah Wood. *Variations:* Elek, Elias, Eliasz, Elie, Eliya, Eliyahu, Ellis, Elya.

ELIRAN (Hebrew) My God is song. *Variations:* Eliron.

ELISHA (Hebrew) God is my salvation. *Variations:* Elish, Elisher, Elishua.

ELIYAHU (Hebrew) The Lord is my God.

ELLARD (German) Noble. *Variations:* Ellerd.

ELLERY (English) Elder trees. *Variations:* Ellary.

ELLIOT (English) God on high. *Notables:* Actor Elliot Gould; law enforcer Eliot Ness. *Variations:* Eliot, Eliott, Elliott.

ELLIS (English) Form of Elias.

ELLISON (English) Son of Ellis. *Variations:* Elison, Ellyson, Elson.

ELMAN (German) Elm tree.

ELMER (English) Noble. *Notables:* Cartoon character Elmer Fudd. *Variations:* Aylmar, Aylmer, Aymer, Ellmer, Elmir.

ELMO (Italian) Helmet.

ELMORE (English) Moor with elm trees. *Notables:* Writer Elmore Leonard.

ELROY Form of Leroy. *Variations:* El Roy, Elroi.

ELTON (English) Ella's town; old town. *Notables:* Singer/songwriter Elton John.

ELVIN (English) Old friend. *Notables:* Singer Elvin Bishop.

ELVIS (Scandinavian) Wise. *Notables:* Singers Elvis Presley and Elvis Costello.

ELWOOD (English) Old wood. *Variations:* Ellwood.

EMBER (English) Ashes.

EMERSON (German) Emery's son.

EMERY (German) Ruler of the house. *Variations:* Emmery, Emory.

EMILE (French) Eager to please. *Notables:* Writer Emile Zola. *Variations:* Emil, Emilek, Emilio, Emilo, Emils.

EMLYN (Welsh) Waterfall.

EMMANUEL (Hebrew) God is among us. *Variations:* Emanuel, Emmanuil, Immanuel, Manny, Manuel.

EMMETT (German) Powerful. *Notables:* Clown Emmett Kelly Jr. *Variations:* Emmet, Emmot, Emmott.

EMRICK (German) Form of Emery.

EMRYS (Welsh) Form of Ambrose.

ENGELBERT (German) Bright as an angel. *Notables:* Singer Engelbert Humperdinck. *Variations:* Englebert.

ENNIS (Gaelic) Island.

ENOCH (Hebrew) Dedicated.

ENOS (Hebrew) Man. *Variations:* Enosa, Enosh.

ENRICO (Italian) Leader of the house. *Notables:* Opera great Enrico Caruso. *Variations:* Enric, Enrikos, Enrique.

ENZO (Italian) Form of Henry.

EOIN (Irish) God is good.

EPHRAIM (Hebrew) Fertile. *Notables:* Actor Efrem Zimbalist Jr. *Variations:* Efraim, Efrain, Efrayim, Efrem, Efren, Ephraim, Ephrain, Ephrayim.

ERASMUS (Greek) Loved. *Variations:* Erasme, Erasmo, Erastus, Rasmus.

ERCOLE (Italian) Gift.

ERHARD (German) Determination. *Variations:* Erhardt, Erhart.

ERIC (Scandinavian) Mighty ruler. *Notables:* Singer/guitarist Eric Clapton; news reporter Eric Severeid; actor Erik Estrada. *Variations:* Erek, Erich, Erick, Erico, Erik.

ERICKSON (English) Son of Eric.

ERLAND (English) Nobleman's land. *Variations:* Erlend, Erlund.

ERNEST (English) Earnest. *Notables:* Writer Ernest Hemingway; actor Ernest Borgnine. *Variations:* Earnest, Ernestino, Ernesto, Ernst.

ERNIE Short form of Ernest. *Notables:* Folk singer Tennessee Ernie Ford; comedian Ernie Kovacs. *Variations:* Erney, Enry.

ERNO (Hungarian) Form of Ernest.

ERROL (English) Form of Earl. *Notables:* Actor Errol Flynn. *Variations:* Erol, Erroll, Erryl.

ERSKINE (Scottish) High cliff.

ERVIN (Hungarian) Form of Erwin. *Notables:* Basketball great Earvin "Magic" Johnson. *Variations:* Earvin, Erving, Ervyn.

ERWIN (English) Boar. *Variations:* Erwinek, Erwyn, Erwynn, Irwin.

ESAU (Hebrew) Rough and hairy.

ESMOND (English) Rich protector.

ESSEX (English) Eastern town.

ESTEBAN (Spanish) Form of Stephen. *Variations:* Estabon, Esteben, Estefan, Estevan.

ETHAN (Hebrew) Steadfast. *Notables:* Patriot Ethan Allen; actor Ethan Hawke. *Variations:* Eathan, Ethe, Ethen.

ETHELBERT (English) Highborn.

ÉTIENNE (French) Crown. Variation of Stephen.

EUCLID (Greek) Intelligent.

EUGENE (Greek) Well-born. *Notables:* Playwright Eugene O'Neill; actor/comedian Eugene Levy; music conductor Eugene Ormandy. *Variations:* Eugen, Eugeni, Eugenio, Eugenius, Gene.

EUSTACE (Greek) Productive. *Variations:* Eustis.

EVAN (Welsh) God is good. *Variations:* Ev, Evann, Evans, Evin, Evon.

EVANDER (Scottish) Good man. *Notables:* Boxer Evander Holyfield.

EVERETT (English) Wild boar. *Variations:* Everard, Everet, Everhard, Everitt.

EVERLEY (English) Boar meadow. *Variations:* Everlea, Everlee.

EVERTON (English) Boar town.

EWAN (Scottish) Form of Eugene. *Notables:* Actor Ewan MacGregor. *Variations:* Euan, Euen, Ewen.

EWING (English) Lawful. *Variations:* Ewynn.

EZEKIEL (Hebrew) The strength of God. *Variations:* Ezekial, Ezequiel, Zeke.

EZRA (Hebrew) Helper. *Notables:* Poet Ezra Pound. *Variations:* Esra, Ezera, Ezri.

FABIAN (Latin) One who grows beans. *Notables:* Fifties singer Fabian Forte. *Variations:* Faba, Fabek, Faber, Fabert, Fabiano, Fabien, Fabio, Fabius, Fabiyan, Fabyan, Fabyen.

FABRICE (French) One who works with his hands. *Variations:* Fabrizio, Fabrizius.

FADEY (Russian) Bold. *Variations:* Faddei, Fadeaushka, Fadeuka.

FADIL (Arabic) Generous.

FAGAN (Irish) Fiery child. *Variations:* Fagin.

FAHD (Arabic) Leopard. *Variations:* Fahad.

FAIRCHILD (English) Fair-haired child.

FAIRFAX (English) Blond.

FAIRLEIGH (English) Meadow with bulls. *Variations:* Fairlay, Fairlee, Fairlie, Farleigh, Farley.

FAISAL (Arabic) Resolute. *Variations:* Faisel, Fasel, Faysal.

FALAN (Hindu) Fertile. *Variations:* Faleen, Falit.

FALKNER (English) Falcon trainer. *Variations:* Falconer, Falconner, Faulkner, Fowler.

FAOLAN (Irish) Little wolf. *Variations:* Felan, Phelan.

FARLEY (English) Sheep meadow. *Notables:* Actor Farley Granger. *Variations:* Farlay, Farleigh.

FARNELL (English) Hill covered with ferns.

FARNHAM (English) Meadow of the ferns. *Variations:* Farnam, Farnum, Fernham.

FARNLEY (English) Field with ferns. *Variations:* Farnlea, Farnleigh, Fernleigh, Fernley.

FARON (English) Unknown definition. Last name. *Variations:* Faran, Farin, Farran, Farrin, Farron, Farrun, Farun.

FAROUK (Arabic) Truth. *Variations:* Faraq, Faroqh.

FARQUHAR (Scottish) Dear one. *Variations:* Farquar, Farquarson, Farquharson, Fearchar.

FARR (English) Wayfarer.

FARRAR (Irish) Blacksmith.

FARRELL (Irish) Courageous man. *Variations:* Farall, Farrel, Farrill, Farryll, Ferrel, Ferrell, Ferrill, Ferryl.

FAUST (Latin) Lucky. *Variations:* Faustino, Fausto, Faustus.

FAVIAN (Latin) Understanding man.

FAXON (English) Long haired.

FAYIZ (Arabic) Winner.

FEIVEL (Yiddish) Bright one. *Variations:* Feiwel.

FELIPE (Spanish) Form of Philip.

FELIX (Latin) Happy-go-lucky. *Variations:* Feliz.

FELTON (English) Field town.

FENWICK (English) Farm on a marsh.

FERDINAND (German) Brave traveler. *Notables:* Explorer Ferdinand Magellan; actor Fernando Lamas. *Variations:* Ferdinando, Ferdynand, Fernand, Fernando.

FERGUS (Scottish) Man of vigor. *Variations:* Fergie, Fergis.

FERGUSON (Scottish) Son of Fergus.

FEROZ (Persian) Lucky.

FERRAND (French) Gray hair. *Variations:* Farand, Farrand, Farrant, Ferrant.

FERRIS (Irish) Rock. *Notables:* Film character Ferris Bueller.

FIDEL (Latin) Faith. *Notables:* Cuban President Fidel Castro. *Variations:* Fidal, Fidele, Fidelio, Fidelis, Fidello.

FIELDING (English) In the field. *Variations:* Field.

FILBERT (English) Brilliant. *Variations:* Philbert.

FILMORE (English) Famous. *Variations:* Fillmore.

FINIAN (Irish) Fair. *Variations:* Finnian, Fionan, Fionn.

FINLAY (Irish) Fair-haired hero. *Variations:* Findlay, Findley, Finleigh, Finley.

FINN (Irish) Short for Finlay or Finnegan.

FINNEGAN (Irish) Fair. *Variations:* Finegan.

FIORELLO (Italian) Little flower. *Notables:* New York City Mayor Fiorello LaGuardia.

FIRTH (English) Forest.

FISHER (English) Fisherman. *Notables:* Actor Fisher Stevens. *Variations:* Fischer.

FISK (English) Fisherman. *Variations:* Fiske.

FITCH (English) Weasel or ferret.

FITZ (English) Son.

FITZGERALD (English) Son of the mighty spear holder.

FITZPATRICK (English) Son of Patrick.

FITZROY (Irish) Son of a king.

FLAMINIO (Spanish) Priest.

FLANNERY (Irish) Red hair. *Variations:* Flaine, Flann, Flannan.

FLAVIAN (Latin) Blond. *Variations:* Flavia, Flavien, Flavio.

FLEMING (English) Man from the valley. *Variations:* Flemming.

FLETCHER (English) One who makes arrows. *Variations:* Fletch.

FLINT (English) Stream. *Variations:* Flynt.

FLIP (American) Short for Philip. *Notables:* Comedian Flip Wilson.

FLORENT (French) Flower. *Variations:* Florenz.

FLORIAN (Latin) In bloom. *Variations:* Florien, Florino, Floryan.

FLOYD (Welsh) Gray haired. *Notables:* Boxer Floyd Patterson.

FLYNN (Irish) Red-haired man's son. *Variations:* Flin, Flinn, Flyn.

FONTAINE (French) Fountain.

FORBES (Scottish) Field.

FORD (English) River crossing.

FOREST (French) Woods. *Notables:* Film character Forrest Gump; newscaster Forrest Sawyer; actors Forrest Whittaker and Forrest Tucker. *Variations:* Forester, Forrest, Forrester, Forster, Foster.

FORTUNÉ (French) Lucky. *Variations:* Fortunato, Fortunatus, Fortunio.

FOSTER (Latin) Woodsman.

FOWLER (English) Bird trapper.

goth baby names

If you're a heavy metal fan, like to dress in black, and find the dark side fun, here's a list of baby names—mostly unisex—for your little Goth-in-training.

Girls	Unisex
Ankha	Lynx
Aunika	Malificent
Elvira	Mysterie
Esperanza	Onyx
Lunaria	Plath
Boys	Rasputin(a)
Crow	Raven
Dickinson	Shelley
Lucifer	
Ozzie	
Voltaire	

Tropical storms make news every year. Each storm is given a male or female name, alternating with each storm. Depending on your perspective, a storm name might be either an interesting choice or one to avoid. Here are the hurricane names selected for 2006:

Alberto	Leslie
Beryl	Michael
Chris	Nadine
Debby	Oscar
Ernesto	Patty
Florence	Rafael
Gordon	Sandy
Helene	Tony
Isaac	Valerie
Joyce	William
Kirk	

FRANCIS (Latin) Frenchman. *Notables:* Lawyer and writer of "The Star-Spangled Banner," Francis Scott Key. *Variations:* Fran, Franchot, Francisco, Franco, Francois.

FRANK (English) Short form of Francis or Franklin. *Notables:* Singers Frank Sinatra, Frank Zappa, and Frankie Valli; architect Frank Lloyd Wright; film directors Frank Capra and Frank Oz. *Variations:* Franc, Frankie.

FRANKLIN (English) A free property owner. *Notables:* U.S. president Franklin D. Roosevelt. *Variations:* Franklyn, Franklynn.

FRANZ (German) Form of Francis. *Notables:* Writer Franz Kafka; composer Franz Liszt. *Variations:* Frans, Franzen, Franzl.

FRASER (French) Strawberry. *Variations:* Fraser, Fraze, Frazer, Frazier.

FRAYNE (English) Foreign. *Variations:* Fraine, Frayn, Freyne.

FRED Short form of Alfred or Frederick. *Notables:* Dancer Fred Astaire; actor Fred MacMurray; children's TV show host Fred Rogers; singers Fred Durst and Freddie Mercury.

FREDERICK (German) Merciful leader. *Notables:* Abolitionist Frederick Douglass; composer Frederick Chopin; philosopher Friedrich Nietzsche. *Variations:* Fred, Freddie, Freddy, Fredek, Frederich, Frederico, Frederik, Fredric, Fredrick, Friedrich, Fritz.

FREEMAN (English) Free man.

FREMONT (German) Protector of liberty.

FREY (Scandinavian) Supreme Lord.

FRICK (English) Brave.

FRITZ (German) Form of Frederick. *Notables:* Film director Fritz Lang. *Variations:* Fritzchen, Fritzroy.

FULLER (English) One who works with cloth.

FULTON (English) Town settlement.

FYFE (Scottish) Town in Scotland. *Variations:* Fife, Fyffe.

FYODOR (Russian) Form of Theodore. *Variations:* Feodor.

GABE (Hebrew) Short form of Gabriel. *Notables:* Comedian Gabe Kaplan.

GABRIEL (Hebrew) Man of God. *Notables:* Writer Gabriel Garcia Marquez; actor Gabriel Byrne. *Variations:* Gab, Gabby, Gabe, Gabi, Gabko, Gabo, Gabor, Gabriele, Gabrielli, Gabriello, Gabris, Gabys, Gavi, Gavriel.

GADIEL (Arabic) Fortune from God. *Variations:* Gaddiel.

GAGE (French) Pledge.

GAINES (English) To gain. *Variations:* Gaynes.

GAIR (Irish) Small one. *Variations:* Gaer, Geir.

GAIUS (Latin) Rejoice.

GALBRAITH (Irish) Scotsman in Ireland.

GALE (Irish) Foreigner. *Variations:* Gael, Gail.

GALEN (Greek) Healer. *Variations:* Galeno.

GALILEO (Italian) From Galilee. *Notables:* Astronomer Galileo Galilei.

GALLAGHER (Irish) Foreign; helper.

GALLOWAY (Irish) Foreigner. *Variations:* Gallway, Galway.

GALVIN (Irish) Sparrow. *Variations:* Gallven, Gallvin, Galvan, Galven.

GAMAL (Arabic) Camel.

GAMLIEL (Hebrew) God is my reward. *Variations:* Gamaliel.

GANESH (Hindu) Lord of them all.

GANNON (Irish) Light-skinned.

GARDNER (English) Gardener.

GAREK (Polish) Wealth with a spear. Variation of Edgar. *Variations:* Garreck, Garrik.

GAREN (English) Form of Gary.

GARETH (Welsh) Gentle. *Variations:* Garith, Garreth, Garyth.

GARFIELD (English) Field of spears. *Notables:* Cartoon cat Garfield.

GARLAND (French) Wreath. *Variations:* Garlan, Garlen, Garlyn.

GARNER (English) To harvest grain. *Variations:* Gar.

GARNET (English) Red precious gem. *Variations:* Garnett.

GARNOCK (Welsh) River of alder trees.

GARRETT (Irish) Brave with a spear. *Variations:* Garett, Garrat.

GARRICK (English) He who rules with a spear. *Variations:* Garreck, Garryck, Garyk.

GARRISON (English) Fort.

GARSON (English) Son of Gar.

GARTH (Scandinavian) Gardener. *Notables:* Country singer Garth Brooks.

GARVEY (Irish) Peace. *Variations:* Garvie, Garvy.

GARVIN (English) Friend with a spear. *Variations:* Garvan, Garven, Garvyn.

GARWOOD (English) Evergreen.

GARY (English) Spearman. *Notables:* Actor Gary Cooper; cartoonist Garry Trudeau; comedian Garry Shandling. *Variations:* Garey, Garrey, Garry.

GASPARD (French) Form of Jasper. *Variations:* Gaspar, Gasper.

GASTON (French) Man from Gascony, France. *Variations:* Gascon.

GAUTIER (French) Powerful leader. *Variations:* Gauther, Gauthier.

GAVIN (Welsh) White falcon. *Notables:* Actor Gavin McLeod. *Variations:* Gavan, Gaven, Gavyn, Gawain, Gawaine, Gawayn, Gawayne, Gawen.

GAYLORD (French) Lively lord.

GAYNOR (Irish) Son of a pale man.

GEARY (English) Changeable. *Variations:* Gearey.

GEMINI (Latin) Twins.

GENOVESE (Italian) From Genoa.

GENE (English) Short form of Eugene. *Notables:* Dancer/actor Gene Kelly; Kiss member Gene Simmons; comedic actor Gene Wilder; actor Gene Hackman; *Star Trek* creator/producer Gene Roddenberry. *Variations:* Genek, Genio, Genka, Genya.

GEOFFREY (German) Peace. Alternative spelling of Jeffrey.

GEORGE (Greek) Farmer. *Notables:* U.S. Presidents George Washington, George H. W. Bush, and George W. Bush; General George Patton; designer Giorgio Armani; actor George Clooney; comedian George Burns. *Variations:* Georg, Georges, Georgi, Georgios, Georgy, Giorgio, Giorgos.

GERALD (German) Ruler with a spear. *Notables:* U.S. President Gerald Ford; TV journalist/host Geraldo Rivera. *Variations:* Geralde, Geraldo, Geraud, Gerrald, Gerrold, Gerry, Jerald, Jeralde, Jeraud, Jerold, Jerrald, Jerrold, Jerry.

GERARD (German) Brave with a spear. *Notables:* Actor Gerard Depardieu. *Variations:* Garrard, Gerhard, Gerrard, Gerrit, Gerry.

GERHARD (German) Form of Gerard. *Variations:* Gerhardt.

GERMAIN (French) From Germany. *Variations:* Germaine, German, Germane, Germayn, Germayne, Jermain, Jermaine, Jermane, Jermayn, Jermayne.

GERONIMO (Italian) Form of Jerome. *Notables:* Geronimo, the famous Apache Indian chief.

GERSHON (Hebrew) Exiled. *Variations:* Gerson.

GERVAISE (French) Honorable. *Variations:* Gervase, Gervais.

GERWIN (Welsh) Fair love. *Variations:* Gerwen, Gerwyn.

popular biblical names

Boys	Girls
Aaron	Bathsheba
Adam	Deborah
Benjamin	Esther
Daniel	Eve
David	Leah
Isaac	Naomi
Joseph	Rachel
Joshua	Rebecca
Noah	Ruth
Samuel	Sarah

names you might want to avoid

Due to certain reputations of the famous (and infamous) who share these names, you might want to think twice about bestowing these on your innocent newborn!

Boys	Girls
Adolph	Delilah
Attila	Imelda
Caligula	Jezebel
Darth	Leona
Judas	Lizzie
Lucifer	Lorena
Momar	Martha
Nero	Omarosa
Osama	Salome
Saddam	Zsa Zsa

GEVARIAH (Hebrew) God's might. *Variations:* Gevaria, Gevarya, Gevaryah, Gevaryahu.

GHALIB (Arabic) Conqueror; dominant.

GIACOMO (Italian) Form of Jacob.

GIAN (Italian) Form of Giovanni (John).

GIANCARLO (Italian) Combination of John and Charles. *Notables:* Actor Giancarlo Giannini.

GIANNI (Italian) Short form of Giovanni (John). *Notables:* Designer Gianni Versace. *Variations:* Giannes, Gianni, Giannos.

GIBSON (English) Son of Gilbert. *Variations:* Gibb, Gibbons, Gibbs, Gibby.

GIDEON (Hebrew) One who cuts down trees. *Variations:* Gideone, Gidon, Gidoni.

GIFFORD (English) Giver. *Variations:* Gifferd, Giffyrd.

GIG (English) Horse carriage. *Notables:* Actor Gig Young.

GILAD (Arabic) Camel's hump. *Variations:* Giladi, Gilead.

GILAM (Hebrew) Joy of a people.

GILBERT (German) Bright pledge. *Notables:* Comedian Gilbert Godfried. *Variations:* Gil, Gilberto.

GILCHRIST (Irish) Servant of Christ.

GILES (English) Young goat. *Variations:* Gil, Gilles, Gyles.

GILLANDERS (Scottish) Servant of St. Andrew. *Variations:* Gille Ainndreis, Gille Anndrai.

GILLEAN (Scottish) Servant of St. John. *Variations:* Gillan, Gillen, Gillian.

GILLESPIE (Irish) Servant of the bishop. *Variations:* Gilleasbuig, Gillis, Giolla Easpaig.

GILLETT (French) Young Gilbert. *Variations:* Gelett, Gelette, Gillette.

GILMORE (Irish) Servant of the Virgin Mary. *Variations:* Gillmore, Gillmour, Gilmour, Giolle Maire.

GILROY (Irish) Son of the king's servant. *Variations:* Gilderoy, Gildray, Gildrey, Gildroy, Gillroy.

GILSON (English) Son of Gilbert.

GINO (Italian) Form of Eugene.

GIONA (Italian) Italian version of Jonah.

GIORGIO (Italian) George. *Notables:* Designer Giorgio Armani.

GIOVANNI (Italian) God is good. Italian version of John.

GIPSY (English) Wanderer. *Variations:* Gypsy.

GIRVIN (Irish) Small, tough child. *Variations:* Girvan, Girven, Girvon.

GIUSEPPE (Italian) God will increase. Italian version of Joseph. *Notables:* Composer Giuseppe Verdi.

GLADWIN (English) Lighthearted. .

GLEN (Irish) Narrow valley. *Notables:* Musician Glenn Miller; actor Glenn Ford; singer Glen Campbell. *Variations:* Glenn.

GLENDON (Scottish) Town in a glen. *Variations:* Glenden, Glendin, Glenton, Glentworth.

GLENDOWER (Welsh) Valley of water.

GODDARD (German) Firm God. *Variations:* Godard, Godart, Goddart, Godhardt, Godhart, Gothart, Gotthard, Gotthardt, Gotthart.

GODFREY (German) God is peace. Variation of Geoffrey. *Notables:* Comedian Godfrey Cambridge. *Variations:* Goddfrey, Godfried, Gotfrid, Gottfrid, Gottfried.

GODWIN (English) God's friend. *Variations:* Godwinn, Godwyn, Godwynn.

GOLDWIN (English) Golden friend. *Variations:* Goldewin, Goldewyn, Goldwinn, Goldwyn, Goldwynn.

GOLIATH (Hebrew) Exiled. *Variations:* Golliath.

GOMER (English) Good fight. *Notables:* TV's Gomer Pyle.

GONZALO (Spanish) Wolf. *Variations:* Gonzales.

GOODWIN (English) Good friend.

GORDON (English) Round hill. *Notables:* Singers Gordon Lightfoot and Gordon Sumner (Sting); hockey player Gordie Howe. *Variations:* Gordan, Gorden, Gordie, Gordy.

GORE (English) Spear.

GORMAN (Irish) Child with blue eyes.

GOTTFRIED (German) Form of Geoffrey.

GOWER (Welsh) Pure. *Notables:* Choreographer Gower Champion.

GRADY (Irish) Famous. *Variations:* Gradey, Graidey, Graidy.

GRAHAM (English) Gray house. *Notables:* Singer Graham Nash; TV chef Graham Kerr; Monty Python comedian Graham Chapman; novelist Graham Greene. *Variations:* Graeham, Graeme, Grahame, Gram.

GRANGER (French) Farmer.

GRANT (French) Great.

GRANTLY (English) Gray meadow. *Variations:* Grantlea, Grantleigh, Grantley.

GRANVILLE (French) Big town. *Variations:* Granvil, Granvile, Granvill, Grenville.

GRAY (English) Gray. *Variations:* Graydon, Grayson, Grey.

GRAYDON (English) Son of gray land. *Notables: Vanity Fair* editor Graydon Carter.

GRAYSON (English) Son of a man with gray hair. *Variations:* Greyson.

GREELEY (English) Gray meadow. *Variations:* Greelea, Greeleigh, Greely.

GREG Short form of Gregory. *Notables:* Actor Greg Kinnear; diver Greg Louganis.

GREGORY (Latin) Observant. *Notables:* Actor Gregory Peck; actor/dancer Gregory Hines. *Variations:* Greg, Gregg, Gregoire, Gregor, Gregorio, Gregorios, Gregos, Greig, Gries, Grigor.

GRIFFIN (Latin) One with a hooked nose. *Notables:* Actor Griffin Dunne. *Variations:* Griff, Griffon, Gryphon.

GRIFFITH (Welsh) Powerful leader. *Variations:* Griff, Griffyth, Gryffyth.

GRISWOLD (German) Gray forest.

GROVER (English) Grove of trees. *Notables:* U.S. President Grover Cleveland.

GUIDO (Italian) A form of Guy.

GUILFORD (English) Ford with yellow flowers. *Variations:* Gilford, Guildford.

GULSHAN (Hindu) Garden.

GULZAR (Arabic) Blooming.

GUNNAR (Scandinavian) Battle. *Variations:* Gun, Gunder.

GUNTHER (Scandinavian) Warrior. *Variations:* Guenther, Gun, Gunnar, Guntar, Gunter, Guntero, Gunthar.

GUS (English) Short form of Augustus or Gustaf.

GUSTAF (Scandinavian) Staff of the gods. *Notables:* Composer Gustav Mahler. *Variations:* Gus, Gustaff, Gustav, Gustave, Gustavo, Gustavs, Gusti, Gustik, Gustus, Gusty.

GUTHRIE (Irish) Windy area. *Variations:* Guthry.

GUY (French) Guide. *Notables:* Designer Guy Laroche; film director and "Mr. Madonna" Guy Ritchie. *Variations:* Gui, Guion, Guyon.

GWYNN (Welsh) Fair.

GYAN (Hindu) Knowledge. *Variations:* Gyani.

more celebrity baby names

Coco Riley
Courtney Cox and David Arquette

Diezel and Denim
Toni Braxton

Dylan and Carys
Michael Douglas and Catherine Zeta Jones

Fifi Trixibelle, Peaches Honeyblossom, and Pixie
Bob Geldof

Finley, Iris, Rafferty, and Rudy
Jude Law and Sadie Frost

Gulliver
Gary Oldman

Heavenly Hiraani Tiger Lily
Michael Hutchence and Paula Yates

Levi Roan Green and Maya
Uma Thurman and Ethan Hawke

HABIB (Arabic) Dear.

HACKETT (German) Wood cutter.

HADAD (Arabic) The Syrian god of virility.

HADAR (Hebrew) Glory.

HADDAD (Arabic) Blacksmith.

HADDEN (English) Hill covered with heather. *Variations:* Haddon.

HADLEY (English) Meadow of heather. *Variations:* Hadlea, Hadlee, Hadleigh, Hadly, Headley, Hedley, Hedly.

HADRIAN (Scandinavian) Black earth.

HADRIEL (Hebrew) God's glory.

HADWIN (English) Friend in war. *Variations:* Hadwinn, Hadwyn, Hadwynne.

HAFIZ (Arabic) Protector.

HAGAN (Irish) Home ruler. *Variations:* Hagen, Haggan.

HAGLEY (English) Surrounded by hedges. *Variations:* Haglea, Haglee, Hagleigh, Haig.

HAIDAR (Arabic) Lion.

HAKEEM (Arabic) Wise. *Variations:* Hakem, Hakim.

HAL (English) Short form of Harold. *Notables:* Actors Hal Linden and Hal Holbrook.

HALBERT (English) Bright hero. *Variations:* Halburt.

HALDAN (Scandinavian) Half Danish. *Variations:* Haldane, Halden.

HALE (English) Healthy. *Variations:* Haley.

HALEEM (Arabic) Gentle. *Variations:* Halim.

HALEN (Scandinavian) Hall.

HALEY (Irish) Clover. *Variations:* Haile, Hailey, Haily.

HALIL (Turkish) Good friend.

HALIM (Arabic) Gentle.

HALLAM (English) Valley.

HALLIWELL (English) Holy well.

HALSEY (English) The island that belongs to Hal. *Variations:* Hallsey, Hallsy, Halsy.

HALSTEAD (English) Grounds of the manor.

HALSTEN (Scandinavian) Rock and stone. *Variations:* Hallstein, Hallsten, Hallston, Halston.

HALYARD (Scandinavian) Defender of the rock. *Variations:* Hallvard, Hallvor, Halvar, Halvor.

HAM (Hebrew) Heat. Short form of Hamilton.

HAMAL (Arabic) Lamb.

HAMID (Arabic) Greatly praised. Derivative of Mohammed. *Variations:* Hammad, Hammed.

HAMILL (English) Scarred. *Variations:* Hamel, Hamell, Hamil, Hammill.

HAMILTON (English) Fortified castle. *Notables:* Politician Hamilton Jordan. *Variations:* Hamelton.

HAMISH (Scottish) He who removes.

HAMLET (English) Village. *Notables:* Hamlet, Shakespeare's tragic Prince of Denmark.

HAMLIN (German) One who loves to stay at home. *Variations:* Hamelin, Hamlen, Hamlyn.

HAMMET (English) Village. *Variations:* Hammett.

HAMMOND (English) Village. *Variations:* Hamond.

HAMPTON (English) A town in England.

HAMUND (Scandinavian) Mythological figure.

HAMZA (Arabic) Powerful. *Variations:* Hamzah, Hamzeh.

popular african-american names

Boys	Girls
Deiondre	Ananda
Denzel	Beyonce
Deshawn	Latanya
Dewayne	Latisha
Jamar	Monisha
Mykelti	Nichelle
Roshaun	Shantell
Shaquille	Talisha
Taurean	Tamira
Tyrell	Taniel

korean names

Boys	Girls
Chin	Cho
Chul	Eun
Chung-Ho	Hea
Hyun-Ki	Hei
Hyun-Su	Hyun
Jin-Ho	Min
Shin	Sook
Suk	Sun
Yon	Young

HANAN (Hebrew) God is good.

HANDEL (German) God is good.

HANDLEY (English) Clearing in the woods. *Variations:* Handleigh, Hanley.

HANIF (Arabic) Believer.

HANK (English) Ruler of the estate. *Notables:* Baseball's Hank Aaron; actor Hank Azaria; country singer Hank Williams.

HANNES (Scandinavian) God is good. Variation of John. *Variations:* Haensel, Hannu, Hans, Hansel, Hansl.

HANNIBAL (English) Unknown definition. *Notables:* Hannibal Lecter from *Silence of the Lambs.*

HANS (Scandinavian) Form of John. *Notables:* Artist Hans Holbein.

HANSEL (Scandinavian) Form of Hans. *Notables:* Fairy tale character from *Hansel and Gretel.*

HANSON (Scandinavian) Son of Hans. *Variations:* Hansen, Hanssen, Hansson.

HARAL (Scottish) Leader of the army. *Variations:* Arailt.

HARB (Arabic) Warrior.

HARBIN (French) Little bright warrior.

HARCOURT (French) Fortified dwelling.

HARDEN (English) Valley of rabbits. *Variations:* Hardin.

HARDING (English) Hardy.

HAREL (Hebrew) Mountain of God. *Variations:* Harell, Harrell.

HARGROVE (English) Grove of hares. *Variations:* Hargreave.

HARI (Hindu) Tawny.

HARISH (Hindu) Lord. *Variations:* Haresh.

HARITH (Arabic) Plowman. *Variations:* Harithah.

HARKIN (Irish) Dark red. *Variations:* Harkan, Harken.

HARLAN (English) Army land. *Notables:* Writer Harlan Coben. *Variations:* Harland, Harlen, Harlenn, Harlin, Harlyn, Harlynn.

HARLEY (English) Rabbit pasture. *Variations:* Arlea, Arleigh, Arley, Harlea, Harlee, Harleiah, Harly.

HARLOW (English) Meadow of the hares.

HARMON (English) Form of Herman.

HAROLD (English) Army ruler. *Notables:* Playwright Harold Pinter; theater producer/director Harold Prince. *Variations:* Hal, Harailt, Harald, Haraldo, Haralds, Haroldas, Haroldo.

HAROUN (Arabic) Exalted.

HARPER (English) Harp player.

HARRIS (English) Form of Harrison.

HARRISON (English) Harry's son. *Notables:* Actor Harrison Ford. *Variations:* Harrisen.

HARRY (English) Ruler at home. Variation of Henry. *Notables:* Britain's Prince Harry; U.S. President Harry Truman; singer Harry Belafonte; illusionist Harry Houdini; popular literary character Harry Potter. *Variations:* Harrey, Harri, Harrie.

HART (English) Form of Hartley.

HARTLEY (English) Deer meadow.

HARTMAN (German) Hard man. *Variations:* Hartmann.

HARTWELL (English) Well where stags drink. *Variations:* Harwell, Harwill.

HARVEY (French) Eager for battle. *Notables:* Actor Harvey Fierstein; comedian Harvey Korman. *Variations:* Herve, Hervey.

HASAD (Turkish) Harvest.

HASHIM (Arabic) Destroyer of evil. *Variations:* Hasheem.

HASIN (Hindu) Laughing.

HASKEL (Hebrew) Wisdom. *Variations:* Chaskel, Haskell, Heskel.

HASLETT (English) Land of hazel trees. *Variations:* Hazlitt.

HASSAN (Arabic) Handsome. *Variations:* Hasan, Hasain, Hassen, Hasson.

HASTINGS (English) Son of a miserly man.

HAVEL (Czech) Small. *Variations:* Hava, Havelek, Havlik.

HAVELOCK (Scandinavian) Sea battler.

HAVEN (English) Sanctuary. *Variations:* Havin.

HAWK (English) Falcon.

HAWKINS (English) Little hawk.

HAWTHORN (English) Where hawthorns grow. *Variations:* Hawthorne.

HAYDEN (English) Hill of heather; (Welsh) Valley with hedges. *Notables:* Actor Hayden Christensen. *Variations:* Aidan, Haddan, Haddon, Haden, Hadon, Hadyn, Haydn, Haydon.

HAYES (English) Hedges. *Variations:* Hays.

HAYWARD (English) Protector of hedged area.

HAYWOOD (English) Hedged forest.

HEATH (English) Heath. *Notables:* Actor Heath Ledger.

HEATHCLIFF (English) Cliff near an open field. *Notables:* Heathcliff the Cat; Heathcliff, tragic hero of Emily Bronte's *Wuthering Heights. Variations:* Heath.

HEATON (English) High place.

HECTOR (Greek) Holding fast. *Notables:* Actor Hector Elizondo; boxer Hector "Macho" Camacho Jr.; composer Hector Berlioz. *Variations:* Hektor.

HEDLEY (English) Meadow of heather.

HEFIN (Welsh) Summer.

HEINRICH (German) Ruler of the estate. Variation of Henry. *Variations:* Heinrick, Heinrik, Henrik, Henrique, Henryk.

HEINZ (German) Henry. *Variations:* Hines, Hynes.

HELMUT (French) Warrior. *Notables:* German chancellor Helmut Kohl; photographer Helmut Newton; fashion designer Helmut Lang.

HENDERSON (English) Son of Henry.

HENLEY (English) High meadow.

HENNING (German) Form of Henry.

HENRICK (Dutch) Form of Henry.

HENRY (German) Ruler of the house. *Notables:* Writers Henry James and Henry David Thoreau; poet Henry Longfellow; actor Henry Fonda; automobile innovator Henry Ford; U.S. Secretary of State Henry Kissinger; explorer Henry Hudson. *Variations:* Henery, Henri, Henrik, Henrique, Henryk.

HERALD (English) Bearer of news.

HERBERT (German) Shining army. *Notables:* U.S. President Herbert Hoover; actor Herbert Lom. *Variations:* Heibert, Herb, Herbie.

HERCULES (Greek) Glory. *Variations:* Herakles, Hercule.

HERMAN (German) Army man. *Notables:* Writers Herman Melville and Herman Hesse. *Variations:* Hermann, Hermon.

HERMES (Greek) Mythological messenger of the Greek gods.

HERNANDO (Spanish) Brave traveler.

HERRICK (German) War ruler.

HERSCHEL (Hebrew) Deer. *Notables:* Actor Herschel Bernardi. *Variations:* Hersch, Hersh, Hershel, Hersz, Hertz, Hertzel, Herz, Herzl, Heschel, Hesh, Hirsch, Hirschel.

HEVEL (Hebrew) Breath.

HEWITT (English) Smart one.

HIAWATHA (Native American) Maker of rivers.

HIDEAKI (Japanese) Wise.

HIERONYMUS (Latin) Form of Jerome. *Notables:* Artist Hieronymus Bosch.

HILARY (Greek) Happy. *Variations:* Hilaire, Hilarie, Hillary, Hillery.

HILLARD (German) Tough soldier. *Variations:* Hilliard, Hillier, Hillyer.

HILLEL (Hebrew) Highly praised.

HILMAR (Scandinavian) Renowned nobleman.

HILTON (English) Town on a hill. *Variations:* Hylton.

HIMESH (Hindu) Snow king.

top names of the 1900s

Boys	Girls
John	Mary
William	Helen
James	Margaret
George	Anna
Joseph	Ruth
Charles	Elizabeth
Robert	Dorothy
Frank	Marie
Edward	Mildred
Henry	Alice

HIPPOCRATES (Greek) The father of medicine.

HIRAM (Hebrew) Most noble man. *Variations:* Hirom, Hyrum.

HIROHITO (Japanese) Emperor.

HIROSHI (Japanese) Generous.

HISHAM (Arabic) Generosity. *Variations:* Hishim.

HO (Chinese) Good.

HOBART (German) Bart's hill.

HOBSON (English) Son of Robert.

HODIAH (Hebrew) God is great. *Variations:* Hodia, Hodiya.

HOGAN (Irish) Youth.

HOKU (Hawaiian) Star.

HOLBROOK (English) Brook on a hollow.

HOLDEN (English) Hollow valley. *Notables:* Holden Caulfield from *Catcher in the Rye*.

HOLLEB (Polish) Dovelike. *Variations:* Hollub, Holub.

HOLLIS (English) Near the holly trees.

HOLMES (English) Islands in a stream.

HOLT (English) Forest.

HOMER (Greek) Hostage. *Notables:* TV cartoon dad Homer Simpson. *Variations:* Homere, Homeros, Homerus, Omer.

HONORE (Latin) Honored.

HORACE (Latin) Punctual. *Notables:* Educator Horace Mann; newspaper editor/politician Horace Greeley. *Variations:* Horacio, Horatio.

HORATIO (Latin) Hour. *Notables:* Writer Horatio Alger; British Navy admiral Horatio Nelson; literary hero Horatio Hornblower.

HORST (German) Undergrowth.

HORTON (English) Gray town. *Variations:* Horten.

HOSEA (Hebrew) Salvation.

HOSNI (Arabic) Excellence. *Variations:* Husni.

HOUGHTON (English) Town on the cliff.

HOUSTON (English) Town on the hill.

HOWARD (English) Observer. *Notables:* Aviator/billionaire/film producer/eccentric Howard Hughes; shock jock Howard Stern; hotelier Howard Johnson. *Variations:* Howie.

HOWE (German) High.

HOWELL (Welsh) Remarkable.

HOWIN (Chinese) A swallow.

HOWLAND (English) Land with hills. *Variations:* Howlan, Howlen.

HOYT (Irish) Spirit. *Notables:* Singer/actor Hoyt Axton.

HU (Chinese) Tiger.

HUANG (Chinese) Wealthy.

HUBERT (German) Bright mind. *Notables:* U.S. Senator Hubert Humphrey. *Variations:* Hubbard, Hube, Huber, Huberto, Huey, Hugh, Hughes, Hugo, Umberto.

HUDSON (English) Son of Hugh.

HUEY (English) Form of Hugh. *Notables:* Singer Huey Lewis; Governor Huey Long; Black Panther Huey Newton.

HUGH (English) Intelligent. *Notables:* Playboy Hugh Hefner; actors Hugh Grant and Hugh Jackson; newscaster Hugh Downs. *Variations:* Hew, Huey, Hughes, Hughie, Huw.

HUGO (Latin) Form of Hugh. *Notables:* Fashion designer Hugo Boss.

HULBERT (German) Shining grace.

HUMBERT (German) Famous warrior. *Notables: Lolita* protagonist Humbert Humbert. *Variations:* Humberto, Umberto.

HUMPHREY (English) Peaceful. *Notables:* Actor Humphrey Bogart. *Variations:* Humfredo, Humfrey, Humfrid, Humfried, Humphery, Humphry.

HUNT (English) To hunt.

HUNTER (English) Hunter. *Notables:* Gonzo journalist Hunter S. Thompson.

HUNTINGTON (English) Hunting estate.

HUNTLEY (English) Meadow of the hunter. *Variations:* Huntlea, Huntlee, Huntleigh, Huntly.

HURLEY (Irish) Sea tide.

HURST (English) Grove of trees. *Variations:* Hearst.

HUSSEIN (Arabic) Little beauty. *Variations:* Husain, Husein.

HUTCHINSON (English) Son of a hutch dweller.

HUTTON (English) House on a ledge.

HUXLEY (English) Hugh's meadow. *Variations:* Hux, Huxlea, Huxlee, Huxleigh, Huxly.

HY (English) Short form of Hyatt or Hyman.

HYATT (English) High gate.

HYDE (English) Measure of land in England in the Middle Ages.

HYMAN (English) Form of Chaim.

HYWEL (Welsh) Famous. *Variations:* Hywell.

I

IAGO (Welsh/Spanish) Holder of the heel. *Notables:* Character in Shakespeare's *Othello*.

IAKOPA (Hawaiian) Form of Jacob.

IAN (Scottish) God is good. Form of John. *Notables:* James Bond creator Ian Fleming; Jethro Tull lead singer Ian Anderson; actors Ian McKellan and Ian McShane. *Variations:* Ean, Iain, Iancu, Ianos.

IARLAITH (Irish) Tributary lord. *Variations:* Iarfhlaith, Jarlath.

IBRAHIM (Arabic) Father of many. Variation of Abraham.

ICARUS (Greek) Follower.

ICHABOD (Hebrew) The glory is no more. *Notables:* Ichabod Crane, character from *The Legend of Sleepy Hollow* by Washington Irving. *Variations:* Ikabod, Ikavod.

ICHIRO (Japanese) First son.

IDAN (Hebrew) Era.

IDRIS (Welsh) Impulsive.

IDWAL (Welsh) Lord of the wall.

IFAN (Welsh) Form of John.

IFOR (Welsh) Archer.

IGGY (Latin) Form of Ignatius. *Notables:* Rock singer Iggy Pop.

IGNAAS (Scandinavian) Fire.

IGNATIUS (English) Fervent; on fire. *Notables:* St. Ignatius of Loyola. *Variations:* Iggy, Ignac, Ignace, Ignacek, Ignacio, Ignatious, Ignatz, Ignaz, Ignazio, Inigo, Nacek, Nacicek.

IGOR (Russian) Form of Ingvar. *Notables:* Composer Igor Stravinsky; aviation pioneer Igor Sikorsky.

IHAB (Arabic) Present.

IKAIA (Hawaiian) God is my savior. *Variations:* Isaia.

IKANI (Polynesian) Small, hot-headed child.

IKE (English) Short for Isaac. *Notables:* Musician Ike Turner. *Variations:* Ikey, Ikie.

ILIAS (Greek) Form of Elijah. *Variations:* Ilia.

ILLINGWORTH (English) Town in Britain.

ILYA (Russian) Nickname for Elias. *Variations:* Ilja.

IMAD (Arabic) Support, pillar.

IMRAN (Arabic) Host.

INDIANA (American) Land of the Indians. *Notables:* Film hero Indiana Jones.

INDIGO (English) Violet-blue.

INGEMAR (Scandinavian) Famous son. *Notables:* Film director Ingmar Bergman. *Variations:* Ingamar, Inge, Ingmar.

INGER (Scandinavian) Son's army. *Variations:* Ingar.

INGRAM (English) Raven. *Variations:* Ingraham, Ingrim.

INGVAR (Scandinavian) Ing's protector.

INIGO (Spanish) From Ignatius. *Notables:* Architect Inigo Jones.

INIKO (African) Hard times.

INMAN (English) Innkeeper.

INNES (Scottish) Island. *Variations:* Inness, Innis, Inniss.

INNOCENZIO (Italian) Innocent. *Variations:* Inocencio, Inocente.

INOKE (Polynesian) Devoted.

INOKENE (Hawaiian) Innocent.

IOAKIM (Russian) God will build.

IONA (Hawaiian) Dove.

IRA (Hebrew) Observant. *Notables:* Lyricist Ira Gershwin; writer Ira Levin.

IRAM (English) Shining.

IRVIN (Scottish) Beautiful. *Variations:* Irvine.

IRVING (English) Sea friend. *Notables:* Composer Irving Berlin; writers Irving Stone

popular names in scotland

Boys	Girls
Lewis	Emma
Jack	Ellie
Cameron	Amy
James	Sophie
Kyle	Chloe
Ryan	Erin
Ben	Rachel
Callum	Lucy
Matthew	Lauren
Jamie	Katie

boys' names from popular songs (part i)

Here's a list of popular songs that include boys' names in the title, along with who performed the ditty:

"Abraham, Martin, and John"
Dion

"Bad, Bad Leroy Brown"
Jim Croce

"Ben"
Michael Jackson

"Chuck E's in Love"
Rickie Lee Jones

"Daniel"
Elton John

"Eli's Coming"
Three Dog Night

"Hey Joe"
Jimi Hendrix

"Hey Jude"
The Beatles

and Irving Wallace; film producer Irving Thalberg. *Variations:* Irv.

IRWIN (English) Form of Irving. *Notables:* Writer Irwin Shaw; film producers Irwin Winkler and Irwin Allen. *Variations:* Erwin, Irwyn.

ISAAC (Hebrew) Laughter. *Notables:* Violinist Isaac Stern; writer and biochemist Isaac Asimov; musician/singer Isaac Hayes; physicist/mathematician Sir Isaac Newton. *Variations:* Isaak, Isak, Itzak, Ixaka, Izaak.

ISAIAH (Hebrew) God helps me. *Notables:* Basketball star Isiah Thomas. *Variations:* Isa, Isaia, Isia, Isiah, Issiah.

ISAM (Arabic) To safeguard.

ISAS (Japanese) Valuable.

ISHA (Hindu) Lord.

ISHAAN (Hindu) Sun. *Variations:* Ishan.

ISHAM (English) Area in Britain.

ISHAQ (Arabic) Laughter.

ISHARA (Hindu) Sign.

ISHMAEL (Hebrew) God will hear. *Variations:* Ismael, Ismail, Yishmael.

ISI (Japanese) Rock.

ISIDORE (Greek) Gift from Isis. *Variations:* Isador, Isadore, Izzy.

ISKANDAR (Arabic) Protector. *Variations:* Iskander.

ISLWYN (Welsh) Grove.

ISMAH (Arabic) God listens. *Variations:* Ismatl.

ISMAT (Arabic) Protector.

ISRAEL (Hebrew) Struggle with God. *Variations:* Yisrael.

ISTVÁN (Hungarian) Crown. *Variations:* Isti.

ITALO (Italian) Italy.

ITHEL (Welsh) Charitable lord.

ITZHAK (Hebrew) Form of Isaac. *Notables:* Musician Itzhak Perlman. *Variations:* Yitzhak.

IVAN (Czech) God is good. *Notables:* Director Ivan Reitman; arbitrageur Ivan Boesky; tennis pro Ivan Lendl; Russian Czar Ivan the Terrible; writer Ivan Turgenev. *Variations:* Ivanchik, Ivanek, Ivano, Ivas.

IVES (English) Yew wood; archer. *Variations:* Ivo, Ivon, Yves.

IVOR (Scandinavian) Bow warrior. *Notables:* Welsh entertainer Ivor Novello. *Variations:* Ivar, Iver.

IVORY (African-American) Ivory.

IZZY (Hebrew) Short form of Isaac.

JABBAR (Hindu/Arabic) One who comforts. *Variations:* Jabar, Jabir.

JABEZ (Hebrew) Born in pain. *Variations:* Jabes, Jabesh, Jabus.

JABIN (Hebrew) God has created.

JACINTO (Spanish) Hyacinth. *Variations:* Ciacintho, Clacinto, Jacindo.

JACK (American) Form of Jacob, Jackson, or John. *Notables:* Actors Jack Nicholson and Jack Lemmon; golfer Jack Nicklaus; CEO Jack Welch; fitness guru Jack LaLanne.

JACKIE (American) Form of Jacob, Jackson, or John. *Notables:* Comedians Jackie Gleason and Jackie Mason. *Variations:* Jacky.

JACKSON (English) Son of Jack. *Notables:* Singer Jackson Browne; artist Jackson Pollack. *Variations:* Jakson.

JACOB (Hebrew) Supplanter; heel. *Notables:* U.S. Senator Jacob Javits. *Variations:* Jaco, Jacobus, Jacoby, Jacquet, Jakab, Jake, Jakie, Jakiv, Jakob, Jakov, Jakub, Jakubek, Kiva, Kivi.

JACOBSON (English) Son of Jacob.

JACY (Native American) Moon. *Variations:* Jace.

JADON (Hebrew) God has heard. *Variations:* Jacdon, Jadon, Jaydon.

JADRIEN (American) Combination of Jay and Adrien.

JAEGAR (German) Hunger.

JAEL (Hebrew) To ascend. *Variations:* Yael.

JAFAR (Arabic) River. *Variations:* Gafar, Jafari.

JAGGER (English) To haul something.

JAGO (English) James.

JAHAN (Arabic) World.

JAIME (Spanish) Form of James.

JAIRUS (Hebrew) God clarifies.

JAKE Short form of Jacob. *Notables:* Boxer Jake LaMotta.

JAKEEM (Arabic) Noble.

JAKUB (Czech) Supplanter. *Variations:* Jakoubek, Kuba, Kubes, Kubicek.

JAL (Gypsy) Wanderer.

JALEEL (Hindu) Revered. *Notables:* Jaleel White (Steve Urkel from TV's *Family Matters*).

JALEN (African-American) Calm.

JAMAINE (Arabic) German.

JAMAL (Arabic) Handsome. *Variations:* Gamal, Gamil, Jamaal, Jamahl, Jamall, Jameel, Jamel, Jamell, Jamil, Jamill, Jammal.

JAMAR (American) Form of Jamal. *Variations:* Jamarr, Jemar, Jimar.

JAMES (English) He who replaces. Variation of Jacob. *Notables:* Singers James Taylor and James Brown; actors James Stewart, James Cagney, James Mason, James Dean, and James Gandolfini. *Variations:* Jacques, Jaime, Jaimey, Jaimie, Jaimito, Jamey, Jamie, Jayme, Jaymes, Jaymie, Jim, Jimi, Jimmey, Jimmie, Jimmy.

JAMESON (English) Son of James. *Variations:* Jamieson, Jamison.

JAMIE (English) Familiar form of James. *Notables:* Comedian Jamie Kennedy; actor Jamey Sheridan. *Variations:* Jamey.

JAMIN (Hebrew) Favored one.

JAN (Slavic) Form of John. *Variations:* Janco, Jancsi, Jando, Janecek, Janek, Janik, Janika, Jankiel, Janne, Jano, Janos, Jenda.

JANSON (Scandinavian) Son of Jan. *Variations:* Jansen, Jantzen, Janzen.

JANUS (Latin) Born in January.

JAPHETH (Hebrew) He increases. *Variations:* Jafet, Japeth, Japhet.

JARAH (Hebrew) Sweet.

JAREB (Hebrew) He struggles. *Variations:* Jarib, Yarev, Yariv.

JARED (Hebrew) Descend. *Notables:* Actor Jared Leto. *Variations:* Jarad, Jarid, Jarod, Jarrad, Jarred, Jerad, Jered, Jerod, Jerrad, Jerrod, Jerryd, Yarden, Yared.

JAREK (Czech) Spring. *Variations:* Jariusz, Jariuszek, Jarousek.

JARELL (Scandinavian) Form of Gerald. *Variations:* Jarel, Jarrel, Jarrell, Jarul.

JARETH (African-American) Newly created. *Variations:* Jarreth, Jerth.

JARMAN (German) German. *Variations:* Jerman.

JARON (Hebrew) To sing or shout. *Variations:* Gerron, Jaran, Jaren, Jarin, Jarran, Jarren, Jarron, Jeran, Jeren, Jeron, Jerrin, Jerron, Yaron.

JARRETT (English) Brave with a spear. *Variations:* Jarret, Jarrete.

JARVIS (German) Honorable. *Variations:* Jervis.

JASON (Hebrew) God is my salvation. *Notables:* Actors Jason Priestley, Jason Robards, and Jason Biggs. *Variations:* Jace, Jacen, Jaison, Jase, Jasen, Jayce, Jaycen, Jaysen, Jayson.

JASPER (English) Wealthy one. *Variations:* Jaspar.

JAVAN (Hebrew) Son of Biblical Japheth. *Variations:* Javin, Javon.

---

zodiac baby: names by astrological sign (part i)

If you enjoy following your daily horoscope, you might like to consider a name for your baby that's influenced by the astrological sign under which he or she is born. Here are some appropriate names suggested by popular New York astrologer Constance Stellas:

Aries

Boys
Benjamin
Mark
Simon

Girls
Holly
Rachel
Scarlett

Taurus

Boys
Edmund
Maurice
Moss

Girls
April
Georgia
Lily

Gemini

Boys
Albert
Bernard
Robert

Girls
Beryl
Crystal
Laurel

baby bottoms up!

If you love a celebration but, as a new parent, your nights out drinking with the friends are behind you, these sparkling names will keep the memories alive!

Boys	Girls
Frangelico	Alize
Glenfiddich	Amaretto
Guinness	Bellini
Hennessy	Chablis
Hiram Walker	Champagne
	Kahlua
Jack Daniel	Margarita
Jim Beam	Merlot
Johnnie Walker	Midori
Jose Cuervo	Syrah

JAVIER (Spanish) Homeowner. Variation of Xavier. *Notables:* Actor Javier Bardem.

JAY (French) Blue jay. *Notables:* TV talk-show host Jay Leno. *Variations:* Jae, Jai, Jave, Jaye, Jeays, Jeyes.

JAYCE (American) Form of Jason.

JAZZ (American) Jazz.

JEAN (French) He replaces. French version of John. *Notables:* Artist/writer/filmmaker Jean Cocteau. *Variations:* Jean-Francois, Jean-Michel, Jean-Phillipe, Jeannot.

JEB (Hebrew) Short form of Jebediah.

JEBEDIAH (Hebrew) A form of Jedidiah.

JEDIDIAH (Hebrew) Beloved of God. *Variations:* Jed, Jedd, Jedediah, Jedidia, Yedidia, Yedidiah, Yedidya.

JEFF (English) Short form of Jefferson or Jeffrey. *Notables:* Race-car driver Jeff Gordon; actors Jeff Goldblum, Jeff Bridges, and Jeff Daniels.

JEFFERSON (English) Son of Jeffrey.

JEFFORD (English) Jeffrey's ford.

JEFFREY (German) Peace. *Notables:* Film studio chief Jeffrey Katzenberg. *Variations:* Geoff, Geoffrey, Geoffry, Gioffredo, Jeff, Jefferies, Jeffery, Jeffries, Jeffry, Jefry.

JELANI (African) Strong. *Variations:* Jalani, Jehlani.

JENDA (Czech) God is good.

JENKIN (Flemish) Little John. *Variations:* Jenkins, Jenkyn, Jenkyns.

JENS (Danish) Form of John.

JENSI (Hungarian) Well born. *Variations:* Jenci, Jens.

JEREMIAH (Hebrew) God will uplift.

JEREMY (Hebrew) The Lord exalts. *Notables:* Actor Jeremy Irons. *Variations:* Jem, Jemmie, Jemmy, Jeramee, Jeramey, Jeramie, Jere, Jereme, Jeremey, Jeremi, Jeremia, Jeremias, Jeremie, Jerimiah, Jeromy, Jerr, Jerrie, Jerry.

JERIAH (Hebrew) God sees.

JERICHO (Arabic) City of the moon.

JERMAINE (German) German. *Variations:* Jermain, Jermane, Jermayne.

JEROME (Latin) Holy. *Notables:* Choreographer Jerome Robbins; composer Jerome Kern. *Variations:* Jeron, Jerone, Jerrome.

JERRICK (American) Combination of Jerry and Derek. *Variations:* Jerick, Jerrie.

JERRY (English) Familiar form of Gerald or Jerome. *Notables:* Comedians Jerry Seinfeld, Jerry Lewis, and Jerry Stiller; singers Jerry Lee Lewis and Jerry Garcia; talk-show host Jerry Springer. *Variations:* Gerry, Jere.

JERVIS (English) Unknown definition. *Variations:* Gervase.

JERZY (Polish) Farmer. *Notables:* Writer Jerzy Kosinski. *Variations:* Jersey.

JESSE (Hebrew) God exists. *Notables:* Rev. Jesse Jackson; Western outlaw Jesse James; Olympic track star Jesse Owens. *Variations:* Jesiah, Jess, Jessey, Jessie, Jessy.

JESUS (Hebrew) The Lord is my salvation.

JETHRO (Hebrew) Fame. *Variations:* Jeth.

JETT (English) Airplane.

JIM (English) Short for James. *Notables:* Comedian Jim Carrey; singers Jim Morrison and Jim Croce; Olympic athlete Jim Thorpe.

JIN (Chinese) Gold.

JIRO (Japanese) Second son.

JIVAN (Hindu) Life. *Variations:* Jivin.

JOAB (Hebrew) Praise the Lord. *Variations:* Jobe.

JOACHIM (Hebrew) God will determine. *Notables:* Actor Joaquin Phoenix. *Variations:* Joaquim, Joaquin.

JOAH (Hebrew) God is his brother.

JOB (Hebrew) Oppressed. *Variations:* Joab, Jobe, Joby.

JOCK (Scottish) Form of Jack or Jacob. *Variations:* Jacques.

JODY (English) Form of Joseph or Jude. *Variations:* Jodie.

JOE (Hebrew) Short for Joseph. *Notables:* Baseball legend Joe DiMaggio; football star Joe Montana. *Variations:* Jo, Joey.

JOEL (Hebrew) God is Lord. *Notables:* Actor Joel Grey.

JOHANN (German) Form of John. *Notables:* Composers Johann Strauss and Johann Sebastian Bach; inventor Johann Gutenberg.

JOHN (Hebrew) God is good. *Notables:* Beatle John Lennon; actors John Wayne, John Travolta, and John Ritter; U.S. Presidents John Adams and John F. Kennedy; writer John Steinbeck. *Variations:* Jack, Jackie, Jacky, Joao, Jock, Jockel, Jocko, Johan, Johann, Johannes, Johnie, Johnnie, Johnny, Jon, Jonam, Jone, Jonelis, Jonnie, Jonny, Jonukas, Jonutis, Jovan, Jovanus, Jovi, Jovin, Jovito, Jovon, Juan, Juanito.

JOHNNY Form of John. *Notables:* TV host Johnny Carson; actor Johnny Depp; singer Johnny Cash; lawyer Johnnie Cochran. *Variations:* Johnnie, Jonny.

JOHNSON (English) Son of John. *Variations:* Johnston, Jonson.

JONAH (Hebrew) Dove; Biblical book. *Variations:* Jonas, Yonah, Yonas, Yunus.

JONAS (Greek) Form of Jonah. *Notables:* Scientist Dr. Jonas Salk.

JONATHAN (Hebrew) Gift from God. *Notables:* Comedian Jonathan Winters; writer Jonathan Swift. *Variations:* Johnathan,

Johnathen, Johnathon, Jon, Jonathen, Jonathon, Jonnie, Jonny, Jonothon.

JONES (Welsh) Son of John.

JOOP (Dutch) Form of Joseph.

JOOST (Dutch) Just.

JORDAN (Hebrew) To descend. *Variations:* Jorden, Jordy, Jori, Jorrin.

JORGE (Spanish) Farmer. *Variations:* Jorgen.

JOSE (Spanish) Form of Joseph. *Notables:* Singer Jose Feliciano; baseball player Jose Canseco.

JOSEPH (Hebrew) God will increase. *Variations:* Jodi, Jodie, Jody, Jose, Josecito, Josef, Joselito, Josephe, Josephus, Josip.

JOSH Short form of Joshua. *Notables:* Singer Josh Groban; actor Josh Brolin.

JOSHA (Hindu) Satisfaction.

JOSHUA (Hebrew) God is my salvation. *Variations:* Josh, Joshuah.

JOSIAH (Hebrew) God supports. *Variations:* Josia, Josias, Josua.

JOSS (Chinese) Fate. *Variations:* Josse, Jossy.

JOVAN (Latin) Majestic.

JUAN (Spanish) Form of John. *Notables:* President of Argentina Juan Peron; Colombian coffee icon Juan Valdez.

JUDAH (Hebrew) Praised.

JUDAS (Latin) Form of Judah.

JUDD (Hebrew) Form of Judah. *Notables:* Actors Judd Hirsch and Judd Nelson.

JUDE (Hebrew) Praise God. *Notables:* Actor Jude Law. *Variations:* Juda, Judah, Judas, Judd, Judson.

JUDSON (English) Son of Judd.

JULES (French) Form of Julius. *Notables:* Writer Jules Verne.

JULIAN (Latin) Saint. Version of Julius. *Notables:* Singer Julian Lennon. *Variations:* Julien, Julion, Julyan.

JULIO (Spanish) Form of Julius. *Notables:* Singer Julio Iglesias.

JULIUS (Latin) Young. *Notables:* Roman emperor Julius Caesar; basketball star Julius Erving. *Variations:* Giulio, Julio.

JUMAH (African: Swahili) Born on Friday. *Variations:* Juma.

JUNIOR (English) Young.

JURGEN (German) Farmer. Variation of George.

JUSTICE (Latin) Just.

JUSTIN (Latin) Just. *Notables:* Singer Justin Timberlake. *Variations:* Justen, Justino, Justo, Juston, Justus, Justyn.

atlantic hurricane names for 2007

Andrea	Lorenzo
Barry	Melissa
Chantal	Noel
Dean	Olga
Erin	Pablo
Felix	Rebekah
Gabrielle	Sebastien
Humberto	Tanya
Ingrid	Van
Jerry	Wendy
Karen	

KABIL (Turkish) Form of Cain.

KADAR (Arabic) Powerful. *Variations:* Kade, Kaedar.

KADEEM (Arabic) Servant. *Notables:* Actor Kadeem Hardison.

KADIN (Arabic) Friend. *Variations:* Kade, Kadeen, Kaden.

KADIR (Arabic) Green. *Variations:* Kadeer.

KADO (Japanese) Entrance.

KAELAN (Gaelic) Powerful soldier. *Variations:* Kalan, Kalen, Kalin.

KAEMON (Japanese) Right-handed.

KAGAN (Irish) Form of Keegan.

KAHIL (Turkish) Young. *Variations:* Cahil, Kahlil, Kaleel, Khaleel, Khalil.

KAI (Hawaiian) Sea.

KAILEN (Irish) Form of Kellen.

KAISER (German) Caesar.

KAJ (Danish) Earth.

KALE (Hawaiian) Man. *Variations:* Kalolo, Karolo.

KALECHI (African) Praise God.

KALEO (Hawaiian) One voice.

KALHANA (Hindu) Name of twelfth-century poet.

KALIL (Arabic) Good friend. *Variations:* Kailil.

KALINO (Hawaiian) Brilliant.

KALIQ (Arabic) Artistic.

KALU (Hindu) Name of founder of the Sikh religion.

KAMAL (Arabic) Perfect. *Variations:* Kameel, Kamil.

KAMAU (African) Warrior.

KAMBAN (Hindu) Twelfth-century poet.

KANALE (Hawaiian) Hawaiian version of Stanley. *Variations:* Sanale.

KANE (Welsh) Beautiful; (Japanese) Golden. *Variations:* Kain, Kaine, Kayne, Keanu.

KANG (Chinese) Healthy.

KANGI (Native American) Raven. *Variations:* Kangee.

KANIEL (Hebrew) Reed. *Variations:* Kan, Kani, Kanny.

KANTU (Hindu) Happy.

KAREEM (Arabic) Generous. *Notables:* Basketball's Kareem Abdul-Jabbar. *Variations:* Karim, Karime.

KAREL (Czech) Form of Carl.

KARIF (Arabic) Born in the fall. *Variations:* Kareef.

KARIO (African-American) Variation of Mario.

KARL (German) Man. *Notables:* Actor Karl Malden; philosopher and father of Communism Karl Marx. *Variations:* Karlen, Karlin.

KARNEY (Irish) The winner. *Variations:* Carney, Carny, Karny.

KARR (Scandinavian) Swamp.

KARSTEN (Greek) Anointed.

KASEKO (African) To tease.

KASI (Hindu) Bright.

KASIB (Arabic) Fertile. *Variations:* Kaseeb.

KASIM (Arabic) Divided. *Variations:* Kaseem.

KASIMIR (Slavic) Destroyer of peace.

KASIYA (African) Trip.

KASPAR (Persian) Protector of wealth. *Variations:* Kasper.

KASS (German) Blackbird.

KAVANAUGH (Irish) Handsome. *Variations:* Kavan.

KAY (Welsh) Joy.

KAYAM (Hebrew) Stable.

KAYIN (African) Famous.

KAZUO (Japanese) Peace. *Notables:* Writer Kazuo Ishiguro.

KEANE (English) Sharp. *Variations:* Kean, Keen, Keene.

KEANU (Irish) Form of Keenan. *Notables:* Keanu Reeves.

KEARN (Irish) Dark. *Variations:* Kern.

KEARNEY (Irish) The winner. *Variations:* Karney, Karny, Kearny.

KEATON (English) Hawk nest. *Variations:* Keeton, Keiton, Keyton.

KEAZIAH (African-American) Cassia.

KEB (Egyptian) Egyptian god.

KEDAR (Hindu) God of mountains.

KEDEM (Hebrew) Old.

KEEFE (Irish) Beloved. *Variations:* Keefer, Keifer.

KEEGAN (Irish) Small and passionate. *Variations:* Kagen, Keagan, Keegen, Kegan.

popular muslim names

Boys	Girls
Abdul	Aliya
Ahmed	Ayishah
Habib	Farah
Hassan	Fatima
Hussein	Jamila
Jamal	Kalila
Khalil	Leila
Mohammed	Malak
Omar	Rana
Salim	Samira
Youssef	Suha
Ziyad	Yasmine

KEELEY (Irish) Handsome.

KEENAN (Irish) Small and old. *Notables:* Comedy writer/producer Keenan Ivory Wayans; actor Keenan Wynn. *Variations:* Keenen, Keenon, Kenan, Kienan, Kienen.

KEFIR (Hebrew) Lion cub.

KEIR (Irish) Dark-skinned; swarthy. *Notables:* Actor Keir Dullea. *Variations:* Keiron, Kerr, Kieran, Kieron.

KEITH (Scottish) Forest. *Notables:* Rolling Stone Keith Richards; The Who's drummer Keith Moon.

KELBY (German) A farm by a spring. *Variations:* Kelbey, Kelbie, Kellby.

KELL (English) Spring.

KELLEN (Irish) Mighty warrior.

KELLY (Irish) Warrior. *Variations:* Kelley, Kellie.

KELSEY (English) Island. *Notables:* TV's *Frasier,* Kelsey Grammer. *Variations:* Kelsie, Kelsy.

KELTON (English) Town of ships. *Variations:* Kelten.

KELVIN (English) Name of a Scottish River. *Variations:* Keloun, Kelvan, Kelven, Kelvyn.

KEMAL (Turkish) Honor.

KEMP (English) Fighter.

KEMPTON (English) Military town.

KEMUEL (Hebrew) To help God.

KEN (English) Short form of Kenneth. *Notables:* Documentary filmmaker Ken Burns; *Jeopardy* champ Ken Jennings.

KENAN (Hebrew) To attain. *Variations:* Cainan.

KENDALL (English) Valley of the River Kent. *Variations:* Kendal, Kendell.

KENDRICK (English) Royal hero. *Variations:* Kendricks, Kendrik, Kendryck.

KENELM (English) Brave helmet.

KENJI (Japanese) Second son.

KENLEY (English) Meadow of the king. *Variations:* Kenlea, Kenlee, Kenleigh, Kenlie, Kenly.

KENNARD (English) Brave; powerful. *Variations:* Kennaird, Kennerd.

KENNEDY (Irish) Helmet head. *Variations:* Canaday, Canady, Kenneday.

KENNETH (Irish) Handsome; sprung from fire. *Notables:* Fashion designer Kenneth Cole; actor Kenneth Branagh. *Variations:* Ken, Kendall, Kenney, Kennie, Kennith, Kenny, Kenyon.

KENT (English) County in England.

KENTON (English) From Kent.

KENTRELL (English) Estate of a king. *Variations:* Kentreal, Kentrel.

KENWARD (English) Brave protector.

KENWAY (English) Brave fighter.

KENYA (African-American) African country.

KENYON (Irish) Blond.

KENZIE (Scottish) Wise leader.

KERMIT (Irish) Free of jealousy. *Notables:* Muppet Kermit the Frog.

KERN (Irish) Dark.

KERR (Scandinavian) Swamp.

KERRICK (English) King's rule.

KERRY (Irish) County in Ireland. *Variations:* Kerrey, Kerrie.

KERSEN (Indonesian) Cherry.

KERWIN (Irish) Dark. *Variations:* Kerwen, Kerwinn, Kerwyn, Kirwin.

KES (English) Falcon.

KESHAWN (American) Combination of prefix "Ke" and first name "Shawn." *Variations:* Keshaun, Keyshawn.

KESTER (English) One who carries Christ in his heart. Variation of Christopher.

KEVIN (Irish) Handsome. *Notables:* Actors Kevin Kline and Kevin Costner. *Variations:* Kavan, Kev, Kevan, Keven, Kevon, Kevyn.

KHAN (Turkish) Prince.

KHOURY (Arabic) Priest.

KIDD (English) Young goat.

KIEFER (German) Barrel maker. *Notables:* Actor Kiefer Sutherland. *Variations:* Keefer.

KIEL (Irish) Form of Kyle.

KIERAN (Irish) Dark. *Variations:* Keiran, Keiren, Keiron, Kieron, Kyran.

KILEY (English) Narrow land.

KILLIAN (Irish) Conflict. *Variations:* Kilian, Killie, Killy.

KIM (Vietnamese) Gold.

KIMBALL (English) Leader in war. *Variations:* Kim, Kimbal, Kimbell, Kimble.

KIMMEL (German) Farmer.

KINCAID (Celtic) Leader in war.

KING (English) King.

KINGSLEY (English) Meadow of the king. *Notables:* Writer Kingsley Amis. *Variations:* Kingslea, Kingslie, Kingsly.

KINGSTON (English) Town of the king. *Variations:* Kinston.

KINNARD (Irish) Top of the hill. *Variations:* Kinnaird.

KINSEY (English) Victorious.

KIPP (English) Hill with a sharp peak. *Variations:* Kip, Kipper, Kippie, Kippy.

KIRAN (Hindu) Ray of light.

KIRBY (English) Village of the church. *Variations:* Kerbey, Kerbi, Kerbie, Kirbey, Kirbie.

KIRIL (Greek) The Lord. *Variations:* Kirillos, Kyril.

KIRK (Scandinavian) Church. *Notables:* Actors Kirk Douglas and Kirk Cameron. *Variations:* Kerk, Kirke.

KIRKLAND (English) Church land.

KIRKLEY (English) Church meadow. *Variations:* Kirklea, Kirklee, Kirklie, Kirkly.

KIT Short form of Christopher.

KIYOSHI (Japanese) Peaceful.

KLAUS (German) Victorious people. Short for Nicholas. *Notables:* Actor Klaus Kinski. *Variations:* Claes, Claus, Clause, Klaas, Klaes.

KLEMENS (Polish) Mild; compassionate. *Variations:* Klement.

KNIGHT (English) Knight.

KNOWLES (English) Grassy slope.

KNOX (English) Hills.

KNUTE (Scandinavian) Knot. *Notables:* Notre Dame football coach Knute Rockne.

KOBE (Japanese) Place name. *Notables:* Hoopster Kobe Bryant.

KOJI (Japanese) Child.

KOJO (Ghanaian) Born on Monday.

KOLYA (Russian) Form of Nikolai.

KONA (Hawaiian) Leader of the world. *Variations:* Dona.

KONG (Chinese) Glorious; sky.

KONTAR (African) Only child.

KOPANO (African) Union.

KORB (German) Basket.

KORDELL (Latin) Warmhearted.

KOREN (Hebrew) Shining. *Variations:* Corin, Korin.

KORESH (Hebrew) To dig. *Variations:* Choreish, Choresh.

KORNEL (Czech) Horn. *Variations:* Kornek, Nelek.

KORT (Scandinavian) Wise counselor.

KOSTI (Scandinavian) Staff of God.

KRISHNA (Hindu) Delightful.

KUBA (Czech) Variation of Jacob. *Variations:* Kubo.

KUMAR (Hindu) Son.

KURT Alternative spelling for Curt. *Notables:* Singer Kurt Cobain; actor Kurt Russell; writer Kurt Vonnegut.

KWAME (African) Saturday born.

KWAN (Korean) Powerful.

KYAN (African-American) Variation of Ryan. *Notables:* TV's *Queer Eye for the Straight Guy* grooming guru Kyan Douglas.

KYLE (Scottish) Narrow land. *Notables:* Actor Kyle MacLachlan. *Variations:* Kiel, Kile, Ky, Kyele, Kyler.

KYROS (Greek) Master.

school daze: names from teachers (part ii)

This selection comes from a third-grade class in Newark, New Jersey.

Diamond	Rstee
Jahid	Sherodasia
Kahlil	Tajia
Mykah	Taloupe
Nyasia	Tawuan
Raymear	Tryee

L

LABAN (Hebrew) White. *Variations:* Leban.

LACHLAN (Scottish) Land of lakes. *Variations:* Lachlann, Laughlin, Lochlain.

LADAN (Hebrew) Witness.

LADD (English) Young man. *Variations:* Lad, Laddey, Laddie, Laddy.

LAEL (Hebrew) Belongs to God.

LAFAYETTE (French) Last name used as a first name.

LAIRD (Scottish) Leader of the land.

LAJOS (Hungarian) Holy.

LAKE (English) Body of water.

LAL (Hindu) Lovely.

LALO (Latin) Singing a lullaby. *Notables:* Composer Lalo Shiffrin.

LAMAR (German) Land. *Variations:* Lamarr, Lemar, Lemarr.

LAMBERT (German) Bright land. *Variations:* Lambard, Lampard.

LAMOND (French) World. *Variations:* Lammond, Lemond.

LAMONT (Scandinavian) Lawyer. *Variations:* Lamonte, Lamond.

LANCE (German) Short form of Lancelot. *Notables:* Tour de France champ Lance Armstrong. *Variations:* Lanz, Launce.

LANCELOT (French) Servant. *Variations:* Lance, Lancelott, Launcelot.

LANDER (English) Landlord. *Variations:* Landers, Landor.

LANDON (English) Grassy meadow. *Variations:* Landan, Landen, Landin.

LANDRY (English) Peaceful ruler. *Variations:* Landre.

LANE (English) One who lives near the lane. *Variations:* Laine, Layne.

LANG (Norse) Tall. *Variations:* Lange.

LANGDON (English) Long hill. *Variations:* Langden.

LANGLEY (English) Long meadow. *Variations:* Langleigh, Langly.

LANGSTON (English) Long town. *Notables:* Poet Langston Hughes. *Variations:* Langsden, Langsdon.

LANGWORTH (English) Long paddock.

LANNY (French) Famous land; (English) Nickname for Landon or Langdon. *Notables:* Golfer Lanny Watkins. *Variations:* Lannie.

LARAMIE (French) Tears of love.

LAREDO (Spanish) Place name.

LARKIN (Irish) Cruel.

LARON (French) Thief.

LARRY (English) Short form of Lawrence. *Notables:* Talk-show host Larry King; basketball great Larry Bird; comedian Larry David; actor Larry Hagman. *Variations:* Larrie, Lary.

LARS (Scandinavian) Crowned with laurel. *Notables:* Film director Lars von Trier. *Variations:* Larse.

LASAIRIAN (Irish) Flame. *Variations:* Laisrian, Laserian.

LASALLE (French) Hall. *Variations:* Lasal, Lascelles.

LASHAWN (American) Combination of prefix "La" and first name "Shawn." *Variations:* Lasean, Lashaun, Lashon, Lashun.

LASSE (Finnish) Form of Nicholas. *Notables:* Writer/director Lasse Hallstrom.

popular names in england

Boys	Girls
Jack	Chloe
Thomas	Emily
James	Megan
Joshua	Charlotte
Daniel	Jessica
Harry	Lauren
Samuel	Sophie
Joseph	Olivia
Matthew	Hannah
Callum	Lucy

top ten
names of
the 1910s

Boys	Girls
John	Mary
William	Helen
James	Dorothy
Robert	Margaret
Joseph	Ruth
George	Mildred
Charles	Anna
Edward	Elizabeth
Frank	Frances
Thomas	Virginia

LASZLO (Hungarian) Famous leader. *Variations:* Laslo, Lazuli.

LATEEF (Arabic) Gentle. *Variations:* Latif.

LATHAM (Scandinavian) Barn.

LATHROP (English) Farm with barns. *Variations:* Lathe, Lay.

LATIMER (English) Interpreter. *Variations:* Latimor, Latymer.

LATRELL (American) Unknown meaning. *Notables:* Basketball player Latrell Sprewell.

LAURENCE (Latin) Alternate spelling of Lawrence. *Notables:* Actors Laurence Olivier and Laurence Fishburne.

LAURENT (French) Form of Lawrence.

LAVALLE (French) Valley. *Variations:* Laval, Lavall, Lavel, Lavell, Levelle.

LAVI (Hebrew) Lion.

LAWFORD (English) Ford on the hill.

LAWLER (Irish) Soft-spoken. *Variations:* Lawlor, Lollar, Loller.

LAWRENCE (English/Latin) Crowned with laurel. *Notables:* Band leader Lawrence Welk; film director Lawrence Kasden. *Variations:* Larry, Laurance, Laurence, Laurencio, Laurens, Laurent, Laurenz, Laurie, Lauris, Laurus, Lawrance, Lawrey, Lawrie, Lawry, Loren, Lorence, Lorencz, Lorens, Lorenzo, Lorin, Lorry, Lowrance.

LAWSON (English) Son of Lawrence. *Variations:* Lawsen, Layson.

LAWTON (English) Town on the hill. *Variations:* Laughton.

LAZAR (Hungarian) Form of Lazarus.

LAZARUS (Hebrew) God's help. *Variations:* Eleazer, Laza, Lazare, Lazaro, Lazzro.

LEANDER (Greek) Lion man. *Variations:* Leandre, Leandro, Leandros.

LEARY (Irish) Herder.

LEBEN (Hebrew) Life.

LEBRUN (French) Brown-haired.

LECH (Polish) From Poland. *Notables:* Polish political leader Lech Walesa.

LEE (English) Meadow. *Notables:* Actor Lee Marvin; automotive business executive Lee Iaccoca; renowned acting teacher Lee Strasberg. *Variations:* Leigh.

LEIBEL (Hebrew) My lion. *Variations:* Leib.

LEIF (Scandinavian) Beloved. *Notables:* Teen idol Leif Garrett; Viking explorer Leif Ericson. *Variations:* Leaf, Lief.

LEIGHTON (English) Town by the meadow. *Variations:* Layton, Leyton.

LEITH (Scottish) Broad river.

LELAND (English) Meadowland. *Variations:* Leeland, Leighland, Leyland.

LEMUEL (Hebrew) Devoted to God.

LEN (German) Short form of Leonard. *Notables:* Actor Len Cariou.

LENNON (Irish) Cape.

LENNOX (Scottish) Land with elm trees. *Variations:* Lenox.

LENNY Form of Leonard. *Notables:* Singer Lenny Kravitz. *Variations:* Lennie.

LEO (Latin) Lion.

LEON (French) Lion. *Notables:* Writer Leon Uris; musician Leon Russell. *Variations:* Leo, Leonas, Leone, Leonek, Leonidas, Leosko.

LEONARD (German) Brave lion. *Notables:* Conductor Leonard Bernstein; actor Leonard Nimoy. *Variations:* Len, Lenard, Lennard, Lenny, Leonardo, Leonek, Leonhard, Leonhards, Leontes, Lienard, Linek, Lynnard.

LEONARDO (Italian) Form of Leonard. *Notables:* Artist/architect Leonardo Da Vinci; actor Leonardo DiCaprio.

LEONID (Russian) Form of Leonard. *Notables:* Soviet leader Leonid Brezhnev.

LEOPOLD (German) Brave people. *Variations:* Leo, Leupold.

LERON (Arabic) My song. *Variations:* Lerone, Liron, Lirone, Lyron.

LEROY (French) The king. *Variations:* Le Roy, LeeRoy, Leeroy, LeRoi, Leroi, LeRoy.

LES (English) Short form of Leslie or Lester. *Notables:* Bandleader Les Brown.

LESLIE (Scottish) Low meadow. *Notables:* Actors Leslie Nielsen and Leslie Howard. *Variations:* Les, Leslea, Lesley, Lesly, Lezly.

LESTER (English) Last name. Leicester, an area in Britain. *Variations:* Leicester.

LEV (Hebrew) Heart.

LEVERETT (French) Young rabbit. *Variations:* Lev, Leveret, Leverit, Leveritt.

LEVI (Hebrew) Attached. *Variations:* Levey, Levin, Levon, Levy.

LEVON (Armenian) Form of Leon. *Notables:* Musician Levon Helm.

LEWIN (English) Beloved friend.

LEWIS (Welsh) Form of Louis. *Notables:* Writer Lewis Carroll.

LEX (English) Short version of Alexander. *Notables:* Superman's nemesis Lex Luthor.

LEYLAND (English) Uncultivated land.

LEYTON (English) Garden of leeks. *Variations:* Layton.

LI (Chinese) Strength.

LIAM (Irish) Form of William.

LIANG (Chinese) Good.

LINCOLN (English) Town by a pool. *Variations:* Linc, Link.

LINDBERG (German) Mountain of linden trees.

LINDELL (English) Valley of the linden trees. *Variations:* Lindall, Lindel, Lyndall, Lyndell.

LINDSAY (English) Island of linden trees. *Notables:* Musician/singer Lindsey Buckingham. *Variations:* Lindsee, Lindsey, Lindsy, Linsay, Linsey, Lyndsay, Lyndsey.

LINFORD (English) Ford of linden trees. *Variations:* Lynford.

LINFRED (German) Gentle peace.

LINLEY (English) Meadow of linden trees. *Variations:* Linlea, Linlee, Linleigh, Linly.

LINTON (English) Town of lime trees. *Variations:* Lintonn, Lynton, Lyntonn.

LINUS (Greek) Flax.

LIONEL (Latin) Little lion. *Notables:* Actor Lionel Barrymore; jazz musician Lionel Hampton. *Variations:* Leonel, Lionell, Lionello, Lonell, Lonnell.

LIOR (Hebrew) Light. *Variations:* Leor.

LIRON (Hebrew) My song. *Variations:* Lyron.

LIVINGSTON (English) Leif's settlement. *Notables:* Singer Livingston Taylor. *Variations:* Livingstone.

LLEWELLYN (Welsh) Lionlike. *Variations:* Lewellen, Lewellin, Llewelin, Llewelleyn.

LLOYD (Welsh) Gray; sacred. *Notables:* Actor Lloyd Bridges. *Variations:* Loyd.

LOCHAN (Hindu) Eyes.

LOCKE (English) Fort. *Variations:* Lock, Lockwood.

LOGAN (Irish) Hollow in a meadow. *Variations:* Logen.

LOMAN (Irish) Little bare one.

LOMBARD (Latin) Long beard.

LON (English) Noble and ready. *Notables:* Actor Lon Chaney. *Variations:* Lonnie, Lonny.

LONDON (English) Place name. *Variations:* Londen, Lunden.

LONNIE (English) Noble and ready. *Variations:* Lonny.

LORCAN (Irish) Little fierce one.

LORD (English) Lord.

LOREN (English) Short form of Lawrence. *Variations:* Lorren, Lorin, Lorrin.

LORENZO (Spanish/Italian) Form of Lawrence. *Notables:* Actor Lorenzo Lamas.

LORIMER (Latin) Harness maker. *Variations:* Lorrimer.

LORING (German) Warrior. *Variations:* Lorring.

LORNE (Scottish) Form of Lawrence. *Notables: Saturday Night Live* producer Lorne Michaels. *Variations:* Lorn.

LOT (Hebrew) Concealed.

boys' names from popular songs (part ii)

Here's another list of popular songs that include names of boys in the title.

"Jimmy Mack"
Martha and the Vandellas

"Johnny Angel"
Shelley Fabares

"Louie, Louie"
The Kingsmen

"Me and Julio Down by the Schoolyard"
Paul Simon

"Mickey"
Toni Basil

"Oliver's Army"
Elvis Costello

"Sweet Baby James"
James Taylor

"Tom Dooley"
The Kingston Trio

Jett and Ella Bleu
John Travolta and Kelly Preston

Makena'lei
Helen Hunt

Maddox and Zahara
Angelina Jolie and Brad Pitt

Madeleine and Kyd
David Duchovny and Tea Leoni

Moon Unit, Dweezil, Ahmet Emuukah Rodan, and Diva Muffin
Frank Zappa

Phinnaeus Walter and Hazel Patricia
Julia Roberts and Danny Moder

Pilot Inspektor
Jason Lee

Presley and Kaia
Cindy Crawford and Rande Gerber

LOTHAR (German) Famous army. *Variations:* Lotario, Lothair, Lothar, Lothario.

LOU (English) Short form of Louis. *Notables:* Singer Lou Rawls; character Lou Grant from TV's *The Mary Tyler Moore Show*. *Variations:* Lew.

LOUDON (German) A low valley. *Notables:* Singer Loudon Wainwright III. *Variations:* Louden, Lowden, Lowdon.

LOUIS (French/German) Famous warrior. *Notables:* Scientist Louis Pasteur; movie mogul Louis B. Mayer; jazz great Louis Armstrong. *Variations:* Lew, Lewe, Lou, Luigi, Luis.

LOWELL (English) Young wolf. *Variations:* Lovel, Lowel.

LUCAS (Latin) Man from Lucania. *Variations:* Loukas, Luc, Lukas, Luke.

LUCIUS (Latin) Light. *Variations:* Luca, Lucan, Lucca, Luce, Lucian, Luciano, Lucias, Lucien, Lucio.

LUCKY (American) Fortunate. *Notables:* Gangster Charles "Lucky" Luciano.

LUDGER (German) Man with spear.

LUDLOW (English) Prince's hill.

LUDWIG (German) Famous soldier. *Notables:* Composer Ludwig van Beethoven.

LUIGI (Italian) Form of Louis.

LUKE (English) Form of Lucas. *Notables:* Actor Luke Perry. *Variations:* Luc, Luk.

LUNDY (Scandinavian) Near an island.

LUNN (Irish) Warlike. *Variations:* Lon, Lonn.

LUNT (Scandinavian) Of the grove.

LUTHER (German) People's army. *Notables:* Singer Luther Vandross.

LYLE (French) Island. *Notables:* Singer Lyle Lovett. *Variations:* Lisle, Ly, Lyall, Lyell, Lysle.

LYMAN (English) Lives in the meadow.

LYNCH (Irish) Mariner.

LYNDON (English) Hill with lime trees. *Notables:* U.S. President Lyndon Johnson. *Variations:* Linden, Lynden, Lydon, Lynne.

LYNTON (English) Town with lime trees. *Variations:* Linton.

LYNN (English) Waterfall. *Notables:* Writer E. Lynn Harris. *Variations:* Lyn.

LYSANDER (Greek) Liberator. *Variations:* Lisandro, Sander.

MAC (Scottish) Son of. *Variations:* Mack.

MACADAM (Scottish) Son of Adam. *Variations:* MacAdam, McAdam.

MACALLISTER (Irish) Son of Alistair. *Variations:* MacAlister, McAlister, McAllister.

MACARTHUR (Scottish) Son of Arthur. *Variations:* MacArthur, McArthur.

MACAULAY (Scottish) Son of the moral one. *Notables:* Actor Macaulay Culkin.

MACBRIDE (Irish) Son of St. Brigid. *Variations:* Macbryde, McBride.

MACCABEE (Hebrew) Hammer. *Variations:* Macabee, Makabi.

MACDONALD (Scottish) Son of Donald. *Notables:* Actor MacDonald Carey. *Variations:* MacDonald, McDonald.

MACDOUGAL (Scottish) Son of the dark stranger. *Variations:* McDougal.

MACGOWEN (Irish) Son of the blacksmith. *Variations:* MacGowan, Magowan, McGowan.

MACKENZIE (Irish) Son of a wise leader. *Variations:* MacKenzie, McKenzie.

son of . . .

"Mac" or "Mc" at the beginning of a name is the Scottish way of indicating "son of . . ." So, Mac-Adam is "son of Adam." Though mostly known as last names, these are now becoming popular as first names. Each can have several variations, such as Macdonald, MacDonald, or McDonald, depending upon tradition or creativity.

Macadam	Macgregor
Macallister	Machenry
Macarthur	Mackay
Macauley	Mackenna
Macauliffe	Mackenzie
Macbride	Mackeon
Maccoy	Mackinley
Macdonald	Maclaine
Macdougal	Maclean
Macdowell	Macmahon
Macfarlane	Macmurray
Macgill	Macneil
Macgowan	

MACKINLEY (Irish) Learned ruler. *Variations:* MacKinley, McKinley.

MACON (English) Maker.

MACY (French) Matthew's estate. *Variations:* Macey.

MADDOX (Welsh) Generous. *Variations:* Maddock, Madock, Madox.

MADISON (English) Son of the mighty warrior. *Variations:* Maddie, Maddison, Maddy, Madisson.

MAGEE (Irish) Son of Hugh. *Variations:* MacGee, McGee.

MAGNUS (Latin) Great. *Variations:* Magnes.

MAGUIRE (Irish) Son of the beige man. *Variations:* MacGuire, McGuire, McGwire.

MAHIR (Arabic) Capable.

MAHMOUD (Arabic) Form of Mohammed. *Variations:* Mahmed, Mahmood.

MAHON (Irish) Bear.

MAITLAND (English) Town in Britain.

MAJID (Arabic) Magnificent. *Variations:* Magid, Majeed.

MAJOR (Latin) Greater. *Variations:* Majar, Majer, Mayer, Mayor.

MAKARIOS (Greek) Blessed. *Variations:* Macario, Macarios, Maccario, Maccarios, Makar.

MAKOTO (Japanese) Honesty.

MAL (Irish) Short form of Malcolm.

MALACHI (Hebrew) Messenger. *Notables:* Writer Malachy McCourt. *Variations:* Malachai, Malachie, Malachy, Malechy.

MALCOLM (Scottish) Follower of St. Columba. *Notables:* Activist Malcolm X; actor Malcolm-Jamal Warner; financier Malcolm Forbes. *Variations:* Malcolum, Malcom, Malkolm.

MALIK (Arabic) King. *Variations:* Maliq, Mallik.

MALIN (English) Little strong warrior. *Variations:* Mallin, Mallon.

MALKI (Hebrew) My king.

MALLORY (French) Sad. *Variations:* Mallery, Mallorie, Malory.

MALONEY (Irish) Regular churchgoer. *Variations:* Malone, Malony.

MALVERN (Welsh) Bare hill.

MANDALA (African) Flowers.

MANDEL (German) Almond. *Variations:* Mandell.

MANDER (Gypsy) From me.

MANFRED (English) Man of peace. *Notables:* Musician Manfred Mann. *Variations:* Manafred, Manafryd, Manfrid, Manfried, Mannfred, Mannfryd.

MANLEY (English) Man's meadow. *Variations:* Manlea, Manleigh, Manly.

MANNING (English) Son of a man.

MANNY (English) Short form of Emmanuel or Manuel.

MANSEL (English) In a clergyman's house. *Variations:* Mansell.

MANSFIELD (English) Field by a river.

MANSUR (Arabic) Divine assistance. *Variations:* Mansour.

MANTON (English) Man's town. *Variations:* Mannton, Manten.

MANUEL (Hebrew) Form of Emmanuel.

MANVILLE (French) Good town. *Variations:* Mandeville, Manvill.

MAOZ (Hebrew) Strength.

MARCEL (French) Form of Marcellus. *Notables:* Mime Marcel Marceau; writer Marcel Proust.

MARCELLO (Italian) Form of Marcellus. *Notables:* Actor Marcello Mastroianni.

MARCELLUS (Latin) Young warrior. *Variations:* Marceau, Marcel, Marcelin.

MARCH (English) One who lives by a border.

MARCO (Italian) Form of Marcus. *Notables:* Explorer Marco Polo.

MARCUS (Latin) Warlike. *Notables:* Social activist Marcus Garvey; TV's Marcus Welby, M.D. *Variations:* Marco, Marcos.

MARDEN (English) Valley with a pool.

MAREK (Czech) Form of Mark. *Variations:* Marecek, Mares, Marik, Marousek.

MARID (Arabic) Defiant.

MARIO (Italian) Roman clan name. *Notables:* Singer Mario Lanza; comedian Mario Cantone; chef Mario Batali.

MARION (French) Bitter; defiant.

MARK (English) Warlike. *Notables:* Roman statesman Mark Antony; writer Mark Twain; actor Mark Wahlberg; Olympic swimmer Mark Spitz. *Variations:* Marc, Marco, Marko, Markos.

MARKHAM (English) Homestead on the border.

MARLEY (English) Meadow near a lake. *Variations:* Marlea, Marleigh, Marly.

MARLON (French) Little hawk. *Notables:* Actor Marlon Brando; comedian Marlon Wayans. *Variations:* Marlin.

MARLOW (English) Hill near a lake. *Variations:* Marlowe.

MARQUIS (African-American) Nobleman. *Variations:* Markeece, Markeese, Markese, Marques, Marqui, Marquise.

MARSDEN (English) Swampy valley. *Variations:* Marsdon.

MARSHALL (French) One who cares for horses. *Notables:* Educator and communications theorist Marshall McLuhan. *Variations:* Marschal, Marsh, Marshal.

MARSTON (English) Town by a marsh.

MARTIN (Latin) Warlike. *Notables:* Dr. Martin Luther King Jr.; religious leader Martin Luther; comedian Martin Short; film director Martin Scorsese; U.S. President Martin Van Buren. *Variations:* Mart, Martan, Martel, Marten, Martey, Martie, Martinas, Martiniano, Martinka, Martino, Martinos, Martins, Marto, Marton, Marty, Martyn, Mertin.

MARTY (English) Short form of Martin. *Notables:* Comedian Marty Feldman.

MARVIN (English) Mariner. *Notables:* Composer Marvin Hamlisch; singer Marvin Gaye. *Variations:* Marv, Marvyn.

MARWOOD (English) Lake in a forest.

MASAHIRO (Japanese) Sage.

MASAMBA (African) Leaves.

MASAO (Japanese) Sacred.

MASATO (Japanese) Justice.

MASLIN (French) Little twin. *Variations:* Maslen, Masling.

MASON (French) Stone carver or worker. *Variations:* Mace, Masson.

MASSEY (English) Twin.

MASUD (Arabic) Lucky. *Variations:* Masiud.

MATANIAH (Hebrew) Gift from God. *Variations:* Matania, Matanya, Matitia, Matitiah, Matityah, Matityahu, Mattaniah, Mattathias, Matya.

MATENI (Polynesian) Warrior.

MATHER (English) Mighty army.

MATT (English) Short form of Matthew. *Notables:* Talk-show host Matt Lauer; actors Matt LeBlanc (from TV's *Friends*) and Matt Dillon.

MATTHEW (Hebrew) Gift of the Lord. *Notables:* Actors Matthew Broderick and Matthew Modine. *Variations:* Mateo, Mateus, Mathe, Mathew, Mathia, Mathias, Mathieu, Matias, Matt, Matteo, Matthaus, Matthia, Matthias, Mattias, Matty.

MAURICE (Latin) Dark-skinned. *Notables:* Bee Gee Maurice Gibb; singer Maurice

zodiac baby: names by astrological sign (part ii)

Cancer

Boys
Andrew
Gabriel
Matt

Girls
Crystal
Delilah
Luna

Leo

Boys
Adam
Leo
Rex

Girls
Judy
Leona
Rose

Virgo

Boys
August
Jasper
Philip

Girls
Celeste
Elizabeth
Stella

The names of popular members of European royal families may add some cachet to your own family.

Boys	Girls
Albert	Beatrice
Andrew	Caroline
Carl	Diana
Charles	Elizabeth
Edward	Eugenie
Henry	Madeleine
Phillip	Stephanie
William	Victoria

Chevalier. *Variations:* Maurey, Mauricio, Maurie, Mauris, Maurise, Maurizio, Maury, Morey, Morice, Morie, Moris, Moriss, Morrice, Morrie, Morris, Morriss, Morry.

MAURO (Italian) Form of Maurice.

MAURY (English) Form of Maurice. *Notables:* Talk-show host Maury Povich.

MAVERICK (American) Nonconformist.

MAX (English) Short for Maximilian or Maxwell. *Notables:* Boxer Max Baer; makeup pro Max Factor.

MAXIMILIAN (Latin) Greatest. *Notables:* Actor Maximilian Schell. *Variations:* Maksim, Maksimka, Maksum, Massimiliano, Massimo, Max, Maxi, Maxie, Maxim, Maxime, Maximilano, Maximiliano, Maximillian, Maximino, Maximo, Maximos, Maxy.

MAXWELL (Scottish) Marcus's well. *Variations:* Max.

MAYER (Latin) Larger. *Variations:* Mayor, Meier, Meir, Meirer, Meuer, Myer.

MAYFIELD (English) Strong man's field.

MAYHEW (English) Gift from the Lord. Variation of Matthew.

MAYNARD (English) Hard strength. *Notables:* Jazz legend Maynard Ferguson. *Variations:* Maynhard, Meinhard, Menard.

MEAD (English) Meadow. *Variations:* Meade, Meed.

MEDGAR (German) Form of Edgar. *Notables:* Civil rights activist Medgar Evers.

MEDWIN (German) Faithful friend.

MEHTAR (East Indian) Prince.

MEINHARD (German) Strong.

MEIR (Hebrew) Bright one. *Variations:* Mayer, Meyer, Myer.

MEL (English) Short for Melvin. *Notables:* Comedian/director Mel Brooks; actor/director Mel Gibson; singer Mel Torme.

MELBOURNE (English) Mill stream. *Variations:* Melborn, Melburn, Milbourne, Milburn, Millburn, Millburne.

MELCHIOR (Hebrew) King.

MELDON (English) Mill on a hill. *Variations:* Melden.

MELVILLE (English) Mill town.

MELVIN (Irish) Great chief. *Notables:* Actors Melvin Van Peebles and Melvyn Douglas. *Variations:* Malvin, Malvinn, Malvon, Malvonn, Mel, Melvern, Melvyn, Melwin, Melwinn.

MENACHEM (Hebrew) Comforting. *Notables:* Israeli statesman Menachem Begin. *Variations:* Menahem, Mendel.

MENDEL (Hebrew) Wisdom. *Variations:* Mendeley, Mendell.

MERCER (English) Shopkeeper. *Variations:* Merce.

MEREDITH (Welsh) Great leader. *Notables:* Broadway composer Meredith Wilson. *Variations:* Meredyth, Merideth, Meridith.

MERLE (French) Form of Merlin or Merrill. *Notables:* Singer Merle Haggard.

MERLIN (English) Falcon. *Notables:* The wizard Merlin from Arthurian legend; actor Merlin Olsen. *Variations:* Marlin, Marlon, Merle, Merlen, Merlinn, Merlyn, Merlynn.

MERRICK (English) Ruler of the sea. *Variations:* Merryck.

MERRILL (English) Bright as the sea. *Variations:* Meril, Merill, Merrel, Merrell, Merril, Meryl.

MERRITT (English) Small and famous. *Variations:* Merit, Meritt, Merrett.

MERV (Welsh) Short form of Mervyn. *Notables:* TV host/producer Merv Griffin.

MERVYN (Welsh) Sea hill. *Notables:* Film producer/director Mervyn LeRoy. *Variations:* Mervin, Murvin, Murvyn.

MESHACH (Hebrew) Artist. *Notables:* Actor Meshach Taylor.

MEYER (German) Farmer. *Notables:* Gangster Meyer Lansky. *Variations:* Mayer.

MICAH (Hebrew) Form of Michael.

MICHAEL (Hebrew) Who is like God. *Notables:* Financier Michael Milken; actors Michael J. Fox and Michael Douglas; "King of Pop" Michael Jackson; basketball great Michael Jordan. *Variations:* Makis, Micah, Micha, Michail, Michak, Michal, Michalek, Michau, Micheal, Michel, Michele, Mick, Mickel, Mickey, Mickie, Micky, Miguel, Mihail, Mihailo, Mihkel, Mikaek, Mikael, Mikala, Mike, Mikelis, Mikey, Mikhail, Mikhalis, Mikhos, Mikkel, Mikko, Mischa, Misha, Mitch, Mitchel, Mitchell.

MICK (English) Short form of Michael. *Notables:* Rolling Stone Mick Jagger; actor Mickey Rooney. *Variations:* Mickey, Micky.

MIKOLAS (Czech) Victorious people. *Variations:* Mikuls.

MILAN (Slavic) Beloved.

MILES (Latin) Soldier. *Notables:* Jazz musician Miles Davis. *Variations:* Milo, Myles.

MILLARD (English) Guard of the mill.

MILLER (English) One who mills grain.

MILLS (English) The mills.

MILO (German) Generous. *Notables:* Actor Milo O'Shea.

MILTON (English) Mill town. *Notables:* "Mr. Television" Milton Berle.

MISHA (Russian) Form of Michael.

MITCH (English) Form of Mitchell. *Notables:* Writer Mitch Albom.

MITCHELL (English) Form of Michael.

MOE (English) Form of Moses. *Notables:* "Stooge" Moe Howard.

MOHAJIT (Hindu) Handsome. *Variations:* Mohan, Mohandas, Mohanshu.

MOHAMMED (Arabic) Greatly praised. *Notables:* Boxer Mohammed Ali. *Variations:* Ahmad, Amad, Amed, Hamdrem, Hamdum, Hamid, Hammad, Hammed, Humayd, Mahmed, Mahmoud, Mahmud, Mehemet, Mehmet, Mohamad, Mohamed, Mohamet, Mohammad, Muhammad.

MOHAN (Hindu) Enchanting.

MONAHAN (Irish) Monk. *Variations:* Monaghan, Monohan.

MONROE (Irish) Mouth of the Roe River. *Variations:* Monro, Munro, Munroe.

MONTAGUE (French) Sharp mountain peak. *Variations:* Montagu, Montaqu, Montaque.

MONTEL (Italian/Spanish) Mountain. *Notables:* Talk-show host Montel Williams.

MONTGOMERY (English) Rich man's mountain. *Notables:* Montgomery Clift. *Variations:* Montgomerie.

MONTY (English) Short form of Montgomery or Montague. *Notables:* Game-show host Monty Hall; comedy troupe Monty Python. *Variations:* Monte.

MORAN (Hebrew) Guide.

MORDECAI (Hebrew) Warlike. *Notables:* Writer Mordecai Richler. *Variations:* Mordche, Mordechai, Mordi, Motche.

MORELAND (English) Uncultivated land. *Variations:* Moorland, Morland.

MORGAN (Welsh) Great and bright. *Notables:* Actor Morgan Freeman. *Variations:* Morgen, Morrgan.

MORLEY (English) Meadow on a moor. *Notables:* News reporter Morley Safer. *Variations:* Moorley, Moorly, Morlee, Morleigh, Morly, Morrley.

MORRIS (English) Form of Maurice. *Notables:* Cat food advertising icon Morris the Cat.

MORRISON (English) Son of Morris. *Variations:* Morrisson.

MORSE (English) Son of Maurice.

MORTIMER (French) Still water. *Variations:* Mort, Mortmer, Mortym.

---

atlantic hurricane names for 2008

Arthur	Laura
Bertha	Marco
Cristobal	Nana
Dolly	Omar
Edouard	Paloma
Fay	Rene
Gustav	Sally
Hanna	Teddy
Ike	Vicky
Josephine	Wilfred
Kyle	

MORTON (English) Town by a moor. *Notables:* Morton Downey Jr. *Variations:* Morten.

MORVEN (Scottish) Mariner.

MOSES (Hebrew) Arrived by water. *Notables:* Basketball player Moses Malone. *Variations:* Moise, Moises, Moisey, Mose, Mosese, Mosha, Moshe, Moss, Moyse, Moze, Mozes.

MOSS (Irish) Giving. *Notables:* Playwright Moss Hart.

MOUSA (Arabic) From water.

MUIR (Scottish) Moor.

MUNIR (Arabic) Bright.

MURDOCH (Scottish) Sailor. *Variations:* Murdo, Murdock, Murtagh.

MURPHY (Irish) Sea fighter.

MURRAY (Scottish) Mariner. *Notables:* DJ Murray the K. *Variations:* Murrey, Murry.

MUSAD (Arabic) Lucky. *Variations:* Misid, Musaed.

MUSTAFA (Arabic) Chosen. *Notables:* Founder of modern Turkey, Mustafa Kemal Ataturk. *Variations:* Mustapha.

MYERS (English) One who lives in a swamp. *Variations:* Myer.

MYRON (Greek) Fragrant. *Notables:* Myron Cohen. *Variations:* Miron, Myreon.

NABIL (Arabic) Noble.

NACHMAN (Hebrew) Comfort. *Variations:* Nahum.

NADIM (Hindu) Friend. *Variations:* Nadeem.

NADIR (Arabic) Precious.

NAGID (Hebrew) Leader. *Variations:* Nageed.

NAIM (Arabic) Happy. *Variations:* Naeem.

NAIRNE (Scottish) River glade. *Variations:* Nairn.

NAJIB (Arabic) Smart. *Variations:* Nagib, Najeeb.

NALDO (Spanish) Strong.

NALIN (Hindu) Lotus.

NAMID (Native American) Star dancer.

NAMIL (Arabic) To achieve.

NAMIR (Hebrew) Leopard.

NANDAN (Hindu) Happiness. *Variations:* Nandin.

NANDO (Spanish) Short form of Fernando. *Variations:* Nandor.

NAOMHAN (Irish) Little holy one. *Variations:* Nevan.

NAPIER (English) Keeper of linens.

NAPOLEON (Greek) Lion of the woods; (Italian) From Naples. *Notables:* General Napoleon Bonaparte; writer Napoleon Hill.

NARAIN (Hindu) Protector.

NARAYANA (Hindu) Man.

NARCISSUS (Greek) Daffodil. *Variations:* Narcisse.

NARD (Persian) Chess game.

NARDO (Spanish) Short form of Bernard.

NAREN (Hindu) Superior man.

NARESH (Hindu) Ruler of men.

NASH (English) Ash tree.

NASHOBA (Native American) Wolf. *Variations:* Neshoba.

NASIM (Persian) Breezy. *Variations:* Naseem, Nassim.

NASSER (Arabic) Victory. *Variations:* Naser, Nasir, Nassir, Nassor.

NAT (English) Short form of Nathan or Nathaniel. *Notables:* Singer Nat King Cole;

boys 99

begins with "da" and "de"

For boys, adding "Da" or "De" (or even "D plus an apostrophe") to the beginning of a popular name creates a trendy new alternative. "Shawn" can become "Dashawn" or "Deshawn" or "D'Shawn." Here are some other ideas.

Damarcus	Deanthony
Damario	Dejon
Dantrell	Dejuan
Daquan (or Daquon)	Demarco
	Deonte
Dashawn (or Dashon)	Dequan
Davonte	Deshawn
Deandre	Dewayne
Deangelo	

should your son be a junior?

Making your son a "Jr." is a personal choice. The upside is that dad's legacy is carried on. The downside is that Little Jimmy might get tired of being called that once the novelty wears off. Junior often grows up being compared to dad and this comparison might create a conflict for the son in finding his own identity.

freedom fighter/slave Nat Turner. *Variations:* Natt, Natty.

NATAL (Spanish) Birthday. *Variations:* Natale, Natalino, Natalio.

NATE (English) Short form of Nathan or Nathaniel.

NATHAN (Hebrew) Giver. *Notables:* American soldier/hero Nathan Hale; actor Nathan Lane. *Variations:* Natan, Nathen, Nathon.

NATHANIEL (Hebrew) Gift from God. *Notables:* Writer Nathanial Hawthorne. *Variations:* Nathanael, Nathanial, Nathanie.

NAV (Hungarian) Name.

NAVARRO (Spanish) Land. *Variations:* Navarre.

NAVEED (Persian) Good news.

NAVEEN (Hindu) New. *Notables:* Actor Naveen Andrews. *Variations:* Naven, Navin.

NAYLAND (English) Island resident.

NED (English) Short form of Edward or Edwin. *Notables:* Actor Ned Beatty; Australian bushranger Ned Kelly.

NEDAVIAH (Hebrew) Charity of the Lord. *Variations:* Nedabiah, Nedavia, Nedavya.

NEHEMIAH (Hebrew) Lord's comfort. *Variations:* Nechemiah, Nechemya.

NEIL (Irish) Champion. *Notables:* Astronaut Neil Armstrong; playwright Neil Simon; singers Neil Sedaka and Neil Young. *Variations:* Neal, Neale, Neall, Nealle, Nealon, Neile, Neill, Neille, Neils, Nels, Niadh, Nial, Niall, Nialle, Niel, Niels, Nigel, Niles, Nilo.

NELLO (Spanish) Form of Daniel.

NELSON (English) Son of Neil. *Notables:* South African President Nelson Mandela; New York Governor and U.S. Vice President Nelson Rockefeller; bandleader Nelson Riddle. *Variations:* Nealson, Neilson, Nilson.

NEMO (Latin) Nobody.

NEPTUNE (Latin) Roman god of the sea.

NERO (Latin) Strong. *Notables:* Roman emperor Nero. *Variations:* Neron, Nerone.

NESBIT (English) Curve in the road. *Variations:* Naisbit, Naisbitt, Nesbitt, Nisbet.

NESTOR (Greek) Traveler.

NETANIAH (Hebrew) God has given. *Variations:* Netania, Netanya, Nethaniah.

NEVADA (Spanish) Snow-covered. *Variations:* Navada, Nevade.

NEVILLE (French) New town. *Notables:* British Prime Minister Neville Chamberlain. *Variations:* Nevil, Nevile, Nevill, Nevyle.

NEVIN (Irish) Holy. *Variations:* Nev, Nevan, Nevins, Niven.

NEWELL (English) New hall. *Variations:* Newall, Newel, Newhall.

NEWLAND (English) New land. *Variations:* Newlan.

NEWLIN (Welsh) New lake. *Variations:* Newlun, Newlyn.

NEWMAN (English) Newcomer. *Variations:* Neiman, Neuman, Numan.

NEWTON (English) New town. *Notables:* Politician Newt Gingrich. *Variations:* Newt.

NICHOLAS (Greek) Victorious. *Notables:* Actor Nicolas Cage; writer Nicholas Sparks. *Variations:* Niccolo, Nichol, Nickolas, Nickolaus, Nicol, Nicolaas, Nicolas, Nikita, Niklas, Niklos, Niko, Nikolais, Nikolas, Nikolaus, Nikolo, Nikolos, Nikos, Nikula.

NICK (English) Short form of Nicholas or Dominic. *Notables:* Singers Nick Lachey and Nick Carter; actor Nick Nolte; writer Nick Hornby. *Variations:* Nic, Nicky, Nik, Nicki.

NICO (Greek) Form of Nicholas. *Variations:* Nicco.

NICODEMUS (Greek) Victory of the people. *Variations:* Nicodem, Nicodemius.

NICOLAI (Russian) Form of Nicholas. *Notables:* Russian writer Nikolai Gogol. *Variations:* Nikolai.

NIEN (Vietnamese) Year.

NIGAN (Native American) In the lead.

NIGEL (Latin) Dark. *Notables:* Actor Nigel Hawthorne. *Variations:* Nigal, Nigiel, Nigil.

NIKE (Greek) Victorious.

NILES (English) Form of Neil. *Variations:* Nyles.

NIMROD (Hebrew) Rebel.

NINO (Spanish) Child.

NIRAM (Hebrew) Fertile meadow.

NIRVAN (Hindu) Bliss.

NISAN (Hebrew) Miracle. *Variations:* Nissan.

NISHAD (Hindu) Seventh note of a scale.

NITIS (Native American) Good friend. *Variations:* Netis.

NIUTEI (Polynesian) Coconut tree.

NIXON (English) Son of Nicholas.

NOADIAH (Hebrew) Meeting with God. *Variations:* Noadia, Noadya.

NOAH (Hebrew) Comfort. *Notables:* Actor Noah Wyle; dictionary writer Noah Webster. *Variations:* Noach, Noak, Noe, Noi, Noy.

NOAM (Hebrew) Delight. *Notables:* Linguist Noam Chomsky.

NOBLE (Latin) Well bred.

NOBU (Japanese) Truth. *Notables:* Japanese chef Nobu Matsuhisa.

NODIN (Native American) The wind. *Variations:* Noton.

NOE (French) Form of Noah.

NOEL (French) Christmas. *Notables:* Actor/playwright/composer Noel Coward. *Variations:* Natal, Natale, Nowel, Nowell.

NOHEA (Hawaiian) Handsome.

NOLAN (Irish) Little proud one. *Notables:* Fashion designer Nolan Miller; baseball star Nolan Ryan. *Variations:* Noland, Nolen, Nolin, Nollan, Nuallan.

NORBERT (German) Bright. *Variations:* Norberto.

NORM (English) Short form of Norman. *Notables:* Comedians Norm McDonald and Norm Crosby.

NORMAN (English) Northerner. *Notables:* Writer Norman Mailer; TV producer Norman Lear; clergyman Norman Vincent Peale. *Variations:* Norm, Normand, Normando, Normen, Normie.

NORRIS (French) Northerner. *Variations:* Noris, Norreys, Norrie, Norriss, Norry.

NORTHCLIFF (English) Northern cliff. *Variations:* Northcliffe, Northclyff, Northclyffe.

NORTHROP (English) Northern farm. *Variations:* Northrup.

NORTON (English) Northern town.

NORVILLE (French) North town. *Variations:* Norval, Norvel, Norvil.

NORVIN (English) Northern friend. *Variations:* Norvyn, Norwin, Norwinn, Norwyn, Norwynn.

NORWARD (English) Guardian of the north.

NORWOOD (English) Northern woods.

NUMA (Arabic) Kindness.

NUNCIO (Italian) Messenger. *Variations:* Nunzio.

NURI (Hebrew/Arabic) Fire. *Variations:* Noori, Nury.

NURIEL (Hebrew/Arabic) Fire of God. *Variations:* Nuria, Nuriah, Nurial.

NYE (Welsh) Noble.

OAKES (English) Oak tree. *Variations:* Oak, Ochs.

OAKLEY (English) Meadow of oak trees. *Variations:* Oaklee, Oakleigh, Oakly.

OBA (African) King.

OBADIAH (Hebrew) Servant of God. *Variations:* Obadias, Obe, Obed, Obediah, Obie, Ovadiach, Ovadiah.

OBASI (African) Honoring God.

OBERON (German) Noble and bearlike. *Variations:* Auberon, Auberron.

OBERT (German) Wealthy and brilliant.

OCEAN (English) Ocean. *Variations:* Oceanus.

OCTAVIUS (Latin) Eighth child. *Variations:* Octave, Octavian, Octavien, Octavio, Octavo, Ottavio.

ODAKOTA (Native American) Friends.

ODELL (English) Forested hill. *Variations:* Ode, Odey, Odi, Odie.

ODHRAN (Irish) Pale green. *Variations:* Odran, Oran.

ODIN (Scandinavian) Inspiration and rage.

ODOLF (German) Wealthy wolf. *Variations:* Adolf, Odolff.

ODYSSEUS (Greek) Full of wrath. *Notables:* Trojan War leader Odysseus.

OG (Aramaic) King. *Notables:* Writer/speaker Og Mandino.

OGDEN (English) Valley of oak trees. *Notables:* Writer Ogden Nash. *Variations:* Ogdan, Ogdon.

OISIN (Irish) Young deer. *Variations:* Ossian, Ossin.

OISTIN (Irish) Respected.

OLAF (Scandinavian) Forefather. *Variations:* Olaff, Olav, Olave, Olen, Olin, Olof, Olov, Olyn.

OLDRICH (Czech) Noble king. *Variations:* Olda, Oldra, Oldrisek, Olecek, Olouvsek.

OLEG (Russian) Holy. *Notables:* Fashion designer Oleg Cassini. *Variations:* Olezka.

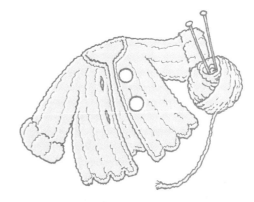

names of u.s. cities and states

Place names have become increasingly popular over the last decade.

Boys	Girls
Arlington	Alexandria
Austin	Atlanta
Boston	Augusta
Dallas	Charlotte
Denver	Cheyenne
Jackson	Dakota
Laramie	Florida
Orlando	Georgia
Reno	Helena
Roswell	Madison
Salem	Montana
Sheridan	Savannah

OLERY (French) Leader.

OLIN (English) Holly. *Variations:* Olen, Olney.

OLIVER (Latin) Olive tree. *Notables:* Comedian Oliver Hardy; film director Oliver Stone. *Variations:* Oliverio, Olivero, Olivier, Olivor, Olley, Ollie, Olliver, Ollivor.

OLNEY (English) Town in Britain.

OMAR (Arabic) High follower of the Prophet. *Notables:* Actor/bridge expert Omar Sharif; General Omar Bradley; poet Omar Khayyam. *Variations:* Omarr, Omer.

OMRI (Hebrew) Bundle of grain.

ONAN (Turkish) Wealthy.

ONDREJ (Czech) Manly. *Variations:* Ondra, Ondravsek, Ondrejek, Ondrousek.

O'NEIL (Irish) Son of Neil. *Variations:* O'Neal, Oneal, Oneil, O'Neill.

ONSLOW (English) Fan's hill. *Variations:* Ounslow.

ONUR (Turkish) Honor.

ORAL (Latin) Verbal. *Notables:* Religious leader Oral Roberts.

ORBAN (Hungarian) Urbanite.

ORDELL (Latin) Beginning.

OREN (Hebrew) Pine tree. *Notables:* U.S. Senator Orrin Hatch *Variations:* Orin, Orran, Orren, Orrin.

ORESTES (Greek) Mountain. *Variations:* Aresty, Oreste.

OREV (Hebrew) Raven.

ORFORD (English) Ford of cattle.

ORI (Hebrew) My light. *Variations:* Orie, Oron, Orrie, Orry.

ORION (Greek) Son of fire or light.

ORLANDO (Italian) Famous land. *Notables:* Actor Orlando Bloom. *Variations:* Ordando, Orland, Orlande, Orlo.

ORMAN (English) Spearman.

ORMOND (German) Serpent. *Variations:* Ormande, Ormonde, Ormondo.

ORPHEUS (Greek) Dark of night.

ORRICK (English) Old oak tree. *Variations:* Orric.

ORSON (Latin) Bearlike. *Notables:* Actors Orson Welles and Orson Bean. *Variations:* Orsen, Orsin, Orsini, Orsino.

ORTON (English) Shore town.

ORUNJAN (African) Born under the noontime sun.

ORVILLE (French) Golden town. *Notables:* Aviator Orville Wright; popcorn maker Orville Redenbacher. *Variations:* Orv, Orval, Orvell, Orvelle, Orvil.

ORVIN (English) Friend with a spear. *Variations:* Orwin, Orwynn.

OSBERT (English) Divine and bright.

OSBORN (English) Divine bear. *Variations:* Osborne, Osbourn, Osbourne, Osburn, Osburne.

OSCAR (English) Divine spear. *Notables:* Writer Oscar Wilde; composer Oscar Hammerstein; boxer Oscar de la Hoya; fashion designer Oscar de la Renta. *Variations:* Oskar, Osker, Ossie.

OSGOOD (English) Divine and good. *Variations:* Oz, Ozzi, Ozzie, Ozzy.

O'SHEA (Irish) Son of Shea. *Variations:* Oshay, Oshea.

OSMAN (Turkish) Ruler.

OSMAR (English) Divine and marvelous.

OSMOND (English) Divine protector. *Variations:* Osman, Osmand, Osmonde, Osmund, Osmunde.

OSRIC (English) Divine ruler. *Variations:* Osrick.

OSTIN (Latin) Esteemed. *Variations:* Austin, Osten, Ostyn.

OSWALD (English) Divine power. *Variations:* Ossie, Osvald, Oswaldo, Oswall, Oswell.

OSWIN (English) Divine friend. *Variations:* Osvin, Oswinn, Oswyn, Oswynn.

OTHELLO (Spanish) Form of Otis.

OTIS (English) Son of Otto.

OTTAH (African) Skinny boy.

OTTO (German) Wealthy. *Notables:* Film director Otto Preminger; German Chancellor Otto von Bismarck. *Variations:* Odo, Otello, Othello, Otho, Othon, Oto, Ottomar.

OVED (Hebrew) Worshiper. *Variations:* Obed.

OVID (Latin) Sheep. *Notables:* Roman poet Ovid (Publius Ovidius Naso).

OWEN (Welsh) Well born. *Notables:* Actor Owen Wilson. *Variations:* Owain, Owin.

OXFORD (English) Oxen river crossing.

OZ (Hebrew) Power.

OZZY (English) Short for Osborne or Osgood. *Notables:* Rock singer Ozzy Osborne; actors Ossie Davis and Ozzie Nelson. *Variations:* Ossie, Ossy, Ozzie.

P

PABLO (Spanish) Form of Paul. *Notables:* Artist Pablo Picasso.

PACE (English) Peace.

PACKARD (English) Packer.

PACO (Spanish) Form of Francisco. *Notables:* Fashion designer Paco Rabanne. *Variations:* Pacorro, Paquito.

PADDY (Irish) Nickname for Patrick. *Notables:* Dramatist Paddy Chayefsky. *Variations:* Paddey, Paddie.

PADGET (English) Young assistant. *Variations:* Padgett, Paget, Pagett.

PAGE (French) Intern. *Variations:* Paige.

PAGIEL (Hebrew) Worships God.

PAINTER (English) Painter.

PAKI (South African) Witness.

PAL (Gypsy) Brother.

PALLADIN (Native American) Fighter. *Variations:* Pallaten, Pallaton.

PALMER (English) Carrying palm branches. *Variations:* Pallmer, Palmar.

PANCHO (Spanish) Nickname for Francisco. *Notables:* Mexican revolutionary Pancho Villa. *Variations:* Panchito.

PANOS (Greek) Rock.

PARAMESH (Hindu) Great.

PARIS (Greek) The city. *Variations:* Paras, Parese, Parris.

PARKER (English) Park keeper. *Notables:* Actor Parker Stevenson. *Variations:* Park, Parke, Parkes, Parks.

PARLAN (Scottish) Farmer.

PARNELL (French) Little Peter. *Variations:* Parkin, Parnel, Parrnell.

PARR (English) Barn; stable. *Variations:* Parrey, Parrie.

PARRISH (English) County; church area. *Variations:* Parish.

PARRY (Welsh) Son of Harry.

PARSONS (English) Clergyman.

PARVAIZ (Persian) Happy. *Variations:* Parvez, Parviz, Parwiz.

PASCAL (French) Easter child. *Variations:* Pascale, Pascalle, Paschal, Pascoe, Pascow, Pasqual, Pasquale.

PASHA (Russian) Form of Paul. *Variations:* Pashka.

PASQUALE (Italian) Form of Pascal. *Variations:* Pasqual, Pasquali.

PAT Short form of Patrick. *Notables:* Singer Pat Boone; comedian Pat Cooper.

pharma-ceutical names

Believe it or not, names of popular prescription and over-the-counter drugs have been making their way to babies. Perhaps that's because some of these names sound exotic enough to be appealing. Or perhaps they are used (with doctor's approval, of course) to successfully treat a condition!

Advair	Diovan
Advil	Flonase
Aleve	Levitra
Allegra	Motrin
Amaryl	Paxil
Anacin	Valium
Avandia	Viagra
Celexa	Xanax
Cialis	Zoloft
Cipro	Zyprexa

great names in sports

Alex (Rodriquez) *Baseball*	Lance (Armstrong) *Cycling*
Andre (Agassi) *Tennis*	Mario (Andretti) *Race-car driving*
Dale (Earnhardt) *Race-Car Driving*	Michael (Jordan) *Basketball*
David (Beckham) *Soccer*	Muhammad (Ali) *Boxing*
Deion (Sanders) *Football*	Shaquille (O'Neal) *Basketball*
Derek (Jeter) *Baseball*	Tiger (Woods) *Golf*
Kobe (Bryant) *Basketball*	Tony (Hawk) *Skateboarding*

PATRICK (Latin) Noble man. *Notables:* Patron saint of Ireland St. Patrick; basketball player Patrick Ewing; actor Patrick Swayze. *Variations:* Paddey, Paddy, Padraic, Padraig, Padruig, Pat, Patek, Patric, Patrice, Patricio, Patricius, Patrik, Patrizio, Patrizius, Patryk.

PATTERSON (English) Son of Pat. *Variations:* Patteson.

PATTON (English) Soldier's town. *Variations:* Paten, Patin, Paton, Patten, Pattin.

PATWIN (Native American) Man.

PAUL (Latin) Small. *Notables:* Beatle Paul McCartney; singer Paul Simon; Revolutionary War hero Paul Revere; actor Paul Newman. *Variations:* Pablo, Pal, Pali, Palika, Pall, Paolo, Pasha, Pashenka, Pashka, Paska, Paulin, Paulino, Paulis, Paulo, Pauls, Paulus, Pauly, Pavel, Pavils, Pavlicek, Pavlik, Pavlo, Pavlousek, Pawel, Pawl, Pol, Poul.

PAVEL (Slavic) Little.

PAXTON (English) Peaceful town. *Variations:* Packston, Pax, Paxon, Paxten.

PAYNE (Latin) Countryman. *Variations:* Paine.

PAZ (Spanish) Peace.

PEADAR (Irish) Rock. *Variations:* Peadair.

PEALE (English) Ring. *Variations:* Peel, Peele.

PEARSON (English) Son of Piers. *Variations:* Pierson.

PEDAHEL (Hebrew) God redeems. *Variations:* Pedael.

PEDAT (Hebrew) Atonement.

PELAGIOS (Greek) From the sea.

PELEKE (Hawaiian) Wise counselor. *Variations:* Ferede.

PELHAM (English) Region in Britain.

PELL (English) Parchment paper.

PEMBROKE (Irish) Rocky hill. *Variations:* Pembrook.

PENLEY (English) Fenced meadow. *Variations:* Penlea, Penleigh, Penly, Pennlea, Pennleigh, Pennley.

PENN (English) Enclosure. *Variations:* Pen.

PENROD (German) Commander.

PEPE (Spanish) Nickname for Jose. *Variations:* Pepito.

PEPIN (German) One who perseveres. *Variations:* Pepi, Peppi, Peppie, Peppy.

PEPPER (English) Pepper.

PER (Scandinavian) Form of Peter.

PERACH (Hebrew) Flower. *Variations:* Perah.

PERACHIAH (Hebrew) God's flower. *Variations:* Perachia, Perachya.

PERCIVAL (French) Pierce the valley. *Variations:* Perceval.

PERCY (French) Valley prisoner. *Notables:* Singer Percy Faith. *Variations:* Pearce, Pearcey, Pearcy, Percey.

PEREGRINE (Latin) Falcon. *Variations:* Peregrin, Peregryn.

PERICLES (Greek) Name of famous Greek orator.

PERKIN (English) Little Peter. *Variations:* Perkins, Perkyn.

PERNELL (French) Form of Parnell. *Notables:* Actor Pernell Roberts.

PERRY (English) Traveler. *Notables:* Singer Perry Como; fashion designer Perry Ellis.

PERSEUS (Greek) To destroy. *Notables:* In mythology, Perseus was the son of Zeus.

PERTH (Irish) Thorny bush.

PERVIS (Latin) Passage.

PESACH (Hebrew) Spared. The name for Passover. *Variations:* Pessach.

PETE (English) Short form of Peter. *Notables:* Pete Rose; singer Pete Seeger.

PETER (Greek) Rock. *Notables:* Actors Peter O'Toole, Peter Sellers, and Peter Ustinov. *Variations:* Pearce, Pears, Pearson, Pearsson, Peat, Peder, Pedro, Peers, Peet, Peeter, Peirce, Petey, Petie, Petras, Petro, Petronio, Petros, Petter, Pierce, Piero, Pierre, Pierrot, Pierrson, Piers, Pierson, Piet, Pieter, Pietro, Piotr, Pyotr.

PETERSON (English) Son of Peter.

PEVERELL (French) Piper. *Variations:* Peverall, Peverel, Peveril.

PEYTON (English) Warrior's estate. *Notables:* Peyton Manning. *Variations:* Payton.

PHARAOH (Egyptian) King. *Variations:* Pharoah.

PHELAN (Irish) Wolf.

PHELPS (English) Son of Philip.

PHIL (American) Short form of Philip. *Notables:* Talk-show host Phil Donahue; TV psychologist Dr. Phil McGraw.

PHILANDER (Greek) Friend of man.

PHILEMON (Greek) Kiss.

PHILIP (Greek) Lover of horses. *Notables:* Prince Philip; writer Philip Roth. *Variations:* Felipe, Felipino, Fil, Filib, Filip, Filipo, Filippo, Fillipek, Fillipp, Fillips, Phil, Philippel, Phill, Phillip, Phillipe, Phillipos, Phillipp, Phillippe, Phillips, Pilib, Pippy.

PHILO (Greek) Loving.

PHINEAS (Hebrew) Oracle. *Notables:* Circus legend Phineas T. Barnum. *Variations:* Pinchas, Pincus.

PHOENIX (Greek) Immortal. *Variations:* Phenix.

PICKFORD (English) Ford at a peak.

PIERCE (English) Form of Peter. *Notables:* Actor Pierce Brosnan. *Variations:* Pearce.

PIERRE (French) Form of Peter.

PILA (Hawaiian) Hawaiian version of Bill.

PILAR (Spanish) Pillar.

PINKY (American) Short for Pincus or Phineas. *Notables:* Comedian Pinky Lee.

PINO (Italian) God will add.

PINON (Native American) Constellation.

PIO (Latin) Pious. *Variations:* Pius.

PIPER (English) Bagpipe player.

PIRAN (English) Unknown definition. *Variations:* Peran, Pieran.

PIRRO (Greek) Red hair.

PITNEY (English) Island of a headstrong man. *Variations:* Pittney.

PITT (English) Ditch.

PLACIDO (Spanish) Peaceful. *Notables:* Opera singer Placido Domingo. *Variations:* Placid, Placidus, Placyd, Placydo.

PLATO (Greek) Broad-shouldered. *Variations:* Platon.

PLATT (French) Flat land. *Variations:* Platte.

POCANO (Native American) Spirits coming.

POLLARD (English) Bald. *Variations:* Poll, Pollerd, Pollurd.

POLLUX (Greek) Crown. *Variations:* Pol, Pollack, Polloch, Pollock.

POLO (Greek) Short form of Apollo.

POMEROY (French) Apple orchard. *Variations:* Pommeray, Pommeroy.

PONCE (Spanish) Fifth. *Notables:* Explorer Ponce de Leon.

PONTUS (Greek) The sea. *Notables:* Roman statesman Pontius Pilate. *Variations:* Pontius.

PORFIRIO (Greek) Purple stone. *Variations:* Porphirios, Prophyrios.

PORTER (Latin) Gatekeeper.

POV (Gypsy) Ground; mud.

POWA (Native American) Rich.

POWELL (English) *Variations:* Powel.

PRADEEP (Hindu) Light.

PRAVIN (Hindu) Capable.

PREM (Hindu) Love.

PRENTICE (English) Apprentice. *Variations:* Pren, Prent, Prentis, Prentiss.

PRESCOTT (English) Priest's cottage. *Variations:* Prescot, Prestcot, Prestcott.

PRESLEY (English) Priest's meadow. *Variations:* Presleigh, Presly, Pressley, Prestley, Priestley, Priestly.

PRESTON (English) Priest's town. *Notables:* Preston Sturgis.

PREWITT (French) Brave little one. *Variations:* Prewett, Prewit, Pruitt.

PRICE (Welsh) Ardent man. *Variations:* Pryce.

PRIMO (Italian) First son. *Notables:* Writer Primo Levi. *Variations:* Preemo, Premo.

PRINCE (Latin) Prince. *Notables:* The Artist Formerly Known as Prince. *Variations:* Prinz, Prinze.

PRINCETON (English) Princely town.

PROCTOR (Latin) Official. *Variations:* Prockter, Procter.

PROSPER (Latin) Fortunate. *Variations:* Prospero.

PRYOR (Latin) Leader of the monastery. *Variations:* Prior.

PURVIS (English) Purveyor. *Variations:* Purves, Purviss.

PUTNAM (English) From the sire's estate.

QABIL (Arabic) Able.

QADIR (Arabic) Powerful.

QAMAR (Arabic) Moon.

QASIM (Arabic) Provider.

QUADE (Latin) Fourth. *Variations:* Quaid.

QUAN (Vietnamese) Soldier.

QUANT (Greek) How much?

QUENNELL (French) Oak tree. *Variations:* Quennel.

QUENTIN (Latin) Fifth. *Notables:* Film director Quentin Tarantino. *Variations:* Quent, Quenten, Quenton, Quint, Quinten, Quintin, Quinton, Quito.

QUIGLEY (Irish) One with messy hair.

QUILLAN (Irish) Cub. *Variations:* Quillen.

QUIMBY (Scandinavian) A woman's house. *Variations:* Quenby, Quim, Quin, Quinby.

QUINCY (French) The estate of the fifth son. *Notables:* Record producer Quincy Jones. *Variations:* Quincey.

QUINLAN (Irish) Strong man. *Variations:* Quindlen, Quinley, Quinlin, Quinly.

QUINN (Irish) Wise. *Notables:* Television producer Quinn Martin. *Variations:* Quin.

QUINTO (Spanish) Home ruler. *Variations:* Quiqui.

QUIRIN (English) A magic spell.

QUIRINUS (Latin) Roman god of war.

QUON (Chinese) Bright.

QUSAY (Arabic) Distant. *Variations:* Qussay.

QUY (Vietnamese) Precious.

RABBI (Hebrew) My master.

RABI (Arabic) Breeze. *Variations:* Rabee.

RABY (Scottish) Famous and bright. *Variations:* Rab, Rabbie.

RACHIM (Hebrew) Compassion. *Variations:* Racham, Rachmiel, Raham, Rahim.

RAD (Arabic) Thunder; (English) Adviser.

RADBORNE (English) Red stream. *Variations:* Rad, Radborn, Radbourn, Radbourne, Radburn, Radburne, Radd.

RADCLIFF (English) Red cliff. *Variations:* Radcliffe, Radclyffe.

RADFORD (English) Red ford; ford with reeds. *Variations:* Rad, Radd, Radferd, Radfurd, Redford.

RADHI (East African) Goodwill.

RADIMIR (Russian/Slavic) Happy and famous. *Variations:* Radim, Radomir.

RADLEY (English) Red meadow. *Variations:* Radlea, Radlee, Radleigh, Radly.

RADMAN (Slavic) Joy.

RADNOR (English) Red shore.

RADU (Romanian) Happy. *Notables:* Celebrity fitness trainer Radu Teodorescu.

RAFAT (Arabic) Merciful.

RAFE (English) Form of Rafferty or Ralph.

RAFFERTY (Irish) Prosperous. *Variations:* Rafer, Raferty, Raff, Raffarty, Raffer, Raffi, Raffy.

RAFFI (Arabic) Exalted; (Hebrew) Form of Raphael. *Notables:* Children's entertainer Raffi Cavoukian. *Variations:* Rafi.

RAFIQ (Arabic) Friend. *Variations:* Rafee, Rafi, Rafiki.

RAGNAR (Norse) Powerful army. *Variations:* Rainer, Rainier, Rayner, Raynor.

RAHIM (Arabic) Compassionate. *Variations:* Raheem.

RAIDEN (Japanese) God of thunder.

RAINE (English) Form of Rainer.

---

cowboy names

If you love Westerns, maybe your little pardner might fair well with a rugged cowboy name.

Audie	Jesse
Boone	Kidd
Buck	Kit
Butch	Laredo
Carson	Ringo
Cassidy	Roy
Cisco	Slim
Cody	Tex
Dallas	Wyatt
Jack	

RAINER (German) Counselor. *Notables:* Monaco's Prince Rainier. *Variations:* Rainier, Rayner, Raynor.

RAJ (Indian) Prince. *Variations:* Rajah.

RAJAB (Arabic) Seventh month. *Variations:* Ragab.

RALEIGH (English) Deer meadow. *Variations:* Rawleigh, Rawley, Rawly.

RALPH (English) Wolf counselor. *Notables:* Fashion designer Ralph Lauren; actor Ralph Fiennes; consumer advocate Ralph Nader. *Variations:* Ralphie, Raoul, Raul, Raulas, Raulo, Rolf, Rolph.

RALSTON (English) Ralph's town.

RAMADAN (Arabic) Ninth month of the Muslim year.

RAMESES (Egyptian) Son of Ra. *Notables:* Egyptian pharaoh Rameses. *Variations:* Ramesses.

RAMIRO (Portuguese) Great judge. *Variations:* Ramirez.

RAMSAY (English) Island of rams. *Notables:* Former U.S. Attorney General Ramsey Clark. *Variations:* Ramsey, Ramsy.

RANCE (African) Borrower. *Variations:* Rancel, Rancell, Ransel, Ransell.

RAND (English) Fighter.

RANDALL (English) Form of Randolph. *Notables:* Football quarterback Randall Cunningham.

RANDOLPH (English) Wolf with a shield. *Notables:* Actor Randolph Scott. *Variations:* Randal, Randall, Randel, Randell, Randey, Randie, Randil, Randle, Randol, Randolf.

RANDY (English) Short form of Randall or Randolph. *Notables:* Record producer and *American Idol* judge Randy Jackson; singer Randy Travis.

RANGER (French) Protector of the forest. *Variations:* Rainger, Range.

RANIT (Hebrew) Song. *Variations:* Ronit.

RANJIT (Indian) Charmed.

RANKIN (English) Shield.

RANON (Hebrew) Joyful song.

RANSFORD (English) Raven ford.

RANSLEY (English) Raven meadow. *Variations:* Ransleigh, Ransly.

RANSOM (English) Son of the protector. *Variations:* Ransome, Ranson.

RAOUL (French) Form of Ralph. *Notables:* Celebrity lawyer Raoul Felder; Swedish diplomat Raoul Wallenberg. *Variations:* Raul.

RAPHAEL (Hebrew) God has healed. *Notables:* Italian painter Raphael (Raffaello Sanzio). *Variations:* Rafael, Rafel, Rafello, Raffaello.

RAPIER (French) As strong as a sword.

RASHAD (Arabic) Moral work. *Variations:* Rashid.

RASHID (Turkish) Righteous. *Variations:* Rasheed, Rasheid, Rasheyd.

RASHAWN (American) Combination of first names "Ray" and "Shawn." *Variations:* Rachan, Rashaan, Rasham, Rashan, Rashawn, Reshaun, Reshawn.

RASMUS (Greek) Beloved.

RAVENEL (English) Raven.

RAVI (Hindu) Sun. *Variations:* Ravee.

RAWDON (English) Craggy hill.

RAWLINS (French) Last name. *Variations:* Rawlinson, Rawson.

RAY (English) Royal. *Notables:* Comedian Ray Romano; singer Ray Charles; writer Ray Bradbury. *Variations:* Rayce, Raydell, Rayder, Raydon, Rayford, Raylen, Raynell.

RAYBURN (English) Brook for deer. *Variations:* Rayborn, Raybourne, Rayburne.

RAYMOND (German) Counselor and protector. *Notables:* Actor Raymond Burr; writer Raymond Chandler. *Variations:* Raimondo, Raimund, Raimunde, Raimundo, Rajmund, Ramon, Ramond, Ramone, Ray, Rayment, Raymonde, Raymondo, Raymund, Raymunde, Raymundo, Reimond.

RAZIEL (Hebrew) The Lord is my secret. *Variations:* Raz, Raziel.

READING (English) Son of the red-haired one. *Variations:* Redding, Reeding, Reiding.

REBEL (American) Rebel.

RED (English) Ruddy or red-haired. *Notables:* Comedians Red Skelton and Redd Foxx; coach Red Auerbach. *Variations:* Redd.

REDFORD (English) Red ford.

REDLEY (English) Red meadow.

REDMOND (Irish) Counselor. Variation of Raymond. *Variations:* Radmond, Radmund, Redmund.

REECE (Welsh) Fiery. *Variations:* Rees, Reese, Reiss, Rhys.

REED (English) Ruddy. *Variations:* Reade, Reed, Reid, Reide, Reyd.

REEVE (English) Bailiff. *Variations:* Reave, Reeves.

REG (English) Short form of Reginald.

REGAN (Irish) Little king. *Variations:* Reagan, Reagen, Regen.

REGGIE (English) Form of Reginald. *Notables:* Baseball player Reggie Jackson.

REGIN (Scandinavian) Judgment.

REGINALD (English) Strong counselor. *Variations:* Reg, Reggie, Reginalt.

REINHARD (German) Form of Reynard. *Variations:* Reinhart.

REMINGTON (English) Family of ravens. *Variations:* Rem, Remee, Remi, Remie, Remmy.

REMUS (Latin) Swift.

REMY (French) From Rheims, a town in central France. *Variations:* Remee, Remi, Remie, Remmy.

RENAUD (French) Powerful.

RENDOR (Hungarian) Policeman.

RENÉ (French) Reborn. *Notables:* French philosopher Rene Descartes. *Variations:* Renat, Renato, Renatus, Renne, Rennie, Renny.

RENFRED (English) Strong peace.

RENFREW (Welsh) Calm river.

RENNY (Irish) Small and mighty.

RENTON (English) Deer habitat.

RENZO (Italian) Laurel. Diminutive form of Lorenzo.

REUBEN (Hebrew) Behold a son. *Variations:* Reuban, Reubin, Reuven, Reuvin, Rube, Ruben, Rubin, Rubu.

REX (Latin) King. *Notables:* Actor Rex Harrison; film critic Rex Reed.

REXFORD (English) King's ford.

REY (Spanish) King. *Variations:* Reyes.

REYNARD (German/English) Brave adviser. *Variations:* Rainard, Reinhard, Renard, Reynard.

REYNOLD (English) Powerful adviser. *Variations:* Ranald, Renald, Renaldo, Renauld, Renault, Reynaldo, Reynaldos, Reynolds, Rinaldo.

RHETT (Welsh) Fiery. *Notables: Gone with the Wind* hero Rhett Butler. *Variations:* Rhys.

RHYS (Welsh) Fiery. Form of Reece.

RHODES (Greek) Island of roses. *Variations:* Rhoades, Rhodas, Rodas.

RICE (English) Form of Reece.

RICH (English) Short form of Richard. *Notables:* Comedian Rich Little.

RICHARD (German) Strong ruler. *Notables:* Actors Richard Burton, Richard Chamberlain, and Richard Attenborough; comedian Richard Lewis; U.S. President Richard M. Nixon. *Variations:* Dic, Dick, Dickie, Dicky, Ricard, Ricardo, Riccardo, Ricciardo, Rich, Richardo, Richards, Richart, Richerd, Richi, Richie, Rick, Rickard, Rickert, Rickey, Rickie, Ricky, Rico, Rihards, Riki, Riks, Riocard, Riqui, Risa, Ritch, Ritchard, Ritcherd, Ritchie, Ritchy, Rostik, Rostislav, Rostya, Ryszard.

RICHMOND (English) Rich mouth.

RICK (English) Short form of Richard. *Notables:* Singers Rick James, Rik Ocasek, and Rick Springfield; actor Rick Schroeder. *Variations:* Rik.

popular names in ireland

Boys	Girls
Sean	Emma
Jack	Sarah
Adam	Aoife
Conor	Ciara
James	Katie
Daniel	Sophie
Michael	Rachel
Cian	Chloe
David	Amy
Dylan	Leah

RICKY (English) Short form of Richard. *Notables:* Singer Ricky Martin. *Variations:* Rickey, Rickie.

RICO (Spanish) Short form of Enrico or Ricardo.

RIDER (English) Horseman. *Variations:* Ridder, Ryder.

RIDGE (English) Ridge. *Variations:* Rigg.

RIDGLEY (English) Meadow on a ridge. *Variations:* Ridgeleigh, Ridgeley, Ridglea, Ridglee, Ridgleigh.

RIDGEWAY (English) Road on a ridge.

RIDLEY (English) Reed meadow. *Notables:* Film director Ridley Scott. *Variations:* Riddley, Ridlea, Ridleigh, Ridly.

RIGBY (English) Ruler's valley.

RIGEL (Arabic) Foot.

RILEY (Irish) Brave. *Variations:* Reilly, Ryley.

RIMON (Arabic) Pomegranate.

RINALDO (Italian) Form of Reynold or Ronald.

RING (English) Ring.

RINGO (Japanese) Apple. *Notables:* Beatle Ringo Starr.

RIO (Spanish) River. *Variations:* Reo.

RIORDAN (Irish) Poet and minstrel. *Variations:* Rearden, Reardon.

RIP (Dutch) Ripe. *Notables:* Actor Rip Torn; comedian Rip Taylor.

RIPLEY (English) Shouting man's meadow. *Variations:* Ripleigh, Riply, Ripp.

RISHON (Hebrew) First.

RISLEY (English) Meadow with shrubs. *Variations:* Rishley, Rislea, Rislee, Risleigh, Risly.

RISTON (English) Town near shrubs.

RITTER (German) Knight.

RIVER (English) River. *Notables:* Actor River Phoenix.

RIYAD (Arabic) Garden. *Variations:* Riyadh.

ROALD (Scandinavian) Famous leader. *Notables:* Children's writer Roald Dahl.

ROAN (English) Form of Rowan.

ROARK (Irish) Mighty. *Variations:* Roarke, Rorke, Rourke.

ROB (English) Short form of Robert. *Notables:* Actor Rob Lowe; director Rob Reiner.

ROBBIE (English) Form of Robert. *Notables:* Singers Robbie Williams and Robbie Robinson; actor/director Robby Benson.

ROBERT (English) Bright fame. *Notables:* U.S. Senator Robert Kennedy; actors Robert Taylor, Robert Wagner, Robert Young, Robert Redford, and Robert De Niro; poets Robert Burns and Robert Frost. *Variations:* Bob, Bobbey, Bobbie, Bobby, Riobard, Rob, Robb, Robbi, Robbie, Robbin, Robby, Rob-byn, Rober, Robers, Roberto, Roberts, Robi, Robin, Robinet, Robyn, Rubert, Ruberto, Rudbert, Ruperto, Ruprecht.

ROBERTSON (English) Son of Robert.

ROBIN (English) Form of Robert. *Notables:* Actor/comedian Robin Williams; *Lifestyles of the Rich and Famous* expert Robin Leach; folklore hero Robin Hood.

ROBINSON (English) Son of Robert. *Notables:* Literary hero Robinson Crusoe. *Variations:* Robbinson, Robeson, Robson, Robynson.

ROCCO (Italian) Rest. *Notables:* Chef Rocco DiSpirito. *Variations:* Rock, Rockie, Rocky.

ROCHESTER (English) Stone fortress.

ROCK (English) Rock; (Italian) Form of Rocco. *Notables:* Rock Hudson. *Variations:* Rockford, Rockie, Rocky.

ROCKFORD (English) Rocky ford.

ROCKLEY (English) Rocky meadow. *Variations:* Rocklee, Rockleigh, Rockly.

ROCKWELL (English) Well by the rocks.

ROCKY (American) Form of Rocco. *Notables:* Boxer Rocky Marciano.

ROD (English) Short form of Roderick or Rodney. *Notables:* Singer Rod Stewart; hockey player Rod Gilbert; writer/producer Rod Serling; actor Rod Steiger. *Variations:* Rodd.

RODDY (English) Form of Roderick. *Notables:* Wrestler "Rowdy" Roddy Piper; writer Roddy Doyle; actor Roddy McDowell.

RODEO (Spanish) Round up.

RODERICK (German) Famous ruler. *Variations:* Rod, Rodd, Roddie, Roddy, Roderic, Roderich, Roderigo, Rodique, Rodrich, Rodrick, Rodrigo, Rodrique, Rurich, Rurik.

RODMAN (English) Famous man.

RODNEY (English) Island clearing. *Notables:* Comedian Rodney Dangerfield. *Variations:* Rodnee, Rodnie, Rodny.

ROGAN (Irish) Redhead.

ROGER (German) Renowned spearman. *Notables:* Actor Roger Moore; rock singer Roger Daltrey; film critic Roger Ebert. *Variations:* Rodger, Rogelio, Rogerio, Rogerios, Rogers, Ruggerio, Ruggero, Rutger, Ruttger.

ROHAN (Hindu) Ascending.

ROLAND (German) Famous land. *Variations:* Rolle, Rolli, Rollie, Rollin, Rollins, Rollon, Rolly, Rolo, Rolon, Row, Rowe, Rowland, Rowlands, Rowlandson.

ROLF (German) Form of Ralph.

ROLLE (Scandinavian) Form of Roland.

ROLLO (English) Form of Roland. *Notables:* Psychologist/writer Rollo May.

ROMAN (Latin) One from Rome. *Notables:* Director Roman Polanski. *Variations:* Romain, Romano, Romanos, Romulo, Romulos, Romulus.

ROMANY (Gypsy) Gypsy.

ROMEO (Italian) Pilgrim visiting Rome. *Notables:* Romeo Montague, hero of Shakespearean tragedy *Romeo and Juliet.*

ROMNEY (Welsh) Curving river.

ROMULUS (Latin) Citizen of Rome.

RON (English) Short form of Ronald or Aaron. *Notables:* Actor/director Ron Howard.

RONALD (English) Powerful adviser. *Notables:* U.S. President Ronald Reagan; McDonald's spokesclown Ronald McDonald. *Variations:* Ranald, Ron, Ronn, Ronney, Ronni, Ronnie, Ronny.

RONAN (Irish) Little seal.

RONDEL (French) Poem.

RONEL (Hebrew) Song of God.

RONI (Hebrew) Joyful.

RONNIE (English) Form of Ronnie. *Notables:* Rock musicians Ronnie Van Zant and Ronnie Lane.

RONSON (English) Son of Ronald.

ROONEY (Irish) Red-haired. *Variations:* Roone, Roonie, Roony.

ROOSEVELT (Dutch) Field of roses. *Notables:* Football player Roosevelt Grier.

ROPER (English) Maker of rope.

RORY (Irish) Red king. *Notables:* Irish singer Rory Gallagher; actor Rory Calhoun. *Variations:* Ruaidri, Ruairi, Ruaraidh.

ROSARIO (Portuguese) The rosary.

ROSCOE (Scandinavian) Deer forest.

ROSLIN (Scottish) Small redheaded child. *Variations:* Roslyn, Rosselin, Rosslyn.

ROSS (Scottish) Cape. *Variations:* Rosse, Rossie, Rossy.

ROSWELL (English) Spring of roses.

ROTH (German) Red.

ROUSSE (French) Red-haired.

ROVER (English) Wanderer.

ROWAN (English) Rowan tree; little red one. *Notables:* Comedic actor Rowan Atkinson. *Variations:* Rowen.

ROWLEY (English) Unevenly cleared meadow. *Variations:* Rowlea, Rowlee, Rowleigh, Rowlie, Rowly.

ROXBURY (English) Town of the rook.

ROY (Irish) Red; (French) King. *Notables:* Country singers Roy Orbison, Roy Clark, and Roy Rogers. *Variations:* Roi.

ROYAL (French) Royal. *Variations:* Royle.

ROYCE (English) Roy's son. *Variations:* Roice, Royse.

ROYDON (English) Rye hill. *Variations:* Royden.

zodiac baby: names by astrological sign (part iii)

Libra

Boys
Charles
Luke
Nathaniel

Girls
Grace
Jewel
Venus

Scorpio

Boys
Alexander
Daniel
Thomas

Girls
Alexandra
Danielle
Topaz

Sagittarius

Boys
Dustin
Earl
James

Girls
Dahlia
Iris
Olivia

ROYSTON (English) Town of Royce. *Variations:* Roystan.

ROZEN (Hebrew) Leader.

RUBE (English) Form of Reuben.

RUBEN (Hebrew) Form of Reuben. *Notables:* Singers Ruben Studdard and Ruben Blades.

RUDD (English) Ruddy skin.

RUDOLPH (German) Famous wolf. *Notables:* New York City mayor Rudolph Giuliani; dancer Rudolf Nureyev; silent film star Rudolph Valentino. *Variations:* Rodolfo, Rodolph, Rodolphe, Rolf, Rolfe, Rolle, Rollo, Rolph, Rolphe, Rudey, Rudi, Rudie, Rudolf, Rudolfo, Rudolpho, Rudolphus, Rudy.

RUDY (English) Short form of Rudolph or Rudyard.

RUDYARD (English) Red yard. *Notables:* Writer Rudyard Kipling.

RUFORD (English) Red ford. *Variations:* Rufford.

RUFUS (Latin) Red-haired. *Notables:* Singer/songwriter Rufus Wainwright. *Variations:* Ruffus, Rufo, Rufous.

RUGBY (English) Rook fortress.

RUMFORD (English) Wide river crossing.

RUNE (Scandinavian) Secret.

RUPERT (German) Bright fame. Variation of Robert. *Notables:* Actor Rupert Everett. *Variations:* Ruperto, Ruprecht.

RURIK (Scandinavian) Famous king. *Variations:* Roar, Rorek, Roth, Rothrekr.

RUSH (English) Red-haired. *Notables:* Radio talk-show host Rush Limbaugh.

RUSHFORD (English) Ford with rushes.

RUSKIN (French) Child with red hair.

RUSS (English) Short form of Russell.

RUSSELL (French) Small red one. *Notables:* Actor Russell Crowe. *Variations:* Russ, Russel.

RUSTY (English) Red-haired. *Notables:* Baseball player Rusty Staub. *Variations:* Rustie.

RUTGER (Dutch) Form of Roger. *Notables:* Actor Rutger Hauer.

RUTHERFORD (English) Cattle crossing. *Variations:* Rutherfurd.

RUTLAND (Norse) Red land.

RUTLEY (English) Red meadow.

RYAN (Irish) Little king. *Notables:* Actors Ryan O'Neil and Ryan Phillippe; singer Ryan Adams. *Variations:* Ryne, Ryon, Ryun.

RYCROFT (English) Field of rye. *Variations:* Ryecroft.

RYE (Polish) Strong ruler.

RYLAND (English) Land of rye. *Variations:* Ryeland, Rylan, Rylyn.

RYMAN (English) Rye seller.

S

SABER (French) Sword. *Variations:* Sabre.

SABIN (Latin) Name of an ancient Roman clan. *Variations:* Sabine, Sabino.

SABIR (Arabic) Patient. *Variations:* Sabri.

SADDAM (Arabic) Powerful ruler. *Notables:* Former Iraqi dictator Saddam Hussein.

SADLER (English) Saddle maker. *Variations:* Saddler.

SAFFORD (English) River crossing at the willows.

SAGE (English) Wise. *Variations:* Sagen, Saige.

SA'ID (Arabic) Happy. *Variations:* Saeed, Saied, Saiyid, Sayeed, Sayid, Syed.

SAKARIA (Scandinavian) God remembers. Variation of Zachariah. *Variations:* Sakari, Sakarias.

SAL (Italian) Short form of Salvatore. *Notables:* Actor Sal Mineo.

SALIM (Arabic) Tranquility. *Variations:* Saleem, Salem, Salima, Selim.

SALTON (English) Town in the willows.

SALVADOR (Spanish) Form of Salvatore. *Notables:* Artist Salvador Dali.

SALVATORE (Latin) Savior. *Variations:* Sal, Salvador, Salvator.

SAM (English) Short form of Samuel. *Notables:* Playwright Sam Shepard; singer Sam Cooke; Wal-Mart founder Sam Walton.

SAMIR (Arabic) Entertainer.

SAMMY (English) Short form of Samuel. *Notables:* Rat Pack singer/dancer Sammy Davis Jr.; rocker Sammy Hagar; baseball player Sammy Sosa.

SAMOSET (Native American) He who walks a lot. *Variations:* Samaset.

SAMSON (Hebrew) Sun. *Variations:* Sampson, Sanson, Sansone.

SAMUEL (Hebrew) God listens. *Notables:* Telegraph inventor Samuel Morse; actor Samuel L. Jackson; American patriot Samuel Adams. *Variations:* Sam, Sammie, Sammy, Samouel, Samuele, Samuello.

top ten names of the 1930s

Boys	Girls
Robert	Mary
James	Betty
John	Barbara
William	Shirley
Richard	Patricia
Charles	Dorothy
Donald	Joan
George	Margaret
Thomas	Nancy
Joseph	Helen

SANBORN (English) Sandy brook.

SANCHO (Latin) Sacred. *Notables:* Don Quixote's sidekick, Sancho Panza. *Variations:* Sauncho.

SANDER (English) Form of Alexander.

SANDFORD (English) Sandy crossing. *Variations:* Sandfurd, Sanford.

SANDY (English) Short form of Sander or Alexander. *Notables:* Baseball great Sandy Koufax.

SANJAY (Hindu) Winner.

SANTIAGO (Spanish) Saint.

SANTO (Spanish) Holy. *Variations:* Santos.

SARGENT (French) Officer. *Notables:* Politician and U.S. Ambassador Sargent Shriver. *Variations:* Sarge, Sergeant.

SASHA (Russian) Form of Alexander. *Variations:* Sacha, Sascha, Sashka.

SATCHEL (Latin) Small sack. *Notables:* Baseball player Satchel Paige.

SAUL (Hebrew) Asked for. *Notables:* Writer Saul Bellow.

SAVILLE (French) Town of willows. *Variations:* Savil, Savile, Savill, Savilla, Savylle.

SAWNEY (Scottish) Protector of men. *Variations:* Sawnie, Sawny.

SAWYER (English) Woodworker. *Variations:* Sayer, Sayers, Sayre, Sayres.

SAXON (English) Sword. *Variations:* Saxe, Saxen.

SCANLON (Irish) Little trapper. *Variations:* Scanlan, Scanlen.

SCHAFER (German) Shepherd.

SCHMIDT (German) Blacksmith.

SCHNEIDER (German) Tailor.

SCHON (German) Handsome.

SCHUYLER (Dutch) Shield. *Variations:* Schuylar, Skuyler, Skylar, Skyler.

SCOTT (English) One from Scotland. *Notables:* Musician Scott Weiland. *Variations:* Scot, Scottie, Scotto, Scotty.

SCULLY (Irish) Town crier.

SEABERT (English) Bright sea. *Variations:* Seibert.

SEAMUS (Irish) He who supplants. Variation of James. *Variations:* Shamus.

SEAN (Irish) God is good. Variation of John. *Notables:* Actors Sean Penn and Sean Connery. *Variations:* Seann, Shaine, Shane, Shaughn, Shaun, Shawn, Shayn, Shayne.

SEARLE (English) Armor.

SEATON (English) Town by the sea. *Variations:* Seeton, Seton.

SEBASTIAN (Latin) One from Sebastia, an ancient Roman city. *Variations:* Seb, Sebastien, Sebbie.

SEDGWICK (English) Sword place. *Variations:* Sedgewick, Sedgewyck, Sedgwyck.

SEELEY (English) Blessed.

SEFTON (English) Town in the rushes.

SEGER (English) Sea warrior. *Variations:* Seager, Seeger.

SELAH (Hebrew) Song.

SELBY (English) Manor in the village. *Variations:* Shelby.

SELDON (English) Willow valley. *Variations:* Selden, Sellden.

SELIG (German) Blessed.

SELWYN (English) From the manor. *Variations:* Selvin, Selwin, Selwinn, Selwynn, Selwynne.

SENIOR (French) Lord.

if your child hates his name

While most children simply accept their names, occasionally a child might find himself developing a strong dislike for his name. Whether it's a name that rhymes with something weird, or your child is made fun of by insensitive kids at school, take his feelings seriously and help find a solution. Regardless of name, he's still the great kid you love!

SENNETT (French) Venerable. *Variations:* Sennet.

SERAPHIM (Greek) The angels; (Hebrew) Fiery. *Variations:* Serafin, Serafino, Seraphimus.

SERENO (Latin) Calm.

SERGEI (Russian) Form of Sergius. *Notables:* Russian composer Sergei Prokofiev.

SERGIO (Italian) Form of Sergius. *Notables:* Spaghetti Western film director Sergio Leone; musician Sergio Mendes.

SERGIUS (Latin) Servant. *Variations:* Serg, Serge, Sergey, Sergi, Sergie.

SETH (Hebrew) To appoint. *Notables:* Actor Seth Greene; TV animator Seth MacFarlane.

SEVERIN (Latin) Severe. *Variations:* Severen.

SEVERN (English) Boundary.

SEWARD (English) Protector of the sea. *Variations:* Sewerd.

SEYMOUR (French) From St. Maur, a village in France. *Variations:* Seamor, Seamore, Seamour, Si, Sy.

SHADRACH (Babylonian) Under the command of Aku (the Babylonian god of the moon). *Variations:* Shad, Shadrack.

SHAKIL (Hindu) Attractive. *Notables:* Basketball great Shaquille O'Neal. Variations: Shakeel, Shaquille.

SHAKIR (Arabic) Grateful. *Variations:* Shakur, Shukri.

SHALOM (Hebrew) Peace. *Notables:* Writer Sholom Aleichem. *Variations:* Sholom.

SHANAHAN (Irish) Wise one.

SHANE (Irish) Form of Sean.

SHANLEY (Irish) Small and ancient. *Variations:* Shanleigh, Shannleigh, Shannley.

SHANNON (Irish) Old. *Variations:* Shannan, Shannen.

SHAREEF (Hindu) Respected. *Variations:* Sharif, Shereef, Sherif.

SHATTUCK (Irish) Little fish.

SHAW (English) Grove of trees.

SHAWN (Irish) Form of Sean. *Variations:* Shaun.

SHEA (English) Requested. *Variations:* Shae, Shai, Shay, Shaye.

SHEEHAN (Irish) Calm.

SHEFFIELD (English) Uneven field.

SHELBY (English) Village on the ledge. *Variations:* Shelbey, Shelbie.

SHELDON (English) Steep valley. *Variations:* Shelden, Sheldin.

SHELLEY (English) Meadow on a ledge. *Notables:* Comedian Shelley Berman. *Variations:* Shelly.

SHELTON (English) Town on a ledge.

SHEM (Hebrew) Famous.

SHEPHERD (English) Sheepherder. *Variations:* Shep, Shepard, Shephard, Shepp, Sheppard, Shepperd.

SHEPLEY (English) Sheep meadow. *Variations:* Sheplea, Shepleigh, Sheply.

SHERBORN (English) Clear brook. *Variations:* Sherborne, Sherbourn, Sherburn, Sherburne.

SHERIDAN (Irish) Wild man. *Variations:* Sheredan, Sheridon, Sherridan.

SHERLOCK (English) Bright hair. *Notables:* Fictional detective Sherlock Holmes. *Variations:* Sherlocke, Shurlock.

SHERMAN (English) One who cuts cloth. *Notables:* Actor Sherman Helmsley. *Variations:* Scherman, Schermann, Shermann.

SHERWIN (English) Bright friend. *Variations:* Sherwind, Sherwinn, Sherwyn, Sherwynne.

SHERWOOD (English) Shining forest. *Variations:* Sherwoode, Shurwood.

SHILOH (Hebrew) Gift from God. *Variations:* Shilo.

SHIMON (Hebrew) Heard. *Variations:* Simeon.

SHIPTON (English) Sheep town.

SHIVA (Hindu) Fortunate. *Variations:* Sheo, Shiv, Sib, Siva.

SHLOMO (Hebrew) Peace.

SHMUEL (Hebrew) Form of Samuel.

popular names in poland

Boys	Girls
Piotr	Anna
Jan	Maria
Andrzej	Katarzyna
Krzysztof	Malgorzata
Stanislaw	Agnieszka
Tomasz	Krystyna
Pawel	Barbara
Jozef	Ewa
Marcin	Ellbieta
Marek	Zofia

most popular names for twins

According the Social Security Administration in 2005, these are the top names Americans are giving to their girl/boy twins.

Taylor and Tyler

Madison and Morgan

Emma and Ethan

Natalie and Nathan

Madison and Matthew

Madison and Mason

Hayden and Hunter

Jordan and Justin

Jordan and Jacob

Megan and Morgan

Brianna and Brian

SID (English) Short form of Sidney. *Notables:* Comedian Sid Caesar; singer Sid Vicious. *Variations:* Syd.

SIDNEY (English) One from Saint Denis, a town in France. *Notables:* Film director Sidney Lumet; actor Sidney Poitier; writer Sidney Sheldon. *Variations:* Sid, Siddie, Sidon, Sidonio, Syd, Sydney.

SIDWELL (English) Wide brook.

SIEGFRIED (German) Victory and peace. *Variations:* Sigfredo, Siegfrid, Sigfrido, Sigfroi, Sigifredo, Sigvard.

SIGMUND (German) Victory shield. *Notables:* Founder of psychoanalysis Sigmund Freud. *Variations:* Siegmund, Sigmond.

SILAS (English) Form of Silvan.

SILVAN (Latin) Forest. *Variations:* Silva, Silvain, Silvano, Silvanus, Silvio, Sylas, Sylvain, Sylvan, Sylvanus.

SIMA (Hebrew) Treasure.

SIMBA (African) Lion.

SIMCHA (Hebrew) Joy.

SIMON (Hebrew) God hears. *Notables:* *American Idol* judge Simon Cowell; South American revolutionary leader Simon Bolivar. *Variations:* Simeon, Simion, Simm, Simms, Simone, Symms, Symon.

SIMPSON (English) Son of Simon. *Variations:* Simson.

SINCLAIR (French) Town in France. *Variations:* Sinclare, Synclair.

SINJIN (English) From St. John. *Variations:* Sinjon, Sinjun.

SIVAN (Hebrew) Ninth month of the Jewish year.

SKEETER (English) Swift. *Variations:* Skeet.

SKIP (Scandinavian) Boss of a ship. *Variations:* Skipp, Skipper, Skippie, Skippy.

SKY (English) Sky.

SKYLAR (Dutch) Scholar. Form of Schuyler.

SLADE (English) Valley. *Variations:* Slayde.

SLANE (Czech) Salty.

SLOAN (Irish) Soldier. *Variations:* Sloane.

SMEDLEY (English) Flat meadow. *Variations:* Smedleigh, Smedly.

SMITH (English) Blacksmith. *Variations:* Smitty, Smyth, Smythe.

SNOWDEN (English) Snowy mountain. *Variations:* Snowdon.

SOCRATES (Greek) Whole power. *Notables:* Greek philosopher Socrates. *Variations:* Socratis, Sokrates.

SOL (Hebrew) Short form of Solomon. *Notables:* Music impresario Sol Hurok.

SOLOMON (Hebrew) Peaceable. *Notables:* Solomon Schechter, founder of Conservative Judaism. *Variations:* Salamen, Salamon, Salamun, Salaun, Salman, Salmon, Salom, Salomo, Salomon, Salomone, Selim, Shelomoh, Shlomo, Sol, Solaman, Sollie, Solly, Soloman, Solomo, Solomonas, Solomone.

SOMERSET (English) Summer estate. *Notables:* Writer W. Somerset Maugham. *Variations:* Sommerset, Summerset.

SOMERTON (English) Summer town. *Variations:* Somervile, Somerville.

SONNY (English) Son. *Notables:* Singer Sonny Bono; boxer Sonny Liston; musician Sonny Rollins. *Variations:* Sonnie.

SOREN (Scandinavian) Apart.

SORLEY (Scottish) Viking.

SORRELL (French) Reddish brown. *Notables:* Actor Sorrell Booke. *Variations:* Sorrel, Sorrelle.

SPALDING (English) Divided field. *Notables:* Writer/actor Spalding Gray. *Variations:* Spaulding.

SPEAR (English) Man with a spear. *Variations:* Speare, Spears, Speer, Speers, Spiers.

SPENCER (English) Seller of goods. *Notables:* Actor Spencer Tracy; musician Spencer Davis. *Variations:* Spence, Spense, Spenser.

SPIKE (English) One with spiky hair. *Notables:* Film directors Spike Lee and Spike Jonze; bandleader and comedian Spike Jones.

SPIRO (Greek) Spirit. *Notables:* U.S. Vice President Spiro Agnew.

SQUIRE (English) Medieval landlord.

STACY (Greek) Fertile. *Notables:* Actor Stacy Keach. *Variations:* Stacey.

STAFFORD (English) Landing with a ford. *Variations:* Stafforde, Staford.

STAN (English) Short form of Stanley. *Notables:* Comedian Stan Laurel; jazz musician Stan Getz.

STANBURY (English) Fort made of stone. *Variations:* Stanberry, Stanbery.

STANDISH (English) Stony park.

STANFORD (English) Stony ford. *Variations:* Stamford, Stan, Standford.

STANHOPE (English) Stony hollow.

STANISLAUS (Polish) Glorious camp. *Variations:* Stach, Stanislao, Stanislas, Stanislau, Stanislav, Stanislaw, Stanislus, Stas, Stash, Stashko, Stasio.

STANLEY (English) Stony meadow. *Notables:* Director Stanley Kubrick. *Variations:* Stan, Stanlea, Stanlee, Stanleigh, Stanly.

STANTON (English) Stony town. *Variations:* Stanten, Staunton.

STANWICK (English) Stone village.

STARR (English) Star.

STAVROS (Greek) Crowned.

STEADMAN (English) One who lives on a farm. *Notables:* Speaker/writer Stedman Graham. *Variations:* Steadmann, Stedman.

STEELE (English) One who resists. *Variations:* Steel.

STEFAN (Scandinavian) Form of Stephen.

STEIN (German) Stone. *Variations:* Steen.

STEPHEN (Greek) Crowned. *Notables:* Composer Stephen Sondheim; writer Stephen King; physicist Stephen Hawking. *Variations:* Stefan, Stefano, Stefanos, Stefans, Steffan, Steffel, Steffen, Stefos, Stepa, Stepan, Stepanek, Stepek, Stephan, Stephane, Stephanos, Stephanus, Stephens, Stephenson, Stepka, Stepousek, Stevan, Steve, Steven, Stevenson, Stevie.

STERLING (English) First-class. *Variations:* Stirling.

STEVE (English) Short form of Steven. *Notables:* Actor Steve McQueen; comedian Steve Martin.

STEVEN (English) Form of Stephen. *Notables:* Film director Steven Spielberg; Aerosmith lead singer Steven Tyler.

STEWART (English) Steward. *Notables:* Actor Stewart Granger; musician Stewart Copeland. *Variations:* Stew, Steward, Stu, Stuart.

STILLMAN (English) Silent man.

STOCKLEY (English) Meadow of tree stumps. *Variations:* Stocklea, Stocklee, Stockleigh.

STOCKTON (English) Town of tree stumps.

STOCKWELL (English) Spring with tree stumps.

STODDARD (English) Protector of horses.

STORM (English) Storm. *Notables:* TV weatherman Storm Field.

STOVER (English) Keeper of the stove.

STOWE (English) Hidden. *Variations:* Stow.

STRATFORD (English) River crossing near a street.

STRATTON (Scottish) River town.

STROM (German) River. *Notables:* U.S. Senator Strom Thurmond.

STRUTHERS (Irish) Brook.

STUART (English) Caretaker. Form of Stewart. *Notables:* Shoe designer Stuart Weitzman; children's book character, mouse Stuart Little. *Variations:* Stu.

STYLES (English) Stile; stairs that go over a wall.

SULLIVAN (Irish) Black-eyed. *Variations:* Sullavan, Sullevan, Sulliven.

SULLY (English) Southern meadow. *Variations:* Sulleigh, Sulley.

SULWYN (Welsh) Bright sun.

SUMNER (English) Summoner. *Notables:* Communications CEO Sumner Redstone.

SUTCLIFF (English) Southern cliff.

SUTHERLAND (Scandinavian) Southern land. *Variations:* Southerland.

SUTTON (English) Southern town.

SVEN (Scandinavian) Youth.

SWAIN (English) Herdsman; knight's attendant.

SWEENEY (Irish) Small hero. *Variations:* Sweeny.

SWINTON (English) Swine town.

SY (English) Short form of Sydney or Sylvester.

SYDNEY (English) Form of Sidney. *Notables:* Director Sydney Pollack.

SYLVESTER (Latin) Forested. *Notables:* Actor Sylvester Stallone. *Variations:* Silvester, Silvestre, Silvestro, Sly.

T

TAB (German) Brilliant. *Notables:* Actor Tab Hunter. *Variations:* Tabb.

TABOR (Hungarian) Encampment.

TAD (Welsh) Father. *Variations:* Tadd.

TAFT (English) River.

TAGGART (Irish) Son of a priest.

TAHIR (Arabic) Pure.

TAHOMA (Native American) Shoreline. *Variations:* Tohoma.

TAI (Vietnamese) Skilled.

TAJ (Hindu) Crown.

TAKIS (Greek) Form of Peter.

TAL (Hebrew) Rain.

TALBOT (English) From the valley. *Variations:* Talbert, Talbott, Tallbot, Tallbott.

TALE (African) Green.

TALIB (Arabic) Searcher.

TALIESIN (Welsh) Radiant brow. *Variations:* Taltesin.

TALON (Hebrew) Claw.

TAM (Scottish) Form of Thomas.

TAMIR (Arabic) Tall as a tree.

TAMMANY (Native American) Friendly. *Variations:* Tamanend.

TANI (Japanese) Valley.

TANK (Polynesian) God of the sky.

TANNER (English) One who tans leather. *Variations:* Tan, Tanier, Tann, Tanney, Tanny.

TARLETON (English) Thor's town.

TARQUIN (Latin) Etruscan king.

TARRANT (Welsh) Thunder. *Variations:* Tarrent.

TATE (English) Happy. *Notables:* Actor Tate Donovan. *Variations:* Tait, Taitt, Tayte.

TAVARES (Aramaic) Misfortune. *Variations:* Tavor.

TAVISH (Irish) Twin. *Variations:* Tavis, Tevis.

TAYLOR (English) Tailor. *Notables:* Film director Taylor Hackford. *Variations:* Tailer, Tailor, Tayler, Taylour.

TEAGAN (Irish) Form of Teague.

TEAGUE (Irish) Poet.

TEARLACH (Scottish) Man.

TED (English) Short form of Edward or Theodore. *Notables:* News anchorman Ted Koppel; singer Ted Nugent; media entrepreneur Ted Turner.

TEDDY (English) Short form of Edward or Theodore. *Notables:* Singer Teddy Pendergrass.

TEGAN (Irish) Doe.

TELEM (Hebrew) Furrow.

TELFORD (French) One who works with iron. *Variations:* Telfer, Telfor, Telfour.

TELLER (English) Storyteller.

TELLY (Greek) Short form of Teller or Theodore. *Notables:* Actor Telly Savalas.

TEMPEST (French) Storm.

TEMPLE (English) Temple.

TEMPLETON (English) Town near the temple. *Variations:* Temple, Templeten.

TENNANT (English) Tenant. *Variations:* Tenant, Tennent.

TENNESSEE (Native American) The state. *Notables:* Playwright Tennessee Williams.

TENNYSON (English) Son of Dennis. *Variations:* Tenney, Tennie, Tenny.

TERACH (Hebrew) Goat. *Variations:* Tera, Terah.

TERENCE (Latin) Roman clan name that could mean smooth. *Notables:* Actor Terence Stamp; playwright Terence McNally. *Variations:* Tarrance, Terencio, Terrance, Terrence, Terrey, Terri, Terry.

atlantic hurricane names for 2009

Anna	Larry
Bill	Mindy
Claudette	Nicholas
Danny	Odette
Erika	Peter
Fred	Rose
Grace	Sam
Henri	Teresa
Ida	Victor
Joaquin	Wanda
Kate	

top ten names of the 1940s

Boys	Girls
James	Mary
Robert	Linda
John	Barbara
William	Patricia
Richard	Carol
David	Sandra
Charles	Nancy
Thomas	Judith
Michael	Sharon
Ronald	Susan

TERRELL (German) Follower of Thor. *Variations:* Terrall, Terrel, Terrill, Terryl, Terryll, Tirrell, Tyrrell.

TERRY (English) Short form of Terence. *Notables:* Football player Terry Bradshaw; director/animator and Monty Python member Terry Gilliam.

TEVA (Hebrew) Nature.

TEVIN (African-American) Variation of Kevin.

TEVIS (Scottish) Form of Thomas.

TEX (American) Nickname for Texas. *Notables:* Country singer/actor Tex Ritter.

THADDEUS (Aramaic) Brave. *Notables:* Polish patriot and soldier Thaddeus Kosciuszko. *Variations:* Taddeo, Tadeo, Tadio, Thad, Thaddaus.

THAI (Vietnamese) Many.

THANE (English) Warrior. *Variations:* Thain, Thaine, Thayn, Thayne.

THANIEL (Hebrew) Form of Nathaniel.

THANOS (Greek) Nobleman.

THATCHER (English) Roof thatcher. *Variations:* Thacher, Thatch, Thaxter.

THAW (English) Melt.

THAYER (German) Of the army.

THEOBALD (German) Brave people. *Variations:* Thebaud, Thebault, Thibault, Thibaut, Tibold, Tiebold.

THEODORE (Greek) Gift from God. *Notables:* U.S. President Theodore Roosevelt. *Variations:* Teador, Ted, Tedd, Teddey, Teddie, Teddy, Tedor, Teodor, Teodoro, Theo, Theodor.

THEODORIC (German) Leader of the people. *Variations:* Thierry.

THERON (Greek) Hunter.

THESEUS (Greek) Ancient mythological figure.

THIASSI (Scandinavian) Ancient mythological figure. *Variations:* Thiazi, Thjazi.

THIERRY (French) Form of Theodore. *Notables:* Fashion designer Thierry Mugler.

THOMAS (Aramaic) Twin. *Notables:* U.S. President Thomas Jefferson; inventor Thomas Edison; writer Thomas Hardy. *Variations:* Tam, Tameas, Thom, Thoma, Thompson, Thomson, Thumas, Thumo, Tom, Tomas, Tomaso, Tomasso, Tomaz, Tomcio, Tomek, Tomelis, Tomi, Tomie, Tomislaw, Tomm, Tommy, Tomsen, Tomson, Toomas, Tuomas, Tuomo.

THOMPSON (English) Son of Thomas.

THOR (Scandinavian) Thunder. *Notables:* Thor, mythological god of thunder; Norwegian explorer Thor Heyerdahl. *Variations:* Tor, Torr.

THORALD (Scandinavian) One who follows Thor. *Variations:* Thorold, Torald.

THORGOOD (English) Thor is good. *Notables:* Civil rights leader Thurgood Marshall. *Variations:* Thurgood.

THORLEY (English) Thor's meadow. *Variations:* Thorlea, Thorlee, Thorleigh, Thorly, Torley.

THORNE (English) Thorn. *Variations:* Thorn.

THORNLEY (English) Thorny meadow. *Variations:* Thornlea, Thornleigh, Thornly.

THORNTON (English) Thorny town. *Notables:* Writer Thornton Wilder.

THORPE (English) Village.

THURLOW (English) Thor's hill.

THURMOND (English) Defended by Thor. *Notables:* Baseball player Thurman Munson. *Variations:* Thurman, Thurmon.

THURSTON (Scandinavian) Thor's stone. *Variations:* Thorstan, Thorstein, Thorsteinn, Thorsten, Thurstain, Thurstan, Thursten, Torstein, Torsten, Torston.

TIBOR (Slavic) Sacred place. *Variations:* Tiebout, Tybald, Tybalt, Tybault.

TIERNAN (Irish) Little lord. *Variations:* Tierney, Tighearnach, Tighearnan.

TIERNEY (Irish) Lordly.

TIGER (American) Tiger. *Notables:* Golfer Tiger Woods. *Variations:* Tyger.

TILDEN (English) Tilted valley.

TIM (Greek) Short form of Timothy. *Notables:* Comedians Tim Allen and Tim Conway; film director Tim Burton.

TIMMY (Greek) Short form of Timothy.

TIMON (Greek) Honorable.

TIMOTHY (Greek) Honoring God. *Notables:* Actors Timothy Hutton and Timothy Dalton. *Variations:* Timmothy, Timo, Timofeo, Timon, Timoteo, Timothe, Timotheo, Timotheus, Timothey, Tymmothy, Tymothy.

TINO (Italian) Small.

TITO (Spanish) To honor. *Notables:* Musician Tito Puente.

TITUS (Greek) Of the giants. *Variations:* Tito, Titos.

TIVON (Hebrew) Lover of nature.

TOAL (Irish) Strong people. *Variations:* Tuathal, Tully.

in defense of middle names

Though rarely used on a daily basis, middle names are still popular, especially since they break the stalemate when each partner has selected a different favorite name for the baby. They also get parents off the hook with family members who hope at least one name used for the baby will honor Grandpa Max or Great-Grandma Irma.

TOBAR (Gypsy) Road.

TOBIAS (Hebrew) God is good. *Variations:* Tobe, Tobey, Tobia, Tobiah, Tobie, Tobin, Toby.

TOBY (English) Short form of Tobias. *Notables:* Country singer Toby Keith; actor Tobey McGuire. *Variations:* Tobey.

TODD (English) Fox. *Notables:* Chef Todd English. *Variations:* Tod.

TOM (English) Short form of Thomas. *Notables:* Actors Tom Cruise and Tom Hanks; rocker Tom Petty. *Variations:* Thom.

TOMLIN (English) Little twin. *Variations:* Tomlinson.

TOMMY (English) Short form of Thomas. *Notables:* Fashion designer Tommy Hilfiger; choreographer Tommy Tune; comedian Tommy Chong.

TONG (Vietnamese) Aromatic.

TONY (Latin) Nickname for Anthony. *Notables:* Singer Tony Orlando; actor Tony Curtis. *Variations:* Toney, Tonie.

TOPHER (English) Form of Christopher. *Notables:* Actor Topher Grace.

TORAO (Japanese) Tiger.

TORD (Scandinavian) Peace of Thor.

TORGER (Scandinavian) Thor's spear. *Variations:* Terje, Torgeir.

TORIN (Irish) Chief.

TORIO (Japanese) Bird's tail.

TORRANCE (Irish) Little hills. *Variations:* Torin, Torrence, Torrin.

TORY (English) Short form of Torrance. *Variations:* Torrey, Torry.

TOWNSEND (English) Town's end.

TRACY (Greek) Brave warrior. *Variations:* Trace, Tracey, Treacy.

TRAVERS (French) Crossroads.

TRAVIS (French) Toll-taker. *Notables:* Singer Travis Tritt. *Variations:* Traver, Travers, Travus, Travys.

TRAYTON (English) Town near trees.

TREMAIN (Celtic) Stone house. *Variations:* Tremaine, Tremayne.

TRENT (Latin) Rushing waters. *Notables:* Singer Trent Reznor; U.S. Senator Trent Lott. *Variations:* Trenten, Trentin, Trenton.

TREVOR (Welsh) Large homestead. *Notables:* Actor Trevor Howard. *Variations:* Trefor, Trev, Trevar, Trever, Trevis.

TREY (English) Three. *Notables:* South Park creator Trey Parker.

TRIG (Scandinavian) Trusty.

TRINI (Latin) Short form of Trinity. *Notables:* Singer Trini Lopez.

TRINITY (Latin) The Holy Trinity.

TRIPP (English) Traveler.

TRISTAN (Welsh) Famous Welsh folklore character. *Variations:* Tris, Tristam.

TRISTRAM (Welsh) Sorrowful. *Notables:* Literary character Tristram Shandy.

TROY (Irish) Soldier. *Notables:* Actor Troy Donahue. *Variations:* Troi, Troye.

TRUITT (English) Small and sincere.

TRUMAN (English) Loyal one. *Notables:* Writer Truman Capote. *Variations:* Trueman, Trumaine, Trumann.

TRUMBALL (English) Strong.

TUAN (Vietnamese) Unimportant.

TUCKER (English) One who works with cloth. *Notables:* TV news commentator Tucker Carlson.

TUDOR (Welsh) Royal dynasty.

TUG (Scandinavian) Pull. *Notables:* Baseball player Tug McGraw.

TULLY (Irish) Peaceful. *Variations:* Tull, Tulley, Tullie.

TUPPER (English) One who keeps rams.

TURK (English) From Turkey.

TURNER (English) Woodworker.

TWAIN (English) Split in two. *Variations:* Twaine, Twayn.

TWITCHELL (English) Narrow alley.

TWYFORD (English) Place where rivers converge.

TY (American) Unknown definition. *Notables:* TV fix-it man Ty Pennington; baseball player Ty Cobb. *Variations:* Tye.

TYDEUS (Greek) Ancient mythological figure.

TYEE (Native American) Chief.

TYLER (English) Tile maker. *Variations:* Ty, Tylar.

TYNAN (Irish) Dark.

TYRONE (Irish) Land of Owen. *Notables:* Actor Tyrone Power. *Variations:* Tiron, Tirone, Ty, Tyron.

TYRRELL (French) To pull. *Variations:* Terrell, Tirell, Tyrrell.

TYRUS (English) Thor.

TYSON (English) Firebrand. *Notables:* Model Tyson Beckford. *Variations:* Tieson, Tison, Tysen.

U

UALAN (Scottish) Valentine.

UALTAR (Irish) Ruler of the army. *Variations:* Uaitcir, Ualteir.

UANG (Chinese) Great.

UBA (African) Wealthy.

UBADAH (Arabic) He who serves God.

UBERTO (Italian) Form of Herbert.

UDAY (Hindu) To rise. *Variations:* Udayan.

UDELL (English) Yew grove. *Variations:* Dell, Eudel, Udall, Udel.

UDO (German) Prosperity.

UDOLF (English) Wealthy wolf. *Variations:* Udolfo, Udolph.

UGO (Italian) Intellect. Form of Hugo.

UILLEOG (Irish) Small protector. *Variations:* Uilleac, Uillioc.

UILLIAM (Irish) Form of William.

UINSEANN (Irish) One who conquers. *Variations:* Uinsionn.

UJALA (Hindu) Shining. *Variations:* Ujaala.

UKIAH (Native American) Deep valley.

ULAN (African) Firstborn of twins.

ULAND (English) Noble country.

ULBRECHT (German) Grandeur.

ULEKI (Hawaiian) Hawaiian version of Ulysses. *Variations:* Ulesi.

ULF (Scandinavian) Wolf. *Variations:* Ulv.

ULL (Scandinavian) Glory.

ULMER (English) Famous wolf. *Variations:* Ullmar, Ulmar.

ULRIC (German) Wolf power; (Scandinavian) Noble ruler. *Variations:* Ulrich, Ulrick, Ulrik, Ulrike.

ULYSSES (Latin) Wrathful. *Notables:* U.S. President Ulysses S. Grant. *Variations:* Ulises, Ulisse.

UMAR (Arabic) To bloom.

UMBERTO (Italian) Famous warrior. Variation of Humbert. *Notables:* Writer Umberto Eco.

UMED (Hindu) Desire.

UMI (African) Life.

UNCAS (Native American) Fox. *Variations:* Wonkas.

UNER (Turkish) Famous.

UNIKA (African) To shine.

UNWIN (English) Enemy. *Variations:* Unwinn, Unwyn.

UPDIKE (English) Upper bank.

UPSHAW (English) Upper forest.

popular names in france

Boys	Girls
Théo	Léa
Hugo	Chloé
Lucas	Emma
Thomas	Camille
Quentin	Manon
Alexandre	Sarah
Antoine	Océane
Maxime	Margaux
Valentin	Mathilde
Clément	Laura

UPTON (English) Hill town. *Notables:* Writer Upton Sinclair.

UPWOOD (English) Forest on a hill.

URBAN (Latin) Man from the city. *Variations:* Urbain, Urbaine, Urbane, Urbano, Urbanus, Urvan.

URI (Hebrew) God's light. *Notables:* Paranormalist Uri Geller. *Variations:* Uria, Uriah, Urias, Urie, Uriel.

URIAH (Hebrew) My light.

URIAN (Greek) Heaven.

URIEN (Welsh) Privileged birth.

URSA (Latin) Bear. *Variations:* Ursan, Urson.

URVIL (Hindu) The sea.

USAMA (Arabic) Lion. *Variations:* Usamah.

USHER (Latin) River mouth. *Notables:* R&B singer Usher Raymond.

USI (African) Smoke.

USTIN (Russian) Just.

UTHER (English) From Arthurian legend, King Arthur's father.

UTHMAN (Arabic) Bird. *Variations:* Othman, Usman.

UTTAM (Hindu) Best.

UZI (Hebrew) My strength.

UZIAH (Hebrew) God is my strength. *Variations:* Uzia, Uziya, Uzziah.

UZIEL (Hebrew) Powerful. *Variations:* Uzziel.

UZOMA (African) Born on a trip.

VACHEL (French) Small cow. *Variations:* Vachell.

VACLAV (Czech) Glory. *Notables:* Writer/ dramatist Vaclav Havel.

VADIN (Hindu) Educated orator.

VAIL (English) From the valley. *Variations:* Vaile, Vale, Vayle.

VAINO (Scandinavian) Wagon builder.

VAL (English) Short form of Valentine. *Notables:* Actor Val Kilmer.

VALDEMAR (German) Famous leader.

VALENTINE (Latin) Strong. *Variations:* Val, Valentin, Valentino, Valentyn.

VALERIAN (Latin) Healthy. *Variations:* Valerie, Valerien, Valerio, Valery, Valeryan.

VALI (Scandinavian) Mythological figure.

VALIN (Hindu) Mighty soldier. *Variations:* Valen, Valyn.

VAN (Dutch) Short form of Vandyke. *Notables:* Actor Van Johnson; pianist Van Cliburn.

VANCE (English) Swampland. *Variations:* Van, Vancelo, Vann.

VANDA (Lithuanian) Ruling people. *Variations:* Vandele.

VANDAN (Hindu) Salvation.

VANDYKE (Dutch) From the dyke. *Notables:* Songwriter Van Dyck Parks. *Variations:* Van Dyck.

VANE (English) Banner.

VANYA (Russian) God is good. Variation of Ivan. *Variations:* Vanek, Vanka.

VARDEN (French) Green mountains. *Variations:* Vardon, Verden, Verdon, Verdun.

VARICK (German) Defending ruler. *Variations:* Varrick.

VARTAN (Armenian) Rose grower.

VARUN (Hindu) God of rain. *Variations:* Varin, Varoon.

VASANT (Hindu) Spring.

VASILIS (Greek) Kingly. *Variations:* Vasile, Vasilek, Vasili, Vasilios, Vasilis, Vasilos, Vasily, Vassily.

VASIN (Hindu) Leader.

VASU (Hindu) Prosperous.

VAUGHN (Welsh) Small. *Variations:* Vaughan.

VEA (Polynesian) Chief. *Variations:* Veamalohi, Veatama.

VEASNA (Cambodian) Lucky.

VELESLAV (Czech) Great glory. *Variations:* Vela, Velek, Velousek.

VENCEL (Hungarian) Wreath.

VENCESLAV (Czech) Glorious government.

VENEDICT (Russian) Blessed. Variation of Benedict. *Variations:* Venedikt, Venka, Venya.

VERE (French) True.

VERED (Hebrew) Rose.

VERLIE (French) Town in France. *Variations:* Verley.

VERLIN (American) Spring. *Variations:* Verle, Verlon.

VERN (Latin) Short form of Vernon. *Notables:* "Mini Me" actor Verne Troyer. *Variations:* Verne.

school daze: names from teachers (part iii)

This selection comes from an elementary school in Santa Barbara, California.

Advil	Mazulabelle
Anjama	Mozelle
Avila	Myrt
Bolden	Mysterium
Bryanna	Ooanh
Champagne	Perlonia
Chance	Philinda
Crysti	Rachael
Deejonay	Rashon
Emari	Shenique
Fantasee	Shenoa
Fuk	Sheona
Grayson	Synge
Jyl	Torston
Lan	Tranquilino
Lyric	Twyla
Klinsmann	Vianey
Kristofor	Yovanka
Malachi	Zern
Marassa	Zuleika
Maverick	Zulema

VERNER (German) Defense army.

VERNON (Latin) Youthful. *Variations:* Vern, Verne.

VERRILL (French) Loyal. *Variations:* Verill, Verrall, Verrell, Verroll, Veryl.

VIAN (English) Lively.

VIC (Latin) Short form of Victor. *Notables:* Actor Vic Morrow.

VICTOR (Latin) Conqueror. *Notables:* Musician Victor Borge; actor Victor Mature. *Variations:* Vic, Vick, Victoir, Victorien, Victorino, Victorio, Viktor, Vitenka, Vitor, Vittore, Vittorio, Vittorios.

VIDAL (Spanish) Vital. *Notables:* Hair stylist Vidal Sassoon.

VIDAR (Scandinavian) Strong and silent.

VIDKUN (Scandinavian) Vast experience.

VIDOR (Hungarian) Happy.

VIGGO (Scandinavian) Warrior. *Notables:* Actor Viggo Mortensen.

VIJAY (Hindu) Victory. *Variations:* Bijay, Vijen, Vijun.

VILHELM (German) Form of William. *Variations:* Vilem, Vilhelms, Villem, Vilmos.

VILIAMI (Polynesian) Protector.

VILJO (Scandinavian) Guardian.

VILMAR (German) Famous.

VILMOS (German) Steady soldier.

VILOK (Hindu) To see.

VIMAL (Hindu) Pure.

VIN (English) Short form of Vincent. *Notables:* Actor Vin Diesel.

VINAY (Hindu) Courteous.

VINCE (English) Short form of Vincent. *Notables:* Football coach Vince Lombardi; country singer Vince Gill.

VINCENT (Latin) To conquer. *Notables:* Actor Vincent Price; artist Vincent van Gogh. *Variations:* Vikent, Vikenti, Vikesha, Vin, Vince, Vincente, Vincenz, Vincenzio, Vincenzo, Vinci, Vinco, Vinn, Vinnie, Vinny.

VINE (English) One who works in a vineyard.

VINNY (English) Short form of Vincent. *Notables:* Football player Vinny Testaverde. *Variations:* Vinnie.

VINOD (Hindu) Fun.

VINSON (English) Son of Vincent.

VINTON (English) Vineyard settlement.

VIRGIL (Latin) Staff bearer. *Notables:* Roman poet Virgil. *Variations:* Vergil, Virgilio.

VISHAL (Hindu) Great.

VISHNU (Hindu) Protector.

VITALE (Italian) Life.

VITALIS (Latin) Life.

VITAS (Latin) Vital. *Notables:* Tennis player Vitas Gerulaitis. *Variations:* Vitus.

VITO (Latin) Alive. *Variations:* Vital, Vitale, Vitalis.

VITTORIO (Italian) Form of Victor.

VIVEK (Hindu) Wisdom. *Variations:* Vivekanand, Vivekananda.

VIVIAN (Latin) Full of life.

VLAD (Slavic/Russian) Short form of Vladimir or Vladislav.

VLADIMIR (Russian) Famous prince. *Notables:* Russian revolutionary Vladimir Lenin; *Lolita* writer Vladimir Nabokov. *Variations:* Vlad, Vladamir, Vladimeer, Vladko, Vladlen.

VLADISLAV (Czech) Glorious ruler. *Variations:* Ladislav.

VOJTECH (Czech) Comforting soldier. *Variations:* Vojta, Vojtek, Vojtresek.

VOLKER (German) Protector of the people.

VOLNEY (German) Spirit of the people.

VOLYA (Russian) Ruler of the people. Variation of Walter. *Variations:* Vova, Vovka.

VON (Scandinavian) Hope.

VUI (Vietnamese) Cheerful.

WABAN (Native American) Easterly wind.

WADE (English) To cross a river. *Notables:* Baseball player Wade Boggs.

WADLEY (English) Meadow near a river crossing. *Variations:* Wadleigh, Wadly.

WADSWORTH (English) Village near a river crossing. *Variations:* Waddsworth.

WAGNER (German) Wagon maker. *Variations:* Waggoner.

WAHID (Arabic) Unique. *Variations:* Waheed.

WAIL (Arabic) One who returns to Allah.

WAINWRIGHT (English) Wagon maker. *Variations:* Wainright, Waynewright.

WAITE (English) Watchman. *Variations:* Waits, Wayte.

WAKEFIELD (English) Damp field. *Variations:* Wake.

WAKELEY (English) Damp meadow. *Variations:* Wakelea, Wakeleigh, Wakely.

WAKEMAN (English) Watchman.

WALCOTT (English) Cottage by the wall. *Variations:* Wallcot, Wallcott, Wolcott.

WALDEMAR (German) Name of a famous ruler.

WALDEN (English) Forested valley. *Variations:* Waldon.

WALDO (German) Strong.

WALDRON (German) Strong raven.

WALERIAN (Polish) Strong. *Variations:* Waleran.

WALFORD (English) River crossing.

WALFRED (German) Peaceful ruler.

WALID (Arabic) Newborn. *Variations:* Waleed.

WALKER (English) Cloth walker.

WALLACE (Scottish) One from Wales. *Notables:* Actors Wallace Shawn and Wallace Beery. *Variations:* Wallach, Wallie, Wallis, Wally, Walsh, Welch, Welsh.

WALLACH (German) Form of Wallace.

WALLER (English) Wall maker.

WALLY (English) Short form of Wallace or Walter. *Notables:* Writer Wally Lamb; cookie maker Wally "Famous" Amos.

WALSH (English) Form of Wallace.

WALT (German) Short form of Walter or Walton. *Notables:* Film and theme-park legend Walt Disney.

WALTER (German) Ruler of the people. *Notables:* Newscaster Walter Cronkite; actor Walter Pidgeon. *Variations:* Walt, Walther.

WALTON (English) Walled town.

WALWORTH (English) Walled farm.

WALWYN (English) Welsh friend. *Variations:* Walwin, Walwinn, Walwynn, Walwynne.

WANETA (Native American) He who charges another.

WANG (Chinese) Hope.

WAPASHA (Native American) Red leaf. *Variations:* Wabasha, Wapusha.

WAPI (Native American) Lucky.

WARBURTON (English) Old fortress.

WARD (English) Guardian. *Variations:* Warde, Warden, Worden.

WARDELL (English) Watchman's hill.

WARDLEY (English) Watchman's meadow. *Variations:* Wardlea, Wardleigh.

WARE (English) Cautious.

WARFIELD (English) Field by the weir (a device placed in a river to catch fish).

WARFORD (English) River crossing by the weir.

honor your heritage and your child

In this melting pot of cultural diversity, honoring ties to family is noble and worthy. Unless you live in a community filled with people with similar family ties, giving your child a unique, foreign-sounding name might pose some challenges. Be mindful and compromise—"Jack" Gravas might be a better choice in the long run than "Latka."

WARLEY (English) Meadow by the weir.

WARNER (German) Army guard.

WARREN (German) Protector. *Notables:* Actor Warren Beatty; U.S. President Warren Harding. *Variations:* Warrin, Warriner.

WARWICK (English) House near a dam. *Variations:* Warick, Warrick.

WASHAKIE (Native American) Gourd.

WASHBURN (English) Flooded river.

WASHINGTON (English) Town of smart men. *Notables:* Writer Washington Irving.

WASILY (Russian) Form of Basil. *Variations:* Wasili, Wasyl.

WASIM (Arabic) Attractive. *Variations:* Waseem, Wassim.

WATFORD (English) Wattle ford.

WATKINS (English) Son of Walter.

WATSON (English) Son of Walter.

WAVERLY (English) Meadow of aspen trees. *Variations:* Waverlee, Waverleigh, Waverley.

WAYLON (English) Roadside land. *Notables:* Singer Waylon Jennings; ventriloquist Waylon Flowers. *Variations:* Way, Waylan, Wayland, Waylen, Waylin.

WAYNE (English) Wagon maker. *Notables:* Singer Wayne Newton; TV host/comedian Wayne Brady; motivational writer/speaker Wayne Dyer. *Variations:* Wain, Wainwright, Wayn, Waynwright.

WEAVER (English) Weaver.

WEBB (English) Weaver.

WEBLEY (English) Weaver's meadow. *Variations:* Webbley, Webbly, Webly.

WEBSTER (English) Weaver. *Variations:* Web, Webb, Weber.

WEKESA (African) Born during the harvest.

WELBORNE (English) Spring-fed river. *Variations:* Welborn, Welbourne, Welburn, Wellborn, Wellbourn, Wellburn.

WELBY (English) Waterside farm. *Variations:* Welbey, Welbie, Wellbey, Wellby.

WELDON (English) Well near a hill. *Variations:* Welden, Welldon.

WELFORD (English) Well near a river crossing. *Variations:* Wellford.

WELLINGTON (English) Temple in a clearing.

WELLS (English) Source of water.

WELTON (English) Well for a town.

WEN (Armenian) Born in winter.

WENCESLAUS (Slavic) Glorious garland. *Variations:* Wenceslas.

WENDELL (German) Wanderer. *Variations:* Wendel, Wendle.

WENTWORTH (English) White man's town.

WENUTU (Native American) Sky clearing.

WERNER (German) Defending army. *Notables:* Film director Werner Herzog. *Variations:* Warner, Wernher.

WES (English) Short form of Wesley or Weston. *Notables:* Film director Wes Craven.

maiden names as middle names

Women who want their children to carry their last names create a hyphenated last name: Jennifer Hathaway becomes Jennifer Hathaway-Zimmerman. Baby then becomes Alexander Gabriel Hathaway-Zimmerman, which is hard for little Alex to write (much less remember!). By making the maiden name the middle name, Mom's name is preserved and baby has one less name.

WESH (Gypsy) Forest.

WESLEY (English) Western meadow. *Notables:* Actor Wesley Snipes. *Variations:* Wes, Wesly, Wessley, Westleigh, Westley.

WESTBROOK (English) Western stream. *Variations:* Wesbrook, West, Westbrooke.

WESTBY (English) Western farm.

WESTCOTT (English) Western cottage. *Variations:* Wescot, Wescott, Westcot.

WESTON (English) Western town. *Variations:* Westen, Westin.

WETHERBY (English) Form of male sheep, known as a wether. *Variations:* Weatherbey, Weatherbie, Weatherby, Wetherbey, Wetherbie.

WETHERELL (English) Sheep corner. *Variations:* Weatherell, Weatherill, Wetherill, Wethrill.

WETHERLY (English) Sheep meadow. *Variations:* Weatherley, Weatherly, Wetherleigh, Wetherley.

WHALLEY (English) Forest by a hill. *Variations:* Whallie.

WHARTON (English) Town on a river bank. *Variations:* Warton.

WHEATLEY (English) Wheat field. *Variations:* Wheatlea, Wheatleigh, Wheatlie, Wheatly.

WHEATON (English) Town of wheat.

WHEELER (English) Wheel maker.

WHISTLER (English) Whistler or piper.

WHIT (English) Short form of Whitney.

WHITBY (English) Farm with white walls. *Variations:* Whitbey, Whitbie.

WHITCOMB (English) White valley. *Variations:* Whitcombe.

WHITELAW (English) White hill. *Variations:* Whitlaw.

WHITEY (English) Fair-skinned; white-haired. *Notables:* Baseball player Whitey Ford.

WHITFIELD (English) White field.

WHITFORD (English) White ford.

WHITLEY (English) White meadow.

WHITLOCK (English) White-haired one.

WHITMAN (English) White-haired man.

WHITMORE (English) White moor. *Variations:* Whitmoor, Whittemore, Witmore, Wittemore.

WHITNEY (English) White island.

WHITTAKER (English) White field. *Variations:* Whitacker, Whitaker.

WICHADO (Native American) Compliant.

WICKHAM (English) Village paddock.

WILBERT (German) Brilliant.

WILBUR (German) Brilliant. *Notables:* Aviator Wilbur Wright. *Variations:* Wilber, Wilburt, Willbur.

WILDER (English) Wilderness.

WILDON (English) Wild valley.

WILEY (English) Water meadow. *Variations:* Willey, Wylie.

WILFORD (English) River crossing by willow trees.

WILFRED (English) Purposeful peace. *Notables:* Character actor Wilfred Brimley. *Variations:* Wilfredo, Wilfrid, Wilfried, Wilfryd.

WILHELM (German) Guardian.

WILKINS (English) Kin of William.

WILKINSON (English) Son of little Will. *Variations:* Wilkes, Wilkie, Wilkins, Willkins, Willkinson.

WILL (German) Short form of William. *Notables:* Comedian/actor Will Farrell; actor Will Smith; humanitarian Will Rogers. *Variations:* Wil.

WILLARD (German) Determined. *Notables:* Weatherman Willard Scott.

WILLIAM (German) Constant protector. *Notables:* Playwright William Shakespeare; actors William Shatner and William Holden. *Variations:* Bill, Billie, Billy, Guillaume, Guillaums, Guillermo, Vas, Vasilak, Vasilious, Vaska, Vassos, Vila, Vildo, Vilek, Vilem, Vilhelm, Vili, Viliam, Vilkl, Ville, Vilmos, Vilous, Wilhelm, Will, Willem, Willi, Williamson, Willie, Willil, Willy, Wilson.

WILLIAMSON (English) Son of William.

WILLIE (German) Short form of William. *Notables:* Singer Willie Nelson. *Variations:* Willy.

WILLIS (English) Form of William.

WILLOUGHBY (English) Willow tree farm. *Variations:* Willoughbey, Willoughbie.

WILMER (German) Resolute fame. *Notables:* Actor Wilmer Valderrama. *Variations:* Willimar, Willmer, Wylmer.

WILMOT (German) Resolute.

WILSON (English) Son of Will. *Notables:* R&B singer Wilson Pickett. *Variations:* Willson.

WILTON (English) Town with a well. *Variations:* Wilt, Wylton.

WINCHELL (English) Road bend.

WINDHAM (English) Friend of the town. *Variations:* Win, Winn, Wyndham, Wynne.

WINDSOR (English) From Windsor. *Variations:* Wyndsor.

WINFIELD (English) Friend's field. *Variations:* Winnfield, Wynfield, Wynnfield.

WINFRIED (German) Peaceful friend.

WING (Chinese) Glory.

WINGATE (English) Winding gate.

WINSLOW (English) Friend's hill. *Notables:* Artist Winslow Homer.

WINSTON (English) Friend's town. *Notables:* British Prime Minister Winston Churchill. *Variations:* Winsten, Winstone, Winstonn, Winton, Wynstan, Wynston.

WINTHROP (English) Friend's village.

WINWARD (English) My brother's forest.

WIT (Polish) Life.

WOJTEK (Polish) Soldier of consolation. *Variations:* Wojteczek.

WOLCOTT (English) Wolf's cottage.

WOLFE (English) Wolf. *Variations:* Wolf, Woolf.

WOLFGANG (German) Wolf fight. *Notables:* Chef Wolfgang Puck; composer Wolfgang Amadeus Mozart.

WOODFORD (English) River crossing in the forest. *Variations:* Woodforde.

WOODROW (English) Row in the woods. *Notables:* U.S. President Woodrow Wilson. *Variations:* Wood, Woody.

WOODVILLE (English) Forest town.

WOODWARD (English) Protector of the forest. *Variations:* Woodard.

WOODY (American) Short form of Woodrow or Woodward. *Notables:* Writer/director Woody Allen; actor Woody Harrelson.

WORTH (English) Enclosed farm.

WORTHY (English) Enclosure. *Variations:* Worthey, Worthington.

WRIGHT (English) Carpenter.

WYATT (French) Little fighter. *Notables:* Cowboy Wyatt Earp. *Variations:* Wiatt, Wyat.

WYBERT (English) Brilliant at war.

WYCLIFF (English) White cliff. *Notables:* Musician Wyclef Jean. *Variations:* Wyclef, Wycliffe.

WYLIE (English) Charming.

WYNDHAM (English) Town near the path. *Variations:* Windham.

WYNN (English) Friend. *Variations:* Win, Winn, Wynne.

WYNONO (Native American) Firstborn son.

XAN (English) Short form of Alexander.

XANDER (Dutch) Form of Alexander.

XANTHUS (Greek) Blond. *Variations:* Xanthos.

XAVIER (English) New house. *Notables:* Musician Xavier Cugat. *Variations:* Saverio, Xaver.

XAYVION (African-American) The new house. *Variations:* Savion, Sayveon, Sayvion, Xavion, Xayveon, Zayvion.

XENON (Greek) Stranger.

XENOPHON (Greek) Foreign voice.

XENOS (Greek) Guest. *Variations:* Xeno, Zenos.

XERXES (Persian) Ruler.

XIANG (Chinese) To soar; fragrant.

XIAOPING (Chinese) Small bottle.

XIMEN (Spanish) Obedient. *Variations:* Ximenes, Ximon, Ximun.

XIMON (Spanish) Simon.

XING-FU (Chinese) Happiness.

XI-WANG (Chinese) Desire.

XUAN (Vietnamese) Spring.

XUN (Chinese) Fast.

XYLON (Greek) One who lives in the forest.

YADID (Hebrew) Beloved.

YADIN (Hebrew) God will judge. *Variations:* Yadon.

YAHYA (Arabic) God is good. *Variations:* Yihya.

YAIR (Hebrew) God will teach. *Variations:* Jair.

YAKECEN (Native American) Song from the sky.

YAKEZ (Native American) Heaven.

YAKIM (Hebrew) God develops. *Variations:* Jakim.

YAKOV (Russian) Form of Jacob. *Notables:* Comedian Yakov Smirnoff. *Variations:* Yankov.

YALE (Welsh) Fertile moor.

YAMAL (Hindu) One of a twin.

YAMIN (Hebrew) Right hand. *Variations:* Jamin.

YANA (Hebrew) He answers. *Variations:* Janai, Jannai, Yan, Yannai.

YANCY (Native American) Englishman. *Variations:* Yance, Yancey, Yantsey.

YANKA (Russian) God is good.

YANKEL (Yiddish) Form of Jacob.

YANNIS (Greek) God is good. Variation of John. *Variations:* Yannakis, Yanni, Yiannis.

YAPHET (Hebrew) Attractive. *Variations:* Japhet, Japheth, Yapheth.

YARDAN (Arabic) King.

YARDLEY (English) Enclosed meadow. *Variations:* Yardlea, Yardlee, Yardleigh, Yardly.

YARIN (Hebrew) To understand.

YARON (Hebrew) To sing.

YASAHIRO (Japanese) Peaceful.

YASAR (Arabic) Wealth. *Variations:* Yaser, Yasir, Yasser, Yassir.

YASH (Hindu) Glorious.

YASHASKAR (Hindu) One who brings fame.

YASIN (Arabic) Prophet.

YASUO (Japanese) Calm.

YATES (English) Gates. *Variations:* Yeats.

YAZID (African) To increase.

names with "ja" and "ke"

Combining "Ja" or "Ke" with boys' names creates interesting new names.

Ja Names	*Ke* Names
Jalen	Keandre
Jamarcus	Kechel
Janeil	Kedarius
Jaquan	Keon
Jareth	Keshawn (or Keyshawn)
Jashon	Keshua
Jathan	

YE (Chinese) Universe.

YECHEZKEL (Hebrew) God strengthens. *Variations:* Chaskel, Chatzkel, Keskel.

YEHOSHUA (Hebrew) God is salvation. *Variations:* Yeshua.

YEHOYAKIM (Hebrew) God will establish. *Variations:* Jehoiakim, Yehoiakim, Yoyakim.

YEHUDI (Hebrew) A man from Judah; someone who is Jewish. *Variations:* Yechudi, Yechudil, Yehuda, Yehudah.

YELUTCI (Native American) Quiet bear.

YEMON (Japanese) Guardian.

YEN (Vietnamese) Calm.

YEOMAN (English) Servant.

YERED (Hebrew) To come down. *Variations:* Jered.

YERIEL (Hebrew) Founded by God. *Variations:* Jeriel.

YERIK (Russian) God is exalted. *Variations:* Yeremey.

YEVGENI (Russian) Well born. *Variations:* Yevgeniy.

YISRAEL (Hebrew) Israel.

YITRO (Hebrew) Plenty. *Variations:* Yitran.

YITZCHAK (Hebrew) Laughter. *Notables:* Israeli statesman Yitzchak Rabin. *Variations:* Itzhak, Yitzhak.

YMIR (Scandinavian) Mythological figure.

YO (Chinese) Bright.

YOAKIM (Slavic) Form of Jacob.

YONATAN (Hebrew) Gift from God.

YONG (Chinese) Brave.

YONG-SUN (Korean) Courageous.

YORATH (English) Worthy god. *Variations:* Iolo, Iorwerth.

YORICK (English) Farmer.

YORK (English) Yew tree. *Variations:* Yorick, Yorke, Yorrick.

YOSEF (Hebrew) God increases. *Variations:* Yoseff, Yosif, Yousef, Yusef, Yusif, Yusuf, Yuzef.

YOSHA (Hebrew) Wisdom.

YOSHI (Japanese) Quiet.

YOSHIRO (Japanese) Good son.

YOTIMO (Native American) Bee flying to its hive.

YOTTOKO (Native American) Mud from the river.

YOUKIOMA (Native American) Flawless. *Variations:* Youkeoma, Yukeoma, Yukioma.

YOUNG (Korean) Forever.

YOUNG-SOO (Korean) Forever rich.

YOUSEF (Arabic) Form of Joseph.

YUAN (Chinese) Round.

YUCEL (Turkish) Noble.

YUKIKO (Japanese) Snow. *Variations:* Yuki, Yukio.

YUL (Chinese) Past the horizon. *Notables:* Actor Yul Brynner.

YULE (English) Christmas.

YUMA (Native American) Son of the chief.

YUNIS (Arabic) Dove. *Variations:* Younis.

YURCHIK (Russian) Farmer. Variation of George. *Variations:* Yura, Yuri, Yurik, Yurko, Yurli, Yury.

YURI (Russian) Farmer.

YUSHUA (Arabic) God's help.

YUSTYN (Russian) Just.

YUSUF (Arabic) God will increase. *Variations:* Youssef, Yousuf, Yusef, Yusif, Yussef.

YUVAL (Hebrew) Brook. *Variations:* Jubal.

YVES (French) Yew wood. *Notables:* Designer Yves St. Laurent; actor Yves Montand. *Variations:* Evo, Iveo, Ives, Yvo, Yvon.

ZACCHEUS (Hebrew) Pure.

ZACH (American) Short form of Zachary or Zachariah. *Notables:* Actor Zach Braff. *Variations:* Zac, Zack, Zak.

ZACHARIAH (Hebrew) The Lord has remembered. *Variations:* Zacaria, Zacarias, Zach, Zacharia, Zacharias, Zachary, Zachery, Zack, Zackariah, Zackerias, Zackery, Zak, Zakarias, Zakarie, Zako, Zeke.

ZACHARIAS (German) Form of Zachariah.

ZACHARY (Hebrew) Popular form of Zachariah. *Notables:* U.S. President Zachary Taylor. *Variations:* Zacary, Zaccary, Zachaery, Zacharay, Zacharey, Zacharie, Zacharry, Zachory, Zachry, Zackary, Zackery, Zackory, Zackury.

ZADOK (Hebrew) Righteous.

ZAFAR (Arabic) To win. *Variations:* Zafir.

ZAHAVI (Hebrew) Gold.

ZAHID (Arabic) Strict.

ZAHIR (Hebrew) Bright. *Variations:* Zaheer, Zahur.

ZAHUR (Arabic) Flower.

ZAIDE (Hebrew) Older.

ZAIM (Arabic) General.

ZAKAI (Hebrew) Pure. *Variations:* Zaki, Zakkai.

ZAKI (Arabic) Smart. Full of virtue.

ZAKUR (Hebrew) Masculine. *Variations:* Zaccur.

ZALE (Greek) Strength from the sea. *Variations:* Zayle.

ZALMAN (Hebrew) Peaceful.

ZAMIEL (German) God has heard. Variation of Samuel.

ZAMIR (Hebrew) Song.

ZAN (Hebrew) Well fed.

ZANDER (Greek) Short form of Alexander.

ZANE (English) God is good. Variation of John. *Notables:* Writer Zane Grey. *Variations:* Zain, Zayne.

ZAREB (African) Guardian.

ZARED (Hebrew) Trap.

ZAREK (Polish) May God protect the king.

ZAVAD (Hebrew) Present. *Variations:* Zabad.

ZAVDIEL (Hebrew) Gift from God. *Variations:* Zabdiel, Zebedee.

ZAVIER (Arabic) Form of Xavier.

ZAYD (Arabic) To increase. *Variations:* Zaid, Zayed, Ziyad.

ZBIGNIEW (Polish) To get rid of anger. *Notables:* Political scientist Zbigniew Brzezinski. *Variations:* Zbyszko.

ZBYHNEV (Czech) Rid of anger. *Variations:* Zbyna, Zbynek, Zbysek.

ZDENEK (Czech) God of wine. *Variations:* Zdenecek, Zdenko, Zdenousek, Zdicek.

ZDESLAV (Czech) Glory is here. *Variations:* Zdik, Zdisek, Zdislav.

ZDZISLAW (Polish) Glory is here. *Variations:* Zdzich, Zdziech, Zdziesz, Zdzieszko, Zdzis, Zdzisiek.

ZEBADIAH (Hebrew) Gift from God. *Variations:* Zeb, Zebediah.

ZEBEDEE (Hebrew) Form of Zebadiah.

ZEBULON (Hebrew) To exalt. *Variations:* Zebulen, Zebulun.

ZEDEKIAH (Hebrew) God is just. *Variations:* Tzedekia, Tzidkiya, Zed, Zedechiah, Zedekia, Zedekias.

ZEEMAN (Dutch) Seaman.

ZE'EV (Hebrew) Wolf.

ZEHARIAH (Hebrew) Light of God. *Variations:* Zeharia, Zeharya.

ZEHEB (Turkish) Gold.

ZEKE (Hebrew) The strength of God.

ZEKI (Turkish) Smart.

ZELIG (Hebrew) Holy.

ZELIMIR (Slavic) Desires peace.

ZEMARIAH (Hebrew) Song. *Variations:* Zemaria, Zemarya.

ZENAS (Greek) Generous. *Variations:* Zeno, Zenon.

ZENDA (Czech) Well born.

ZENO (Greek) Cart.

ZEPHANIAH (Hebrew) Protection. *Variations:* Zeph, Zephan.

ZEPHYR (Greek) West wind.

ZERACH (Hebrew) Light. *Variations:* Zerachia, Zerachya, Zerah.

ZEREM (Hebrew) Stream.

ZERIKA (Hebrew) Rain shower.

ZERO (Arabic) Worthless. *Notables:* Actor Zero Mostel.

ZEROUN (Armenian) Respected.

ZESIRO (African) Firstborn of twins.

---

everyone has an opinion—so what?

The baby-name search is not just an enjoyable experience—it's also a personal one! Friends and family members will probably ask which names you've chosen, and they've got opinions, too. Unless you've asked for their opinions, ignore them! Once you find a name you and your partner like, don't cave in to any undo pressure from "buttinskies."

ZEUS (Greek) Living. King of the gods. *Variations:* Zeno, Zenon, Zinon.

ZEV (Hebrew) Short form of Zebulon.

ZEVACH (Hebrew) Sacrifice. *Variations:* Zevachia, Zevachtah, Zevachya, Zevah.

ZEVADIAH (Hebrew) God bestows. *Variations:* Zevadia, Zevadya.

ZEVID (Hebrew) Present.

ZEVULUN (Hebrew) House. *Variations:* Zebulon, Zebulun, Zevul.

ZHIXIN (Chinese) Ambitious.

ZHONG (Chinese) Second brother.

ZHU (Chinese) Wish.

ZHUANG (Chinese) Strong.

ZIGFRIED (Russian) Form of Siegfried.

ZIGGY (American) Form of Siegfried or Sigmund.

ZIGMUND (Russian) Form of Sigmund.

ZIKOMO (African) Thank you.

ZIMRA (Hebrew) Sacred. *Variations:* Zemora, Zimrat, Zimri, Zimriah.

ZIMRAAN (Arabic) Celebrated.

ZINAN (Japanese) Second son.

ZINDEL (Hebrew) Protector of mankind. *Variations:* Zindil.

ZION (Hebrew) Guarded land. *Variations:* Tzion, Zyon.

ZIPKIYAH (Native American) Big bow. *Variations:* Zipkoeete, Zipkoheta.

ZISKIND (Yiddish) Sweet child.

ZITKADUTA (Native American) Red bird.

ZITOMER (Czech) To live in fame. *Variations:* Zitek, Zitousek.

ZIV (Hebrew) To shine. *Variations:* Zivan, Zivi.

ZIVAN (Czech) Alive. *Variations:* Zivanek, Zivek, Zivko.

ZIVEN (Slavic) Lively. *Variations:* Ziv, Zivon.

ZIYA (Arabic) Light. *Variations:* Zia.

ZIYAD (Arabic) To increase.

ZLATAN (Czech) Golden. *Variations:* Zlatek, Zlaticek, Zlatik, Zlatko, Zlatousek.

ZOHAR (Hebrew) Bright light.

ZOLLY (Hebrew) Form of Solly (Solomon). *Variations:* Zollie, Zolio.

ZOLTIN (Hungarian) Life. *Variations:* Zoltan.

ZOMEIR (Hebrew) One who prunes trees. *Variations:* Zomer.

ZORBA (Greek) Live to fullest.

ZORYA (Slavic) Star.

ZOWIE (Greek) Life.

ZUBIN (Russian) Toothy. *Notables:* Music conductor Zubin Mehta.

ZUHAYR (Arabic) Young flowers. *Variations:* Zuhair.

ZURIEL (Hebrew) The Lord is my rock.

ZVI (Hebrew) Deer.

ZWI (Scandinavian) Gazelle.

ZYGMUNT (Polish) Victorious protection.

girls'
names

AALIYAH (Hebrew) To ascend. Form of Aliyah. *Notables:* R&B singer/actress Aaliyah.

ABBY (English) Short form of Abigail. *Variations:* Abbe, Abbey, Abbi, Abbie.

ABELIA (Hebrew) A sigh. *Variations:* Abela, Abella, Abelle.

ABELINA (American) Feminine version of Abel.

ABIAH (Hebrew) God is my father. *Variations:* Abiela, Abiella, Avia, Aviah, Aviela, Aviella, Aviya.

ABIGAIL (Hebrew) Father's joy. *Notables:* Advice columnist Abigail Van Buren (more commonly known as Dear Abby); second U.S. first lady Abigail Adams. *Variations:* Abagael, Abagail, Abagale, Abbey, Abbi, Abbie, Abbigael, Abbigail, Abbigale, Abby, Abbye, Abbygael, Abbygail, Abbygale, Abigale, Abigayle, Avigail.

ABIRA (Hebrew) Strong. *Variations:* Abi.

ABRA (Hebrew) Mother of many children.

ABRIELLE (French) Protection. *Variations:* Abriella.

ACACIA (Greek) Of the acacia tree. *Variations:* Cacia, Casia.

ACADIA (Native American) Village.

ADA (German) Nobility. *Variations:* Adah, Aida, Aidah.

ADALIA (Hebrew) God as protector.

ADAMINA (Hebrew) Woman of the earth. Feminine version of Adam. *Variations:* Adama.

ADARA (Greek) Lovely woman.

ADELAIDE (English) Noble and quiet. *Variations:* Adal, Adala, Adalaid, Adalaide, Adalee, Adali, Adalie, Adalley, Addal, Adele, Adelia, Adelice, Adelicia, Adeline, Adelis, Adell, Adella, Adelle, Della, Edeline, Eline.

ADELE (French) Form of Adelaide. *Variations:* Adela, Adelia, Adelina, Adeline.

ADELPHA (Greek) Caring sister. *Variations:* Adelfa.

ADESINA (African) Child of many more to come.

ADHITA (Hindu) Student.

ADIBA (Arabic) Cultured, refined. *Variations:* Adibah.

ADILA (Arabic) Just. *Variations:* Adilah.

ADINA (Hebrew) Delicate. *Variations:* Adeana, Adin, Adine.

ADIVA (Arabic) Gentle.

ADOLPHA (German) Noble wolf. Feminine version of Adolph. *Variations:* Adolfa.

ADONIA (Greek) Beauty. *Variations:* Adona, Adoniah, Adonna.

ADORA (Latin) Much adored. *Variations:* Adoree, Adoria, Adorlee, Dora, Dori, Dorie, Dorrie.

ADRIA (Latin) Dark; from the sea. *Variations:* Adrea, Adreea, Adria, Adriah.

ADRIANA (Italian/Spanish/English) Dark, exotic one. *Variations:* Adrian, Adriane, Adrianna, Adriannah, Adrianne, Adrien, Adriena, Adrienah, Adrienne.

ADRIEL (Hebrew) God's flock.

AEGINA (Greek) Ancient mythological figure.

AENEA (Greek) Worthy.

AFRA (Hebrew) Young doe. *Variations:* Aphra.

AFRICA (Celtic) Pleasant. *Variations:* Afrika.

AFTON (English) From Afton, England. *Variations:* Aften, Aftin.

AGATHA (Greek) Good. *Notables:* Mystery writer Agatha Christie. *Variations:* Aga, Agace, Agacia, Agafia, Agasha, Agata, Agate, Agathe, Agathi, Agatta, Ageneti, Aggi, Aggie, Aggy, Akeneki.

popular names in the netherlands

Boys	Girls
Daan	Emma
Sem	Anna
Thomas	Sanne
Lars	Iris
Milan	Isa
Thijs	Maud
Lucas	Lotte
Bram	Anouk
Jesse	Lisa
Tim	Julia

AGNES (English/German/French/Scandinavian) Chaste. *Notables:* Actress Agnes Moorhead. *Variations:* Agnella, Agnesa, Agnesca, Agnese, Agnesina, Agneska, Agness, Agnessa, Agneta, Agneti, Agnetta, Agnola, Agnolah, Agnolla, Agnolle, Nesa, Ness, Nessa, Nessi, Nessia, Nessie, Nessy, Nesta, Senga, Ynes, Ynesita, Ynez.

AGRIPPINA (Latin) Born feet first. *Variations:* Agrafina, Agrippine.

AHAVA (Hebrew) Beloved. *Variations:* Ahavah, Ahavat, Ahouva, Ahuda, Ahuva.

AIDA (Arabic) Reward. *Notables:* Actress Aida Turturro.

AIDAN (Irish) Fire. *Variations:* Aidana, Aydana, Edana.

AIKO (Japanese) Little one.

AILEEN (Scottish) Light. *Variations:* Ailee, Ailene, Ailey, Aleen, Alene, Aline, Alleen, Allene, Alline, Eileen, Ilene.

AIMEE (French) Beloved. Form of Amy. *Variations:* Aimie, Amie.

AINSLEY (Scottish) A meadow. *Variations:* Ainslee, Ainsleigh, Ainslie, Ansley, Aynslee, Aynsley.

AISHA (Arabic/African) Life. *Notables:* TV personality Aisha Tyler. *Variations:* Aishah, Aisia, Aisiah, Asha, Ashah, Ashia, Ashiah, Asia, Asiah, Ayeesa, Ayeesah, Ayeesha, Ayeeshah, Ayeisa.

AISLING (Irish) Dream. *Variations:* Aislinn, Ashling, Isleen.

AJA (Hindu) Goat. *Variations:* Aija, Ajia.

AKELA (Hawaiian) Noble. *Variations:* Akala.

AKIVA (Hebrew) Shelter. *Variations:* Kiba, Kibah, Kiva, Kivah.

ALA (Hawaiian) Fragrant.

ALAIA (Arabic) Virtuous.

ALALA (Greek) Protected.

ALANA (English) Pretty. *Notables:* TV personality Alana Stewart. *Variations:* Alaina, Alane, Alanna, Alannah, Alayna, Alayne, Alena, Alene, Alenne, Aleyna, Aleynah, Aleyne, Allaine, Allayne, Alleen, Alleine, Allena, Allene, Alleynah, Alleyne, Allina, Allinah, Allyna, Allynn, Allynne, Alynne.

ALANI (Hawaiian) Orange.

ALANNIS (English) Form of Alana. *Notables:* Singer Alanis Morissette.

ALARICE (Greek) Noble. *Variations:* Alarica.

ALBA (Latin) White. *Variations:* Albane, Albina, Albine, Albinia, Albinka, Alva.

ALBERGA (Latin) Noble; inn. *Variations:* Alberge.

ALBERTA (English) Noble. *Variations:* Albertina, Albertine.

ALBINA (Italian) White. *Variations:* Alba, Albertine, Albertyna, Albinia, Albinka,

Alverta, Alvinia, Alwine, Elberta, Elbertina, Elbertine, Elbi, Elbie, Elby.

ALCINA (Greek) A sorceress. *Variations:* Alcine, Alcinia, Alsina, Alsinia, Alsyna, Alzina.

ALDA (Italian) Old. *Variations:* Aldabella, Aldea, Aldina, Aldine, Aleda, Alida.

ALDARA (Greek) A winged gift. *Variations:* Aldora.

ALEGRIA (Spanish) Joy. *Variations:* Alegra, Allegria.

ALETA (Greek) Truth. *Notables:* Singer Aleta Adams. *Variations:* Aletta, Alette.

ALETHEA (Greek) Truth. *Variations:* Alathea, Alathia, Aleethia, Aletea, Aletha, Alethia, Alithea, Alithia.

ALEX (Greek) Short form of Alexandra or Alexis.

ALEXA (Greek) Short form of Alexis. *Variations:* Alexia.

ALEXANDRA (Greek) One who defends. *Variations:* Alejandrina, Aleka, Aleksasha, Aleksey, Alesia, Aleska, Alessandra, Alessa, Alessi, Alexanderia, Alexanderina, Alexena, Alexene, Alexina, Alexiou.

ALEXIS (Greek) Helper. *Notables:* Actress Alexis Bledel. *Variations:* Aleksi, Alessa, Alexa, Alexi, Alexia, Lexi, Lexy.

ALFREDA (English) Wise counselor. Feminine version of Alfred. *Variations:* Alfre,

Alfredah, Alfredda, Alfreeda, Alfrieda, Alfryda, Allfrieda, Allfry, Allfryda, Elfre, Elfrea, Elfrida, Elfrieda Elva, Freda, Freddi, Freddie, Freddy, Fredi, Fredy, Freeda, Freedah, Frieda, Friedah, Fryda, Frydah.

ALI (Greek) Short for Alexandra, Alexis, or Allison. *Variations:* Allee, Alley, Allie, Ally, Aly.

ALICE (Greek) Truthful; (German) Noble. *Notables:* Writer Alice Walker. *Variations:* Alis, Alles, Allice, Allyce, Alyce.

ALICIA (English/Spanish) Truthful. Form of Alice. *Notables:* Singer Alicia Keyes. *Variations:* Alesha, Alesia, Alisha, Alissa, Alycia, Alysha, Alyshia, Alysia, Ilysha.

ALIDA (Spanish) Winged. *Variations:* Alaida, Alda, Aldina, Aldine, Aldyne, Aleda, Alidah, Alidia, Alita, Allda, Alleda, Allida, Allidah, Allidia, Allidiah, Allyda, Allydah, Alyda, Alydah.

ALINA (Scottish/Russian) Fair and bright. *Variations:* Aleen, Aleena, Alenah, Aline, Alline, Allyna, Alyna, Alynah, Alyne, Leena, Leenah, Lena, Lenah, Lina, Lyna, Lynah.

ALISA (Hebrew) Happiness. *Variations:* Alisah, Alisanne, Alissa, Alissah, Aliza, Allisa, Allisah, Allissa, Allissah, Allyea, Allysah, Alyssa, Alyssah.

ALIYAH (Hebrew/Arabic) Exalted. *Variations:* Aaliyah, Aliya, Aliye, Allyah, Alya.

ALIZA (Hebrew) Joyful. *Variations:* Alitza, Alitzah, Aliz, Alizka.

ALLEGRA (Latin/Italian) Joyful.

ALLISON (German) A form of Alice. *Notables:* Actress Allison Janney. *Variations:* Alisann, Alisanne, Alison, Alisoun, Alisun, Allcen, Allcenne, Allicen, Allicenne, Allie, Allisann, Allisanne, Allisoun, Ally, Allysann, Allysanne, Allyson, Alyeann, Alysanne, Alyson.

ALMA (Latin) Nurturing one. *Variations:* Allma, Almah.

ALMEDA (Latin) Determined; destined for success. *Variations:* Allmeda, Allmedah, Allmeta, Almedah, Almeta, Almetah, Almida, Almidah, Almita.

ALMERA (Arabic) Refined woman. *Variations:* Allmeera, Allmera, Almeria, Almira, Almyra, Elmerya, Elmyrah, Meera, Merei, Mira, Mirah, Myra, Myrah.

ALMOND (English) Nut.

ALOHA (Hawaiian) Kind. *Variations:* Alohalani, Alohi, Alohilani, Alohinani.

ALONA (Hebrew) Oak tree. *Variations:* Allona, Allonia, Alonia, Eilona.

ALONSA (Spanish) Ready to fight. *Variations:* Alonza.

ALOUETTE (French) Lark. *Variations:* Allouette, Alouetta.

ALPHA (Greek) First letter of the Greek alphabet. *Variations:* Alfa.

ALTA (Latin) High. *Variations:* Allta.

ALTAIR (Arabic) Bird.

ALTHEA (Greek) Healer. *Notables:* Tennis player Althea Gibson. *Variations:* Altha, Althaia, Altheta, Althia.

ALTHEDA (Greek) Blossom.

ALVA (Spanish) Fair-skinned. *Variations:* Alvah, Alvy, Elva, Elvy.

ALVINA (English) Noble friend. *Variations:* Alvedine, Alveena, Alveene, Alveenia, Alverdine, Alvine, Alvineea, Alvinia, Alwinna, Alwyna, Alwyne, Elveena, Elvena, Elvene, Elvenia, Elvina, Elvine, Elvinia.

ALVITA (Latin) Energetic.

ALYA (Arabic) To rise up.

ALYSSA (Greek) To flourish. *Variations:* Alissa, Elyssa, Ilyssa, Lyssa.

AMADEA (Latin) Lover of God. *Variations:* Amadee, Amedee.

AMADORE (Italian) Gift of love. *Variations:* Amadora.

AMALA (Hindu) Pure. *Variations:* Amalah.

Here's a list of popular songs that include names of girls in the title, along with who performed the ditty:

"Alison"
Elvis Costello

"Angie"
The Rolling Stones

"Barbara Ann"
The Beach Boys

"Beth"
Kiss

"Carrie Anne"
The Hollies

"Cathy's Clown"
The Everly Brothers

"Cecilia"
Simon & Garfunkel

"Dawn (Go Away)"
The Four Seasons

AMANA (Hebrew) Loyal. *Variations:* Amania, Amaniah, Amanya.

AMANDA (Latin) Loved. *Notables:* Actresses Amanda Peet and Amanda Bynes. *Variations:* Amandi, Amandie, Amandine, Amandy, Amata, Manda, Mandaline, Mandee, Mandi, Mandie, Mandy.

AMARA (Greek) Forever lovely. *Variations:* Amarande, Amaranta, Amarante, Amarantha, Amarinda, Amarra, Amarrinda, Mara, Marra.

AMARIS (Hebrew) Covenant with God. *Variations:* Amaria, Amariah.

AMARYLLIS (Greek) Fresh flower. *Variations:* Amarillis.

AMAYA (Japanese) Night rain.

AMBER (French) Semiprecious stone. *Notables:* Actress Amber Tamblyn. *Variations:* Ambar, Amberetta, Amberly, Ambur.

AMBROSINE (Greek) Immortal. *Variations:* Ambrosia, Ambrosina, Ambrosinetta, Ambrosinette, Ambroslya, Ambrozetta, Ambrozia, Ambrozine.

AMELIA (Latin) Hardworking. *Notables:* Aviatrix Amelia Earhart. *Variations:* Amalea, Amalie, Amelcia, Ameldy, Amelie, Amelina, Amelinda, Amelita, Amella.

AMETHYST (English) Semiprecious violet quartz stone.

AMICA (Italian) Close friend. *Variations:* Amice, Amici.

AMIDA (Hebrew) Moral. *Variations:* Amidah.

AMINA (Arabic) Honest. *Variations:* Ameena, Aminah, Amine, Amineh, Amna.

AMIRA (Arabic) Highborn. *Variations:* Amera, Amyra, Merah, Mira.

AMITY (Latin) Friendship. *Variations:* Amiti, Amitie.

AMOR (Spanish) Love. *Variations:* Amora, Amoretta, Amorette, Amorita.

AMY (English) Loved. *Notables:* Singer Amy Grant; actress Amy Brenneman. *Variations:* Aimee, Aimie, Amada, Amata, Ami, Amice, Amie, Amil.

ANAIS (French) Grace. *Notables:* Writer Anaïs Nin.

ANASTASIA (Greek) Resurrection. *Variations:* Anastace, Anastacia, Anastacie, Anastase, Anastasie, Anastasija, Anastasiya, Anastassia, Anastatia, Anastazia, Anastice, Anastyce.

ANAT (Hebrew) To sing.

ANATOLA (Greek) Easterly.

ANCI (Hungarian) Grace of God.

ANDELA (Czech) Angel. *Variations:* Andel, Andelka.

ANDIE (American) Short form of Andrea. *Notables:* Actress Andie MacDowell.

ANDREA (Latin) Womanly. *Notables:* Actress/comedian Andrea Martin. *Variations:* Andera, Andra, Andreana, Andree, Andreea, Andrene, Andrette, Andria, Andriana, Andrianna, Andrienne, Andrietta, Andrina, Andrine.

ANDROMEDA (Greek) One who ponders.

ANGELA (Greek) Messenger of God, angel. *Notables:* Actresses Angela Lansbury and Angela Bassett. *Variations:* Aingeal, Ange, Angel, Angele, Angelene, Angelia, Angelita, Angie, Angiola, Anngilla.

ANGELICA (Latin) Angelic. *Notables:* Actress Anjelica Huston. *Variations:* Angelika, Angelique, Anjelica.

ANGELINA (Italian) Form of Angela. *Notables:* Actress Angelina Jolie. *Variations:* Angeline, Anjolina.

ANGIE (Greek) Short form of Angela. *Notables:* Actress Angie Dickinson.

ANGHARAD (Welsh) Beloved.

ANINA (Hebrew) Answer to a prayer.

ANITA (Spanish) Form of Anna. *Notables:* Singer Anita Baker.

ANN (English) Grace. *Notables:* Advice columnist Ann Landers; fashion designer Ann Taylor. *Variations:* Ana, Anita, Anitra, Anitte,

Anna, Annah, Anne, Annie, Annita, Annitra, Annitta, Hannah, Hannelore.

ANNA (English) Form of Ann. *Notables:* Actress/model Anna Nicole Smith.

ANNABELLE (English) Graceful and beautiful. *Notables:* Actress Annabella Sciorra. *Variations:* Anabel, Anabele, Anabell, Anabelle, Annabel, Annabell, Annabella.

ANNALISA (English) Combined form of Ann and Lisa. *Variations:* Annalise.

ANNEMARIE (English) Combination of first names "Anne" and "Marie." Annamaria, Annamarie.

ANNETTE (French) Form of Ann. *Notables:* Actresses Annette Bening and Annette Funicello.

ANNIE (English) Gracious. Form of Ann. *Variations:* Annee, Anni, Anny.

ANNISA (Arabic) Friendly. *Variations:* Anisa, Anissa, Annissa.

ANNUNCIATA (Latin) The Annunciation. *Variations:* Annunziate, Anonciada, Anunciacion, Anunciata, Anunziata.

ANSONIA (Greek) Son of the divine.

ANTHEA (Greek) Flower. *Variations:* Anthe, Annthea, Antia.

ANTOINETTE (French) Priceless. *Notables:* Actress/director Antoinette Perry, for whom theater's Tony Award is named.

Variations: Antonella, Antonetta, Antonette, Antonia, Antonie, Antonieta, Antonietta, Antonina, Antonine, Tonelle, Tonette, Toney, Toni, Tonia, Tonie, Tony.

ANTONIA (Latin) Priceless. *Variations:* Antonea.

ANWEN (Welsh) Fair, beautiful. *Variations:* Anwyn.

ANYA (Russian) Grace of God. *Variations:* Anyuta.

APHRODITE (Greek) The goddess of love and beauty.

APOLLONIA (Greek) Strength. *Variations:* Apolinara, Apolinia.

APPLE (English) Apple fruit. *Variations:* Appell.

APRIL (Latin) To open up; springlike. *Notables:* Singer Avril Lavigne. *Variations:* Abrial, Abril, Aprilete, Aprilette, Aprili, Aprille, Apryl, Averil, Avril.

ARABELLA (English) Answered in prayer. *Variations:* Arabel, Arabela, Arbell, Arbella, Bel, Bella, Belle, Orabella, Orbella.

ARCADIA (Greek) Pastoral. *Variations:* Arcadie.

ARCELIA (Spanish) Treasure chest.

ARDELLE (Latin) Enthusiastic. *Variations:* Arda, Ardelia, Ardelis, Ardella, Arden, Ardia, Ardra.

ARDEN (Latin) Excited. *Variations:* Ardena, Ardin, Ardyn.

ARELLA (Hebrew) Angel. *Variations:* Arela.

ARETHA (Greek) Virtuous. *Notables:* Singer Aretha Franklin. *Variations:* Areta, Arete, Arethi, Arethusa, Aretina, Aretta, Arette.

ARIA (Italian) Melody.

ARIADNE (Greek) Most holy. *Variations:* Ariadna.

ARIANA (Greek) Holy. *Variations:* Ariane, Arianie, Arianna, Arianne.

ARIEL (Hebrew) Lioness of God. *Notables:* Ariel the Mermaid from the film *The Little Mermaid*. *Variations:* Aeriel, Aeriela, Ari, Ariela, Ariella, Arielle, Ariellel.

ARISTA (Greek) Harvest.

ARLEN (Irish) Devoted. *Variations:* Arlin, Arlyn.

ARLENE (English) Pledge. *Notables:* Actresses Arlene Francis and Arlene Dahl. *Variations:* Arleen, Arlie, Arliene, Arlina, Arline, Arlise, Arlys.

ARLETTE (French) Devoted. *Variations:* Arlet, Arletta.

ARMINA (German) Woman of war. *Variations:* Armida, Armine.

ARNELLE (German) Eagle. *Variations:* Arnell, Arnella.

trendy names from tv

Many popular names are derived from characters in television shows. These recently popular shows, as you can see, have turned a few uncommon names into everyday monikers.

Bree
Desperate Housewives

Carrie
Sex and the City

Gabrielle
Desperate Housewives

Lorelei
Gilmore Girls

Marissa
The O.C.

Miranda
Sex and the City

Paige
Charmed

Piper
Charmed

Rory
Gilmore Girls

Summer
The O.C.

Trista
The Bachelor; The Bachelorette

Willow
Buffy the Vampire Slayer

atlantic hurricane names for 2010

Alex	Lisa
Bonnie	Matthew
Colin	Nicole
Danielle	Otto
Earl	Paula
Fiona	Richard
Gaston	Shary
Hermine	Tomas
Igor	Virginie
Julia	Walter
Karl	

ARNETTE (English) Small eagle. *Variations:* Arnet.

ARTEMISIA (Greek) Perfection. *Variations:* Artemesia.

ARTHURINA (Gaelic) Rock; nobility. *Variations:* Artheia, Arthelia, Arthene, Arthuretta, Arthurine, Artina, Artis, Artri.

ARVINDA (Hindu) Lotus.

ASCENCION (Spanish) Ascension.

ASELA (Spanish) Ash tree.

ASHANTI (African) Africa tribal name. *Notables:* Singer Ashanti. *Variations:* Ashaunta, Ashuntae.

ASHBY (English) Ash trees.

ASHIRA (Hebrew) Wealthy.

ASHLEY (English) Ash tree meadow. *Notables:* Actresses Ashley Judd and Ashley Olsen. *Variations:* Ashely, Ashla, Ashlan, Ashlea, Ashlee, Ashleigh, Ashlie, Ashly, Ashton.

ASHLYN (Irish) Dream. *Variations:* Aislinn, Ashlin.

ASHTON (English) Ash tree town.

ASIA (Greek) Reborn. *Variations:* Aisia, Asiah, Asya, Aysia.

ASPEN (English) Tree. *Variations:* Aspin.

ASTERA (Hebrew) Star. *Variations:* Asta, Asteria, Asteriya, Astra.

ASTRAEA (Greek) Starry skies. *Variations:* Astrea.

ASTRID (Scandinavian) Godlike beauty and strength. *Notables:* Jazz singer Astrid Gilberto. *Variations:* Astrud, Astryd.

ATALANTA (Greek) Athletic hunter. *Variations:* Atlanta.

ATARA (Hebrew) Crown.

ATHALIA (Hebrew) Praise the Lord. *Variations:* Atalia, Ataliah, Atalie, Atalya, Athalee, Athalie, Athalina.

ATHENA (Greek) Goddess of wisdom. *Variations:* Athene, Athina.

AUBREY (German) Noble; (French) Blonde leader. *Variations:* Aubre, Aubree, Aubri, Aubria, Aubrianna, Aubrie.

AUDREY (English) Nobility and strength. *Notables:* Actress Audrey Hepburn. *Variations:* Audey, Audi, Audie, Audra, Audre, Audree, Audreen, Audri, Audria, Audrie, Audry, Audrye, Audy.

AUGUSTA (Latin) Majestic. *Variations:* Agusta, Augustia, Augustina, Augustine, Augustyna, Augustyne, Austina, Austine, Austyna, Austyne.

AURA (Greek) Slow breeze. *Variations:* Aure, Aurea, Auria.

AURELIA (English) Gold. *Variations:* Arela, Arella, Aurene, Aureola, Aureole, Auriel, Aurielle.

AURORA (Latin) Roman goddess of dawn. *Variations:* Aurore.

AUTUMN (English) Autumn.

AVA (English) Life. *Notables:* Actress Ava Gardner. *Variations:* Aualee, Avah, Avelyn, Avia, Aviana, Aviance, Avilina, Avis, Aviva.

AVALON (Gaelic) Island paradise.

AVELINE (French) Birdlike. *Variations:* Avaline, Avalina, Avelina.

AVERY (English) Noble leader. *Variations:* Averi, Averie.

AVIVA (Hebrew) Spring. *Variations:* Abiba, Abibah, Abibi, Abibit, Avivah, Avivi, Avivit.

AXELLE (French) Father of peace.

AYANNA (Hindu) Innocent. *Variations:* Ayana.

AYELET (Hebrew) Deer.

AYLA (Hebrew) Oak tree.

AZALEA (Latin) Flower. *Variations:* Azalia.

AZARIA (Hebrew) Helped by God. *Variations:* Azariah, Azelia.

AZIZA (African) Loved.

AZRIELA (Hebrew) God is my strength. *Variations:* Azriella.

AZURA (French) Blue. *Variations:* Azor, Azora, Azure, Azzura, Azzurra.

BABE (Latin) Short form of Barbara; nickname of endearment. *Notables:* Olympic athlete Babe Didrikson Zaharias.

BABETTE (French) Little Barbara.

BABS (American) Familiar form of Barbara.

BABY (American) Baby.

BAILA (Spanish) To dance. *Variations:* Bayla, Beyla, Byla.

BAILEY (English) Bailiff. *Variations:* Bailee, Baylee, Bayley, Baylie.

BAMBI (Italian) Child. *Variations:* Bambie, Bambina, Bamby.

BANITA (Hindu) Woman.

BAPTISTA (Latin) One who baptizes. *Variations:* Baptiste, Batista, Battista, Bautista.

BARA (Hebrew) To choose. *Variations:* Bari, Barra.

BARB (American) Short form of Barbara.

BARBARA (Greek) Foreign. *Notables:* U.S. first lady Barbara Bush; actresses Barbara Stanwyck and Barbra Streisand. *Variations:* Babb, Babbett, Babbette, Babe, Babett, Babette, Babita, Babs, Barb, Barbary, Barbe, Barbette, Barbey, Barbi, Barbie, Barbra,

Barby, Basha, Basia, Vaoka, Varenka, Varina, Varinka, Varka, Varvara, Varya, Vava.

BARBIE (American) Short form of Barbara. *Notables:* Playboy model/singer Barbie Benton.

BARRIE (Irish) Spear. Feminine version of Barry. *Variations:* Bari, Barri.

BASIA (Hebrew) Daughter of God. *Notables:* Singer Basia. *Variations:* Basha, Basya.

BASILIA (Greek) Royal. *Variations:* Basila, Basilea, Basilie.

BASIMA (Arabic) To smile. *Variations:* Basimah, Basma.

BATHIA (Hebrew) Daughter of God. *Variations:* Basha, Baspa, Batia, Batya, Bitya, Peshe, Pessel.

BATHILDA (German) Female soldier. *Variations:* Bathild, Bathilde, Berthilda, Berthilde.

BATHSHEBA (Hebrew) Daughter of Sheba. *Notables:* Mistress/wife of King David. *Variations:* Bathseva, Batsheba, Batsheva, Batshua, Sheba.

BEA (English) Short form of Beatrice. *Notables:* Actress Bea Arthur. *Variations:* Bee.

BEATA (Latin) Blessed. *Variations:* Beate.

BEATHA (Irish) Life. *Variations:* Betha.

BEATRICE (Latin) Bringing joy. *Notables:* Writer Beatrix Potter. *Variations:* Bea, Beatrisa, Beatrise, Beatrix, Beatriz, Beattie, Bebe, Bee, Beitris, Beitriss.

BEBE (Spanish) Form of Beatrice. *Variations:* Bibi.

BEBHINN (Irish) Sweet woman.

BECCA (Hebrew) Short form of Rebecca. *Variations:* Bekka.

BECHIRA (Hebrew) Chosen.

BECKY (American) Short form of Rebecca. *Variations:* Beckey, Becki, Beckie, Bekki.

BEDELIA (Irish) Form of Bridget. *Variations:* Bidelia, Delia.

BEDRISKA (Czech) Peaceful ruler.

BEGONIA (Spanish) Flower.

BEHIRA (Hebrew) Bright light.

BELÉN (Spanish) Bethlehem.

BELIA (Spanish) Oath of God. *Variations:* Belica, Belicia.

BELINDA (English) Dragon. *Notables:* Singer Belinda Carlyle. *Variations:* Belynda.

BELITA (Spanish) Little beauty.

BELLA (Italian) Beautiful.

BELLE (French) Beautiful. *Variations:* Bela, Bell, Bella, Belva, Belloma.

school daze: names from teachers (part iv)

Here's another selection of names from an elementary school in Santa Barbara, California:

Acachia	Maralisbeth
Adagio	Mia
Adonis	Mweya
Alisan	Omigali
Alitha	Ona
Allondra	Oona
Amairani	Orion
Aradia	Raven
Blue	Remington
Flora and	Seita
Fauna	Seneca
(twins)	Seven
Gael	Shadean
Gennipher	Shale
Herculana	Shama
Jayson	Shamsedeen
Jazzman	Shyama
Jenniffer	Soxchil
Kathe	Stone
Keyani	Tombe
Lemongelo	Torin
and Organ-	Uriah
elo *(twins)*	Usmail

names for brunettes

Boys	Girls
Adrian	Adriana
Bronson	Auburn
Colby	Blake
Donavan	Brunelle
Duncan	Ciara
Kerwin	Darcy
Kiernan	Kerry
Lebrun	Kyrie
Nigel	Melanie
Tynan	Tawny

BELVA (Latin) Beautiful view. *Notables:* Writer Belva Plain.

BENA (Hebrew) Wise.

BENEDETTA (Italian) Blessed. *Variations:* Benedicta, Benedicte, Benedikta, Benetta, Benita, Benni, Benoite.

BENEDICTA (Latin) Blessed. *Variations:* Benedictine.

BENITA (Latin) God has blessed. *Variations:* Bena, Benitri, Bennie, Binnie.

BENTLEY (English) Meadow of grass. *Variations:* Bentlea, Bentlee, Bentleigh, Bently.

BERA (German) Bear.

BERDINE (Greek) Bright maiden. *Variations:* Berdie, Berdina, Berdine, Burdine.

BERIT (Scandinavian) Magnificent. *Variations:* Beret, Berette.

BERKLEY (Scottish) Birch tree meadow. *Variations:* Berkeley, Berkly.

BERLYN (English) Combination of Bertha and Lynn. *Variations:* Berlynn.

BERNADETTE (French) Brave as a bear. *Notables:* Actress Bernadette Peters. *Variations:* Berna, Bernadene, Bernadett, Bernadina, Bernadine, Bernarda, Bernardina, Bernardine, Bernetta, Bernette, Berni, Bernie, Bernita, Berny.

BERNICE (Greek) Bringing victory. *Variations:* Berenice, Bernelle, Bernetta, Bernette, Bernicia, Bernie, Bernyce.

BERNIE (English) Form of Bernice. *Variations:* Bernee, Berni, Berney.

BERNITA (African) Form of Bernice.

BERRY (American) Berry. *Variations:* Berri, Berrie.

BERTHA (German) Bright. *Variations:* Berta, Berthe, Berti, Bertie, Bertilda, Bertilde, Bertina, Bertine, Bertuska, Bird, Birdie, Birdy, Birtha.

BERTILDE (German) Bright warrior. *Variations:* Bertille.

BERTINA (German) Bright.

BERURIA (Hebrew) Chosen by God.

BERYL (Greek) Green gemstone. *Variations:* Beril, Berrill, Berry, Beryla, Beryle.

BESS (English) Short form of Elizabeth. *Notables:* U.S. first lady Bess Truman. *Variations:* Bessie.

BETA (Czech) Grace of God. *Variations:* Betka, Betuska.

BETH (Hebrew) House of God. *Notables:* Singer Beth Nielsen Chapman.

BETHANY (English) House of God. *Variations:* Bethanee, Bethani, Bethanie, BethAnn, Bethann, Bethanne, Bethannie, Bethanny.

BETHEL (Hebrew) Temple.

BETHESDA (Hebrew) House of mercy.

BETHIA (Hebrew) Daughter of Jehovah. *Variations:* Betia, Bithia.

BETSY (American) Short form of Elizabeth. *Notables:* American flag seamstress Betsy Ross; fashion designer Betsy Johnson. *Variations:* Betsey, Betsi, Betsie.

BETTE (French) Form of Betty. *Notables:* Actress Bette Davis; singer/actress Bette Midler.

BETTINA (English) Form of Betty. *Variations:* Bettine.

BETTY (English) Short form of Elizabeth. *Notables:* Actress Betty White; cartoon siren Betty Boop. *Variations:* Betti, Bettie.

BETUEL (Hebrew) Daughter of God. *Variations:* Bethuel.

BETULAH (Hebrew) Dedicated. *Variations:* Bethula, Bethulah, Betula.

BEULAH (Hebrew) Married. *Variations:* Bealah, Beula.

BEV (English) Short form of Beverly.

BEVERLY (English) Beaver meadow. *Notables:* Actress Beverly D'Angelo; model Beverly Johnson. *Variations:* Bev, Beverelle, Beverle, Beverlee, Beverley, Beverlie, Beverlye.

BEVIN (Gaelic) Singer. *Variations:* Beven, Bevena, Bevina, Bevinn, Bevan.

BEYONCE (African) Beyond others. *Notables:* Singer Beyonce Knowles.

BIANCA (Italian) White. *Notables:* Former model Bianca Jagger. *Variations:* Beanka, Biancha, Bionca, Bionka, Blanca, Blancha.

BIBI (Arabic) Lady. *Notables:* Actress Bibi Andersen. *Variations:* Bibiana, Bibianna, Bibianne, Bibyana.

BIBIANA (Latin) Lively. *Variations:* Bibiane.

BIDDY (Irish) Short form of Bridget.

BIENVENIDA (Spanish) Welcome.

BIJOU (French) Sassy. *Notables:* Hollywood "Wild Child" Bijou Phillips. *Variations:* Bejeaux, Bejou, Bijue.

BILLIE (English) Constant protector. *Notables:* Singer Billie Holiday; tennis champ Billie Jean King. *Variations:* Billa, Billee, Billey, Billi, Billy.

BINA (Hebrew) Knowledge. *Variations:* Bena, Binah, Byna.

BINALI (Hindu) Musical instrument.

BINTI (African) Daughter.

BINYAMINA (Hebrew) Right hand. Feminine form of Benjamin.

BIRA (Hebrew) Fortress. *Variations:* Biria, Biriya.

BIRCIT (Scandinavian: Norwegian) Power. *Variations:* Birgit.

BIRDIE (English) *Variations:* Bird, Birdey, Byrd, Byrdie.

BIRGITTE (Scandinavian) Bridget. *Variations:* Birget, Birgetta, Birgit, Birgitta.

BITSIE (American) Small; short form of Elizabeth. *Variations:* Bitzee, Bitzi, Bitzie.

BJORK (Icelandic) One of a kind. *Notables:* Singer Bjork.

BLAINE (Gaelic) Thin. *Variations:* Blane, Blayne.

BLAIR (English) A flat piece of land. *Variations:* Blaire, Blayre.

BLAISE (Latin) One who stutters. *Variations:* Blaize, Blase, Blaze.

BLAKE (English) Dark. *Variations:* Blakeley, Blakely.

BLANCA (Italian) White.

BLANCHE (English) White. *Notables:* Blanche DuBois, character in the play *A Streetcar Named Desire*. *Variations:* Blanca, Blanch, Blancha, Blanka, Blanshe, Blenda.

BLANCHEFLEUR (French) White flower.

BLANDA (Latin) Seductive. *Variations:* Blandina, Blandine.

BLASIA (Latin) Stutterer. *Variations:* Blaise.

BLATH (Irish) Flower. *Variations:* Blaithm, Blathnaid, Blathnait.

BLESSING (English) To sanctify. *Variations:* Bless.

BLIMA (Hebrew) Blossom. *Variations:* Blimah, Blime.

BLISS (English) Joy.

BLODWEN (Welsh) White flower. *Variations:* Blodwyn, Blodyn.

BLONDELLE (French) Blonde one. *Variations:* Blondell.

BLONDIE (American) Blonde-haired. *Variations:* Blondee, Blondi, Blondy.

BLOSSOM (English) Flower. *Notables:* TV character Blossom Russo.

BLUEBELL (English) Flower. *Variations:* Bluebelle.

BLUM (Hebrew) Flower. *Variations:* Blom, Bluma.

BLYTHE (English) Happy. *Variations:* Blithe, Blyth.

BO (Chinese) Precious. *Notables:* Actress Bo Derek.

BOBBI (English) Bright fame. Feminine version of Robert. *Notables:* Cosmetics queen Bobbi Brown. *Variations:* Bobbee, Bobbette, Bobbie, Bobby, Bobbye, Bobina.

BODIL (Scandinavian) Battle. *Variations:* Bothild, Botilda.

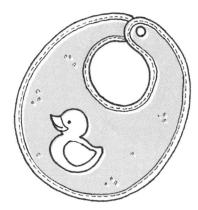

BOGDANA (Polish) Gift from God. *Variations:* Boana, Bocdana, Bogna, Bohdana, Bohna.

BOLADE (African) Honor is here.

BOLANILE (African) Wealth in our house.

BONFILIA (Italian) Good daughter.

BONITA (Spanish) Pretty. *Variations:* Bo, Boni, Bonie, Nita.

BONNIE (English) Pretty. *Notables:* Singer Bonnie Raitt. *Variations:* Boni, Bonie, Bonne, Bonnebell, Bonnee, Bonni, Bonnibel, Bonnibell, Bonnibelle, Bonny.

BOSKE (Hungarian) Lily.

BRACHA (Hebrew) Blessing. *Variations:* Brocha.

BRADLEY (English) Wide meadow. *Variations:* Bradlee, Bradleigh, Bradlie, Bradly.

BRAEDEN (English) Broad hill.

perfume and cologne names

Designer fragrances not only delight our senses, they often have names as captivating as their scents, especially when the creators honor themselves with an eponymous product.

Boys	Girls
Adolfo	Anais
Aramis	Arpege
Armani	Cacharel
Bijon	Calandre
Boucheron	Chanel
Casmir	Chantilly
Claiborne	Chloe
Cristobal	Coriandre
Dior	Desirade
Giorgio	Detchema
Givenchy	Escada
Guerlain	Jontue
Halston	Kantara
Jivago	Katia
Jovan	Mahora
Lanvin	Norell
Tresor	Pavlova
Valentino	Shalimar
Versace	Sirene
Xeryus	Tiffany

BRANCA (Portuguese) White.

BRANDA (Hebrew) Blessing.

BRANDY (English) A liquor. *Notables:* Singer/actress Brandy Norwood. *Variations:* Brandais, Brande, Brandea, Brandee, Brandi, Brandice, Brandie, Brandye, Branndea.

BREANA (Celtic) Strong. Feminine version of Brian. *Variations:* Breann, Breanna, Breanne, Briana, Briane, Briann, Brianna, Brianne, Briona, Bryanna, Bryanne.

BRECK (Gaelic) Freckled.

BREE (Irish) Uplifting. *Variations:* Brea, Bria, Brielle.

BRENDA (English). Sword. *Notables:* Comic-strip heroine Brenda Starr. *Variations:* Bren, Brendalynn, Brenn, Brennda, Brenndah.

BRENNA (English) Raven; black hair.

BRETISLAVA (Czech) Glorious noise. *Variations:* Breeka, Breticka.

BRETT (Latin) From Britain. *Variations:* Brette.

BRIA (Irish) Form of Brianna.

BRIANNA (English) Noble.

BRICE (English) Quick. *Variations:* Bryce.

BRIDGET (Irish) Strength. *Notables:* Actress Bridget Fonda; fictional diary writer Bridget Jones. *Variations:* Birgit, Birgitt, Birgitte,

Breeda, Brid, Bride, Bridgett, Bridgette, Bridgitte, Brigantia, Brighid, Brigid, Brigida, Brigit, Brigitt, Brigitta, Brigitte, Brygida, Brygitka.

BRIDIE (Irish) Form of Bridget. *Variations:* Bridey.

BRIER (French) Heather. *Variations:* Briar.

BRIGITTE (French) Form of Bridget. *Notables:* Actresses Brigitte Bardot and Brigitte Nielsen. *Variations:* Brigitta.

BRINA (Slavic) Defender. *Variations:* Breena, Brena, Brinna, Bryn, Bryna, Brynn, Brynna, Brynne.

BRISA (Spanish) Beloved. *Variations:* Breezy, Brisha, Brisia, Brissa, Briza, Bryssa.

BRITT (English) From Britain. *Variations:* Brit, Britty.

BRITTA (Swedish) Strong. *Variations:* Brita.

BRITTANY (English) From Brittany, France. *Notables:* Singer Britney Spears; actress Brittany Murphy. *Variations:* Brinnee, Britany, Britney, Britni, Brittan, Brittaney, Brittani, Brittania, Brittanie, Brittannia, Britteny, Brittni, Brittnie, Brittny.

BROGAN (Irish) Shoe.

BRONISLAWA (Polish) Glorious protection. *Variations:* Bronya.

BRONWYN (Welsh) Pure of breast. *Variations:* Bronwen.

BROOKE (English) One who lives by a brook. *Notables:* Actress and child model Brooke Shields. *Variations:* Brook.

BROOKLYN (American) Combination of Brooke and Lynn.

BRUCIE (French) Thick brush. Feminine version of Bruce. *Variations:* Brucina, Brucine.

BRUNA (Italian) Having brown skin or brown hair. Feminine version of Bruno.

BRUNELLE (French) Little brown-haired girl. *Variations:* Brunella, Brunetta, Brunette.

BRUNHILDA (German) Armor-clad maiden who rides into battle. *Variations:* Brunhild, Brunhilde, Brunnhilda, Brunnhilde, Brynhild, Brynhilda.

BRYNN (Welsh) Hill. *Variations:* Brinn, Bryn, Brynne.

BRYONY (English) Vine. *Variations:* Briony, Bronie, Bryonie, Bryonie.

BUENA (Spanish) Very good.

BUFFY (American) Form of Elizabeth. *Variations:* Buffee, Buffey, Buffi, Buffie.

BUNNY (English) Rabbit. *Variations:* Bunni, Bunnie.

BURGUNDY (French) Wine. *Variations:* Burgandy.

C

CADENCE (Latin) Rhythmic. *Variations:* Cadena, Cadenza, Kadena, Kadence, Kadenza.

CADY (English) Happiness. *Variations:* Cade, Cadee, Cadey, Cadie, Kade.

CAESARIA (Greek) Ruler. Feminine form of Caesar. *Variations:* Cesaria, Cesarina.

CAIA (Latin) Rejoice.

CAILIDORA (Greek) Gift of beauty.

CAILIN (Scottish) Triumphant people. *Variations:* Caelan, Caileen, Cailyn, Calunn, Cauleen, Caulin.

CAITLIN (Irish) Pure. *Variations:* Caitilin, Caitlan, Caitlion, Caitlon, Caitlyn, Caitlynne, Catlin, Kaitlin, Kaitlyn, Kaitlynn, Kaitlynne, Katelin, Katelynn.

CALANDRA (Greek) Lark. *Variations:* Cal, Calandria, Calendra, Calendre, Calinda, Kalandra.

CALANTHA (Greek) Flower. *Variations:* Calanth, Calantha, Calanthe.

CALEDONIA (Latin) From Scotland.

CALIDA (Greek) Most beautiful; (Spanish) Affectionate, warm. *Variations:* Callida.

CALISTA (Greek) Beautiful. *Notables:* Actress Callista Flockhart. *Variations:* Cala, Calesta, Cali, Calissa, Calisto, Callie, Callista, Cally, Callysta, Calysta, Kala, Kallie.

CALLA (Greek) Lily. *Variations:* Cala.

CALLIE (Greek) Lovely. *Variations:* Caleigh, Caley, Callee, Calleigh, Calley, Cali, Calli, Calley, Cally, Kali, Kallee, Kalley, Kallie.

CALLIOPE (Greek) Pretty muse. *Variations:* Kalliope, Kallyope.

CALLULA (Latin) Little beauty.

CALTHA (Latin) Yellow flower. *Variations:* Kaltha.

CALVINA (Latin) Without hair. Feminine version of Calvin. *Variations:* Calvine.

CALYPSO (Greek) Girl in hiding.

CAMBRIA (Welsh) From Wales. *Variations:* Cambrie, Cambry.

CAMELLIA (Italian) Flower. *Variations:* Camalia, Camela, Camelia, Kamelia.

CAMEO (Italian) Piece of profile jewelry. *Variations:* Cammeo.

CAMERON (Scottish) Crooked nose. *Notables:* Actress Cameron Diaz. *Variations:*

Camaran, Camaron, Camren, Camron, Camryn.

CAMI (American) Short form of Cameron or Camille. *Variations:* Camey, Camie, Cammie, Cammy.

CAMILLE (French) Assistant in the church. *Notables:* Feminist/writer Camille Paglia. *Variations:* Cam, Cama, Camala, Cami, Camila, Camile, Camilia, Camilla, Cammi, Cammie, Cammy, Cammylle, Camyla, Kamila, Kamilka.

CANADA (Native American) Horizon. *Variations:* Caneadea, Kanada.

CANDACE (Latin) White. *Notables:* Writer Candace Bushnell; actress Candice Bergen. *Variations:* Candice, Candie, Candis, Candiss, Candyce, Kandace, Kandice, Kandyce.

CANDIDA (Latin) White. *Variations:* Candide.

CANDRA (Latin) Radiant. *Variations:* Candria, Kandra.

CANDY (English) Short form of Candace. *Variations:* Candee, Candi, Candie, Kandee, Kandi, Kandie, Kandy.

CANTARA (Arabic) Small bridge. *Variations:* Kantara.

CAPRICE (Italian) On a whim. *Variations:* Caprece, Capricia, Caprie, Kapri, Kaprice, Kapricia, Kaprisha.

top ten names of the 1960s

Boys	Girls
Michael	Lisa
David	Mary
John	Karen
James	Susan
Robert	Kimberly
Mark	Patricia
William	Linda
Richard	Donna
Thomas	Michelle
Jeffrey	Cynthia

the pleasures and pitfalls of alternate spellings

Love a trendy, popular name but want to distinguish it from the crowd? Consider an alternate spelling, like Ashley to Ashleigh or Jacob to Jakob. Or, how about "Keighriynne" (Karen)? Creativity knows no limit. Be aware, however, that others may mispronounce the name on paper or spell it the old-fashioned way.

CAPUCINE (French) Collar. *Variations:* Cappucine, Capucina.

CARA (Italian) Dear. *Variations:* Caralea, Caralee, Caralisa, Carella, Carita, Carra, Kara, Karah, Karry.

CAREN (Greek) Pure. Form of Karen. *Variations:* Carin, Carine, Caron, Carrin, Caryn, Karen, Karena, Karin, Karina, Karine, Karon, Karyn, Karyna, Karynn.

CARESSA (French) Loving touch. *Variations:* Caresa, Caress, Caresse.

CAREY (Welsh) Near a castle. *Notables:* Actress Carey Lowell. *Variations:* Caree, Carree, Carrie.

CARIDAD (Spanish) Generous love.

CARINA (Italian) Darling. *Variations:* Careena, Carena, Cariana, Carin, Carinna, Karina.

CARISSA (Greek) Refined. *Variations:* Carisa, Carisse, Karissa.

CARITA (Italian) Charity. *Variations:* Caritta, Carrita.

CARLA (Italian) Woman. Feminine version of Carl, Carlo, or Charles. *Notables:* Actress Carla Gugino. *Variations:* Carli, Carlie, Carly, Carlye, Karla.

CARLENE (English) Woman. Form of Caroline. *Notables:* Singer Carlene Carter. *Variations:* Carleen, Carlina, Carline, Karleen, Karlene.

CARLOTTA (Italian/Spanish) Form of Charlotte. *Variations:* Carletta, Carlette, Carlita, Carlota, Karlotta.

CARLY (English) Feminine form of Carl or Charles. *Notables:* Singer Carly Simon. *Variations:* Carlee, Carley, Carli, Carlie, Karlee, Karley, Karli, Karlie.

CARMEL (Hebrew) Garden. *Variations:* Carmeli, Carmelina, Carmelita, Carmia, Carmiela, Carmit, Carmiya, Karmel, Karmeli, Karmia, Karmit, Karmiya.

CARMELA (Italian) Form of Carmel. *Variations:* Carmelia, Carmella, Karmela, Karmella.

CARMEN (Latin) Song. *Notables:* Actress Carmen Electra. *Variations:* Carma, Carman, Carmina.

CARNA (Arabic) Horn. *Notables:* Singer Carnie Wilson. *Variations:* Carney, Carni, Carnia, Carnie, Carniela, Carniella, Carniya, Carny, Karni, Karnia, Karniela, Karniella, Karniya.

CAROL (German) Woman. *Notables:* Comedian Carol Burnette; singer Carole King. *Variations:* Carel, Carley, Carlin, Caro, Carola, Carole, Carolee, Caroll, Carroll, Caru, Caryl, Caryle, Caryll, Carylle, Karel, Karil, Karol, Karole, Karyl.

CAROLINE (German) Woman. *Notables:* Presidential "first daughter" Caroline Kennedy; Princess Caroline of Monaco. *Variations:* Carilyn, Carilynn, Carlyn, Carlynn, Carolenia, Carolin, Carolina, Karolin, Karolina, Karoline.

CAROLYN (English) Woman. Form of Caroline. *Notables:* Medical intuitive/writer Carolyn Myss. *Variations:* Carolynn, Carolynne, Karolyn, Karolyna, Karolyne, Karolynn, Karolynne.

CARON (Welsh) Love. *Variations:* Carren, Carrin, Carron, Carrone, Caryn, Carynn.

CARRIE (English) Form of Caroline. *Notables:* Writer Carrie Fisher. *Variations:* Carey, Cari, Carri, Carrie, Carry, Cary, Kari, Karie, Karri, Karrie, Karry, Karrye.

CARSON (Scottish) Child of Carr.

CARYS (Welsh) Loved.

CASEY (Irish) Observant. *Variations:* Cacia, Casee, Casie, Cassie, Caycey, Caysey, Kacey, Kacia, Kasee, Kasie, Kaycey, Kaysey.

CASILDA (Latin) House.

CASS (English) Short form of Cassandra. *Notables:* Singer Mama Cass Elliot.

CASSANDRA (Greek) Protector. *Variations:* Casandera, Casandra, Cass, Cassandre, Cassaundra, Casson, Cassondra, Kasandera, Kasandra, Kass, Kassandra, Kassandre, Kassaundra, Kassie, Kasson, Kassondra.

CASSIA (Greek) Cinnamon.

CASSIE (English) Short form of Cassandra. *Variations:* Cassee, Casi, Cassi, Cassey, Cassy.

CASSIDY (Irish) Clever. *Variations:* Cassidee, Cassidey, Cassidi, Cassidie, Kasady, Kassidey, Kassidi, Kassidie, Kassidy.

CASTALIA (Greek) Mythological nymph.

CATE (English) Short form of Catherine. *Notables:* Actress Cate Blanchett. *Variations:* Cait, Caty, Kate, Katee, Katey, Kait, Kati, Katie, Katy.

CATHERINE (English) Pure. *Notables:* Actress Catherine Zeta-Jones. *Variations:* Catalina, Catarina, Catarine, Cateline, Catharin, Catharine, Catharyna, Catharyne, Cathee, Cathelin, Cathelina, Cathelle, Catherin, Catherina, Catrin, Catrina, Catrine, Catryna, Kai, Kaila, Kaitlin, Kata, Kataleen,

Katalin, Katalina, Katarina, Kateke, Katerina, Katerinka, Katharin, Katharina, Katharine, Katharyn, Kathereen, Katherin, Katherina, Kathren, Kathrine, Kathryn, Kathryne, Katia, Katica, Katina, Katrina, Katrine, Katriona, Katryna, Kattrina, Katushka, Katya, Kay, Kisan, Kit, Kitti, Kittie, Kitty, Kotinka, Kotryna.

CATHLEEN(Irish) Pure. Form of Catherine. *Variations:* Cathelin, Cathlene, Cathlyn, Kathleen, Kathlyn, Kathlynn.

CATHY(English) Short form of Catherine. *Notables:* Cartoonist Cathy Guisewite. *Variations:* Cathe, Cathee, Cathey, Cathi, Cathie, Kaethe, Kathe, Kathey, Kathi, Kathie, Kathy.

CECE(Latin) Blind. Short form of Cecilia. *Variations:* CeeCee, Ceci.

CECILIA(Latin) Blind. Feminine version of Cecil. *Notables:* Opera singer Cecilia Bartolli. *Variations:* C'Ceal, Cacilia, Cecely, Ceci, Cecia, Cecile, Cecilie, Cecille, Cecilyn, Cecyle, Cecylia, Ceil, Cele, Celenia, Celia, Celie, Celina, Celinda, Celine, Celinna, Celle, Cesia, Cespa, Cicely, Cicilia, Cycyl, Sessaley, Seslia, Sessile, Sessilly, Sheelagh, Sheelah, Sheila, Sheilagh, Sheilah, Shela, Shelah, Shelia, Shiela, Sisely, Sissie, Sissy.

CEDRICA(English) Chief. *Variations:* Cedricka.

CEIL(Latin) Short form of Cecilia. *Variations:* Ciel.

CELANDINE(Greek) Yellow flower. *Variations:* Celand, Celanda.

CELENA(Greek) Moon goddess. *Notables:* Singer Celine Dion. *Variations:* Celina, Celene, Celine, Selena.

CELESTE(Latin) Heavenly. *Variations:* Cela, Celesse, Celesta, Celestia, Celestiel, Celestina, Celestine, Celestyn, Celestyna, Celinka, Celisse, Cesia, Seleste, Selestia, Selinka.

CELIA(Italian/Spanish) Heaven. *Notables:* Queen of Salsa, Celia Cruz.

CERELIA(Latin) In springtime. *Variations:* Cerella.

CERES(Latin) Roman goddess of agriculture.

CERISE(French) Cherry. *Variations:* Cherice, Cherise, Cherrise, Sarise, Sharise, Sherice, Sherise, Sheriz.

CHABLIS(French) White wine.

CHAKA(Sanskrit) Energy. *Notables:* Singer Chaka Khan.

CHAKRA(Sanskrit) Circle of energy.

CHALICE(French) Goblet. *Variations:* Chalace, Chalyse.

CHALINA(Spanish) A rose.

CHAMPAGNE(French) Sparkling wine.

CHANA(Hebrew) Grace. *Variations:* Chanah, Hannah.

CHANDELLE(French) Candle. *Variations:* Chandal, Chandell, Shan, Shandell, Shandelle.

CHANDRA (Sanskrit) Moon-like. *Variations:* Chandre, Shandra, Shandre.

CHANEL (French) Name inspired by the French designer Coco Chanel. *Variations:* Chanell, Chanelle, Channell, Channelle, Shanell, Shanelle, Shannelle.

CHANIA (Hebrew) Grace of the lord. *Variations:* Chaniya, Hania, Haniya.

CHANTAL (French) Song. *Variations:* Chandal, Chantala, Chantale, Chantalle, Chante, Chantel, Chantele, Chantelle, Shanta, Shantae, Shantal, Shantalle, Shantay, Shante, Shanteigh, Shantel, Shantell, Shantella, Shantelle, Shontal, Shontalle, Shontelle.

CHANTERELLE (French) Cup. *Variations:* Chantrelle.

CHANTILLY (French) Lace. *Variations:* Chantille.

CHARDONNAY (French) White wine. *Variations:* Chardonnae, Shardonnay.

CHARIS (Greek) Grace. *Variations:* Chara, Charece, Charice, Charisse.

CHARISMA (Latin) Charismatic. *Notables:* Actress Charisma Carpenter. *Variations:* Carisma, Karisma.

CHARITY (Latin) Kindness. *Variations:* Charita, Charitee, Charitey, Sharitee.

CHARLENE (English) Womanly. Feminine version of Charles. *Variations:* Charla, Charlaine, Charlayne, Charlena, Charli,

---

great names in sports

Anna (Kournikova)
Tennis

Babe (Didrikson Zaharias)
Track and field

Billie Jean (King)
Tennis

Martina (Navratilova)
Tennis

Mary Lou (Retton)
Gymnastics

Mia (Hamm)
Soccer

Nadia (Comaneci)
Gymnastics

Oksana (Baiul)
Skating

Picabo (Street)
Skiing

Rebecca (Lobo)
Basketball

Serena (Williams)
Tennis

Sheryl (Swoopes)
Basketball

Steffi (Graf)
Tennis

Tara (Lipinski)
Skating

Venus (Williams)
Tennis

Here's another list of popular songs that include names of girls in the title.

"Delilah"
Tom Jones

"Donna"
Ritchie Valens

"Gloria"
Laura Branigan

"Help Me Rhonda"
The Beach Boys

"Lola"
The Kinks

"Lucille"
Little Richard

"Lucy in the Sky with Diamonds"
The Beatles

"Maggie May"
Rod Stewart

"Mandy"
Barry Manilow

Charlie, Charlina, Charline, Cherlene, Cherline, Sharlayne, Sharleen, Sharlene.

CHARLIZE (French) Womanly. *Notables:* Actress Charlize Theron.

CHARLOTTE (French) Small beauty. Variant of Charles. *Notables:* Writer Charlotte Bronte. *Variations:* Carlotta, Charlet, Charlett, Charletta, Charlette, Charlot, Charlotta.

CHARMAINE (French) Song. *Variations:* Charma, Charmagne, Charmain, Charmane, Charmayne, Charmin, Charmine.

CHARMIAN (Greek) Joy. *Variations:* Charmion.

CHARO (Spanish) Rose. *Notables:* Singer/actress Charo. *Variations:* Charro.

CHASIA (Hebrew) Protected by God. *Variations:* Chasya, Hasia, Hasya.

CHASINA (Hebrew) Strong. *Variations:* Hasina.

CHASTITY (Latin) Purity. *Notables:* Cher's daughter, Chastity Bono. *Variations:* Chasta, Chastina, Chastine.

CHAVA (Hebrew) Life. *Variations:* Chabah, Chapka, Chavah, Chavalah, Hava.

CHAVIVA (Hebrew) Beloved.

CHAVON (Hebrew) God is good. *Variations:* Chavona, Chavonna, Chavonne, Shavon.

CHAYA (Hebrew) Life. *Variations:* Chayah, Haya

CHELSEA (English) Ship port. *Notables:* Presidential "first daughter" Chelsea Clinton. *Variations:* Chelcy, Chelsa, Chelsee, Chelsey, Chelsi, Chelsie, Chelsy.

CHEMDIAH (Hebrew) God is my hope. *Variations:* Chemdia, Chemdiya, Hemdia, Hemdiah.

CHENIA (Hebrew) Grace of God. *Variations:* Chen, Chenya, Hen, Henia, Henya.

CHENOA (Native American) White dove. *Variations:* Shonoa.

CHER (French) Dearest. *Notables:* Singer/ actress Cher. *Variations:* Cherise, Sher, Shereen, Shereena, Sherena, Sherene, Sheri, Sherianne, Sherina, Sherry.

CHERIE (French) Dear. *Variations:* Chere, Cherey, Cheri, Cherice, Cherie, Sheri, Sheree, Sherry.

CHERILYN (American) Combination of Cher or Cheryl and Lynn. *Variations:* Cheralyn, Cherilin, Cherilynn, Cherilynne, Cherlin, Cherlyn, Cherylin, Sheralynne, Sherilin, Sherralin, Sherrilyn, Sherrylene, Sherryline, Sherrylyn, Sherylin, Sherylyn.

CHERISH (English) To treasure. *Variations:* Charish, Charisha, Cherrish.

CHERRY (French) Cherry. *Notables:* Actress Cherry Jones. *Variations:* Chere, Cheree, Cherey, Cherida, Cherise, Cherita, Cherreu, Cherri, Cherrie.

CHERYL (French) Beloved. *Notables:* Actress Cheryl Ladd. *Variations:* Cherill, Cherrill, Cherryl, Cheryle, Cheryll, Sherill, Sherryll, Sheryl.

CHEYENNE (Native American) Specific tribe. *Variations:* Cheyanna, Cheyanne, Chiana, Chianna, Shayann, Sheyenne.

CHIARA (Italian) Light. *Variations:* Cheara, Chiarra.

CHICA (Spanish) Girl.

CHIDORI (Japanese) Bird.

CHINA (English) Country. *Notables:* Singer Chynna Phillips. *Variations:* Chinah, Chinna, Chyna, Chynna.

CHIQUITA (Spanish) Little girl. *Variations:* Chaqueta, Chaquita, Chiqueta.

CHITA (Italian) Pearl. *Notables:* Actress/ singer Chita Rivera.

CHLOE (Greek) Young blade of grass. *Notables:* Actress Chloe Sevigny *Variations:* Clo, Cloe.

CHO (Japanese) Butterfly.

CHRIS (English) Short form of Christina. *Notables:* Tennis champ Chris Evert. *Variations:* Chrissie, Chrissy, Cris, Kris.

CHRISTABEL (Latin) Fair Christian. *Variations:* Christabelle, Christabella, Cristabel.

CRISTAL (Latin) Form of Crystal. *Variations:* Christel, Christelle.

CHRISTINA (Greek) Anointed one. *Variations:* Chris, Chrissa, Chrissy, Christa, Christen, Christi, Christiana, Christiane, Christiann, Christianna, Christie, Christina, Christy, Krista, Kristina, Kristine, Kristy, Teena, Teina, Tena, Tina, Tinah.

CHUMANI (Native American) Dew.

CIANNAIT (Irish) Ancient. *Variations:* Ciannata.

CIARA (Irish) Black. *Variations:* Ceara, Ciarra, Ciera, Cierra.

CICELY (Latin) Form of Cecilia. *Variations:* Cicelie, Cicilie, Cicily, Cilla, Sicely.

CINDY (Greek) Moon goddess. Short form of Cynthia. *Notables:* Columnist Cindy Adams; supermodel Cindy Crawford; singer Cyndi Lauper. *Variations:* Cinda, Cindee, Cindi, Cindie, Cyndee, Cyndi, Cyndie, Cyndy, Sindee, Sindi, Sindie, Sindy, Syndi, Syndy.

CIPRIANA (Greek) From Cyprus. *Variations:* Cipriane, Ciprianna, Cypriana, Cyprienne.

CISSY (American) Short form of Cecilia. *Variations:* Ciss, Cissey, Cissi, Cissie, Sissi, Sissy.

CLAIRE (Latin/French) Bright. *Notables:* Actress Claire Danes. *Variations:* Clare, Clairy.

CLARA (English) Bright. *Notables:* Red Cross founder Clara Barton. *Variations:* Clair, Claire, Clairette, Clairine, Clare, Claresta, Clareta, Clarette, Clarice, Clarie, Clarinda, Clarine, Claris, Clarisa, Clarissa, Clarisse, Clarita, Claryce, Clerissa, Clerisse, Cleryce, Clerysse, Klara, Klari, Klarice, Klarissa, Klaryce, Klaryssa.

CLARICE (French) Clear. *Variations:* Clairice, Clareece, Clarise.

CLARISSA (Latin) Brilliant. *Variations:* Clairissa, Claressa, Clarisa, Clerissa, Clarista, Claritza, Klarissa.

CLAUDETTE (French) French form of Claudia. *Notables:* Actress Claudette Colbert. *Variations:* Claudet.

CLAUDIA (Latin) Lame. Feminine version of Claude. *Notables:* Cover girl Claudia Schiffer. *Variations:* Claudelle, Claudette, Claudina, Claudine.

CLELIA (Latin) Glorious.

CLEMATIS (Greek) Vine; flower. *Variations:* Clematia.

CLEMENTINE (English) Gentle. *Variations:* Clementia, Clementina, Clemenza.

CLEO (Greek) Acclaim. Short form of Cleopatra. *Variations:* Clea.

CLEOPATRA (Greek) Her father's renown. *Notables:* Cleopatra, Queen of the Nile. *Variations:* Clea, Cleo.

CLEVA (English) One who lives on a hill.

CLIANTHA (Greek) Flower. *Variations:* Cleantha, Cleanthe, Clianthe.

CLIO (Greek) Proclaimer. *Variations:* Klio.

CLODAGH (Irish) A river.

CLORIS (Latin) White, pure. *Notables:* Actress Cloris Leachman. *Variations:* Chloris.

CLOTILDA (German) Famous in battle. *Variations:* Clothilda, Clothilde, Clotilde, Tilda, Tilly.

CLOVER (English) Flower.

CLYMENE (Greek) Famous.

CLYTIE (Greek) Lovely. *Variations:* Clyte, Clytia.

COCO (Spanish) Coconut. *Notables:* Fashion designer Coco Chanel. *Variations:* Koko.

CODY (English) Cushion. *Variations:* Codee, Codi, Codie, Kodi, Kodie.

COLBY (English) Coal village.

COLETTE (French) Triumphant people. *Notables:* French novelist Colette. *Variations:* Coletta, Collet, Collete, Collett.

COLLEEN (Irish) Young girl. *Variations:* Coleen, Colene, Coline, Colline, Kolleen.

COLUMBA (Latin) Dove. *Variations:* Colombe, Columbia, Columbina, Columbine.

COMFORT (English) To comfort.

CONCEPCION (Latin) Conception.

CONCHETTA (Spanish) Pure. *Variations:* Concetta, Concettina, Conchita.

zodiac baby: names by astrological sign (part iv)

Capricorn

Boys
Matthew
Nick
Oliver

Girls
Annie
Ivy
Julia

Aquarius

Boys
Arnold
Lawrence
Raymond

Girls
Amethyst
Jane
Viola

Pisces

Boys
Clement
Jude
Randall

Girls
Faith
Lavender
Orchid

popular names in norway

Boys	Girls
Mathias	Emma
Martin	Julie
Andreas	Ida
Jonas	Thea
Tobias	Nora
Daniel	Emilie
Sander	Maria
Magnus	Ingrid
Andrian	Malin
Henrik	Tuva

CONCORDIA (Greek) Harmonious.

CONNIE (English) Short form of Constance. *Notables:* Actress Connie Stevens; singer Connie Francis. *Variations:* Conni, Conny.

CONNOR (Irish) Praised. *Variations:* Connar, Conner, Connery, Conor.

CONSTANCE (Latin) Steady. *Variations:* Connie, Constancia, Constancy, Constanta, Constantia, Constantina, Constanza, Constanze.

CONSUELA (Spanish) Consolation. *Variations:* Consolata, Consuelo.

COOKIE (American) Cookie.

CORA (Greek) Maiden. *Variations:* Corah, Coralee, Coralie, Coretta, Corissa, Corra.

CORAL (English) Coral. *Variations:* Corall, Coralle, Corel, Coryl, Koral.

CORAZON (Spanish) Heart.

CORBY (English) Town in Great Britain.

CORDELIA (English) Warmhearted. *Variations:* Cordalia, Cordella, Cordelle, Cordi, Cordilia, Cordy.

COREY (Irish) The hollow. *Variations:* Cori, Corie, Corri, Corrie, Corry, Kori, Korie, Korey.

CORINNE (French) Maiden. *Variations:* Carine, Carinna, Carinne, Carynna, Corina, Corine, Corinna, Correna, Corrianne, Corrienne, Corrine, Corrinn, Korina, Korinne, Korrina.

CORINTHIA (Greek) Woman from Corinth.

CORKY (American) Sprite. *Variations:* Corkee, Corkey, Corki, Corkie, Korky.

CORNELIA (English) Horn. Feminine version of Cornelius. *Variations:* Cornela, Cornelie, Cornella, Corney, Neelia, Neely, Neelya, Nela, Nelia, Nila.

CORONA (Spanish) Crown. *Variations:* Coronetta.

CORVINA (Latin) A raven.

COSETTE (French) Victorious. *Variations:* Cosetta, Cossette, Cozette.

COSIMA (Greek) Order. Feminine version of Cosmo. *Variations:* Cosma, Kosima.

COURTNEY (English) Dweller in the court. *Notables:* Singer Courtney Love; actress Courteney Cox. *Variations:* Cortney, Courtenay, Courteney, Courtnie, Courtny.

CRESCENT (French) Crescent-shaped. *Variations:* Crescentia, Cressant, Cressent, Cressentia.

CRESSIDA (Greek) Gold. *Variations:* Cressa, Cressie.

CRICKET (American) Insect; pet name.

CRISPINA (Latin) Curly hair. Feminine version of Crispin. *Variations:* Crispa.

CRYSTAL (Latin) Clear. *Variations:* Christal, Chrystal, Cristal, Cristalle, Cristel, Crystol, Kristal, Kristle, Kristol, Krystal, Krystalle, Krystel, Krystle.

CULLEN (Irish) Pretty. *Variations:* Cullan.

CYANEA (Greek) Blue as the sky. *Variations:* Cyan, Cyanne.

CYBELE (Greek) Goddess of nature.

CYBILL (Latin) Prophet. *Notables:* Actress Cybill Shepherd. *Variations:* Cybil, Cybille, Sibyl, Sybil.

CYDNEY (English) Form of Sydney.

CYMA (Greek) Blossoming. *Variations:* Syma.

CYNARA (Greek) Thistle plant. *Variations:* Cynarra, Zinara.

CYNTHIA (Greek) Goddess of the moon. *Notables:* Actress Cynthia Nixon. *Variations:* Cindi, Cindie, Cindy, Cinthia, Cintia, Cyndi, Cynth, Cynthie, Cyntia, Cyntie, Synthia, Syntia.

CYPRIS (Greek) From Cyprus. *Variations:* Cypress, Cypriss, Cyprus.

CYRA (Persian) Sun.

CYRENE (Greek) Siren. *Variations:* Cyreen, Cyren, Cyrena.

CYRILLA (Latin) Godly. Feminine version of Cyril. *Variations:* Cirilla.

CYTHEREA (Greek) From the island of Cythera. *Variations:* Cytheria.

CZARINA (Russian) Empress. *Variations:* Cyzarina, Cyzarine.

D

DABORA (Czech) To fight far away. *Variations:* Dalena, Dalenka.

DACEY (Irish) From the south. *Variations:* Dacee, Daci, Dacia, Dacie, Dacy, Daicee.

DAFFODIL (French) Flower. *Variations:* Daffi, Daffie, Daffy.

DAGANA (Hebrew) Grain. *Variations:* Dagan, Dagania, Deganya.

DAGMAR (German) Glory. *Variations:* Daga, Daggi, Dagi, Dagmara.

DAGNY (Scandinavian) New day. *Variations:* Dagna, Dagne, Dagney.

DAHLIA (Scandinavian) Flower. *Variations:* Dahla, Dalia, Daliah.

DAI (Japanese) Grand.

DAISY (English) Flower. *Notables:* TV personality Daisy Fuentes. *Variations:* Dacey, Dacia, Dacy, Daisey, Daisha, Daisi, Daisie, Daizy, Daysi, Deyci.

DAKOTA (Native American) Friend. *Notables:* Child actress Dakota Fanning.

DALAL (Arabic) To flirt. *Variations:* Dhelal.

DALE (English) Valley. *Notables:* Country/Western actress/singer Dale Evans. *Variations:* Dael, Daelyn, Dahl, Dalena, Dalene, Dalenna, Dalina, Dallana, Daly, Dayle.

DALILA (African) Gentle. *Variations:* Dahlila, Dalia, Dalilah, Dalice.

DALIT (Hebrew) Running water.

DALYA (Hebrew) Branch. *Variations:* Dalia, Daliya.

DAMARIS (Greek) Calf. *Variations:* Damara, Damaress, Dameris, Dameryss, Damiris.

DAMIANA (Greek) To tame.

DAMITA (Spanish) Princess.

DANA (English) From Denmark. *Notables:* Actress Dana Delaney. *Variations:* Daina, Danay, Danaye, Dane, Danee, Danet, Danna, Dayna, Denae.

DANAE (Greek) Pure and bright. *Variations:* Danay, Danea, Denae.

DANI (Hebrew) Short for Danielle. *Variations:* Danee, Danie, Danni, Dannie.

DANIAH (Hebrew) God's judgment. *Variations:* Dania, Daniya, Danya.

DANICA (Slavic) Morning star. *Notables:* Actress Danica McKellar. *Variations:* Danika, Dannika, Dannica.

DANIELLE (French) God is my judge. Feminine version of Daniel. *Notables:* Writer Danielle Steele. *Variations:* Danee, Danela, Danele, DaNell, Danella, Danette, Daney, Dani, Dania, Danica, Danice, Danie, Daniela, Daniella, Danika, Danila, Danita, Danyelle.

DANUTA (Polish) Given by God.

DAPHNE (Greek) Ancient mythological nymph who was transformed into a laurel tree. *Notables:* Writer Daphne du Maurier. *Variations:* Dafne, Daphney, Daphny.

DARA (Hebrew) Wisdom. *Variations:* Dahra, Dareen, Darice, Darissa, Darra, Darrah.

DARBY (English) Place where deer graze. *Variations:* Darbi, Darbie.

DARCI (Irish) Dark one. *Variations:* D'Arcy, Darcee, Darcey, Darcie, Darcy, Darsi, Darsie.

DARDA (Hebrew) Pearl of wisdom.

DARIA (Greek) Luxurious. *Variations:* Darea, Dari, Darian, Darianna, Dariele, Darielle, Darienne, Darrelle.

DARIAN (English) Precious. *Variations:* Darien, Darienne, Derian.

DARLA (English) Short form of Darlene. *Variations:* Darly.

DARLENE (English) Darling. *Variations:* Darla, Darleane, Darleen, Darleena, Darlena, Darlina, Darline.

DARNELLE (English) Hiding place. *Variations:* Darnel, Darnell, Darnella, Darnetta.

DARON (Irish) Great. *Variations:* Daren, Darian, Darron.

DARVA (American) Unknown definition. *Variations:* Darvah, Darvy.

DARYL (French) Beloved. *Notables:* Actress Daryl Hannah. *Variations:* Darel, Darielle, Darrel, Darrell, Darrelle, Darryl, Darrylene, Darrylin, Darryline, Darrylyn, Darylin, Daryline.

DARYN (Greek) Gift. *Variations:* Daryan, Darynne.

DASHA (Russian) Dear one. *Variations:* Dashia, Dasia.

DASHIKI (African) Loose shirt. *Variations:* Dashi, Dashika, Dashka, Deshiki.

DAVIDA (Hebrew) Beloved. Feminine version of David. *Variations:* Daveen, Davene, Davia, Daviana, Daviane, Davianna, Davidine, Davina, Davine, Davinia, Davita, Davonna, Davy, Davynn.

DAVINA (Scottish) Form of Davida. *Variations:* Dava, Davean, Daveen, Daveena, Davene, Davi, Davianna, Davin, Davinia, Davinna, Davonna, Deveen, Devina.

DAWN (English) Sunrise, the dawn. *Variations:* Dawna, Dawne, Dawnelle, Dawnetta, Dawnette, Dawnielle, Dawnika, Dawnn.

DAY (English) Day. *Variations:* Dae.

DAYANA (Arabic) Divine. *Variations:* Dayanara, Dayani, Dayanna, Dyana.

DAYTONA (English) Bright town. *Variations:* Dayton, Daytonia.

DEANDRA (American) Divine. Form of Diana. *Variations:* Deanda, Deandrea, Deandria, Deeandra, Dianda, Diandra, Diandre.

DEANNA (English) Valley. *Notables:* Actress Deanna Durbin. *Variations:* Deana, Deane, Deanie, Deann, Deanne, Deeana, Deeann, Deeanna, Deena, Deona, Deondra, Deonna, Deonne.

DEBBIE (American) Short form of Deborah. *Notables:* Actress Debbie Reynolds; singer Debbie Gibson. *Variations:* Deb, Debi, Debbi, Debby, Debbye.

DEBORAH (Hebrew) Bee. *Notables:* Blondie lead singer Deborah Harry. *Variations:* Deb, Debbi, Debbie, Debby, Debi, Debora, Deborrah, Debra, Debrah, Devora, Devorah, Devra.

DEBRA (Hebrew) Variation of Deborah. *Notables:* Actresses Debra Winger and Debra Messing.

DECIMA (Latin) Tenth.

DEE (Welsh) Black.

DEEDEE (English) Nickname for girls' names beginning with "D." *Variations:* D.D., Didee, Didi.

DEIRDRE (Irish) Sorrow. *Notables:* Soap opera actress Deirdre Hall. *Variations:* Dedra, Deidra, Deirdra, Deirdrie, Diedre, Dierdre.

DEITRA (Greek) Earth mother. Short form of Demetria. *Variations:* De'Atra, Deetra, Detria.

DEJA (French) Seen before. *Variations:* Dejah, Dejanae, Dejon.

DELANEY (Irish) Child of a competitor. *Variations:* Delaina, Delaine, Delane, Delayna, Delayne.

DELIA (Greek) From Delos. *Notables:* Writer Delia Ephron. *Variations:* Del, Delise, Delya, Delys, Delyse.

DELICIA (Latin) Delight. *Variations:* Daleesha, Dalicia, Dalisia, Delcia, Delcina, Delcine, Deleesha, Delesha, Delesia, Delice, Delisa, Delise, Delisha, Delisia, Delys, Delyse.

DELILAH (Hebrew) Delicate. *Notables:* Radio personality Delilah. *Variations:* Dalila, Delila.

DELLA (English) Noble. *Notables:* Actress Della Reese. *Variations:* Del, Dela, Dell, Delle.

DELORA (Spanish) From the ocean.

DELPHINE (Greek) From Delphi. *Variations:* Delfina, Delpha, Delphe, Delphi, Delphia, Delphina.

DELTA (Greek) Fourth letter of the Greek alphabet. *Notables:* Actress Delta Burke.

DELWYN (Welsh) Pretty and fair.

DELYTH (Welsh) Pretty.

DEMETRIA (Greek) Earth mother. *Variations:* Demeter, Demetra, Demetris, Demi, Demitra, Demitras, Dimetria.

DEMI (Greek) Short form of Demetria. *Notables:* Actress Demi Moore.

DENISE (French) Wine goddess. Feminine version of Dennis. *Notables:* Fitness guru Denise Austin; actress Denise Richards. *Variations:* Denese, Deni, Denice, Deniece, Denisha, Denize, Dennise, Denyce, Denys.

DENISHA (American) Form of Denise. *Variations:* Deneesha, Deneisha, Denesha, Deneshia, Denishia.

DERIKA (German) Ruler. *Variations:* Dereka, Derica, Derrica.

DERRY (Irish) Red-haired. *Variations:* Deri, Derrie.

DERYN (Welsh) Bird. *Variations:* Derren, Derrin, Derrine, Derron, Deryn.

DESDEMONA (Greek) Misery. *Variations:* Desdemonia.

popular names in iceland

Boys	Girls
Sigurdur	Gudrun
Gudmundur	Sigrídur
Jon	Kristín
Gunnar	Margret
Olafur	Ingibjorg
Magnus	Sigrun
Einar	Helga
Kristjan	Johanna
Bjorn	Anna
Bjarni	Ragnheidur

DESIRE (English) Desired.

DESIRÉE (French) Desired. *Variations:* Desarae, Desira, Desyre, Dezarae, Dezirae, Diseraye, Diziree, Dsaree.

DESTINY (French) Fate. *Variations:* Destanee, Destina, Destine, Destinee, Destini, Destinie.

DEVA (Hindu) Divine. *Variations:* Devanee, Devee, Devi, Devika.

DEVANY (Gaelic) Dark-haired. *Variations:* Davanfe, Devaney, Devenny, Devinee, Devony.

DEVI (Hindu) Goddess. *Variations:* Devia, Devie, Devri.

DEVIN (Irish) Poet. *Variations:* Deva, Devan, Devinne.

DEVON (English) From Devon, a region in southern England. *Variations:* Devan, Devana, Devanna, Devona, Devondra, Devonna, Devonne, Devyn, Devynn.

DEVORA (Hebrew) Form of Deborah. *Variations:* Devorah, Devore, Devra.

DEWANDA (African-American) Combination of prefix "De" and first name "Wanda."

DEXTRA (Latin) Skilled. *Variations:* Dexter, Dexy.

DHARMA (Hindu) Believe. *Variations:* Darma.

DI (Latin) Short form of Diana or Diane. *Variations:* Dy.

DIAMOND (English) Jewel. *Variations:* Diamanda, Diamante, Diamonique, Diamontina.

DIANA (Latin) Divine. *Notables:* Great Britain's Princess Diana; singer Diana Ross. *Variations:* Dee, Dianna, Didi, Dyana.

DIANE (Latin) Divine. Form of Diana. *Notables:* TV news personality Diane Sawyer; fashion designer Diane von Furstenberg; actresses Diahann Carroll, Diane Lane, and Dyan Cannon. *Variations:* Diahann, Dian, Dianne, Dyan.

DIANTHA (Greek) Divine flower. *Variations:* Diandre, Dianthe, Dianthia.

DIDO (Greek) Ancient mythological figure. *Notables:* British singer Dido Armstrong.

DIELLE (French) God. *Variations:* Diella.

DILYS (Welsh) Faithful. *Variations:* Dylis, Dyllis, Dylys.

DINAH (Hebrew) God will judge. *Notables:* Singer/TV host Dinah Shore. *Variations:* Deena, Denora, Dina, Dinorah, Diondra, Dyna, Dynah.

DIONNE (Greek) Divine ruler. *Notables:* Singer Dionne Warwick. *Variations:* Deonne, Dion, Diona, Dione, Dionia, Dionna, Dionysia.

DITA (English/Spanish) Derivative of Edith. *Variations:* Ditka.

DIVINE (Latin) Divine. *Variations:* Divina, Divinia.

DIXIE (French) Tenth. *Notables:* Actress Dixie Carter. *Variations:* Dix, Dixee, Dixy.

DIZA (Hebrew) Joy. *Variations:* Ditza, Ditzah.

DODIE (Hebrew) Beloved. *Variations:* Dodee, Dodi, Dody.

DOLLY (English) Doll. *Notables:* U.S. first lady Dolly Madison; country singer Dolly Parton. *Variations:* Doll, Dollee, Dolley, Dollie.

DOLORES (Spanish) Sorrow. *Notables:* Actress Dolores Del Rio. *Variations:* Delores, Doloras, Doloris, Doloritas.

DOMINA (Latin) Woman. *Variations:* Domini.

DOMINIQUE (French) Of the Lord. *Notables:* Actress Dominique Sanda. *Variations:* Domenica, Domini, Dominica, Dominika.

DOÑA (Spanish) Lady. *Variations:* Donella, Donelle, Donetta.

DONALDA (Scottish) Ruler of the world. Feminine form of Donald. *Variations:* Donaldina.

DONATA (Latin) Give. *Variations:* Donada, Donatha, Donatta.

DONATELLA (Italian) Given. *Notables:* Fashion designer Donatella Versace.

DONNA (Italian) Woman of the home. *Notables:* Actress Donna Reed; disco songstress Donna Summer; fashion designer Donna Karan. *Variations:* Dahna, Donetta, Donielle, Donisha, Donnalee, Donnalyn, DonnaMarie, Donni, Donnie, Donya.

DORA (Greek) Gift. *Notables:* Children's TV character Dora the Explorer. *Variations:* Doralia, Doralyn, Doralynn, Doreen, Dorelia, Dorelle, Dorena, Dorenne, Dorette, Dori, Dorie, Dorinda, Dorita, Doru.

DORCAS (Greek) Gazelle. *Variations:* Doreka.

DOREEN (Irish) Gloomy. *Variations:* Doireann, Dorene, Dorine, Dorinnia, Doryne.

DORIAN (Greek) A region in Greece. *Variations:* Doriana, Dorianne, Dorrian, Dorryen.

DORINDA (Spanish) Form of Dora.

DORIS (Greek) From Doria, a region in Greece. *Notables:* Actresses Doris Day and Doris Roberts. *Variations:* Dorice, Dorisa, Dorlisa, Dorolice, Dorosia, Dorrie, Dorrys, Dorys, Doryse.

DORIT (Hebrew) Generation. *Variations:* Dorrit.

DOROTHY (Greek) Gift from God. *Notables:* Writer Dorothy Parker. *Variations:* Dollie, Dolly, Dorethea, Doro, Dorotea, Dorotha, Dorothea, Dorothee, Dorothia, Dorrit, Dortha, Dorthea, Dot, Dottie, Dotty.

DORY (English) Yellow-haired girl. *Variations:* Dori, Dorri, Dorrie, Dorry.

DOTTIE (English) Nickname for Dorothy. *Notables:* Singer Dottie West. *Variations:* Dot, Dotty.

DREA (Greek) Courageous. *Variations:* Dree.

DREW (Greek) Strong. Diminutive of Andrew. *Notables:* Actress Drew Barrymore. *Variations:* Dru.

DRINA (Greek) Protector. *Variations:* Dreena, Drena.

DRISILLA (Latin) Strong. *Variations:* Drewsila, Drucella, Drucie, Drucilla, Drucy, Druscilla.

DULCIE (Latin) Sweet. *Variations:* Delcina, Delcine, Delsine, Dulce, Dulcea, Dulci, Dulcia, Dulciana, Dulcibella, Dulcibelle, Dulcina, Dulcine, Dulcinea.

DUSANA (Czech) Spirit. *Variations:* Dusa, Dusanka, Dusicka, Duska.

DUSCHA (Russian) Sweet.

DUSTY (English) Feminine form of Dustin. *Notables:* Singer Dusty Springfield. *Variations:* Dustee, Dusti, Dustie.

DYANI (Native American) Deer.

DYLAN (Welsh) Born of the sea. *Variations:* Dylana.

EARLENE (English) Leader. Feminine version of Earl. *Variations:* Earla, Earleen, Earley, Earlie, Earlinda, Earline, Erlene, Erlina, Erline.

EARTHA (English) Earth. *Notables:* Singer Eartha Kitt. *Variations:* Erta, Ertha, Hertha.

EASTER (English) Named for the holiday.

EBERTA (German) Bright.

EBONY (English) Black wood. *Variations:* Ebbony, Eboney, Eboni, Ebonie.

ECATERINA (Romanian) Form of Katherine. *Variations:* Ekaterina.

ECHO (Greek) Sound.

EDA (English) Happy. *Variations:* Edda, Edde.

EDDA (Scandinavian) Mythological figure.

EDDIE (English) Protector of property. Feminine version of Edward. *Variations:* Eddi, Eddy, Eddye.

EDELINE (German) Noble. *Variations:* Edalene, Edalyne, Ediline, Lena.

EDEN (Hebrew) Place of pleasure. *Variations:* Eaden, Eadin, Edana, Edena, Edenia, Edin.

EDIE (English) Form of Edith. *Notables:* Actress Edie Falco. *Variations:* Edia, Ediya, Edya, Edyah, Eydie.

EDINA (English) One from Edinburgh, capital of Scotland. *Variations:* Edeena, Edena, Edyna, Idina.

EDITH (English) Prosperity in war. *Notables:* Novelist Edith Wharton; costume designer Edith Head. *Variations:* Edie, Edita, Edithe, Edy, Edyth, Edytha, Edythe, Eydie, Eydith.

EDLYN (English) Small noble girl. *Variations:* Edlan, Edland, Edlin.

EDMONDA (English) Rich protector. Feminine version of Edmund. *Variations:* Edmunda.

EDNA (Hebrew) Youthful. *Notables:* Writer Edna St. Vincent Millay. *Variations:* Ednah.

EDRICE (English) Strong property owner. Feminine version of Edric. *Variations:* Edris, Edryce, Edrys, Eidris, Eydris.

EDWARDINE (English) Rich protector. Feminine version of Edward. *Variations:* Edwarda, Edwardeen, Edwardene, Edwardyne.

EDWIGE (French) Joyful war. *Variations:* Edvig, Edwig, Hedwig, Hedwige, Yadwigo.

EDWINA (English) Rich friend. Feminine version of Edwin. *Variations:* Edween, Edweena, Edwena, Edwiena, Edwuna, Edwyna.

EFFIE (Greek) Singing talk. *Variations:* Eff, Effy, Ephie, Eppie, Euphemia, Euphemie, Euphie.

EGLANTINE (English) Sweetbriar. *Variations:* Eglantilne, Eglantyne.

EGYPT (English) Egypt.

EIBHLIN (Irish) Shining. Derivative of Helen.

EIDEL (Yiddish) Delicate.

EILAH (Hebrew) Oak tree. *Variations:* Aila, Ailah, Ala, Ayla, Eila, Eilona, Ela, Elona, Eyla.

EILEEN (Irish) Shining, bright. Familiar version of Helen. *Variations:* Aileen, Ailene, Alene, Aline, Ayleen, Eilean, Eilleen, Ilene.

EIRWEN (Welsh) Fair. *Variations:* Eirwyn.

EKELA (Hawaiian) Noble. *Variations:* Etela.

ELAINE (French) Bright, shining. Derivative of Helen. *Notables:* Actress Elaine Stritch; writer/director Elaine May. *Variations:* Alaina, Alayna, Alayne, Allaine, Elaina, Elana, Elane, Elanna, Elayn, Elayne, Eleana, Elena, Eleni, Ellaina, Ellaine, Ellane, Ellayne.

ELAMA (Hebrew) God's people.

ELAMMA (Hindu) Mother goddess. *Variations:* Ellama.

ELATA (Latin) Held in high esteem. *Variations:* Elatt, Elota.

ELBERTA (English) Noble, shining. Feminine version of Elbert. *Variations:* Elbertina, Elbertine, Elbie.

ELDORA (Spanish) Coated by gold. *Variations:* Eldoree, Eldoria, Eldoris.

ELDREDA (English) Elderly counselor.

ELEANOR (English) Light. Derivative of Helen. *Notables:* U.S. first lady Eleanor Roosevelt. *Variations:* Eleanore, Elenore, Eleonora, Eleonore, Elinor, Ellinor.

ELECTRA (Greek) Shining one. *Variations:* Elektra.

ELENA (Greek/Spanish/Russian) Light. Form of Helen. *Variations:* Elana, Eleana, Eleni, Ilena.

ELENOLA (Hawaiian) Bright. *Variations:* Elenoa, Elenora, Elianora.

but she doesn't look like a blanche!

Even if you give your baby the perfect name, you might discover, months later, that her name doesn't really suit her. Baby Blanche (meaning white), once tow-headed, has transformed into an adorable brunette toddler and now looks more like a Kerry. No problem. You can easily file papers to make the appropriate legal changes you request.

ELERI (Welsh) Smooth.

ELFREDA (English) Strong as an elf. *Variations:* Elfrida, Elfrieda, Elfryda.

ELGA (Slavic) Holy.

ELI (Scandinavian) Light.

ELIANA (Hebrew) God has answered my prayers. *Variations:* Eliane.

ELIEZRA (Hebrew) God is salvation.

ELIKA (Hawaiian) Forever ruler.

ELILI (Polynesian) Periwinkle.

ELIORA (Hebrew) God is light. *Variations:* Eleora.

ELISE (English) Form of Elizabeth. *Variations:* Elisse, Elyse, Elysse.

ELISHA (Hebrew) Consecrated to God. *Variations:* Eleasha, Elecia, Eleesha, Elesha.

ELITA (Latin) Chosen. *Variations:* Elida, Ellita, Ilita.

ELIVAH (Hebrew) God is able. *Variations:* Eliava.

ELIZA (English) Form of Elizabeth.

ELIZABETH (Hebrew) Pledged to God. *Notables:* Actress Elizabeth Taylor; Great Britain's Queen Elizabeth. *Variations:* Alzbeta, Babette, Bess, Bessey, Bessi, Bessie, Bessy, Bet, Beta, Beth, Betina, Betine, Betka, Betsey, Betsi, Betsy, Bett, Betta, Bette, Betti, Bettina, Bettine, Betty, Betuska, Boski, Eilis, Elis, Elisa,

flower names for girls

There's a lovely association with a name that evokes the scents and colors of flowers.

Blossom	Jasmine
Clover	Lily
Dahlia	Marigold
Daisy	Pansy
Flora	Petunia
Heather	Poppy
Holly	Posey
Hyacinth	Rose
Iris	Violet
Ivy	Zinnia

school daze: names from teachers (part v)

Here's yet another selection of names from an elementary school in Santa Barbara, California.

Abhay	Keir
Avis	Kiara
Brady	Levi
Briseida	Logan
Christophe	Lorolie
Cian	Maisy
Davita	Martinique
Deshaun	Maura
Fisher	Meleton
Gopal	Milocsz
Greir	Muhammed
Jasmyne	Murphy
Jhon	Nayeli
Jiaya	Otto
Kaden	Ronan
Kai	Saliah
Karime	Sequoia
Katya	Shahir
Keighriynne	Somerset
Keiji	Soren

Elisabet, Elisabeta, Elisabeth, Elisabetta, Elisabette, Elisaka, Elisauet, Elisaveta, Elise, Eliska, Elissa, Elisueta, Eliza, Elizabetta, Elizabette, Elliza, Elsa, Elsbet, Elsbeth, Elsbietka, Elschen, Else, Elsee, Elsie, Elspet, Elspeth, Elyse, Elyssa, Elyza, Elzbieta, Elzunia, Isabel, Isabelita, Liazka, Lib, Libbee, Libbey, Libbie, Libby, Libbye, Lieschen, Liese, Liesel, Lis, Lisa, Lisbet, Lisbete, Lisbeth, Lise, Lisenka, Lisettina, Lisveta, Liz, Liza, Lizabeth, Lizanka, Lizbeth, Lizka, Lizzi, Lizzie, Lizzy, Vetta, Yelisaveta, Yelizaueta, Yelizaveta, Ysabel, Zizi, ZsiZsi.

ELK (Hawaiian) Black.

ELKANA (Hebrew) God has created. *Variations:* Elkanah.

ELKE (German) Noble. *Notables:* Actress Elke Sommers. *Variations:* Elka, Elkie.

ELLA (German) Other. *Notables:* Jazz singer Ella Fitzgerald.

ELLE (French) She. *Notables:* Supermodel Elle MacPherson.

ELLEN (English) Light. Variation of Helen. *Notables:* Actresses Ellen Barkin and Ellen DeGeneres. *Variations:* Elan, Elen, Elena, Eleni, Elenyl, Ellan, Ellene, Ellie, Ellon, Ellyn, Elyn, Lene.

ELLIE (English) Short form of Eleanor. *Variations:* Elli, Elly.

ELLICE (Greek) Noble. Feminine version of Elias. *Variations:* Elyce.

ELMA (Greek) Helmet; (Turkish) Apple. Feminine version of Elmo.

ELMIRA (English) Princess; (Spanish) True.

ELOISE (French) Wise. *Variations:* Eloisa, Eloisia, Eloiza, Elouise.

ELORA (Hindu) God gives the laurel to the winner. *Variations:* Ellora.

ELSA (German/Scandinavian) Noble. *Notables:* Style maven Elsa Klensch; actress Elsa Lancaster. *Variations:* Ellsa, Elsah.

ELSIE (German) Hard-worker. *Variations:* Else, Elsie, Elsy.

ELSPETH (English) Form of Elizabeth. *Variations:* Elsbeth.

ELUNED (Welsh) Image. *Variations:* Eiluned.

ELVA (English) Variation of Olivia.

ELVINA (English) Elf friend. Feminine version of Alvin. *Variations:* Elvie, Elvy, Elwina.

ELVIRA (Spanish/Latin) Blonde. *Notables:* Elvira, Mistress of the Dark. *Variations:* Elva, Elvera, Elvia, Elvirah, Elvire.

ELYSSA (Greek) Sweet. *Variations:* Elisa, Elissa, Elysa, Elysia, Ilyssa, Lyssa.

ELYSIA (Latin) Blissful. *Variations:* Eliese, Elise, Elisia, Elyse, Ileesia, Iline, Illsa, Ilyse, Ilysia.

EMELINE (French) Form of Emily. *Variations:* Emelie, Emelina, Emmaline, Emmalynn, Emmeline.

EMERA (English) Swift.

EMERALD (English) Jewel.

EMILY (German) Industrious. *Notables:* Etiquette maven Emily Post; writers Emily Bronte and Emily Dickinson. *Variations:* Aimil, Amalea, Amalia, Amalie, Amelia, Amelie, Ameline, Amy, Eimile, Em, Ema, Emalee, Emalia, Emelda, Emelene, Emelia, Emelina, Emeline, Emelyn, Emelyne, Emera, Emi, Emie, Emila, Emile, Emilea, Emilia, Emilie, Emilka, Emlyn, Emlynne, Emma, Emmalee, Emmali, Emmaline, Emmalynn, Emmele, Emmeline, Emmiline, Emylin, Emylynn.

EMMA (German) Embracing all. *Notables:* Actress Emma Thompson. *Variations:* Em, Emmi, Emmie, Emmy.

EMMANUELLE (French) God is with us. Feminine version of Emanuel. *Variations:* Em, Emmanuela, Emmie, Emmy.

EMMY (English) Short form of Emily or Emmanuelle. *Variations:* Emi, Emmi, Emmie.

EMMYLOU (American) Combination of first names "Emmy" and "Lou." *Notables:* Singer Emmylou Harris.

EMUNA (Hebrew) Faithful.

ENA (Irish) Bright, shining. Possibly a derivative of Helen.

ENID (Welsh) Life. *Variations:* Eanid, Enidd, Enud, Enudd.

ENNIS (Irish) A town in western Ireland. *Variations:* Inis.

ENRICA (Italian) Leader of the house. Feminine version of Henry. *Variations:* Enrieta, Enriqueta.

ENYA (Irish) Fiery. *Notables:* New Age singer Enya.

EPPIE (English) Short form of Euphemia.

ERELA (Hebrew) Angel.

ERIANTHE (Greek) Lover of flowers.

ERICA (Scandinavian) Leader forever. Feminine version of Eric. *Variations:* Airica, Airika, Ayrika, Enrica, Enricka, Enrika, Ericka, Erika, Errika, Eyrica.

ERIN (Gaelic) Nickname for Ireland. *Notables:* Activist Erin Brockovich. *Variations:* Erene, Ereni, Eri, Erina, Erinn, Eryn.

ERINA (Hindu) Speech. *Variations:* Erisha.

ERLINDA (Hebrew) Spirit.

ERMA (German) Whole. Variation of Irma.

ERMINE (French) Weasel. *Variations:* Ermina, Erminia, Erminie, Ermy.

ERNA (Scandinavian) Capable.

ERNESTINA (English) Earnest. *Variations:* Erna, Ernaline, Ernesta, Ernestine, Ernestyna.

ERROLYN (English) Area in Britain. Feminine version of Errol. *Variations:* Erroline.

ERWINA (English) Boar; friend. Feminine version of Erwin.

ESME (French) Esteemed. *Variations:* Esma, Esmee, Esmie.

ESMERELDA (Spanish) Emerald. *Variations:* Emerant, Emeraude, Esma, Esmaralda, Esmarelda, Esmiralda, Esmirelda, Ezmeralda.

ESPERANZA (Spanish) Hope. *Variations:* Esperance, Esperantia.

ESTEE (English) Bright star. Form of Estelle. *Notables:* Cosmetics icon Estee Lauder. *Variations:* Esti, Estie, Esty.

ESTELLE (French) Star. *Notables:* Actresses Estelle Parsons and Estelle Getty. *Variations:* Essie, Essy, Estee, Estela, Estelita, Estella, Estrelita, Estrella, Estrellita, Stelle.

ESTHER (Hebrew) Star. *Notables:* Aquatic film star Esther Williams. *Variations:* Essie, Essy, Esta, Ester, Etti, Ettie, Etty.

ESTRELLA (French) Child of the stars. *Variations:* Estrelle.

ETHEL (English) Noble. *Notables:* Actress/singer Ethel Merman. *Variations:* Ethelda, Etheline, Ethelyn, Ethelynne, Ethille, Ethlin, Ethyl.

ETHELINDA (German) Noble serpent. *Variations:* Etheleen, Ethelena, Ethelende, Ethelina, Ethelind, Ethylinda.

ETTA (English) Diminutive. Short form of Henrietta. *Notables:* R&B singer Etta James.

EUDORA (Greek) Altruistic gift. *Variations:* Eudore.

EUGENIA (Greek) Well born. Feminine version of Eugene. *Notables:* Princess Eugenie is the Duke and Duchess of York's second daughter. *Variations:* Eugena, Eugenie, Eugina.

EULALIA (Greek) Well spoken. *Variations:* Eula, Eulala, Eulia, Eulie.

EUNICE (Greek) Victorious. *Variations:* Eunise, Euniss, Eunys.

EUPHEMIA (Greek) Of good reputation. *Variations:* Eufemia.

EURYDICE (Greek) Greek mythological figure; wife of Orpheus. *Variations:* Euridice.

EUSTACIA (Greek) Fruitful. *Variations:* Eustace, Stacey.

EVA (Hebrew) Giver of life. *Notables:* Actress Eva Longoria. *Variations:* Ebba, Evaine, Evathia, Evchen, Eve, Evelina, Eveline, Evi, Evicka, Evike, Evita, Evka, Evonne, Evy, Ewa, Yeuka, Yeva.

EVANGELINE (Greek) Good news. *Variations:* Evangelia, Evangelina, Evangeliste.

EVANIA (Irish) Spirited youth. *Variations:* Evanna.

EVE (Hebrew) Life. *Notables:* Singer Eve; actress Eve Arden. *Variations:* Evie.

top ten names of the 1980s

Boys	Girls
Michael	Jessica
Christopher	Jennifer
Matthew	Amanda
Joshua	Ashley
David	Sarah
Daniel	Stephanie
James	Melissa
Robert	Nicole
John	Elizabeth
Joseph	Heather

EVELYN (Irish) Young and lively. *Variations:* Aveline, Eoelene, Evaline, Eveline, Evelyne, Evelynn, Evelynne, Evlin, Evline, Evlun, Evlynn.

EVETTE (French) Form of Yvette.

EVITA (Spanish) Life. *Notables:* Argentina's first lady Evita Peron.

EVONNE (French) Form of Yvonne.

EZRELA (Hebrew) God is my strength.

FABIA (Latin) One who grows beans. Feminine version of Fabian. *Variations:* Fabiana, Fabiane, Fabianna, Fabienne, Fabiola.

FABRIZIA (Italian) One who works with her hands. *Variations:* Fabrice, Fabricia, Fabrienne, Fabritzia.

FADILA (Arabic) Virtue. *Variations:* Fadilah.

FAHIMA (Arabic) Smart.

FAIDA (Arabic) Abundant. *Variations:* Fayda.

FAIRUZA (Arabic) Turquoise.

FAITH (English) Faith. *Notables:* Singer Faith Hill; actress Faith Ford. *Variations:* Faithe, Faythe.

FAIVA (Polynesian) Game.

FAIZAH (Arabic) Triumphant.

FALDA (Icelandic) Folded wings.

FALINE (Latin) Catlike. *Variations:* Faleen, Falene, Fayleen, Faylene, Fayline.

FALLON (Irish) Related to a leader. *Variations:* Falan, Fallan, Fallyn, Falon, Falyn.

FANCY (French) Engaged. *Variations:* Fancey, Fanci, Fancie.

FANNY (English) Short form of Frances. *Notables:* Actress/comedian Fanny Brice. *Variations:* Fani, Fannie.

FANTASIA (Greek) Imaginative. *Notables:* American Idol Fantasia Barrino. *Variations:* Fantasha, Fantasya, Fantazia.

FAREWELL (English) Goodbye; beautiful spring.

FARICA (German) Leader of peace.

FARIDA (Arabic) Unique. *Variations:* Faridah, Farideh.

FARIHA (Arabic) Happy. *Variations:* Farihah.

FARRAH (English) Pleasant; (Arabic) Beautiful. *Notables:* Actress Farrah Fawcett. *Variations:* Fara, Farah, Farra.

FARREN (English) Wandering. *Variations:* Faren, Farin, Faron, Farrin, Farron, Faryn.

FATHIYA (Arabic) Victorious.

FATIMA (Arabic) To abstain. *Variations:* Fatimah, Fatma, Fatuma.

FAUSTINE (Latin) Lucky. Feminine version of Faust. *Variations:* Fausta, Fauste, Faustia, Faustiana, Faustina.

FAWN (French) Young deer. *Variations:* Faina, Fanya, Fauan, Faun, Faunia, Fawna, Fawne, Fawnia, Fawnya.

FAY (French) Fairy. Diminutive version of Faith. *Notables:* Actress Fay Wray; writer Fay Weldon. *Variations:* Fae, Faye, Fayette, Fayla, Fayleen, Faylene, Fey.

FAYZA (Arabic) Winner. *Variations:* Faiza, Faizah, Fawzia.

FEDORA (Greek) Gift from God.

FEIGEL (Hebrew) Bird. *Variations:* Faga, Faiga, Faige, Feiga, Feigel.

FELDA (German) From the field. *Variations:* Felde, Feldy.

FELICIA (Latin) Happy; lucky. Feminine version of Felix. *Variations:* Falecia, Falicia, Falicie, Falisha, Falishia, Felice, Feliciana, Felicidad, Felicienne, Felicita, Felicitas, Felicity, Felise, Felisha, Felita, Feliz, Feliza, Phylicia.

FELICITY (English) Happy.

FELORA (Hawaiian) Flower. *Variations:* Felorena, Folora, Polola, Pololena.

FEMI (African) Seeking love. *Variations:* Femie, Femmi, Femmie, Femmy.

FENIA (Scandinavian) Ancient mythological figure. *Variations:* Fenja, Fenya.

FEODORA (Russian) Gift from God. Feminine version of Theodore. *Variations:* Fedora, Fedoria.

FERN (English) Fern. *Variations:* Ferne, Ferny.

FERNANDA (German) Brave traveler. Feminine version of Ferdinand. *Variations:* Ferdinanda, Fernande, Fernandette, Fernandina.

FERNLEY (English) Valley of ferns. *Variations:* Fern, Ferne, Fernlee, Fernleigh, Fernly.

FIALA (Czech) Violet.

FIAMMA (Italian) Fiery.

FIDELIA (Latin) Faithful. *Variations:* Fidela, Fidele, Fidella, Fidelle.

FIDELITY (Latin) Faithful. *Variations:* Fidelina, Fidelma.

FIFI (French) Nickname of Josephine. *Variations:* FeeFee, Fifine, Fina.

Boys	Girls
Giuseppe	Maria
Giovanni	Anna
Antonio	Giuseppina
Mario	Rosa
Luigi	Angela
Francesco	Giovanna
Angelo	Teresa
Vincenzo	Lucia
Pietro	Carmela
Salvatore	Caterina

FILIA (Greek) Friendship. *Variations:* Filea, Filiah.

FILIPPA (Italian) Lover of horses. Feminine version of Philip. *Variations:* Felipa, Filipa, Filipina, Filippina, Philippa.

FILOMENA (Italian) Strong friend. *Variations:* Philomena.

FINOLA (Irish) White shoulders. *Variations:* Effie, Ella, Fenella, Finella, Fionnaghuala, Fionneuala, Fionnghuala, Fionnuala, Fionnula, Fionola, Fynella, Nuala.

FIONA (Irish) Fair, white. *Variations:* Fionna, Fionne.

FIORELLA (Italian) Little flower.

FLAIR (English) With style. *Variations:* Flaire, Flare.

FLAMINIA (Latin) Priest.

FLANNA (Irish) Red hair. *Variations:* Flana, Flanagh.

FLANNERY (Irish) Red hair. *Notables:* Writer Flannery O'Connor.

FLAVIA (Latin) Yellow hair. *Variations:* Flavie, Flaviere, Flavyere, Flayia.

FLEUR (French) Flower. *Variations:* Fleura, Fleuree, Fleuretta, Fleurette.

FLO (American) Short form of Florence.

FLORA (Latin) Flower. *Notables:* Actress Flora Birch. *Variations:* Fiora, Fiore, Fiori, Fleur, Fleurette, Fleurine, Flo, Flor, Florann,

Floranne, Flore, Florella, Florelle, Floretta, Florette, Flori, Floria, Floriana, Florie, Floriese, Florina, Florine, Floris, Florrie, Florry, Floss, Flossey, Flossie.

FLORENCE (Latin) Flourishing. *Notables:* Actress Florence Henderson. *Variations:* Fiorentina, Fiorenza, Florance, Florencia, Florentia, Florentyna, Florenze.

FLORIDA (Spanish) Flowery. *Variations:* Floridia, Florinda, Florita.

FLORIMEL (Latin) Flower plus honey.

FLOSSIE (English) Short form of Florence.

FLOWER (English) Flower.

FLYNN (Irish) Red-headed. *Variations:* Flinn, Flyn.

FONDA (Spanish) Inn.

FONTANNA (French) Fountain. *Variations:* Fontaine, Fontana, Fontane, Fontanne, Fontayne.

FORSYTHIA (Latin) Flower.

FORTUNA (Latin) Lucky. *Variations:* Fortunata, Fortune.

FRAN (Latin) Short form of Frances. *Notables:* Actress Fran Drescher. *Variations:* Frann, Franni, Frannie, Franny.

FRANCES (Latin) One who is from France. Feminine version of Francis. *Notables:* Actress Frances McDormand. *Variations:* Fan, Fancy, Fania, Fannee, Fanney,

Fannie, Fanny, Fanya, Fran, Franca, Francee, Franceline, Francena, Francene, Francesca, Francetta, Francette, Francey, Franchesca, Francie, Francina, Francine, Francisca, Francoise, Frank, Frankie, Franni, Frannie, Franzetta, Franziska, Paquita.

FRANCESCA (Italian) Form of Frances. *Variations:* Franchesca, Franzetta.

FRANCINE (French) Form of Frances. *Variations:* Francene, Francina, Francyne.

FRANÇOISE (French) From France.

FRANKIE (American) Nickname for Frances or Francine. *Variations:* Franke, Franki, Franky.

FRANTISKA (Czech) Free woman. *Variations:* Frana, Franka.

FRAYDA (Hebrew) Happy. *Variations:* Fradel, Frayde, Freida, Freide.

FREDA (German) Peaceful. *Notables:* Artist Frida Kahlo. *Variations:* Freada, Freeda, Freida, Frida, Frieda, Fritzi, Fryda.

FREDDI (English) Nickname for Frederica or Winifred. *Variations:* Freddie, Freddy.

FREDERICA (German) Peaceful ruler. *Notables:* Model Frederique Van Der Wal. *Variations:* Federica, Frederika, Frederike, Frederique.

FREESIA (English) Flower.

FRENCHIE (American) From France. *Variations:* Frenchee, Frenchi, Frenchy.

FREYA (Scandinavian) Noble lady. *Variations:* Freja, Freyja, Froja.

FRIGG (Scandinavian) Beloved. *Variations:* Frigga.

FRITZI (German) Short form of Frederica. *Variations:* Fritze, Fritzie, Fritzy.

FUJI (Japanese) Wisteria. *Variations:* Fujiko.

FULVIA (Latin/Italian) Blonde. *Variations:* Fulvie.

FUSCHIA (Latin) Purple flower.

GABRIELLE (French) Devotion to God. Feminine version of Gabriel. *Notables:* Volleyball player Gabrielle Reese; tennis star Gabriela Sabatini. *Variations:* Gabrela, Gabriela, Gabriell, Gabriella.

GABY (French) Short form of Gabrielle. *Variations:* Gabi, Gabby.

GADA (Hebrew) Lucky. *Variations:* Gadah.

GAETANA (Italian) From Gaeta, Italy. *Variations:* Gaetane.

GAFNA (Hebrew) Vine.

GAIA (Greek) Earth. *Variations:* Gaea, Gaioa, Gaya.

GAIL (Hebrew) My father rejoices. *Notables:* Writer Gail Sheehy. *Variations:* Gael, Gaelen, Gaila, Gailah, Gaile, Gale, Gayle.

GALA (French) Festive. *Variations:* Galla.

GALADRIEL (Sindarin, a literary language) Radiant maiden. Name of elf princess from J.R.R. Tolkien's *Lord of the Rings* trilogy.

GALATEA (Greek) White as milk. *Variations:* Galatee.

GALEN (Irish) Lively. *Variations:* Gaelen, Gaylen, Gaylene.

GALENA (Greek) Healer.

GALI (Hebrew) Hill, mound. *Variations:* Gal, Galice.

GALIA (Hebrew) Wave. *Variations:* Gal.

GALIENA (German) High one. *Variations:* Galiana, Galianna.

GALILANI (Native American) Friendly.

GALINA (Russian) Bright or shining one. Variation of Helen. *Variations:* Galenka, Galia, Galiena, Galinka.

GALYA (Hebrew) God has redeemed. *Variations:* Galia, Gallia, Gallya.

GAMBHIRA (Hindu) Noble.

GAMILA (Arabic) Beautiful. *Variations:* Jamila.

GAMMA (Greek) Third letter of the Greek alphabet.

GANESA (Hindu) Goddess of wisdom.

GANYA (Hebrew) Garden of God. *Variations:* Gana, Ganice.

GARDENIA (English) Flower.

GARI (German) Spear. Feminine version of Gary.

GARIMA (Hindu) Importance.

GARLAND (French) Wreath. *Variations:* Garlanda, Garlande, Garlandera.

GARNET (English) Jewel. *Variations:* Garnetta, Garnette.

GASHA (Russian) Good. Russian version of Agatha. *Variations:* Gashka.

GAVRILLA (Hebrew) Heroine.

GAY (French) Joyful. *Variations:* Gae, Gai, Gaye.

GAYLE (Hebrew) Rejoicing. Form of Gail. *Variations:* Gayla, Gaylah, Gaylene, Gaylyn.

GAYORA (Hebrew) Valley of light.

GAZELLE (Latin) Gazelle; graceful. *Variations:* Gazella.

GAZIT (Hebrew) Smooth stone.

girls' names from popular songs (part iii)

Here's a final list of popular songs that include names of girls in the title:

"Melissa"
The Allman Brothers

"Michelle"
The Beatles

"My Sharona"
The Knack

"Rhiannon"
Fleetwood Mac

"Rosanna"
Toto

"Roxanne"
The Police

"Sara Smile"
Hall and Oates

"Sherry"
The Four Seasons

"Susie Q"
Creedence Clearwater Revival

"Valleri"
The Monkees

african names

Boys	Girls
Adisa	Etana
Amadi	Imani
Imamu	Kamaria
Jelani	Malaika
Kgosi	Morowa
Mfalme	Nafisa
Obataiye	Razina
Paki	Sanura
Sefu	Thema
Thabo	Zuri

GEFEN (Hebrew) Vine. *Variations:* Gafna, Gafnit, Gaphna, Geffen.

GELILAH (Hebrew) Rolling hills. *Variations:* Gelalia, Gelalya, Gelila, Gelilia, Geliliya.

GELSEY (English) Last name. *Variations:* Gelsi, Gelsie, Gelsy.

GELYA (Russian) Messenger.

GEMINI (Greek) Twin. *Variations:* Gemella, Gemelle, Gemina, Geminine.

GEMMA (Italian) Precious stone. *Variations:* Gem, Gema, Gemmie, Jemma.

GENA (French) Form of Gena, Geneva, or Genevieve. *Variations:* Geena, Genah, Genia.

GENELL (American) Form of Janelle.

GENEROSA (Spanish/Italian) Generous.

GENESEE (Native American) Wonderful valley.

GENESIS (Hebrew) Beginning. *Variations:* Genessa, Genisa, Genisia, Genisis, Jenessa.

GENEVA (French) Juniper. *Variations:* Geneeva, Geneieve, Geneve, Janeva, Jeneva.

GENEVIEVE (French) White. *Notables:* Actress Genevieve Bujold. *Variations:* Genavieve, Geneva, Geneve, Geneveeve, Genivieve, Gennie, Genny, Genovera, Genoveva, Gina, Janeva, Jenevieve.

GENIE (English) Short form of Eugenia or Eugenie. *Variations:* Geeni, Geenie, Geeney.

GENNA (English) Variation of Jenna.

GENNIFER (English) Variation of Jennifer. *Variations:* Gen, Genifer, Genny.

GEONA (Hebrew) Glorification. *Variations:* Geonit.

GEORGIA (Latin) Farmer. Feminine version of George. *Notables:* Artist Georgia O'Keeffe. *Variations:* Georgeann, Georgeanne, Georgena, Georgene, Georgetta, Georgette, Georggann, Georgganne, Georgiana, Georgianne, Georgie, Georgienne, Giorgia, Giorgina, Giorgyna, Jorga, Jorgia, Jorgina, Jorja.

GEORGINA (English) Form of Georgia. *Variations:* Georgie, Georgine, Georgy.

GERALDINE (German) One who rules with a spear. Feminine version of Gerald. *Notables:* Politician Geraldine Ferraro. *Variations:* Ceraldina, Deraldene, Geralda, Geraldeen, Geralyn, Geralynne, Geri, Gerianna, Gerianne, Gerilynn, Geroldine, Gerry, Jeraldeen, Jeraldene, Jeraldine, Jeralee, Jere, Jeri, Jerilene, Jerrie, Jerrileen, Jerroldeen, Jerry.

GERILYN (American) Combination of Geraldine and Lynn. *Variations:* Geralyn, Geralynn, Gerilynn.

GERANIUM (Latin) Flower.

GERDA (Scandinavian) Guarded. *Variations:* Gard, Gerd.

GERI (American) Nickname for Geraldine. *Variations:* Gerri, Gerry, Jeri.

GERIANNE (American) Combined form of first names "Gerry" and "Anne."

GERMAINE (French) One from Germany. *Notables:* Writer Germaine Greer. *Variations:* Germain, Germana, Germane, Germayn.

GERTIE (German) Short form of Gertrude. *Variations:* Gert, Gerti, Gerty.

GERTRUDE (German) With the strength of a spear. *Notables:* Writer Gertrude Stein. *Variations:* Gerti, Gertie, Gertina, Gertraud, Gertrud, Gertruda, Gerty, Truda, Trude, Trudey, Trudi, Trudie, Trudy, Trudye.

GERUSHAH (Hebrew) Banishment. *Variations:* Gerusha.

GERVAISE (French) Spear. *Variations:* Gervaisa.

GESSICA (American) Form of Jessica. *Variations:* Gesica, Gesika.

GEVA (Hebrew) Hill.

GEVIRAH (Hebrew) Queen. *Variations:* Gevira.

GHADA (Arabic) Graceful. *Variations:* Ghadah, Ghayda.

GHALIYA (Arabic) Pleasant odor. *Variations:* Ghaliyah.

GHITA (Italian/Greek) Pearl.

GHUFRAN (Arabic) To forgive.

GIA (Italian) Queen.

GIACINTA (Italian) Hyacinth.

GIALIA (Italian) Youthful. Feminine version of Giulio. *Variations:* Giala, Gialiana, Gialietta.

GIANNA (Italian) God is good. Feminine version of John. *Variations:* Giancinthia, Gianetta, Gianina, Giannina, Giannine, Jacenda, Jacenta, Jacey, Jacie, Jacinda, Jacindia, Jacinna, Jacinta, Jacinth, Jacintha, Jacinthe, Jacinthia, Jacynth, Jacyntha, Jacynthe.

GIBORAH (Hebrew) Strong. *Variations:* Gibora.

GIDGET (American) Petite girl.

GIGI (French) Short form of Georgina, Gilberte, or Virginia. *Notables:* Tennis player Gigi Fernandez.

GILA (Hebrew) Joy. *Variations:* Gela, Gilah.

GILADAH (Hebrew) Hill of testimony. *Variations:* Galat, Geela, Gila, Gili, Gilia.

GILANAH (Hebrew) Happy. *Variations:* Gilana.

GILDA (English) Golden. *Notables:* Comedian Gilda Radner.

GILBERTE (French) Shining pledge. Feminine version of Gilbert. *Variations:* Gilberta, Gilbertina, Gilbertine, Gill, Gillie, Gilly.

GILIAH (Hebrew) God's joy. *Variations:* Gilia, Giliya, Giliyah.

GILL (English) Downy. *Variations:* Gilli, Gillie.

GILLIAN (English) Youthful. *Variations:* Gilian, Gillaine, Gillan, Gillianne, Gillyanne.

GILSEY (English) Jasmine.

GIN (Japanese) Silver.

GINA (Italian) Nickname for names such as Regina and Angelina. *Notables:* Italian actress Gina Lollobrigida; actress Geena Davis. *Variations:* Geena, Gena, Ginat, Ginia.

GINGER (English) The spice. Diminutive of Virginia.

GINNY (English) Diminutive of Virginia. *Variations:* Ginney, Ginni, Ginnie.

GIOVANNA (Italian) God is good. Feminine version of John. *Variations:* Giovana.

GISELLE (German/French) Oath; pledge. *Notables:* Model Giselle Bundchen. *Variations:*

Gelsi, Gelsy, Gisela, Gisele, Gisella, Gizela, Gizella, Gizelle.

GITA (Sanskrit) Song. *Variations:* Geeta, Gitah, Gitta.

GITANA (Spanish) Gypsy. *Variations:* Gitane, Gitanna.

GIULIA (Italian) Form of Julia. *Variations:* Giuliana, Giulietta.

GLADIOLA (Italian) Flower.

GLADYS (Welsh) Lame. Form of Claudia. *Notables:* Singer Gladys Knight. *Variations:* Gladis, Gladiz, Gwladus, Gwladys.

GLENDA (Welsh) Holy and good. *Notables:* Actress Glenda Jackson. *Variations:* Glinda, Glynda.

GLENNA (Irish) Narrow valley. *Notables:* Actress Glenn Close. *Variations:* Glen, Glenn, Glennette.

GLORIA (Latin) Glory. *Notables:* Feminist Gloria Steinem; actress Gloria Swanson; clothing designer Gloria Vanderbilt; singer Gloria Estefan. *Variations:* Gloree, Glori, Glorianna, Glorianne, Glorie, Glorielle, Glorria, Glory.

GLYNIS (Welsh) Small valley. *Notables:* Actress Glynnis O'Connor. *Variations:* Glenice, Glenis, Glenise, Glennis, Glennise, Glennys, Glenyse, Glenyss, Glynnis.

GODIVA (English) Gift from God.

wicca baby names

Forget Samantha, Serena, Tabitha, and Endora! Real Wiccans have far more bewitching names to offer, courtesy of Wiccan writer Brenda Knight, author of *Gem Magic* and *Rituals For Life*.

Boys	Girls
Angel	Bree
Forest	Cerridwen
Hawk	Coventina
Mars	Freya
Puck	Gaia
Ocean	Marah
Sage	Pandora
Silver	Raven
Spider	Rhiannon

popular names in chile

Boys	Girls
Jose	Maria
Juan	Ana
Luis	Rosa
Carlos	Claudia
Jorge	Patricia
Manuel	Carolina
Victor	Camila
Francisco	Daniela
Cristian	Margarita
Pedro	Juana

GOLDA (English) Golden. *Notables:* Israeli Prime Minister Golda Meir. *Variations:* Goldarina, Goldarine, Goldia, Goldie, Goldif.

GOLDIE (English) Golden. *Notables:* Actress Goldie Hawn. *Variations:* Goldi, Goldy.

GRACE (Latin) Grace. *Notables:* Singers Grace Slick and Grace Jones; actress Grace Kelly. *Variations:* Engracie, Graca, Gracelle, Gracey, Graci, Gracia, Graciana, Gracie, Graciela, Gracy, Grasiela, Gratia, Grazyna.

GRAINNE (Irish) Goddess of grain. *Variations:* Grainnia, Grania, Granna.

GRAZIELLA (Italian) Form of Grace. *Variations:* Grazia, Grazie, Grazielle, Graziosa.

GREER (Scottish) Observant. *Notables:* Actress Greer Garson. *Variations:* Grear, Grier.

GREGORIA (Latin) Alert. Feminine form of Gregory. *Variations:* Gregoriana, Gregorina.

GRETA (Scandinavian/German) Pearl. *Notables:* Actress Greta Garbo. Short form of Margaret. *Variations:* Grete, Gretie, Grette.

GRETCHEN (German) Pearl. Form of Margaret. *Notables:* Actress Gretchen Mol. *Variations:* Grechen, Grechyn, Gretchin, Gretchyn.

GRETEL (German) Short form of Margaret. *Variations:* Gretal, Grettel, Gretelle.

GRISELDA (German) Gray fighting maid. *Variations:* Grizelda, Zelda.

GUADALUPE(Spanish) Valley of wolves. *Variations:* Lupe.

GUDRUN(Scandinavian) Fight. *Variations:* Gudren, Gudrin, Gudrinne, Gudruna, Guro.

GUIDA(Italian) Guide.

GUINEVERE(Welsh) Fair; yielding. *Variations:* Gaenor, Gayna, Gaynah, Gayner, Gaynor.

GULL(Scandinavian) Gold.

GUNHILDA(Scandinavian) Woman warrior. *Variations:* Gunda, Gunhilde, Gunilda, Gunilla.

GUSSIE(English) Short form of Augusta. *Variations:* Gussy.

GUSTA(Latin) Short form of Augusta.

GUSTAVA(Scandinavian: Swedish) Staff of the gods. Feminine version of Gustav. *Variations:* Gusta, Gustha.

GWEN(Welsh) Short form of Gwendolyn or Guinevere. *Notables:* Singer Gwen Stefani. *Variations:* Guin, Gwenn, Gwyn.

GWENDOLYN(Welsh) White brow. *Notables:* Poet Gwendolyn Brooks. *Variations:* Guendolen, Guenna, Gwen, Gwenda, Gwendaline, Gwendia, Gwendolen, Gwendolene, Gwendolin, Gwendoline, Gwendolynn, Gwendolynne, Gwenette, Gwennie, Gwenn, Gwenna, Gwenny.

GWYNETH(Welsh) Happiness. *Notables:* Actress Gwyneth Paltrow. *Variations:* Gwenith, Gwenyth, Gwynedd, Gwynith, Gwynn, Gwynna, Gwynne, Gwynneth.

GYPSY(English) Wanderer. *Variations:* Gipsi, Gipsy, Gypsi, Gypsie.

HABIBA(Arabic) Cherished. *Variations:* Habibah, Haviva.

HACHI(Japanese) Good luck.

HADARA(Hebrew) Beauty. *Variations:* Hadar, Hadarah.

HADASSAH(Hebrew) Myrtle. *Variations:* Hada, Hadas, Hadasa, Hadassa, Hodel.

HADIYA(African) Gift. *Variations:* Hadiyah.

HADLEY(English) Meadow of heather. *Variations:* Hadlea, Hadlee, Hadleigh.

HADRIA(Latin) From Hadria. *Variations:* Hadriana, Hadriane, Hadrienne.

HADYA(Arabic) Guide. *Variations:* Hadi, Hadia.

HAFSAH (Arabic) Lioness. *Variations:* Hafza.

HAGAR (Hebrew) Stranger. *Variations:* Haggar.

HAIDEE (Greek) Modest. *Variations:* Haydee.

HAILEY (English) Hay meadow. Form of Hayley. *Variations:* Haile, Hailee, Haileigh, Haily.

HALA (Arabic) Halo. *Variations:* Halah.

HALCYON (Greek) Kingfisher. *Variations:* Halcion, Halcione, Halcyone.

HALDANA (Scandinavian) One who is half Danish. *Variations:* Halda, Haldaine, Haldane, Haldayne, Haldi, Haldie.

HALIA (Hawaiian) Remembering a loved one.

HALIMA (Arabic) Gentle. *Variations:* Halimah.

HALIMEDA (Greek) Of the sea.

HALINA (Russian) Shining one. Russian version of Helen.

HALKU (Hawaiian) Flower.

HALLIE (English) Form of Hayley. *Notables:* Actress Halle Berry. *Variations:* Haleigh, Hali, Halie, Halle, Hallee, Hally.

HALONA (Native American) Good luck. *Variations:* Halonna.

HAMA (Japanese) Beach. *Variations:* Hamako.

HAMIDA (Arabic) To praise. *Variations:* Hameedah, Hamidah.

HANA (Japanese) Flower. *Variations:* Hanae, Hanako.

HANIA (Hebrew) Resting place. *Variations:* Haniya.

HANITA (Hindu) Grace.

HANNAH (Hebrew) Grace. *Variations:* Chana, Hana, Hanah, Hanna, Hanne, Hannele, Hannelore, Hannie, Honna.

HANSA (Hindu) Swan. *Variations:* Hansika, Hansila.

HANSINE (Scandinavian) God is good.

HAPPY (English) Glad. *Variations:* Happi.

HAQIKAH (Arabic) Truthful.

HARA (Hindu) Tawny.

HARALDA (Scandinavian) Army power. Feminine version of Harold. *Variations:* Harilda.

HARITA (Hindu) The wind.

HARLEY (English) Rabbit pasture. *Variations:* Harlea, Harlee, Harleigh, Harlie, Harly.

HARMONY (Latin) Harmony. *Variations:* Harmonee, Harmoni, Harmonia, Harmonie.

HARPER (English) Harp player. *Notables:* Writer Harper Lee.

HARRIET (German) Leader of the house. Feminine version of Harry. *Notables:* Writer Harriet Beecher Stowe. *Variations:* Harrie, Harrietta, Harriette, Harriot, Harriott, Hatsie, Hatsy, Hattie, Hatty.

HARSHA (Hindu) Happiness. *Variations:* Harshida, Harshika, Harshina.

HARU (Japanese) Born in spring. *Variations:* Harue, Haruko.

HASANATI (Arabic) Good.

HASIKA (Hindu) Laughter.

HASINA (African) Lovely and good. *Variations:* Haseena, Hasena, Hassina.

HASNA (Arabic) Strong.

HATEYA (Native American) Push with the foot.

HATHOR (Egyptian) The goddess of love.

HATHSHIRA (Arabic) Seventh daughter.

HATSU (Japanese) Firstborn.

HATTIE (English) Form of Harriet. *Variations:* Hatty.

HAUKEA (Hawaiian) Snow.

HAULANI (Hawaiian) Royalty.

HAUMA (Hindu) Gentle. *Variations:* Haleema, Halimah.

HAVEN (English) Refuge. *Variations:* Havin.

top ten names of the 1990s

Boys	Girls
Michael	Ashley
Christopher	Jessica
Matthew	Emily
Joshua	Sarah
Jacob	Samantha
Andrew	Brittany
Daniel	Amanda
Nicholas	Elizabeth
Tyler	Taylor
Joseph	Megan

Boys	Girls
Maximilian	Marie
Alexander	Sophie
Paul	Maria
Leon	Anna
Lukas	Leonie
Luca	Leah
Felix	Laura
Jonas	Lena
Tim	Katharina
David	Johanna

HAVIVA (Hebrew) Beloved. *Variations:* Havivah.

HAYDEN (English) Valley of hay. *Variations:* Haydon, Hadyn.

HAYLEY (English) Meadow of hay. *Notables:* Child actress Hayley Mills. *Variations:* Hailee, Hailey, Haley, Halie, Halley, Halli, Hallie, Hally, Haylee, Hayleigh, Haylie.

HAZEL (English) Name of a tree. *Variations:* Hazal, Hazeline, Hazell, Hazelle, Hazle.

HEATHER (English) Flower. *Notables:* Actresses Heather Locklear and Heather Graham.

HEAVEN (English) Paradise. *Variations:* Heavan, Heavenly, Heavin.

HEBE (Greek) Youth. *Variations:* Heebee.

HEDDA (English) Warfare. *Notables:* Gossip columnist Hedda Hopper. *Variations:* Heda, Heddi, Heddie, Hetta.

HEDIAH (Hebrew) Echo of God. *Variations:* Hedia, Hedya.

HEDVIKA (Czech) War of strife.

HEDWIG (German) Struggle. *Variations:* Hadvig, Hadwig, Hedvig, Hedviga, Hedvige, Hedwiga, Hedwige.

HEDY (Greek) Wonderful. *Notables:* Actress Hedy Lamarr. *Variations:* Hedi, Hedia, Hedyla.

HEIDI (German) Noble. *Variations:* Hedie, Heida, Heide, Heidie, Hydie.

HELAINE (French) Light. Form of Helen.

HELEN (Greek) Light. *Notables:* Actresses Helen Hayes and Helen Hunt; writer Helen Keller. *Variations:* Hela, Hele, Hellen, Helli.

HELENA (Scandinavian) Form of Helen. *Notables:* Actress Helena Bonham Carter.

HELENE (French) Form of Helen. *Variations:* Heline.

HELGA (German) Holy.

HELIA (Greek) Sun. *Variations:* Helya.

HELMA (German) Helmet. *Variations:* Hillma, Hilma.

HELMINE (German) Constant protector. Feminine version of William.

HELOISE (French) Famous in war. *Notables:* "Household Hints" columnist Heloise. *Variations:* Heloisa.

HELSA (Danish) Glory to God.

HEMALI (Hindu) Golden.

HENRIETTA (German) Leader of the home. Feminine version of Henry. *Variations:* Hattie, Hatty, Hendrika, Henka, Hennie, Henrie, Henrieta, Henriette, Henrika, Hetta, Hettie.

HEPHZIBAH (Hebrew) Delight. *Variations:* Hephsibah, Hephzabah, Hepzibah.

HERA (Greek) Queen. *Notables:* In mythology, queen of the goddesses and wife of Zeus. *Variations:* Herra.

HERLINDIS (Scandinavian) Gentle army.

HERMIA (Greek) Messenger. Feminine version of Hermes.

HERMINA (German) Soldier. *Variations:* Herma, Hermia.

HERMIONE (Greek) Earthly. *Notables:* In literature, Harry Potter's friend Hermione Granger. *Variations:* Hermina, Hermine, Herminia.

HERMOSA (Spanish) Beautiful.

HERNANDA (Spanish) Brave traveler. Feminine form of Hernando.

HERODIAS (Greek) To watch over.

HERTHA (German) Earth. *Variations:* Heartha.

HESPER (Greek) Evening star. *Variations:* Hespera, Hesperia, Hespira.

HESTER (Greek) Star. Variation of Esther. *Notables: The Scarlet Letter* heroine, Hester Prynne. *Variations:* Hesther, Hestia.

HETA (Native American) Rabbit hunt.

HIBERNIA (Latin) Latin name for Ireland.

HIBISCUS (Latin) Flower.

HIDE (Japanese) Excellent. *Variations:* Hideko, Hideyo.

HIKMAT (Arabic) Wise.

HILARY (Latin) Cheerful. *Notables:* Actresses Hilary Swank and Hilary Duff; U.S. Senator Hillary Clinton. *Variations:* Hilaria, Hilarie, Hillary, Hillery, Hilliary.

HILDA (German) Battle woman. *Variations:* Hilde, Hildie, Hildy, Hylda.

HILDEGARDE (German) Battle. *Variations:* Hildagaarde, Hildegard.

HILDEMAR (German) Famous in battle.

HILMA (German) Nickname for Wilhelmina.

HIMANI (Hindu) Snow-covered. *Variations:* Heemani.

HINDA (Hindu) Female deer. *Variations:* Hindel, Hindelle, Hynda.

HIPPOLITA (Greek) Horse freer. *Variations:* Hippolyta.

HISA (Japanese) Everlasting. *Variations:* Hisae, Hisako, Hisayo.

HISANO (Japanese) Meadow.

HOA (Vietnamese) Flower.

HOLDA (German) Hidden. *Variations:* Holde, Holle, Hulda.

HOLLIS (English) Near the holly. *Variations:* Holice.

HOLLY (English) Plant. *Notables:* Actress Holly Hunter. *Variations:* Holley, Holli.

HONEY (English) Sweetener; term of affection.

HONORA (English) Honorable woman. *Variations:* Honner, Honnor, Honnour, Honor, Honorah, Honorata, Honore, Honoria, Honorina, Honorine, Honour.

HOPE (English) Hope.

HORATIA (Latin) Timekeeper. Feminine version of Horatio. *Variations:* Horacia.

HORTENSE (Latin) From the garden. *Variations:* Hortensia.

HOSANNA (Hebrew) Deliver us. *Variations:* Hosana, Hosannah, Hosannie.

HOSHI (Japanese) Star. *Variations:* Hoshiko, Hoshiyo.

HUBERTA (German) Intelligent. Feminine version of Hubert. *Variations:* Huette.

HULDA (Scandinavian/German) Loved one. *Variations:* Huldah, Huldie, Huldy.

HUNTER (English) Hunter.

HYACINTH (Greek) Flower name.

I

IANA (Scottish) God is gracious. Feminine form of Ian (John). *Variations:* Ianna, Iyana.

IANEKE (Hawaiian) God is good. *Variations:* Ianete, Iani.

IANTHE (Greek) Flower. *Variations:* Iantha, Ianthia, Ianthina.

IDA (German) Hard working. *Notables:* Actress Ida Lupino. *Variations:* Idalene, Idalia, Idalina, Idaline, Idalya, Idalyne, Ide, Idell, Idella, Idelle, Idetta, Idette, Idia.

IDELLE (Welsh) Form of Ida.

IDINA (English) From Edinburgh, Scotland. Form of Edina. *Notables:* Actress Idina Mendel.

IDONY (Scandinavian) Goddess of spring. *Variations:* Idonea, Idun.

IDRA (Hebrew) Fig tree.

IDRIYA (Hebrew) Duck. *Variations:* Idria.

IDUNA (Scandinavian) Beloved. *Variations:* Idonia.

IGNACIA (Latin) On fire. Feminine version of Ignatius. *Variations:* Ignatia, Ignazia, Iniga.

IHAB (Arabic) To give.

IHSAN (Arabic) Benevolent. *Variations:* Ihsana, Ihsanah.

IKABELA (Hawaiian) Pledged to God. *Variations:* Ikapela.

IKIA (Hebrew) God helps me.

IKU (Japanese) Nurturing. *Variations:* Ikuko.

ILA (Hungarian) Form of Helen.

ILANA (Hebrew) Tree. *Variations:* Elana, Elanit, Ilanit, Ileana.

ILENE (English) Variation of Eileen. *Variations:* Ileen, Ilena.

ILESHA (Hindu) God of the earth.

ILIA (English) One who comes from the town of Troy, also known as Ilium.

ILIANA (Greek) From Troy.

ILIMA (Hawaiian) Flower.

ILISA (Scottish) Form of Alisa. *Variations:* Ilysa.

ILKA (Slavic) Admirer.

ILMA (English) Variation of William.

ILONA (Hungarian) Light. Form of Helen.

ILSA (German) Pledge of God. Variation of Elizabeth. *Variations:* Ilse, Ilsie.

IMA (Japanese) Now. *Variations:* Imae, Imako.

IMALA (Native American) Disciplined.

IMAN(Arabic) Faith. *Notables:* Model Iman. *Variations:* Imani.

IMELDA(German) Embracing the fight. *Notables:* Philippines First Lady and shoe fanatic Imelda Marcos. *Variations:* Imalda.

IMIN(Arabic) Conviction.

IMMACULADA(Spanish) Innocent. *Variations:* Immaculata.

IMOGEN(Latin) Innocent. *Notables:* Comedian Imogene Coca. *Variations:* Imogenia.

IMPERIA(Latin) Imperial.

INA(Greek) Pure. *Variations:* Ena.

INAM(Arabic) Charitable. *Variations:* Enam.

INANNA(Babylonian) The goddess of war.

INAS(Arabic) Friendly. *Variations:* Inaya, Inayah.

INDIA(English) From India. *Variations:* Indya.

INDIGO(Latin) Dark blue.

INDIRA(Hindu) Beauty. *Notables:* Indian prime minister Indira Gandhi.

INDRA(Hindu) Supreme god; god of the sky. *Variations:* Indre.

INDU(Hindu) Moon.

INÉS(Spanish) Pure. Variation of Agnes. *Variations:* Inesita, Inessa, Inetta, Inez, Ynez.

INGA(Scandinavian) Protected by Ing, Norwegian god of peace. *Variations:* Ingaar, Inge, Ingo, Ingvio.

INGEBORG(Scandinavian) Protector of Ing, Norwegian god of peace. *Variations:* Ingaberg, Ingaborg, Ingeberg, Inger, Ingmar.

INGEGERD(Scandinavian) Ing's fortress. *Variations:* Ingegard, Ingjerd.

INGRID(Scandinavian) Beautiful. *Notables:* Actress Ingrid Bergman. *Variations:* Ingred.

INOA(Hawaiian) Name.

INOCENCIA(Spanish) Innocence. *Variations:* Inocenta, Inocentia, Innocence.

INOLA(Native American) Black fox.

IOLA(Greek) Dawn. *Variations:* Iole.

IOLANA(Hawaiian) To soar. *Variations:* Iolani.

IOLANTHE(English) Violet.

IONA(Greek) Scottish island. *Variations:* Ionia.

IONE(Greek) Violet. *Variations:* Ionie.

IOSEPINE(Hawaiian) God adds. *Variations:* Iokepina, Iokepine, Kepina.

IPHIGENIA(Greek) Sacrifice. *Variations:* Iphigenie.

IRELAND(English) From Ireland. *Variations:* Irelyn.

IRENE(Greek) Peace. *Notables:* Actresses Irene Ryan and Irene Cara. *Variations:* Arina, Arinka, Eirena, Eirene, Erena, Erene, Errena, Irayna, Ireen, Irena, Irenee, Irenka, Irina, Irine,

Irini, Irisha, Irka, Irusya, Iryna, Orina, Orya, Oryna, Reena, Reenie, Rina, Yarina, Yaryna.

IRINA (Russian) Form of Irene.

IRIS (Greek) Rainbow. *Notables:* Latina TV personality Iris Chacon. *Variations:* Irisa, Irisha.

IRMA (German) Complete. *Variations:* Erma.

IRVETTE (English) Friend of the sea. Feminine version of Irving.

ISABEL (Spanish) Pledge to God. Version of Elizabeth. *Notables:* Actresses Isabelle Adjani and Isabella Rossellini. *Variations:* Isa, Isabeau, Isabelita, Isabella, Isabelle, Isobel, Issi, Issie, Issy, Izabel, Izabele, Izabella, Izabelle, Izebela, Ysabel.

ISADORA (Greek) Gift from Isis. Feminine version of Isidore. *Notables:* Dancer Isadora Duncan. *Variations:* Isidora.

ISEULT (Irish) Ruler of the ice. *Variations:* Hisolda, Isolda, Isolde, Ysenit, Ysolte.

ISHA (Hebrew) Woman; (Hindu) Protector.

ISHANA (Hindu) Desire. *Variations:* Ishani.

ISHI (Japanese) Stone. *Variations:* Ishie, Ishiko, Ishiyo, Shiko, Shiuo.

ISIS (Egyptian) Goddess of ancient Egypt.

ISLA (Scottish) Name of a river in Scotland.

ISMAELA (Hebrew) God listens. *Variations:* Isma, Mael, Maella.

most popular names for twin girls

According to the Social Security Administration in 2005, these are the top names Americans are giving to their twin girls.

Faith and Hope

Madison and Morgan

Hailey and Hannah

Anna and Emma

Ella and Emma

Ashley and Emily

Elizabeth and Katherine

Jennifer and Jessica

Abigail and Emma

Gabriella and Isabella

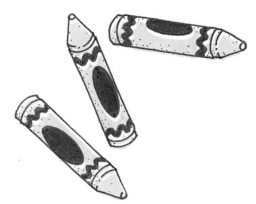

ISOKA (African) Gift from God. *Variations:* Isoke, Soka.

ISOLDE (Welsh) Fair maiden. *Variations:* Isolda, Isolt, Yseult.

ISTVAN (Hungarian) Crowned with laurels.

ITA (Irish) Thirsty.

ITALIA (Latin) From Italy. *Variations:* Talia.

ITIAH (Hebrew) God is here. *Variations:* Itia, Itiel, Itil, Itiya.

IUANA (Native American) Wind blowing over a bubbling stream.

IULIA (Hawaiian) Form of Julia. *Variations:* Iuliana, Kulia, Kuliana.

IUNIA (Hawaiian) Good victory. *Variations:* Eunika.

IUSITINA (Hawaiian) Righteous. Form of Justine. *Variations:* Iukikina.

IVA (Slavic) Short form of Ivana. *Variations:* Ivah.

IVANA (Slavic) God is good. Feminine version of Ivan. *Notables:* Donald Trump's ex-wife Ivana Trump. *Variations:* Ivania, Ivanka, Ivanna, Ivannia.

IVEREM (African) Good luck.

IVETTE (French) Alternate form of Yvette.

IVONNE (French) Alternate form of Yvonne.

IVORY (Latin) Ivory. *Variations:* Ivoree, Ivoreen, Ivori, Ivorie, Ivorine.

IVRIA (Hebrew) From the land of Abraham. *Variations:* Ivriah, Ivrit.

IVY (English) Plant. *Variations:* Iva, Ivee, Ivey, Ivie.

IWA (Japanese) Rock.

IWALANI (Hawaiian) Sea bird.

IYABO (African) Mother comes back.

IYANA (Hebrew) Form of Iana (feminine form of John). *Notables:* Writer/motivational speaker Iyanla Vansant. *Variations:* Iyanla, Iyanna, Iyannia.

IYRIA (Hebrew) In Abraham's land. *Variations:* Ivriah, Ivrit.

IZDIHAR (Arabic) Blossoming.

IZEGBE (African: Nigerian) Long-awaited child. *Variations:* Izebe.

IZUSA (Native American) White stone.

IZZY (American) Short form of Isabel.

J

JACEY (American) Undetermined meaning. *Variations:* J.C., Jace, Jacee, Jaci, Jacie, Jacy.

JACINTA (Spanish) Hyacinth. Feminine version of Jacinto. *Variations:* Glacinda, Glacintha, Jacinda, Jacintha, Jacinthe, Jacinthia, Jacki, Jacky, Jacquetta, Jacqui, Jacquie, Jacynth, Jacyntha, Jacynthe.

JACKIE (English) Nickname for Jacqueline. *Notables:* Writer Jackie Collins. *Variations:* Jacki, Jacky, Jacqui, Jakki.

JACOBINA (Hebrew) Supplanter. Feminine version of Jacob. *Variations:* Jacoba.

JACQUELINE (French) He who replaces. Feminine version of Jacob. *Notables:* U.S. first lady Jacqueline Kennedy (Onassis); actress Jacqueline Bisset. *Variations:* Jacaline, Jacalyn, Jackalin, Jackalyn, Jackeline, Jackelyn, Jacketta, Jackette, Jacki, Jackie, Jacklin, Jacklyn, Jacky, Jaclyn, Jaclynn, Jacoba, Jacobette, Jacobina, Jacolyn, Jacqualine, Jacqualyn, Jacqualynn, Jacquelean, Jacquelene, Jacquelin, Jacquelyn, Jacquelyne, Jacquelynn, Jacquelynne, Jacqueta, Jacquetta, Jacquiline, Jacquline, Jacqulynn, Jaculine, Jakelyn, Jaqueline, Jaquelyn, Jaquith.

JADE (Spanish) Jade stone. *Notables:* Actress Jada Pinkett. *Variations:* Jada, Jadda, Jadee, Jaden, Jadi, Jadira, Jady, Jadyn, Jaid, Jaida, Jaide, Jayde, Jaydra.

JAE (Latin) Jaybird. *Variations:* Jaya, Jaylee, Jayleen, Jaylene, Jaylynn.

JAEL (Hebrew) Mountain goat. *Variations:* Jaela, Jaeli, Jaelyn.

JAIRA (Spanish) God teaches. *Variations:* Jairah.

JAFFA (Hebrew) Beautiful. Feminine version of Yaffa. *Variations:* Jaffe, Jaffi, Jaffice, Jaffit, Jafit.

JALEESA (American) Combined form of first names "Jay" and "Lisa." *Variations:* Ja Leesa, Ja Lisa, Jalisa.

JALENA (America) Combined form of first names "Jay" and "Lena." *Variations:* Jalana, Jalani, Jalanie, Jalean, Jaleena, Jalen, Jalene, Jalina, Jaline, Jalyn, Jalynn, Jelena, Jelina, Jelyna.

JALILA (Arabic) Great. *Variations:* Jalile.

JALINDA (American) Combination of Jay and Linda. *Variations:* Jalynda, Jelinda, Jelynda.

JAMAICA (English) The island country. *Notables:* Writer Jamaica Kincaid. *Variations:* Jameika, Jameka, Jamica, Jamika.

the family jewels

Each of these gemstones also makes a jewel of a name.

Boys	Girls
Agate	Amber
Alexandrite	Amethyst
Garnet	Beryl
Iolite	Citrine
Jasper	Coral
Kunzite	Emerald
Lapis Lazuli	Jade
Morganite	Onyx
Peridot	Opal
Tanzanite	Pearl
Topaz	Ruby
Zircon	Sapphire

JAMIE (English) One who replaces. Feminine version of James. *Notables:* Actress Jamie Lee Curtis. *Variations:* Jaima, Jaime, Jaimee, Jaimey, Jaimi, Jaimie, Jaimy, Jamea, Jamee, Jami, Jamia, Jamiah, Jayme, Jaymee, Jaymi, Jaymie.

JAMILA (Arabic) Beautiful. *Variations:* Gamila, Gamilah, Jameela, Jamelia, Jamilah, Jamilla, Jamillah, Jamille, Jamillia.

JAN (Hebrew) God is good. *Variations:* Jana, Janina, Janine, Jann, Janna.

JANAE (Hebrew) God answers. *Variations:* Janai, Janais, Janay, Janaya, Janaye, Jannae, Jeanae, Jeanay, Jenae, Jenai, Jenay, Jenaya, Jenee, Jennae, Jennay.

JANE (English) God's grace. *Notables:* Actress Jane Fonda; writer Jane Austen. *Variations:* Janey, Janica, Janice, Janicia, Janie, Janiece, Janis, Janise, Jannice, Jannis, Jayne, Sheenagh, Sheenah, Sheina, Shena.

JANELLE (French) God is good. *Variations:* Janel, Janela, Janele, Janelis, Janell, Janella, Janiel, Jenelle, Nell.

JANESSA (American) Combination of Jan and Vanessa. *Variations:* Janesse, Janissa, Jannessa, Jenessa.

JANET (English) Diminutive of Jane. *Notables:* Singer Janet Jackson; actress Janet Leigh. *Variations:* Janeta, Janeth, Janett, Janetta, Janette, Jannet, Janneth, Jannetta, Jenet, Jenett, Jenetta, Jenette, Jennetta,

Jennette, Joanet, Sinead, Siobahn, Sioban, Siobhan.

JANICE (English) Form of Jane. *Notables:* Supermodel Janice Dickinson; singer Janis Joplin. *Variations:* Janess, Janessa, Janesse, Janiece, Janis, Janyce.

JANIKA (Slavic) Form of Jane, Janet, or Janice. *Variations:* Janaca, Janeca, Janecka, Janica, Janicka, Jannica.

JANINE (English) God is good. Feminine version of John. *Notables:* Comedian Janeane Garofalo. *Variations:* Janeane, Janina, Jannine, Jeneen, Jenine.

JANNA (Hebrew) Form of Johanna. *Variations:* Jannah.

JANOAH (Hebrew) Quiet. *Variations:* Janowa.

JARDENA (French) Garden. *Variations:* Jardan, Jardana, Jardane, Jardania, Jardee, Jardenia, Jardine, Jardyn.

JARITA (Arabic) Water urn. *Variations:* Jara, Jari, Jaria, Jarica, Jarida, Jarietta, Jarika, Jarina, Jaritta, Jaritza, Jarrina, Jarrine.

JARKA (Czech) Spring. *Variations:* Jaruse, Jaruska.

JARMILA (Czech) One who loves spring.

JASMINE (Persian) Flower. *Notables:* Actress Jasmine Guy. *Variations:* Jasmeen, Jasmin, Jasmina, Jazmin, Jazmine, Jessamine, Jessamyn, Yasiman, Yasman, Yasmine.

JASWINDER (Hindu) The god of the sky's thunder.

JAVANA (Malaysian) From Java. *Variations:* Javan, Javanna, Javanne, Javon, Javona, Javonna.

JAVIERA (Spanish) Shining. *Variations:* Javeera, Xaviera.

JAY (Latin) Happy. *Variations:* Jai, Jaie, Jaye.

JAYA (Hindu) Victory. *Variations:* Ja Wanti, Janatika, Jayamala, Jayanti, Jayashree, Jayna, Jayt.

JAYLA (American) Feminine form of Jay. *Variations:* Jaila, Jaylah, Jaylan.

JAYLENE (English) Blue jay. *Variations:* Jae, Jaye, Jayleen, Jayline, Jaynell.

JAZLYN (American) Combined form of first names "Jasmine" and "Lynn." *Variations:* Jasleen, Jaslyn, Jaslynn, Jazlynn, Jazzalyn, Jazzlyn.

JAZZ (American) Jazz. Short form of Jasmine. *Variations:* Jas, Jassie, Jaz, Jazzi, Jazzy.

JEAN (Scottish) God is good. Feminine version of John. *Notables:* Actress Jean Harlow; Weight Watchers founder Jean Niditch. *Variations:* Jeana, Jeanette, Jeanna, Jeanne, Jeannie, Jennette.

JEANNETTE (English) Form of Jean or Jane. *Variations:* Janette, Janetta, Jeannetta, Jenet, Jenett, Jenette, Jennette.

JEANNINE (French) Form of Jean or Jane. *Variations:* Janeane, Janine, Jeanene, Jeanine, Jenine, Jennine.

JELENA (Russian/Serbian) Light. *Variations:* Jelaina, Jelaine, Jelana, Jelane, Jilena.

JEMIMA (Hebrew) Dove. *Notables:* Breakfast icon Aunt Jemima. *Variations:* Jamima, Jemimah, Jemmie, Jemmimah, Jemmy, Mima, Mimma.

JEMINA (Hebrew) Right-handed. *Variations:* Jem, Jemi, Jemine, Jemma, Jemmi, Jemmie, Jemmy, Mina.

JEMMA (English) Precious stone. *Variations:* Gemma.

JENA (Hindu) Patience.

JENDAN (African) Thankful.

JENDAYA (African) To give thanks.

JENELLE (English) Yielding. Version of Guinevere.

JENICA (Romanian) Form of Jane.

JENILEE (American) Combination of Jennifer and Lee. *Variations:* Jenelea, Jenalee, Jenaleigh, Jenalie, Jenelee, Jeneleigh, Jenileigh, Jennalea, Jennalee, Jennilee, Jennileigh.

JENILYN (American) Combined form of first names "Jennifer" and "Lynn." *Variations:* Jenalyn, Jenilynn, Jennalyn, Jennalynn, Jennilyn.

JENNA (English) Form of Jennifer. *Notables:* Actress Jenna Elfman. *Variations:* Jannarae, Jena, Jenesi, Jenn, Jennabel, Jennah, Jennalee, Jennalyn, Jennasee.

JENNICA (English) God is good. *Variations:* Jenica.

JENNIFER (Welsh) White; smooth; soft. Variation of Guinevere. *Notables:* Actress/singer Jennifer Lopez; actress Jennifer Garner. *Variations:* Genn, Gennifer, Genny, Ginnifer, Jen, Jena, Jenalee, Jenalyn, Jenarae, Jenene, Jenetta Jenita, Jeni, Jenice, Jeniece, Jenifer, Jeniffer, Jenilee, Jenilynn, Jenise, Jenn, Jennessa, Jenni, Jennie, Jennika, Jennilyn, Jennis, Jennyann, Jennylee, Jeny, Jinny.

JENNY (Welsh) Short form of Jennifer. *Notables:* Actress Jenny McCarthy; diet guru Jenny Craig. *Variations:* Jenee, Jennee, Jeni, Jenni, Jennie.

JERALYN (American) Combination of Jeri and Lynn. *Variations:* Jerelyn, Jerilee, Jerilyn, Jerilynn, Jerralyn, Jerrilyn.

JEREMIA (Hebrew) The Lord is great. Feminine version of Jeremiah.

JERI (English) Short form of Geraldine or Jeralyn; feminine form of Gerald or Jerry. *Variations:* Geri, Jerri, Jerry.

JERICA (American) Combination of Jeri and Erica. *Variations:* Jerika, Jerrica, Jerrika.

JERMAINE (French) Form of Germaine. *Variations:* Jermayne.

JERSEY (English) Place name.

JERUSHA (Hebrew) Possession; inheritance.

JESSALYN (English) Combined form of first names "Jessica" and "Lynn." *Variations:* Jesalin, Jesaline, Jesalyn, Jesilyn, Jeslyn.

JESSENIA (Arabic) Flower. *Variations:* Jesene, Jesenia.

JESSICA (Hebrew) He beholds. *Notables:* Singer Jessica Simpson; actress Jessica Alba. *Variations:* Jesica, Jess, Jessa, Jesse, Jesseca, Jessey, Jessi, Jessie, Jessika.

JETHRA (Hebrew) Plenty.

JETTE (Scandinavian) Black. *Variations:* Jetta.

JEWEL (French) Jewel. *Notables:* Singer Jewel Kilchner. *Variations:* Jewelle.

JEZEBEL (Hebrew) Unexalted. *Variations:* Jessabel, Jez, Jezabel, Jezzie.

JIA (Chinese) Beauty.

JILL (English) Young. Short version of Jillian. *Notables:* Actresses Jill Ireland, Jill Clayburgh, and Jill St. John. *Variations:* Gil, Gill, Gyl, Gyll, Jil, Jilli, Jillie, Jilly, Jyl, Jyll.

JILLIAN (English) Young. *Notables:* TV personality Jillian Barberie. *Variations:* Gilli, Gillian, Gillie, Jilaine, Jilane, Jilian, Jiliana, Jillana, Jilleen, Jilliana, Jillianne, Jilliyanne, Jillyan, Jillyanna.

JIMENA (Spanish) Heard.

JIN (Japanese) Tender.

JINNAT (Hindu) Heaven.

JINX (Latin) Spell. *Variations:* Jynx.

popular greek names

Boys	Girls
Alexander	Ariadne
Aristotle	Athena
Constantine	Calista
Demos	Dimitria
Dimitri	Helena
Lucas	Ionia
Nicholas	Katrina
Nikos	Nia
Stefanos	Olga
Theo	Philana
Vasilis	Theodora
	Zoe

top ten names of 2000

Boys	Girls
Jacob	Emily
Michael	Hannah
Matthew	Madison
Joshua	Ashley
Christopher	Sarah
Nicholas	Alexis
Andrew	Samantha
Joseph	Jessica
Daniel	Taylor
Tyler	Elizabeth

JO (English) Short form of Joanna, Josephine, or any name beginning with "Jo." *Variations:* Jojo.

JOAN (Hebrew) God is good. *Notables:* Actresses Joan Crawford, Joan Allen, and Joan Cusack. *Variations:* Joani, Joanie, Joannie, Jonee, Joni.

JOANNA (English) Form of Joan. *Variations:* Joana, Joannah, Johanna.

JOANNE (English) God is good. *Notables:* Actress Joanne Woodward. *Variations:* JoAnn, JoAnne, Johanna, Johanne.

JOAQUINA (Spanish) Flower; (Hebrew) God will establish. *Variations:* Joaquine.

JOBETH (American) Combination of first names "Jo" and "Beth." *Notables:* Actress JoBeth Williams.

JOBY (Hebrew) Persecuted. Feminine version of Job. *Variations:* Jobi, Jobie.

JOCASTA (Greek) Shining moon.

JOCELYN (Latin) Joyous. *Variations:* Jocelin, Joceline, Jocelyne, Joci, Jocie, Josaline, Joscelin, Josceline, Joscelyn, Joseline, Joselyn, Joselyne, Josiline, Josline.

JOCOSA (Latin) Playful.

JODELLE (French). *Variations:* Jo Dell, Jodell.

JOELLE (French) God is Lord. Feminine version of Joel. *Variations:* Joda, Joell, Joella, Joellen, Joellyn, Joely.

JODHA (Hindu) Sixteenth-century Hindu woman.

JODY (Hebrew) Praised. *Notables:* Actress Jodie Foster. *Variations:* Jodi, Jodie.

JOHANNA (German) Form of Joanna. *Variations:* Johana, Johnna.

JOLÁN (Hungarian) Purple flower.

JOLANDA (Greek) Form of Yolanda.

JOLÁNTA (Czech) Violet. *Variations:* Jolana.

JOLENE (American) Combination of first name "Jo" and the suffix "lene." *Variations:* Jolean, Joleen, Jolian, Jolin, Joline, Jolinn, Jolinne, Jolyn, Jolynn, Jolynne, Jolyon.

JOLIE (French) Pretty. *Variations:* Jolee, Joley, Joli, Joline, Joly.

JOLISA (American) Combination of Jo and Lisa.

JONATHA (Hebrew) Gift of God. Feminine form of Jonathan.

JONELLE (English). *Variations:* Johnelle, Jonell, Jonella, Jonnell.

JONI (American) Familiar form of Joan. *Notables:* Singer Joni Mitchell. *Variations:* Joanie, Jonie.

JONINA (Hebrew) Dove. *Variations:* Jona, Jonati, Jonit, Jonita, Yona, Yonit, Yonita.

JONNA (English) God is good. Feminine version of John. *Variations:* Jahnna, Johnna.

JONQUIL (English) Flower. *Variations:* Jonquila, Jonquille.

JORA (Hebrew) Autumn rain. *Variations:* Jorah.

JORDAN (English) To descend. *Variations:* Jordain, Jordaine, Jordana, Jordanna, Jordon, Jordyn, Jourdan.

JORI (Hebrew) Form of Jordan or short form of Marjorie. *Variations:* Joree, Jorie, Jorri, Jory.

JOSELYN (Latin) Form of Jocelyn.

JOSEPHINE (Hebrew) God will add. Feminine version of Joseph. *Variations:* Jo, Joey, Jojo, Josefa, Josefina, Josefine, Josepha, Josephe, Josephene, Josephina, Josetta, Josette.

meeting in the middle

What happens when you and your partner completely disagree? Or if you each detest the name the other loves most? One solution is to go through your lists of favorites and choose from only those names you *both* selected. You can always save the other names for a middle name or try again with your next baby.

JOSIE (English) Familiar form of Josephine. *Variations:* Josee, Josey, Josi.

JOVANA (Latin) Majestic. *Variations:* Jovan, Jovanna, Jovannah, Jovanne, Jovenna, Jovenne.

JOVITA (Latin) Gladden.

JOY (English) Happiness. *Notables:* Comedian Joy Behar. *Variations:* Gioia, Joi, Joie, Joya, Joye.

JOYCE (Latin) Joyous. *Notables:* Columnist/ therapist Dr. Joyce Brothers; writer Joyce Carol Oates. *Variations:* Joice, Joycee, Joyousa.

JOYITA (Spanish) Jewel.

JUANA (Spanish) God is good. Feminine form of Juan (John). *Variations:* Juanna.

JUANITA (Spanish) God is good. Feminine form of Juan (John). *Variations:* Juanetta, Juanita.

JUBILEE (Hebrew) Jubilant.

JUDE (Latin) Praised.

JUDITH (Hebrew) Admired, praised. *Variations:* Jitka, Jucika, Judey, Judi, Judie, Judit, Judita, Judite, Juditha, Judithe, Judy, Judye, Jutka.

JUDY (English) Short form of Judith. *Notables:* Singer Judy Garland. *Variations:* Judee, Judi, Judie.

JULA (Polish) Form of Julia.

JULES (English) Form of Julia. *Notables:* TV host Jules Asner.

JULIA (Latin) Young. *Notables:* Actress Julia Roberts; TV chef Julia Child. *Variations:* Giulia, Iulia, Jula, Julcia, Julee, Juley, Juli, Juliana, Juliane, Julianna, Julianne, Julica, Julie, Julina, Juline, Julinka, Juliska, Julissa, Julka, Yula, Yulinka, Yuliya, Yulka, Yulya.

JULIANA (Italian) Form of Julia. *Notables:* Actresses Julianna Margulies and Julianne Moore. *Variations:* Julian, Juliane, Julianna, Julianne.

JULIE (English) Young. Form of Julia. *Notables:* Actress Julie Andrews. *Variations:* Jule, Julee, Juli.

JULIET (English) Form of Julia. *Variations:* Julieta, Julietta, Juliette, Julita.

JULISA (American) Combination of Julia and Lisa. *Variations:* Julessa, Julissa.

JUMANA (Arabic) Pearl. *Variations:* Jumanah.

JUN (Chinese) Truth of life. *Variations:* Junko.

JUNE (Latin) The month. *Notables:* Singer June Carter Cash. *Variations:* Junae, Junel, Junella, Junelle, Junette.

JUNIPER (English) Juniper tree.

JUNO (Latin) Queen of heaven.

JUSTINE (French) Just. Feminine version of Justin. *Variations:* Justeen, Justeena, Justena, Justina, Justinna, Justyna, Justyne.

JYOTI (Hindu) Light of the moon. *Variations:* Jyotsana.

KACEY (English) Vigilant. Variation of Casey. *Variations:* K.C., Kace, Kacee, Kaci, Kacia, Kacie, Kacy, Kasey, Kasie, Kaycee, Kayci, Kaycie, Kaysie.

KACHINA (Native American) Sacred dancer.

KACIA (Greek) Short form of Acacia. *Variations:* Kasia, Kaycia.

KADESHA (American) Combination of Kady and Aisha.

KADY (English) Variation of Cady or Katy. *Variations:* Kadee, Kadie.

KAELIN (Irish) Pure. Form of Cailin. *Variations:* Kaelan, Kaelen, Kaeline, Kaelyn, Kaelynn, Kailin, Kailyn.

KAI (Hawaiian) Sea. *Variations:* Kae.

KAITLIN (Irish) Pure. Form of Katherine. *Variations:* Caitlin, Kaitlinn, Kaitlinne, Kaitlynn, Katelin, Katelyn, Katelynne.

KALANI (Hawaiian) Of the heavens. *Variations:* Kalauni, Kaloni.

KALI (Hindu) The black one. *Variations:* Kala, Kalli.

KALILA (Arabic) Beloved. *Variations:* Kaila, Kailey, Kaleela, Kaleigh, Kalie, Kalilla, Kaly, Kayle, Kaylee, Kayleen, Kayleigh, Kaylene, Kayley, Kaylie, Kaylil, Kylila.

KALINA (Slavic) Flower. *Variations:* Kaleen, Kaleena, Kalena, Kalene.

KALINDA (Hindu) The sun. *Variations:* Kaleenda, Kalindi.

KALISA (American) Combination of Kay and Lisa. *Variations:* Kaleesa, Kalisha, Kallisa, Kaylisa.

KALLISTA (Greek) Most beautiful. *Variations:* Cala, Calesta, Calista, Callie, Cally, Kala, Kalesta, Kali, Kalie, Kalika, Kalista, Kalli, Kallie, Kally, Kallysta.

KAMA (Sanskrit) Beloved.

KAMALI (African) Guardian angel.

chinese names

Boys	Girls
An	Ai
Cheng	Bao
Ho	Chan
Hu	Dai
Jin	Hua
Kong	Jiao
Li	Jun
Liang	Li
Ning	Lin
Po	Ling
Qiang	Mei
Shing	Ping
Wen	Qian
Wing	Ting
Yong	Xian
Yu	Yan

KAMEA (Hawaiian) Only one.

KAMI (Polynesian) Love.

KAMILA (Arabic) Perfect. *Variations:* Kamala, Kameela, Kamilah, Kamilia, Kamilla, Kamillah, Kamla.

KANA (Hindu) Tiny. *Variations:* Kanika.

KANANI (Hawaiian) Beautiful.

KANYA (Hindu) Virginal. *Variations:* Kania.

KARA (Greek) Dear. *Variations:* Kaira, Karah, Karalee, Karalyn, Karalynn, Kari, Kariana, Karianna, Karianne, Karie, Karielle, Karrah, Karrie, Kary.

KAREN (Greek) Pure. Form of Katherine. *Notables:* Singer Karen Carpenter. *Variations:* Caren, Carin, Caron, Carren, Carrin, Carron, Caryn, Kareen, Karenna, Karin, Karina, Karon, Karyn, Keren, Kerena, Kerran, Kerrin, Kerron, Keryn.

KARIDA (Arabic) Virginal. *Variations:* Kareeda.

KARIMA (Arabic) Noble. *Variations:* Kareema, Karimah.

KARIS (Greek) Grace.

KARISMA (English) Variation of Charisma.

KARISSA (Greek) Dear.

KARLA (German) Woman. Feminine form of Carl.

KARLENE (Latvian) Woman. Feminine version of Charles. *Variations:* Karleen, Karlen, Karlena, Karlina.

KARMA (Hindu) Fate.

KARMEL (Hebrew) Garden of grapes. *Variations:* Cami, Carmel, Carmia, Karmeli, Karmi, Karmia, Karmiel, Karmielle.

KARMEN (Latin) Song. Variation of Carmen. *Variations:* Karmina, Karmine, Karmita.

KAROLINA (Polish) Form of Caroline. *Variations:* Karalina, Karaline, Karoline, Karolyn.

KARUNA (Hindu) Compassion.

KASMIRA (Slavic) Bringing peace. Feminine version of Casimir.

KAT (Greek) Pure. Short form of Katherine.

KATE (Greek) Short form of Katherine and its derivatives. *Notables:* Actress Kate Winslet. *Variations:* Cate, Kait.

KATIE (English) Short form of Katherine. *Notables:* TV news host Katie Couric. *Variations:* Katee, Katey, Kati, Katy.

KATHERINE (Greek) Pure. *Notables:* Actress Katherine Hepburn. *Variations:* Caitriona, Caren, Caron, Caryn, Caye, Kaethe, Kai, Kaila, Kaitlin, Karen, Karena, Karin, Karina, Karine, Karon, Karrin, Karyn, Karyna, Karynn, Kata, Kataleen, Katalin, Katalina, Katarina, Kateke, Katerina, Katerinka, Katharin, Katharina, Katharine, Katharyn, Kathereen, Katherin, Katherina, Kathey, Kathi, Kathie, Kathleen, Kathlyn, Kathlynn, Kathren, Kathrine, Kathryn, Kathryne, Kathy, Katia, Katica, Katina, Katrina, Katrine, Katriona, Katryna, Kattrina, Katushka, Katya, Kay, Kisan, Kit, Kitti, Kittie, Kitty, Kotinka, Kotryna, Yekaterina.

KATHLEEN (Irish) Form of Katherine. *Notables:* Actress Kathleen Turner. *Variations:* Cathleen, Cathlene, Cathlyn, Kathlyn.

KATHY (English) Short form of Katherine. *Notables:* Actress Kathy Bates; comedian Kathy Griffin. *Variations:* Kathe, Kathee, Kathi, Kathie.

KATIA (Russian) Form of Katherine.

KATRIEL (Hebrew) Crowned by God.

KATRINA (Scandinavian) Form of Katherine. *Variations:* Katreena, Katrine.

KATSU (Japanese) Triumphant. *Variations:* Katsuko.

KAYLA (English) Pure; (Irish) Girl. *Variations:* Kaela, Kaelee, Kaeleigh, Kaelene, Kaeli, Kaelie, Kaelin, Kaelyn, Kaila, Kailan, Kailee, Kaileen, Kailene, Kailey, Kailin, Kailynne, Kalan, Kalee, Kaleigh, Kalen, Kaley, Kalie, Kalin, Kalyn, Kayana, Kayanna, Kaye, Kaylan, Kaylea, Kayleen, Kayleigh, Kaylene, Kayley, Kayli, Kaylle.

KAZIA (Polish) Destroyer of peace.

KEARA (Irish) Dark. *Notables:* Actress Keira Knightley. *Variations:* Keera, Keira, Kera, Kiara, Kiera.

KEELY (Irish) Brave. Form of Kelly. *Variations:* Kealee, Kealey, Kealy, Keeley, Keeli, Keelie, Keighley, Keilie, Keyley, Kieley, Kiely.

KEENA (Irish) Brave. *Variations:* Kina.

KEESHA (African) Favorite. *Variations:* Keisha, Keshia, Kiesha.

KEIKI (Hawaiian) Child. *Variations:* Keikana.

KEIKO (Japanese) Joyful child.

KELA (Hawaiian) Valley. *Variations:* Dela.

KELBY (English) Farm by the river. *Variations:* Kelbi, Kelbie.

KELDA (Scandinavian) Fountain; spring. *Variations:* Kilde.

KELILA (Hebrew) Crown. *Variations:* Kaile, Kaille, Kalia, Kayla, Kayle, Keila, Keilah, Kellila, Kellula, Kyle, Kylia.

KELINA (Hawaiian) Moon goddess.

KELLY (Irish) Brave soldier. *Notables:* Singer Kelly Clarkson; talk-show host Kelly Ripa. *Variations:* Kealey, Kealy, Keeley, Keelie, Keellie, Keely, Keighley, Keiley, Keilly, Keily, Kellee, Kelley, Kellia, Kellie, Kellina, Kellisa.

KELSEY (Scottish) Island. *Variations:* Kelcey, Kelci, Kelcie, Kelcy, Kellsie, Kelsa, Kelsea, Kelsee, Kelseigh, Kelsi, Kelsie, Kelsy.

KELULA (Yiddish) Girlfriend.

KENDA (Native American) Magic. *Variations:* Kenada, Kenadi, Kendi, Kendie, Kendy, Kennda, Kenndi, Kenndie, Kenndy.

KENDALL (English) Valley of Kent, England. *Variations:* Kendal, Kendel, Kendell, Kendelle.

KENDRA (English) Knowledgeable. *Variations:* Kena, Kenadrea, Kendria, Kenna, Kindra, Kinna, Kyndra.

KENISHA (American) Beautiful woman. *Variations:* Keneisha, Keneshia, Kennesha.

KENNA (Scottish) Attractive. Feminine form of Kenneth. *Variations:* Kennae, Kennina.

KENNICE (English) Beautiful. *Variations:* Kennise.

KENTON (English) Place name.

KENYA (English) African country. *Variations:* Kenia, Kenyatta.

KENZIE (Scottish) Attractive. *Variations:* Kensey, Kensie, Kenzi.

KERANI (Hindu) Sacred bells. *Variations:* Kera, Kerie, Kery.

KEREN (Hebrew) Horn. *Variations:* Kerrin, Keryn.

KERENSA (Cornish) Love. *Variations:* Karensa, Karenza, Kerenza.

KERRY (Irish) Dark haired. *Notables:* Actress Keri Russell. *Variations:* Kera, Keree, Keri, Keriana, Keriann, Kerianna, Kerianne, Kerra, Kerrey, Kerri, Kerrianne, Kerrie.

KESIA (American) Favorite. *Variations:* Kecia, Keishia, Keshia.

KETIFA (Hebrew) To pick. *Variations:* Ketipha.

KETINA (Hebrew) Girl.

KETURAH (Hebrew) Perfume. *Variations:* Ketura.

KEVINA (Irish) Handsome. Feminine version of Kevin. *Variations:* Keva, Kevia, Kevine, Kevinne, Kevonna, Kevyn.

KEWANEE (Native American) Prairie hen. *Variations:* Kewaunee.

KEZIAH (Hebrew) Cassia tree. *Variations:* Kazia, Kesiah, Ketzi, Ketziah, Kezi, Kezia, Keziah, Kissie, Kizzie, Kizzy.

KHALIDA (Arabic) Eternal. *Variations:* Khali, Khalia.

KIANA (Hawaiian) Variation of Diana. *Variations:* Kia, Kiana, Kianah, Kianna.

KIARA (American) Dark. Form of Ciara. *Variations:* Keira, Kiarra, Kiera, Kierra.

KIKI (Spanish) Short form of Enriqueta. *Variations:* Kikee.

KIKILIA (Hawaiian) Blind.

KILEY (Gaelic) Handsome. *Variations:* Kilee, Kilia, Kylee, Kylie.

KIM (English) Short form of Kimberly. *Notables:* Actress Kim Basinger. *Variations:* Kimmie, Kimmy, Kym.

top ten names of 2004

Boys	Girls
Jacob	Emily
Michael	Emma
Joshua	Madison
Matthew	Olivia
Ethan	Hannah
Andrew	Abigail
Daniel	Isabella
William	Ashley
Joseph	Samantha
Christopher	Elizabeth

KIMBERLY (English) King's meadow. *Notables:* Actresses Kim Novak and Kim Stanley; singer Lil' Kim. *Variations:* Kim, Kimba, Kimba Lee, Kimball, Kimber, Kimberlea, Kimberlee, Kimberlei, Kimberley, Kimberli, Kimberlie, Kimberlyn, Kimbley, Kimmi, Kimmie, Kymberlee.

KINSEY (English) Offspring. *Variations:* Kinsee, Kinsley.

KIOKO (Japanese) Happy child. *Variations:* Kiyoko.

KIRAN (Hindu) Light. *Variations:* Kirina.

KIRBY (English) Farm near a church. *Variations:* Kirbee, Kirbi, Kirbie.

KIRI (Hindu) Amaranth. *Variations:* Kirsi.

KIRIAH (Hebrew) Village. *Variations:* Kiria, Kirya.

KIRIMA (Eskimo) Hill.

KIRSTEN (Scandinavian) Christian. *Notables:* Actress Kirsten Dunst. *Variations:* Karsten, Keerstin, Kersten, Kerstin, Kiersten, Kierstin, Kirsta, Kirstin, Kirstine, Kirstyn, Kyrstin.

KIRSTIE (Scandinavian) Form of Kirsten. *Notables:* Actress Kirstie Alley. *Variations:* Kersti, Kerstie, Kirsti, Kirstie, Kirsty.

KISA (Russian) Kitten. *Variations:* Keesa, Kysa.

KISHANDA (American) Newly created.

KISMET (Arabic) Destiny.

KIT (Greek) Short form of Katherine. *Variations:* Kitt.

KITRA (Hebrew) Wreath.

KITTY (English) Short form of Katherine. *Notables:* Actress Kitty Carlyle. *Variations:* Kiti, Kittee, Kittey, Kitti, Kittie.

KIZZY (American) Short form of Keziah. *Variations:* Kissee, Kissie, Kizzee, Kizzi, Kizzie.

KLARA (Hungarian) Bright. Form of Clara. *Variations:* Klari, Klarice, Klarika.

KLARISSA (German) Bright. Form of Clarissa. *Variations:* Klarisa, Klarise.

KOFFI (African) Born on Friday. *Variations:* Kofi, Koffe, Koffee.

KOLINA (Scandinavian) Form of Katherine or Colleen.

KONA (Hawaiian) Female. *Variations:* Koni, Konia.

KORA (Greek) Girl. *Variations:* Cora, Corabel, Corabella, Corabelle, Corabellita, Corake, Coralyn, Corella, Corena, Coretta, Corey, Cori, Corilla, Corinna, Corinne, Corissa, Corlene, Corri, Corrin, Corrissa,

Corry, Cory, Coryn, Coryna, Corynn, Korabell, Koree, Koreen, Korella, Korenda, Korette, Korey, Kori, Korie, Korilla, Korissa, Korri, Korrie, Korrina, Korry, Kory, Korynna, Koryssa.

KORINA(English) Maiden. *Variations:* Corinna, Corinne, Korine, Korinna, Korinne, Korrina.

KRIS(Scandinavian) Short form of Kristina or Kristin.

KRISTIN(Scandinavian/German) Form of Christine. *Notables:* Actresses Kristin Davis and Kristin Chenoweth. *Variations:* Kristen, Krysten, Krystin.

KRISTINA(Greek/Scandinavian) Christian. Form of Christina. *Variations:* Krista, Kristeen, Kristeena, Kristena, Kristi, Kristie,

Kristine, Kristy, Krysine, Krysta, Krysti, Krystie, Krystina, Krysty.

KRYSTAL(American) Clear and bright. Form of Crystal. *Variations:* Kristel, Kristell, Kristelle, Kristle, Krystle.

KYLE(Scottish) Attractive. *Variations:* Kyla, Kylia.

KYLIE(Irish) Graceful. *Notables:* Singer Kylie Minogue. *Variations:* Kiley, Kye, Kyla, Kylene.

KYOKO(Japanese) Mirror.

KYRA(Greek) Lady. *Notables:* Actress Kyra Sedgwick. *Variations:* Keera, Keira, Kira, Kyrene, Kyria.

KYRIE(Irish) Dark.

LACEY(Latin) Cheer. *Notables:* Actress Lacey Chabert. *Variations:* Lace, Laci, Lacie.

LADONNA(American/Italian) The woman. *Variations:* Ladon, Ladonne, Ladonya.

LADY(English) Woman. *Variations:* Ladey, Laydie.

LAEL(Hebrew) From God.

LAILA(Hebrew/Arabic) Night. *Variations:* Lailah, Laliah, Layla.

LAINA(English) Road.

LAINE(English) Bright one. Variation of Helen. *Variations:* Lainey, Lane, Layne.

LAKEISHA(American) The favorite or the woman. Combination of prefix "La" and first names "Ayesha" or "Keisha." *Variations:* Lakecia, Lakeesha, Lakesha, Lakeshia, Laketia, Lakeysha, Lakeyshia, Lakicia, Lakiesha, Lakisha, Lakitia, Laquiesha, Laquisha, Lekeesha, Lekeisha, Lekisha.

A popular trend in girls' names is to combine the prefix "La" with a favorite name, forming a brand new name. "La" and "Donna" create "Ladonna" (or "LaDonna"), while "La" and "Yvonne" create "Lavonne." If you find a name you like, see how starting it with "La" sounds. You could be onto something!

Lachandra	Laquita
Lachelle	Lashana
Lachina	Lashay (or Lashea)
Ladawn	
Lajuana	Lashawna
Lakeisha	Lashonda
Lakendra	Latanya
Lakenya	Latavia
Lamonica	Latesha (or Latisha)
Laneisha	
Laportia	Latricia
Laqueena	Lavonna
Laquinta	Lawanda
Laquisha	

LALA (Slavic) Tulip. *Variations:* Lalah.

LALLY (English) Babbler. *Variations:* Lalley, Lalli, Lallie.

LAMIS (Arabic) Soft.

LAMYA (Arabic) Dark lips. *Variations:* Lama.

LAN (Chinese) Orchid. *Variations:* Lang.

LANA (English) Rock. Variation of Alanna. *Notables:* Actress Lana Turner. *Variations:* Lanae, Lanice, Lanna, Lannette.

LANE (English) Road. *Variations:* Laine, Lainey, Laney, Lanie, Layne, Laynie.

LANI (Hawaiian) Sky. *Variations:* Lanai, Lenai.

LANTHA (Greek) Purple flower. *Variations:* Lanthe, Lanthia, Lanthina.

LARA (Greek) Cheerful. *Notables:* Actress Lara Flynn Boyle; *Tomb Raider*'s Lara Croft. *Variations:* Laralaine, Laramae, Lari, Larina, Larinda, Larita.

LAREINA (Spanish) The queen. *Variations:* LaRayne, Lareine, Larena, Larraine.

LARISSA (Greek) Happy. *Variations:* Laresa, Laressa, Larisa, Laryssa.

LARK (English) Bird. *Variations:* Larke.

LATIFAH (Arabic) Kind. *Notables:* Actress/singer Queen Latifah. *Variations:* Lateefa, Lateefah, Latifa.

LATONA (Latin) Powerful goddess. *Variations:* Latonna.

LATOYA (American) Newly created. *Notables:* Singer LaToya Jackson. *Variations:* Latoia, Latoyia, Latoyla.

LAUDOMIA (Italian) Praise the house.

LAUFEIA (Scandinavian) Leafy island. *Variations:* Laufey.

LAURA (Latin) Laurel. *Notables:* Media psychologist Dr. Laura Schlessinger; actresses Laura Linney and Laura Dern. *Variations:* Larette, Laure, Laureana, Laurena, Lauret, Laureta, Lauretta, Laurette, Lora, Loret, Loreta, Loretta, Lorette, Lorin, Lorita.

LAUREL (Latin) Laurel tree. *Variations:* Laural, Laurell, Laurelle, Lorel, Lorrell, Lorella.

LAUREN (English) Feminine form of Laurence. *Notables:* Actress Lauren Bacall; model Lauren Hutton. *Variations:* Laurin, Lauryn, Loren, Lorena, Lorrin, Loryn.

LAURIE (English) Form of Lauren and Laura. *Notables:* Singer Laurie Anderson. *Variations:* Laure, Lauri, Laury, Lori, Lorie, Lorrie, Lorry, Lory.

LAVEDA (Latin) Pure. *Variations:* Lavetta.

LAVENDER (English) Lavender flower.

LAVERNE (French) Springlike. *Notables:* Laverne DeFazio, character on classic TV show *Laverne and Shirley*. *Variations:* Lavern, Laverna, Lavyrn, Lavyrne, Verna.

LAVINIA (Latin) Roman woman. *Variations:* Lavena, Lavenia, Lavina, Laviner, Lavinie, Levina, Levinia, Livinia, Lovina.

LAYLA (Hebrew/Arabic) Night. *Variations:* Laela, Laila, Lala, Leila.

LEAH (Hebrew) Weary. *Notables:* Actress Leah Remini; *Star Wars's* Princess Leia. *Variations:* Lea, Leia, Leigha, Lia, Liah.

LEALA (French) Loyal. *Variations:* Lealia, Lealie, Leola.

LEANDRA (English) Lioness. *Variations:* Leanda, Leodora, Leoine, Leoline, Leona, Leonanie, Leonelle, Leonette, Leonice, Leonissa.

LEANNA (English) Flowering vine. *Notables:* Singer LeAnn Rimes. *Variations:* Leana, Leane, Leann, Leanne, Lee Ann, Lee Anne, Leeann, Leeanne, Leianna, Leigh Ann, Leighann, Leighanne, Liana, Liane, Lianne.

LECIA (Latin) Short for Alicia, Felicia, or Letitia. *Variations:* Lecy, Lisha, Lishia.

LEDA (Greek) Woman. *Variations:* Leida, Lida.

LEE (English) Meadow. *Notables:* Actresses Lee Grant and Lee Remick. *Variations:* Lea, Leigh.

LEIGH (English) Meadow. *Variations:* Lea, Lee.

LEIKO (Japanese) Proud.

LEILA (Arabic) Night. *Variations:* Laila, Layla, Leela, Leelah, Leilah, Leilia, Lela, Lelah, Lelia, Leyla, Lila, Lilah.

LEILANI (Hawaiian) Heavenly child.

LELIA (Greek) Well spoken. *Variations:* Leliah, Lellia.

LEMUELA (Hebrew) Devoted to God. Feminine version of Lemuel. *Variations:* Lemuella.

LENA (English) Bright one. Variation of Helen. *Notables:* Singer Lena Horne; actress Lena Olin. *Variations:* Leena, Lenah, Lene, Leni, Lenia, Lina, Linah, Line.

LENIS (Latin) Smooth, silky. *Variations:* Lenice, Lennice. Lennis.

LENKA (Czech) Light.

LENNA (German) The strength of a lion. *Variations:* Lenda, Lennah.

LENORE (Greek) Light. Form of Eleanor.

LEONA (Latin) Lion. Feminine version of Leon. *Notables:* Hotel owner Leona Helmsley. *Variations:* Leonia, Leonie, Leonine, Leonissa, Leontyne, Liona.

LEONARDA (German) Brave lion. *Variations:* Lenda, Leonarde.

LEONIE (French) Lioness. *Variations:* Leona, Leonda, Leondra, Leondrea, Leonela.

LEONORA (English) Bright one. Variation of Helen. *Variations:* Leanor, Leanora, Lenor, Lenora, Lenorah, Lenore, Leonara, Leonore.

LESLIE (Scottish) Gray castle. *Notables:* Actresses Leslie Caron and Lesley Ann Warren. *Variations:* Leslea, Leslee, Lesley, Lesli, Lesly, Lezlee, Lezley, Lezli, Lezlie.

LETA (Latin) Happy. *Variations:* Lida, Lita.

LETICIA (Latin/Spanish) Happiness. *Notables:* Social arbiter Letitia Baldrige. *Variations:* Letecia, Letisha, Letitia, Lettice.

LETTY (English) Short form of Letitia. *Variations:* Letti, Lettie.

LEVANA (Hebrew) White moon. *Variations:* Lewana, Livana.

LEVINA (Latin) Streak of lightning.

LEXA (English) Protector of man. Short form of Alexandra or Alexis. *Variations:* Lexi, Lexia, Lexie, Lexina, Lexine, Lexy.

LIAN (Chinese) Graceful tree.

LIANA (French) Twist like a vine. *Variations:* Li, Lia, Lian, Liane, Liann, Lianna, Lianne.

LIAT (Hebrew) You belong to me.

LIBBY (English) Short form of Elizabeth. *Variations:* Libbey, Libbi, Libbie.

LIBENA (Czech) Love. *Variations:* Liba, Libenka, Libuse, Libuska, Luba.

LIBERTY (English) Freedom.

LIDA (Greek) Woman.

LIDIA (Greek) Form of Lydia. *Variations:* Lidea, Lidiya, Lidya.

LIDDY (English) Nickname for Lydia. *Variations:* Liddi, Liddie.

LIESL (German) Nickname for Elizabeth. *Variations:* Leizl, Liesa, Liese, Liesel, Liezel, Lisel, Lisl, Lisle.

LILA (Hindu) Dance of God. *Variations:* Lilah, Lilia, Lyla.

LILAC (English) Flower.

LILITH (Arabic) Of the night. *Variations:* Lillis, Lillith.

LILLIAN (English) Flower. Combination of Lily and Ann. *Notables:* Writer Lillian Hellman. *Variations:* Lileana, Lilian, Liliana, Lilias, Lilika, Lillia, Lillianne, Lillyan, Lillyanna, Lilyan.

LILY (Latin) Flower. *Variations:* Lili, Lilia, Lilie, Lilli, Lillie, Lillye, Lilye.

LINA (Greek) Light. *Variations:* Lena, Linah.

LINDA (Spanish) Pretty one. *Notables:* Singer Linda Ronstadt; actress Lynda Carter. *Variations:* Lin, Linday, Linde, Lindee, Lindi, Lindie, Lindy, Linn, Lyn, Lynada, Lynadie, Lynda, Lynde, Lyndy, Lynn, Lynnda.

LINDSAY (English) Island of linden trees. *Notables:* Actresses Lindsay Lohan and Lindsay Wagner. *Variations:* Lindsaye, Lindsey, Lindsi, Lindsie, Lindsy, Linsay, Linsey, Linzey, Lyndsay, Lyndsey, Lynsay, Lynsey.

LINETTE (Welsh) Idol. *Variations:* Lanette, Linet, Linetta, Linnet, Linnetta, Linnette, Lynetta, Lynette, Lynnet, Lynnette.

LING (Chinese) Delicate.

LINNEA (Scandinavian) Lime tree. *Variations:* Linae, Linia, Linnia.

LIORA (Hebrew) Light. *Variations:* Leora, Lior.

LISA (English) Pledged by oath to God. Version of Elizabeth. *Notables:* Actress Lisa Kudrow. *Variations:* Leesa, Leeza, Leisa, Liesa, Liese, Lisanne, Lise, Liseta, Lisetta, Lisette, Lissa, Lissette, Liza, Lizana, Lizanne, Lizette.

LISBETH (Hebrew) Form of Elizabeth. *Variations:* Lisbet, Lizbet, Lizbeth.

LISETTE (French) Short form of Elizabeth. *Variations:* Lisett, Lissette, Lysette.

LISSA (Greek) Bee. Short form of Melissa. *Variations:* Lyssa.

LIV (Scandinavian) Life. *Notables:* Actresses Liv Tyler and Liv Ullmann.

LIVIA (Latin) Form of Olivia. *Variations:* Liviya, Livya.

LIZ (English) Short form of Elizabeth. *Variations:* Lizzi, Lizzie, Lizzy.

LIZA (English) Short form of Elizabeth. *Notables:* Singer Liza Minnelli.

LOIS (English) Famous soldier. Feminine version of Louis. *Notables:* Superman's love, Lois Lane.

LOLA (Spanish) Sorrow. Nickname for Dolores. *Variations:* Loleta, Loletta, Lolita.

LOLLY (English) Lollipop. *Variations:* Lolli, Lollie.

LONI (English) Ready for battle. Feminine version of Lonnie. *Notables:* Actress Loni Anderson. *Variations:* Lona, Lonee, Lonie, Lonna, Lonni, Lonnie.

LORELEI (German) Rocky cliff on the Rhine River. *Variations:* Loralee, Loralie, Loralyn, Lorilee, Lura, Lurette, Lurleen, Lurline.

LORELLE (American) Form of Laurel.

LORENA (English) Form of Lauren. *Variations:* Loreen.

LORENZA (Italian) Feminine form of Lorenzo.

LORETTA (English) Laurel. *Notables:* Country singer Loretta Lynn. *Variations:* Lauretta.

LORI (English) Variation of Laurie. *Notables:* Actress Lori Loughlin. *Variations:* Lorie.

LORINDA (Spanish) Form of Linda. *Variations:* Larenda, Larinda, Lorenda.

LORNA (Scottish) Area in Scotland. *Notables:* Singer Lorna Luft; literary character Lorna Doone. *Variations:* Lorrna.

LORRAINE (French) From Lorraine, an area in France. *Notables:* Actress Lorraine Bracco; comedian Laraine Newman. *Variations:* Laraine, Lauraine, Laurraine, Lorain, Loraine, Lorayne, Lorine, Lorrayne.

LOTTA (Scandinavian) Woman. *Variations:* Lotte.

LOTTIE (German) Short form of Charlotte. *Variations:* Lotie, Lotte, Lottey, Lotti, Lotty.

LOTUS (Greek) Lotus flower.

LOU (English) Short form of Louise.

LOUISE (French) Warrior. Feminine form of Louis. *Notables:* Writer Louise Erdrich. *Variations:* Louisa, Louisette, Louisiane, Luisa, Luise.

LOURDES (French) From Lourdes, France.

LOVE (English) Love. *Variations:* Lovey, Lovi, Lovie.

LUANN (English) Combination of Lou and Ann. *Variations:* Louann, Louanne, Luanna, Luanne.

LUBA (Russian) Love. *Variations:* Lubna, Lubov, Lyuba.

LUCASTA (Latin) From Lucania, feminine form of Lucas; (English) Name from English poem.

LUCIA (Italian) Form of Lucille. *Variations:* Luciana.

LUCIENNE (French) Light. *Variations:* Lucianne.

LUCILLE (French) Light. *Notables:* Comedy legend Lucille Ball. *Variations:* Loucille, Lucilla.

LUCINDA (Latin) Beautiful light. *Notables:* Singer Lucinda Williams.

LUCKY (English) Fortunate. *Variations:* Luckie, Luckye.

LUCRETIA (Latin) Roman clan name. *Notables:* Lucretia Borgia, Duchess of Ferrara. *Variations:* Lacrecia, Lacretia, Lucrece, Lucrecia, Lucreecia, Lucrezia.

LUCY (English) Light. Short form of Lucille. Feminine version of Lucius. *Notables:* Actresses Lucy Liu and Lucy Lawless. *Variations:* Lucetta, Lucette, Lucia, Luciana, Lucie, Lucienne, Lucilla, Lucille, Lucina, Lucinda, Lucita.

LUDMILA (Czech) Loving people. *Variations:* Lidka, Lidmila, Lidunka, Liduse, Liduska, Ludmilla, Luduna, Lyudmila.

hindu names

Boys	Girls
Aditya	Aditi
Arjun	Chandi
Arnav	Devi
Dalal	Garesa
Hardeep	Maya
Nikhil	Natesa
Pranav	Shreya
Rahul	Sita
Rishi	Tara
Samir	Veda

LUELLA (English) Combined form of first names "Lou" and "Ella." *Variations:* Louella, Louelle, Luelle.

LUISA (Spanish) Form of Louisa.

LULU (German) Short form of Louise. *Notables:* British singer Lulu. *Variations:* LouLou.

LUNA (Latin) Roman moon goddess. *Variations:* Lunetta, Lunette, Lunneta.

LUPE (Spanish) Short form of Guadalupe. *Variations:* Lupi, Lupita.

LURLEEN (German) Temptress. *Variations:* Lura, Lurlene, Lurlie, Lurline.

LUZ (Spanish) Light.

LYDIA (Greek) Woman from Lydia, a region in ancient Greece. *Variations:* Lidi, Lidia, Lidie, Lidka, Likochka, Lydiah, Lydie.

LYNETTE (French) Form of Linette.

LYNN (English) Pretty. Diminutive of Linda. (Welsh) Lake. *Notables:* Actress Lynn Redgrave. *Variations:* Lin, Lina, Linell, Linelle, Linn, Linne, Lyn, Lyndall, Lyndel, Lyndell, Lyndelle, Lynelie, Lynell, Lynna, Lynne, Lynnelle.

LYRIC (Greek) Songlike.

LYRIS (Greek) Lyre; small harp. *Variations:* Lyra.

LYSANDRA (Greek) Variation of Alexandra.

LYSISTRATA (Greek) Loosen the army.

MAB (Irish) Joy. *Notables:* Queen Mab, the legendary Irish fairy queen.

MABEL (English) Lovable. *Variations:* Mabelle, Mable, Maybel, Maybell, Maybelle.

MACARIA (Spanish) Blessed. *Variations:* Macarea, Macarie.

MACKENNA (Irish) Child of the handsome one.

MACKENZIE (Irish) Child of a handsome leader. *Notables:* Actress Mackenzie Phillips.

Variations: Mac, MacKenzie, Mackenze, Mackenzi, McKenzie, Mckenzie.

MACY (English) Matthew's estate; (French) Weapon. *Notables:* Singer Macy Gray.

MADELINE (French) From Magdalen. *Notables:* Actress Madeline Kahn; U.S. Secretary of State Madeleine Albright. *Variations:* Mada, Madalena, Maddalena, Madalyn, Madelaine, Madelayne, Madeleine, Madelena, Madelene, Madelina, Madelyn, Madge, Madilin, Madiline, Madilyn, Madolyn, Magda.

MADIA (Arabic) To praise. *Variations:* Madiha, Madihah.

MADDIE (English) Short form of Madeline. *Variations:* Maddi, Maddy.

MADGE (Greek) Short form of Margaret or Madeline. *Variations:* Madgie.

MADISON (English) Child of Maud. *Variations:* Maddison, Madisen, Madisson, Madyson.

MADONNA (Latin) My lady. *Notables:* Singer Madonna.

MAE (English) Variation of May. *Notables:* Actress Mae West.

MAEVE (Irish) Intoxicating. *Notables:* Writer Maeve Binchy. *Variations:* Maive, Mave, Mayve.

MAGDA (Russian/Slavic) Form of Magdalen.

MAGDALEN (Greek) From Magdala, area in the Middle East. *Variations:* Magdala, Magdaleen, Magdalena, Magdalene, Magdaline, Magdalyn, Magdelen.

MAGENA (Native American) New moon.

MAGGIE (English) Short for Magdalen or Margaret. *Notables:* Actresses Maggie Smith and Maggie Gyllenhaal. *Variations:* Magi, Maggi, Maggy.

MAGNOLIA (Latin) Flowering tree.

MAHALA (Hebrew) Tenderness. *Notables:* Singer Mahalia Jackson. *Variations:* Mahalah, Mahalia, Mahaliah, Mahalla, Mahelia, Mehalia.

MAHOGANY (Spanish) Rich; strong.

la, de, da . . .

The African-American community has cleverly spawned a creative trend in baby naming. By adding or combining "La," "Da," "De," "Ja," and "Ke" to the beginning of a classic name, the name becomes modern and unique: Dajuan, Dewayne, Latanya, Jalinda, Keshawn. Makes a fun alternative to Datom, Jadick, and Keharry.

MAIA (Greek) Mother. *Variations:* Maiya, Maya, Mya.

MAIDA (English) Maiden. *Variations:* Maidie, Mayda.

MAIRE (Irish) Form of Mary. *Variations:* Mair, Maira, Mairin.

MAISIE (Scottish) Pearl. Short form of Margaret. *Variations:* Maisey, Maisy, Maizie.

MALI (Thai) Flower.

MALKAH (Hebrew) Queen. *Variations:* Malcah, Malka, Malkia, Malkiah, Malkie, Malkit, Malkiya.

MALKIN (German) Battle maiden.

MALLORY (French) Unfortunate. *Notables:* Mallory Keaton, character on TV's *Family Ties*. *Variations:* Malloreigh, Mallorey, Mallorie, Malorey, Malori, Malorie, Malory.

seafaring names

For those who love to sail, fish, swim, or just enjoy the ocean, these names are defined as "from the sea," "friend of the sea," or "protector of the sea."

Boys	Girls
Colbert	Chelsea
Dylan	Dylana
Hurley	Marielle
Irving	Marina
Mervin	Marissa
Morgan	Meredith
Murdoch	Meryl
Murphy	Nerida
Murray	Nerissa
Seabert	Ondine
Seward	Pacifica
Zane	Thalassa

MALVA (English) Form of Melba. *Variations:* Melva.

MALVINA (Scottish) Feminine form of Melvin. *Variations:* Malvi.

MAMIE (English) Form of Margaret. *Notables:* U.S. first lady Mamie Eisenhower; actress Mamie Van Doren. *Variations:* Mame, Mamee.

MANDA (Latin) Short form of Amanda.

MANDY (English) Lovable. Short form of Amanda. *Notables:* Singer Mandy Moore. *Variations:* Mandee, Mandey, Mandi, Mandie.

MANETTE (French) Defiant.

MANGENA (Hebrew) Song. *Variations:* Mangina.

MANON (French) Bitterness. Form of Marie.

MANSI (Native American) Picked flower. *Variations:* Mancey, Manci, Mancie, Mancy, Mansey, Mansie, Mansy.

MANUELA (Spanish) God is among us. Feminine version of Emanuel. *Variations:* Manuelita.

MANYA (Russian) Form of Maria.

MARA (Hebrew) Bitter. *Variations:* Marah.

MARABEL (English) Beautiful sea. *Variations:* Marabelle, Marable, Marbella.

MARCELLA (Latin) Warlike. *Variations:* Marcela, Marcelle.

MARCIA (Latin) Warlike. Feminine version of Mark. *Notables:* Actress Marcia Cross;

lawyer Marcia Clark. *Variations:* Marce, Marcee, Marcela, Marcelia, Marcella, Marcelle, Marcena, Marcene, Marcey, Marci, Marcie, Marcina, Marcy, Marsha.

MARCY (English) Short form of Marcia or Marcella. *Variations:* Marcee, Marcey, Marci.

MARELLA (English) Combination of Mary and Elle. *Variations:* Marelle.

MAREN (Latin) Sea. *Variations:* Marin, Marren, Marrin.

MARETTA (English) Defiant. *Variations:* Marette.

MARGARET (English) Pearl. *Notables:* Former British Prime Minister Margaret Thatcher; actress Margaret Hamilton. *Variations:* Greeta, Greetje, Grere, Gret, Greta, Gretal, Gretchen, Gretel, Grethal, Gretje, Gretl, Gretta, Groer, Maggi, Maggie, Maggy, Mair, Maire, Mairi, Mairona, Margara, Margareta, Margarethe, Margarett, Margaretta, Margarette, Margarita, Margarite, Marge, Margeret, Margerey, Margery, Margrett, Marguerette, Marguerite, Marjorie, Meagan, Meaghan, Meaghen, Meg, Megan, Megen, Meggi, Meggie, Meggy, Meghan, Meghann, Peg, Pegeen, Pegg, Peggey, Peggi, Peggie, Peggy, Reet, Reeta, Reita, Rieta, Ritta.

MARGARITA (Spanish/Italian) Form of Margaret.

MARGE (English) Short form of Margaret or Marjorie. *Notables:* Actress Marg Helgenberger; TV cartoon mom Marge Simpson. *Variations:* Marg.

MARGIE (English) Short form of Margaret or Marjorie. *Variations:* Margi, Margy, Marjie, Marjy.

MARGO (French) Form of Margaret. *Notables:* Actresses Margo Kidder and Margaux Hemingway. *Variations:* Margaux, Margot.

MARIA (Latin/Italian/Spanish) Form of Mary. *Notables:* Tennis pro Maria Sharapova; opera singer Maria Callas. *Variations:* Marea, Mariah, Marie, Marya.

MARIAH (Hebrew) Form of Mary. *Notables:* Singer Mariah Carey. *Variations:* Moriah.

MARIAN (French) Combination of first names "Mary" and "Ann." *Notables:* Singer Marian Anderson. *Variations:* Mariana, Mariane, Mariann, Marianna, Marianne, Marion, Marrian, Marrion, Mary Ann, Maryann, Maryanna, Maryon, Maryonn.

MARIE (French) Variation of Mary. *Notables:* Scientist Marie Curie; former queen of France Marie Antoinette. *Variations:* Maree.

MARIEL (Dutch) Form of Mary. *Notables:* Actress Mariel Hemingway. *Variations:* Mariella, Marielle.

MARIETTA (French) Form of Mary. *Notables:* Actress Mariette Hartley. *Variations:* Mariette.

MARIGOLD (English) Flower.

MARILYN (English) Combination of first names "Mary" and "Lynn." *Notables:* Actress Marilyn Monroe. *Variations:* Maralin, Maralynn, Marelyn, Marilee, Marilin, Marilynne, Marralynn, Marrilin, Marrilyn, Marylin, Marylyn.

MARINA (Latin) From the sea. *Variations:* Marena, Marinda, Marine, Marinna, Marna.

MARION (French) Form of Marian or Mary. *Notables:* Actress Marion Ross.

MARIS (Latin) Star of the sea. *Variations:* Marieca, Marisa, Marise, Marish, Marisha, Marissa, Marisse, Meris, Merisa, Merissa.

MARISOL (Spanish) Sunny sea.

MARISSA (Latin) Of the sea. *Notables:* Actress Marisa Tomei. *Variations:* Marisa.

MARIT (Scandinavian) Form of Margaret.

MARITA (Spanish) Form of Mary.

MARITZA (Arabic) Blessed.

MARJORIE (Greek) Form of Margaret. *Notables:* Literary heroine Marjorie Morningstar. *Variations:* Margery, Marjery, Marjori, Marjory.

MARKIE (Latin) Warlike. Feminine form of Mark. *Notables:* Actress Markie Post. *Variations:* Marki, Marky.

MARLA (English) Short form of Marlene. *Notables:* Actresses Marla Gibbs and Marla Maples. *Variations:* Marlee, Marley, Marlo, Marly.

MARLENE (English) Combined form of first and last names "Mary Magdalene." *Notables:* Actress Marlene Dietrich. *Variations:* Marla, Marlaina, Marlaine, Marlana, Marlane, Marlayne, Marlea, Marlee, Marleen, Marleina, Marlena, Marley, Marlie, Marlina, Marlinda, Marline, Marlyn.

MARLO (English) Form of Mary or Marlene. *Notables:* Actress Marlo Thomas. *Variations:* Marlow, Marlowe.

MARNI (Hebrew) To rejoice. *Variations:* Marna, Marne, Marney, Marnia, Marnie, Marnina, Merina.

MARONA (Hebrew) Flock of sheep.

MARQUITA (Spanish) Ruler. *Variations:* Marqueda, Marquisa.

MARSHA (Latin) Warlike. Form of Marcia. *Notables:* Comedian Marsha Warfield.

MARTA (Spanish/Italian/Portuguese) Form of Martha.

MARTHA (Aramaic) Lady. *Notables:* Domestic diva Martha Stewart. *Variations:* Marcia, Marit, Marite, Marlet, Mart, Marta, Martell, Marth, Marthe, Marthena, Marti, Martie, Martina, Martita, Martus, Martuska, Marty, Martyne, Martynne, Masia, Matti, Mattie.

MARTI (English) Short form of Martha or Martina. *Variations:* Martie, Marty.

MARTINA (Latin) Warlike. Feminine version of Martin. *Notables:* Tennis pro Martina

Navratilova; singer Martina McBride. *Variations:* Martine.

MARVA (English) Famous friend. Feminine version of Marvin.

MARVEL (French) Marvel. *Variations:* Marva, Marvela, Marvele, Marvella, Marvelle.

MATTHEA (Hebrew) Gift from God. Feminine version of Matthew. *Variations:* Mathea, Mathia, Mattea, Matthia, Mattia.

MARY (Hebrew) Bitterness. *Notables:* Singer Mary J. Blige; actress Mary Tyler Moore. *Variations:* Maree, Marella, Marelle, Mari, Marial, Marieke, Mariel, Mariela, Mariele, Mariella, Marielle, Marika, Marike, Maryk, Maura, Moira, Moll, Mollee, Molley, Molli, Mollie, Molly, Mora, Moria, Moyra.

MASHA (Russian) Form of Mary.

MATILDA (German) Maiden in battle. *Variations:* Maddi, Maddie, Maddy, Mat, Matelda, Mathilda, Mathilde, Matilde, Mattie, Matty, Matusha, Matylda, Maud, Maude, Tila, Tilda, Tildie, Tildy, Tilley, Tilli, Tillie, Tilly, Tylda.

MAUD (English) Short form of Madeline or Matilda. *Notables:* Actress/model Maud Adams. *Variations:* Maude.

MAURA (Irish) Form of Mary. *Notables:* Actress Maura Tierney. *Variations:* Moira.

MAUREEN (Irish) Variation of Mary. *Notables:* Actresses Maureen O'Sullivan, Maureen

popular names in spain

Boys	Girls
Alejandro	Lucia
Daniel	Maria
Pablo	Paula
David	Laura
Javier	Marta
Adrian	Andrea
Alvaro	Alba
Sergio	Sara
Carlos	Claudia
Hugo	Ana

O'Hara, and Maureen McCormick. *Variations:* Maurene, Maurine, Moreen, Moureen.

MAUVE (French) Mallow plant.

MAVIS (French) Thrush. *Variations:* Mayvis.

MAXINE (English) Greatest in excellence. *Notables:* Singer Maxine Nightingale. Feminine version of Maximilian. *Variations:* Maxene, Maxi, Maxie, Maxima, Maximina, Maxina.

MAY (English) Calendar month. *Variations:* Mae, Mai, Mayleen, Maylene.

MAYA (Hindu) Illusion. *Notables:* Writer Maya Angelou. *Variations:* Maia, Mya.

MAYBELLINE (Latin) Form of Mabel. *Variations:* Maybeline.

MAYIM (Hebrew) Water. *Notables:* Actress Mayim Bialik.

MAYSA (Arabic) Walk proudly. *Variations:* Maisah.

MEAD (Greek) Wine of honey. *Variations:* Meade, Meede.

MEDEA (Greek) Ruling.

MEDINA (Arabic) City in Saudi Arabia.

MEDORA (English) Gift from mother.

MEG (English) Short form of Margaret or Megan. *Notables:* Actress Meg Ryan.

MEGAN (Irish) Form of Margaret. *Notables:* Actress Megan Mullaly. *Variations:* Magan, Magen, Maygen, Meagan, Meaghan, Megane, Megann, Megen, Meggen, Meghan.

MEGGIE (English) Familiar form of Margaret or Megan. *Variations:* Meggi, Meggy.

MEHITABEL (Hebrew) Benefited by God. *Variations:* Mehetabel.

MEIYING (Chinese) Beautiful flower.

MEL (English) Short form of Melanie or Melody.

MELANIE (Greek) Dark-skinned. *Notables:* Actress Melanie Griffith. *Variations:* Mel, Mela, Melaine, Melana, Melane, Melani, Melaniya, Melanka, Melany, Melanya, Melashka, Melasya, Melenia, Melka, Mellanie, Mellie, Melloney, Mellony, Melly, Meloni, Melonie, Melony, Milena, Milya.

MELBA (English) From Melbourne, Australia. *Notables:* Singer Melba Moore. *Variations:* Mellba, Mellva, Melva.

MELINA (Greek) Honey. Actress Melina Kanakaredes.

MELINDA (Greek) Honey. *Variations:* Malina, Malinda, Malinde, Mallie, Mally, Mel, Meleana, Melina, Melinde, Meline, Mellinda, Melynda, Mindi, Mindie, Mindy.

MELIORA (Latin) Better. *Variations:* Melora.

MELISANDE (French) Form of Melissa or Millicent. *Variations:* Melasandre, Mellisande.

MELISSA (Greek) Bee. *Notables:* Singer Melissa Etheridge; actress Melissa Joan Hart. *Variations:* Melisa, Melisande, Melisandra, Melisandre, Melissande, Melissandre, Melisse, Mellisa, Mellissa.

MELODY (Greek) Song. *Variations:* Melodee, Melodey, Melodia, Melodice, Melodie.

MELVINA (Irish) Great chief. Feminine form of Melvin. *Variations:* Malva, Malvina, Melva, Melvena, Melvine.

MENA (Dutch) Strength. *Notables:* Actress Mena Suvari. *Variations:* Menna.

MENIA (Scandinavian) Ancient mythological figure. *Variations:* Menja.

MERCEDES (Spanish) Mercy. *Notables:* Actress Mercedes Ruehl. *Variations:* Merced, Mercedez.

MERCIA (English) Ancient British kingdom.

MERCY (English) Merciful. *Variations:* Mercey, Merci, Mercia, Mercie, Mersey.

MEREDITH (Welsh) Great leader. *Notables:* TV host Meredith Viera; actress Meredith Baxter Birney. *Variations:* Meredithe, Merideth, Meridith, Merridith.

MERI (Scandinavian) Ocean. *Variations:* Meriata.

MERIEL (Irish) Brilliant seas. *Variations:* Merial, Meriol, Merrill.

MERLE (French) Blackbird. *Notables:* Actress Merle Oberon. *Variations:* Merl, Merla, Merlin, Merlina, Merline, Merlyn.

MERRY (English) Happy. *Variations:* Meri, Merri, Merrie, Merrilee, Merrily.

MERYL (English) Bright as the sea. *Notables:* Actress Meryl Streep. *Variations:* Merill, Merrall, Merrel, Merrell, Merrill, Meryle, Meryll.

MESSINA (Latin) Middle.

MIA (Italian) Mine. *Notables:* Actress Mia Farrow.

MICHAELA (Hebrew) Who is like God? Feminine version of Michael. *Variations:* Makaela, Micaela, Mical, Micala, Michael, Michaella, Michal, Michala, Mickaula, Mikaela, Mikayla, Mikella, Mikelle, Mychaela.

MICHELLE (French) Who is like God? *Notables:* Singer Michelle Branch; actress Michelle Pfeiffer. *Variations:* Michele, Mishell, Mishelle.

MICKI (American) Short form of Michaela or Michelle. *Variations:* Mickee, Mickey, Micky, Miki, Mikki.

MIDGE (English) Form of Margaret.

MIDORI (Japanese) Green.

MIGNON (French) Petite. *Variations:* Mignonette, Minyon.

MILA (Slavic) Loved by the people. *Notables*: Actresses Milla Jovovich and Mila Kunis. *Variations*: Milla.

MILADA (Czech) My love. *Variations*: Mila.

MILAGROS (Spanish) Miracle. *Variations*: Milagro, Milagrosa.

MILANA (Italian) From Milan, Italy.

MILDRED (English) Tender strength. *Variations*: Mildrid.

MILENA (Czech) Grace. *Variations*: Milada, Miladena, Miladka, Milana, Milanka, Milenka, Milka, Miluse, Miluska, Mlada, Mladena, Mladka, Mladuska.

MILETA (German) Generous.

MILLICENT (German) Born to power. *Variations*: Melicent, Meliscent, Mellicent, Milicent, Milley, Milli.

MILLIE (English) Short form of Millicent. *Variations*: Mili, Mille, Millee, Milly.

MIMI (French) Form of Miriam or Marie. *Notables*: Actress Mimi Rogers. *Variations*: Mim, Mimsie.

MINA (German) Protector. Short form of Wilhelmena. *Variations*: Mena, Minah.

MINDY (English) Short form of Melinda. *Notables*: Country singer Mindy McCready. *Variations*: Mindee, Mindi, Mindie.

MINERVA (Latin) Wise. The Roman goddess of wisdom,

MINETTA (English) Feminine nickname of William; (French) Faithful defender. *Variations*: Minette, Minna.

MING (Chinese) Tomorrow; shiny.

MINNA (German) Short form of Wilhelmina.

MINNIE (English) Short form of Minerva or Wilhelmina. *Notables*: Actress Minnie Driver. *Variations*: Mini, Minni, Minny.

MIRA (Spanish) To gaze. *Notables*: Actress Mira Sorvino.

MIRABEL (Latin) Wonderful. *Variations*: Mirabell, Mirabella, Mirabelle.

MIRACLE (Latin) Marvel.

MIRANDA (Latin) Admirable. *Notables*: Actress Miranda Richardson. *Variations*: Maranda, Meranda, Mira, Myranda, Randa, Randee, Randene, Randey, Randi, Randie, Randy.

MIREILLE (French) To admire. *Variations*: Mirela, Mirella, Mirelle.

MIRENA (Hawaiian) Beloved. *Variations*: Milena.

MIRIAM (Hebrew) Bitterness. *Variations*: Mariam, Merian, Miri, Miriama, Miriem, Mirriam, Mirrian, Miryam, Myriam.

MISHA (Russian) Form of Michaela. *Notables*: Actress Mischa Barton. *Variations*: Mischa.

MISSY (English) Short form of Melissa. *Notables:* Singer Missy Elliot. *Variations:* Missee, Missey, Missi, Missie.

MISTY (English) In a mist. *Variations:* Mistee, Misti, Mistie, Mysti, Mysty.

MITZI (German) Form of Mary. *Notables:* Actress Mitzi Gaynor. *Variations:* Mitzee, Mitzie, Mitzy.

MO (English) Short form of Maureen.

MODESTY (Latin) Modesty. *Variations:* Modesta, Modestia, Modestina, Modestine.

MOESHA (African-American) Drawn from water. *Variations:* Moeshia.

MOIRA (Irish) Pure. *Variations:* Moirah, Moire, Moirin.

MOLLY (English) Form of Mary. *Notables:* Actress Molly Ringwald. *Variations:* Molli, Mollie.

MONA (Irish) Noble. *Notables:* DaVinci subject Mona Lisa. *Variations:* Mony.

MONDAY (English) Day of the week.

MONICA (Latin) Adviser or nun; (Greek) Solitary. *Notables:* White House intern Monica Lewinsky. *Variations:* Monika, Monique.

MONIQUE (French) Form of Monica.

MONTANA (Spanish) Mountain. *Variations:* Montanna.

MORELA (Polish) Apricot.

MORGAN (Welsh) Great and bright. *Notables:* Actress Morgan Fairchild. *Variations:* Morgana, Morganna, Morganne, Morgen.

MORWENNA (Welsh) Maiden. *Variations:* Morwen, Morwynna.

MURIEL (Irish) Bright as the sea. *Notables:* Writer Muriel Spark. *Variations:* Muirgheal, Murial, Muriell, Murielle.

MURPHY (Irish) Sea warrior.

MYRA (Latin) Scented oil. Feminine version of Myron. *Variations:* Murah, Myria, Myriah.

MYRNA (Irish) Beloved. *Notables:* Actress Myrna Loy. *Variations:* Merna, Mirna, Muirna.

MYRTLE (English) Plant. *Variations:* Myrta, Myrtilla.

MYSTIQUE (French) Mysterious. *Variations:* Mistique, Misty, Mystica.

NABILA (Arabic) Highborn. *Variations:* Nabeela, Nabilah.

NADETTE (German) Brave bear; (French) Form of Bernadette.

NADIA (Russian) Hope. *Notables:* Gymnast Nadia Comaneci. *Variations:* Nada, Nadene, Nadina, Nadine, Nadiya, Nadja, Nadya, Natka.

NADINE (French) Form of Nadia. *Variations:* Nadeen, Nadene, Nadyne.

NADIRA (Arabic) Precious.

NAIDA (Greek) Water nymph. *Variations:* Naiad, Nayad, Nyad.

NAILAH (Arabic) One who succeeds. *Variations:* Naila.

NAIMA (Arabic) Content. *Variations:* Naeemah, Naimah.

NAIRI (Armenian) Land of rivers. *Variations:* Nyree.

NALANI (Hawaiian) Heavenly calm.

NAN (English) Grace. Variation of Ann; short form of Nancy or Nanette.

NANALA (Hawaiian) Sunflower.

NANCY (Hebrew) Grace. *Notables:* U.S. first lady Nancy Reagan; fictional detective Nancy Drew; Olympic skater Nancy Kerrigan. *Variations:* Nan, Nana, Nance, Nancee, Nancey, Nanci, Nancie, Nancsi, Nanette, Nann, Nanna, Nanncey, Nanncy, Nanni, Nannie, Nanny, Nanscey, Nansee, Nansey.

NANDANA (Hindu) Happiness. *Variations:* Nandini, Nandita.

NANETTE (French) Form of Nancy. *Notables:* Actress Nanette Fabray.

NANISE (Polynesian) Gracious.

NAOMI (Hebrew) Pleasant. *Notables:* Country singer Naomi Judd; actress Naomi Watts; supermodel Naomi Campbell. *Variations:* Naoma, Naomia, Naomie, Neoma, Noami, Noemi, Noemie, Nyomi.

NARA (Japanese) Oak tree.

NARCISSA (Greek) Daffodil. *Variations:* Narcisa, Narcisse, Narkissa.

NARDA (Latin) Scented lotion.

NARELLE (English) Woman from the sea.

NARESHA (Hindu) Leader.

NASIRA (Arabic) To help.

NASRIN (Arabic) Rose. *Variations:* Nasreen.

NASTASIA (Russian) Resurrection. Form of Anastasia. *Notables:* Actress Nastassja Kinski. *Variations:* Nastassia, Nastassja, Nastasya, Nastya.

NASYA (Hebrew) Miracle of God. *Variations:* Nasia.

NATA (Native American) Creator.

NATALIE (Latin) Christmas. *Notables:* Singers Natalie Cole and Natalie Merchant; actresses Natalie Portman and Natalie Wood. *Variations:* Natala, Natalee, Natalene, Natalia, Natalina, Nataline, Natalka, Natalya, Natelie, Nathalia, Nathalie.

NATANIAH (Hebrew) Gift of God. Feminine version of Nathan. *Variations:* Natania, Nataniela, Nataniella, Natanielle, Natanya, Nathania, Nathaniella, Nathanielle, Netana, Netanela, Netania, Netaniah, Netaniella, Netanya, Nethania, Nethaniah, Netina.

NATASHA (Russian) Christmas. Form of Natalie. *Notables:* Actress Natasha Richardson. *Variations:* Nastasia, Nastassya, Natashia, Tashi, Tashia, Tasis, Tassa, Tassie.

NATESA (Hindu) Lord of the dance. *Variations:* Natisa.

NATIVIDAD (Spanish) Christmas.

NATKA (Russian) Promise.

NATSUMI (Japanese) Summer. *Variations:* Natsuko, Natsuyo.

NAYANA (Hindu) Beautiful eyes.

popular names in sweden

Boys	Girls
William	Emma
Filip	Maja
Oscar	Ida
Lucas	Elin
Erik	Julia
Emil	Linnéa
Isak	Hanna
Alexander	Alva
Viktor	Wilma
Anton	Klara

NAYO (African) She is our joy.

NAZIHAH (Arabic) Trustworthy.

NAZIRA (Arabic) Equal. *Variations:* Nazirah.

NEALA (Irish) Champion. Feminine version of Neil. *Variations:* Nealie, Nealy, Neeli, Neelie, Neely, Neila, Neile, Neilla, Neille.

NECI (Latin) On fire.

NEDA (Czech) Born on Sunday. *Variations:* Nedia, Neida.

NEDAVIAH (Hebrew) God is charitable. *Variations:* Nedavia, Nedavya, Nediva.

NEDDA (English) Prosperous family. *Variations:* Neddi, Neddie, Neddy.

NEDRA (English) Underground.

NEEMA (African) Born during good times.

NEENAH (Native American) Running water.

NEFERTITI (Egyptian) Coming of the beautiful one. *Notables:* Egyptian queen Nefertiti.

NELL (English) Light. *Notables:* Actress Nell Carter. *Variations:* Nella, Nelley, Nelli, Nellie, Nelly.

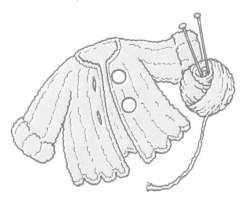

NEMERA (Hebrew) Leopard.

NENET (Egyptian) Goddess.

NEOLA (Greek) Young girl. *Variations:* Neolah.

NEOMA (Greek) New moon.

NEPA (Arabic) Walking backward.

NERA (Hebrew) Candlelight. *Variations:* Neria, Neriah, Neriya.

NERIDA (Greek) Sea nymph. *Variations:* Nereida, Nerice, Nerina, Nerine, Nerisse, Neryssa.

NESSA (English) Short form of Vanessa.

NERISSA (Greek) Sea nymph. *Variations:* Nerisa, Nerise.

NESSIE (English) Form of Agnes or Vanessa. *Variations:* Nessi, Nessy.

NETTIE (English) Form of Nanette, Annette, or Antoinette. *Variations:* Neti, Netti, Netty.

NEVA (Spanish) Snow. *Notables:* Actress Neve Campbell. *Variations:* Neve, Nieve, Nieves.

NEVADA (Spanish) Snow covered.

NEVIAH (Hebrew) Forecaster. *Variations:* Nevia.

NEVINA (Irish) Worshipper. *Variations:* Nivena, Nivina.

NEZA (Slavic) Chaste. Form of Agnes. *Variations:* Neysa.

NIA (Irish) Bright. Form of Niamh. *Notables:* Actresses Nia Vardalos and Nia Peeples.

NIABI (Native American) Fawn.

NIAMH (Irish) Bright.

NIBAL (Arabic) Arrow.

NICKI (American) Short form of Nicole. *Notables:* Actress Nikki Cox. *Variations:* Nicky, Nikki.

NICOLE (French) People of victory. Feminine version of Nicholas. *Notables:* Actresses Nicole Kidman and Nicole Richie. *Variations:* Nichol, Nichola, Nichole, Nicholle, Nicki, Nickola, Nickole, Nicola, Nicoleen, Nicolene, Nicoletta, Nicolette, Nicolina, Nicoline, Nicolla, Nicolle, Nikki, Nikola, Nikoletta, Nikolette.

NICOLETTE (French) Form of Nicole. *Notables:* Actress Nicolettte Sheridan.

NIDIA (Latin) Nest. *Variations:* Nydia.

NIGELLA (Irish) Champion. Feminine form of Nigel. *Notables:* TV chef Nigella Lawson. *Variations:* Nigelia.

NIKA (Russian) Short form of Nikita or Veronica. *Variations:* Nica, Nieka.

NIKE (Greek) Victory. *Variations:* Nika.

NIKITA (Russian) Victorious.

NILSINE (Scandinavian) Victory of the people.

NINA (Spanish) Girl; (Hebrew) Grace of God. *Notables:* Jazz singer Nina Simone. *Variations:* Neena, Ninelle, Ninet, Nineta, Ninete, Ninetta, Ninette, Ninita, Ninnette, Ninotchka, Nynette.

NINON (French) Form of Ann.

NIRVANA (Sanskrit) Bliss.

NISSA (Hebrew) Sign. *Variations:* Nisa.

NITA (Spanish) Short form of Juanita or Anita. *Variations:* Neeta, Nitali.

NITARA (Hindu) Grounded.

NIXIE (German) Water nymph. *Variations:* Nixee, Nixi.

NOELANI (Hawaiian) Heavenly.

NOELLE (French) Christmas. *Variations:* Noel, Noela, Noele, Noelene, Noeline, Noell, Noella, Noelline, Noleen, Nowell.

NOGA (Hebrew) Morning light.

NOIRIN (Irish) Honorable light.

NOLA (Irish) White shoulder. Form of Fionnula. *Variations:* Nolah, Nolana.

NOLETA (Latin) Reluctant. *Variations:* Nolita.

NONA (Latin) Ninth. *Variations:* Nonah, Noni, Nonie, Nonna, Nonnah.

NOOR (Arabic) Light. *Notables:* Queen Noor of Jordan. *Variations:* Noora.

NORA (Greek) Light. Form of Eleanor or Leonora. *Notables:* Writer/film director Nora Ephron; singer Norah Jones. *Variations:* Norah.

NORBERTA (German) Renowned northerner. Feminine form of Norbert.

NOREEN (Irish) Form of Nora or Eleanor. *Variations:* Noreena, Norina, Norine.

NORMA (Latin) From the North. Feminine form of Norman. *Notables:* Actress Norma Shearer. *Variations:* Normah.

NORMANDY (French) Area of northern France. *Variations:* Normandie.

NORNA (Scandinavian) Fate; goddess of time.

NOVA (Latin) New. *Variations:* Novah.

NOVELLA (Spanish) New little thing.

NOVIA (Spanish) Girlfriend.

NUALA (Irish) White shoulders. Form of Fionnula.

NUBIA (African) Area in ancient Africa.

NUNZIA (Italian) Messenger. Short form of Annunciata. *Variations:* Nunciata.

NURA (Aramaic) Light. *Variations:* Noor, Noora, Noura, Nurah, Nuri, Nuria, Nuriel.

NURITA (Hebrew) Flower. *Variations:* Nurit.

NYALA (African) Antelope.

NYDIA (Latin) Nest. *Variations:* Nidia.

NYLA (Irish) Champion. *Variations:* Nila.

NYUSHA (Russian) Form of Agnes. *Variations:* Nyushka.

OBEDIENCE (English) Loyalty. *Variations:* Obey.

OBELIA (Greek) Needle.

OCEANA (Greek) Ocean. *Variations:* Oceania.

OCTAVIA (Latin) Eighth. *Variations:* Octave, Octavie, Ottavia, Tavia, Tavie.

ODDRUN (Scandinavian) Point. *Variations:* Oda, Odd, Oddr.

ODE (African) Born while traveling.

ODEDA (Hebrew) Powerful.

ODELE (German) Wealthy; (Greek) Melody. *Variations:* Oda, Odeela, Odela, Odelia, Odelinda, Odell, Odella, Odelle, Odelyn, Odila, Odile, Odilia.

ODELETTE (French) Little song. *Variations:* Odelet, Odette.

ODELIA (Greek) Melody. *Variations:* Odeleya.

ODELLA (English) Wood hill. *Variations:* Odela, Odelle.

ODERA (Hebrew) Plow.

ODESSA (Greek) Long journey. *Variations:* Adessa, Odessia.

ODETTE (French) Wealthy. *Variations:* Odetta.

ODILE (French) Success in battle.

ODINA (Native American) Mountain.

ODIYA (Hebrew) Song of God.

OFIRA (Hebrew) Gold. *Variations:* Ofra.

OKSANA (Russian) Praise to God. *Notables:* Olympic gold medalist Oksana Baiul.

OLA (Scandinavian) Ancestor. *Variations:* Olah, Olesia, Olesya.

OLEDA (Spanish) Noble. *Variations:* Oleta, Olethea, Olida, Olita.

OLENA (Russian) Brilliant light. *Variations:* Oleena, Olenka, Olenna, Olenya.

OLESIA (Greek) Protector of humanity. *Variations:* Olecia, Olisha.

OLGA (Scandinavian/Russian) Holy. *Notables:* Gymnast Olga Korbut. *Variations:* Elga, Ola, Olenka, Olesya, Olia, Olina, Olka, Olli, Olly, Olunka, Oluska, Olva, Olya, Olyusha.

OLIANA (Hawaiian) Oleander.

OLINA (Hawaiian) Happy. *Variations:* Oleen, Oline.

OLINDA (Latin) Perfumed.

OLISA (African) God.

OLIVE (Latin) Olive tree. *Variations:* Olyve.

OLIVIA (Latin) Olive tree. *Notables:* Actress Olivia de Havilland; singer Olivia Newton-John. *Variations:* Liv, Olia, Oliva, Olive, Olivet, Olivette, Olivine, Ollie, Olva.

OLWEN (Welsh) White footprint. *Variations:* Olwenn, Olwin, Olwyn, Olwyne.

OLYMPIA (Greek) Mount Olympus, home of the Greek gods. *Notables:* Actress Olympia Dukakis. *Variations:* Olimpia, Olympya, Pia.

OMA (Hebrew) Devout. *Variations:* Omah.

OMAIRA (Arabic) Red. *Variations:* Omara, Omarah, Omaria.

OMANA (Hindu) Lady.

OMEGA (Greek) Final.

ONATAH (Native American) Child of the earth.

ONDINE (Latin) Little wave. *Variations:* Ondina, Ondyne, Undina, Undine.

ONDREA (Czech) Fierce woman. *Variations:* Ondra.

ONEIDA (Native American) Anticipation. *Variations:* Oneeda, Onida, Onyda.

ONELLA (Greek) Light.

ONORA (Latin) Honor. *Variations:* Ona, Onoria, Onorine.

OONA (Irish) Unity. *Variations:* Oonagh, Oonah.

OPA (Native American) Owl.

OPAL (English) Gem. *Variations:* Opalina, Opaline.

OPHELIA (Greek) Help. *Variations:* Ofelia, Ofilia, Ophelie.

OPHIRA (Hebrew) Gold. *Variations:* Ofira.

OPRAH (Hebrew) A fawn. *Notables:* Talk-show personality Oprah Winfrey. *Variations:* Ofra, Ofrat, Ofrit, Ophra, Ophrah, Ophrat, Ophrit, Orpa, Orpah, Orpha, Orphy.

ORA (Latin) Prayer. *Variations:* Orra.

ORABELLA (Latin) Form of Arabella.

ORALIE (French) Golden. *Variations:* Oralee, Oralia, Orelie, Oriel, Orielle, Orlena, Orlene.

ORMANDA (Latin) Noble.

ORANGE (English) Orange. *Variations:* Orangetta.

ORELA (Latin) Revelation. *Variations:* Oralla, Orella, Orelle.

ORENDA (Native American) Magic spell. *Variations:* Orinda.

ORETHA (Greek) Form of Aretha.

ORIANA (Latin) Sunrise. *Variations:* Oraine, Oralia, Orane, Orania, Orelda, Orelle, Oriane, Orianna, Orianne.

ORINA (Russian) Form of Irene. *Variations:* Orena.

ORIOLE (English) Bird. *Variations:* Auriel, Orella, Oriel, Oriola.

ORIT (Hebrew) Light.

ORLA (Irish) Golden.

ORLANDA (German) Famous in the land.

ORLENDA (Russian) Female eagle. *Variations:* Orlinda.

ORLY (Hebrew) Light of mine. *Variations:* Orli, Orlie.

ORMANDA (Latin) Noble.

ORNA (Irish) Pale green.

ORNELLA (Italian) Flowering tree.

ORNICE (Hebrew) Cedar tree. *Variations:* Orna, Ornit.

ORQUIDEA (Spanish) Orchid.

ORSA (Latin) Female bear. *Variations:* Orsala, Orsaline, Orsel, Orselina, Orseline, Orsola.

ORTENSIA (Italian) Form of Hortense.

ORTHIA (Greek) Straight.

ORVA (French) Golden.

ORYA (Russian) Peace. *Variations:* Oryna.

OSANA (Latin) Praise the lord. *Variations:* Osanna.

OSEN (Japanese) Thousand.

OSEYE (African) Happy one.

OSMA (English) Divine protector. *Variations:* Ozma.

OTTHILD (German) Successful in battle. *Variations:* Ottila, Ottilia, Ottilie, Otylia.

OTYLIA (Polish) Wealth.

OURANIA (Greek) Heavenly one.

OVIA (Latin) Egg.

OWENA (Welsh) Well born. Feminine version of Owen. *Variations:* Owenna, Owina.

OZARA (Hebrew) Treasure. *Variations:* Otzara.

P

PAAVANA (Hindu) Pure.

PAAVANI (Hindu) The Ganges River.

PACA (Spanish) From France. Form of Francisca.

PACIFICA (Spanish) Peaceful.

PADMA (Hindu) Lotus. *Variations:* Padmasundara, Padmavati, Padmini.

PAGE (English) Intern. *Notables:* TV host Paige Davis. *Variations:* Paige.

PAGET (English) Little page. *Variations:* Padget, Padgett, Pagett, Pagette.

PAKA (African) Kitten.

PALILA (Hawaiian) Bird.

PALLAS (Greek) Goddess of wisdom.

PALMA (Latin) Palm.

PALMER (English) Palm tree.

PALMIRA (Italian) Pilgrim. *Variations:* Palmyra.

PALOMA (Spanish) Dove. *Notables:* Fashion designer Paloma Picasso. *Variations:* Palloma, Palometa, Palomita, Peloma.

PAM (English) Short form of Pamela. *Notables:* Actress Pam Dawber.

PAMELA (Greek) Honey. *Notables:* Actress Pamela Anderson. *Variations:* Pam, Pamala, Pamalia, Pamalla, Pamelia, Pamelina, Pamella, Pamilia, Pamilla, Pammela, Pammi, Pammie, Pammy.

PANCHA (Spanish) From France.

PANA (Native American) Partridge.

PANDITA (Hindu) Scholar.

PANDORA (Greek) All-gifted. *Variations:* Panda, Pandorra, Panndora.

PANGIOTA (Greek) All holy.

PANNA (Hindu) Emerald.

PANPHILA (Greek) She loves all. *Variations:* Panfila, Panfyla, Panphyla.

PANSY (English) Flower. *Variations:* Pansey, Pansi, Pansie, Panzie, Panzy.

PANTHEA (Greek) All the gods.

PANYA (African) Mouse.

PANYIN (African) Firstborn of twins.

PAOLA (Italian) Form of Paula. *Variations:* Paolina.

PAPINA (Native American) Vine on an oak tree.

PAQUITA (Spanish) Form of Frances.

PARADISA (Greek) Garden. *Variations:* Paradise.

PARIS (Greek) The city. *Notables:* Hotel heiress Paris Hilton. *Variations:* Parisa, Parris, Parrish.

PARKER (English) Park keeper. *Notables:* Actress Parker Posey.

PARMENIA (Spanish) Studious.

PARNELLE (French) Small rock. *Variations:* Parnel, Parnell.

PARTHENIA (Greek) Virginal. *Variations:* Parthania, Parthena, Parthenie, Parthina, Parthine, Pathania, Pathena, Pathenia, Pathina.

PARVANI (Hindu) Full moon. *Variations:* Parvina.

PARVATI (Hindu) Child of the mountain.

PARVIN (Hindu) Star. *Variations:* Parveen.

PASCALE (French) Child of Easter. Feminine version of Pascal. *Variations:* Pascalette, Pascaline, Pascalle, Pascasia, Paschale.

PASHA (Greek) Of the ocean. *Variations:* Palasha.

PASSION (Latin) Passion.

PASTORA (Spanish) Shepherd.

PAT (Latin) Short form of Patricia. *Notables:* Singer Pat Benatar.

disney names

Favorite Walt Disney films are bound to inspire parents (or big brothers and sisters) to choose a favorite character's name for the new baby.

Boys	Girls
Aladdin	Alice
Chip	Ariel
Dale	Aurora
Donald	Bambi
Eric	Belle
Jiminy	Cinderella
Louie	Esmeralda
Maurice	Jasmine
Mickey	Minnie
Peter	Mulan
Phillip	Pocahontas
Sebastian	Wendy

PATIA (Spanish) Leaf.

PATIENCE (English) Patience. *Variations:* Paciencia, Patient.

PATRICE (French) Form of Patricia.

PATRICIA (Latin) Noble. Feminine version of Patrick. *Notables:* Actresses Patricia Heaton and Patricia Arquette; writer Patricia Cornwell. *Variations:* Pat, Patreece, Patreice, Patria, Patric, Patrica, Patrice, Patricka, Patrizia, Patsy, Patti, Pattie, Patty, Tricia, Trish, Trisha.

PATSY (Irish/English) Form of Patricia. *Notables:* Singer Patsy Cline. *Variations:* Patsi.

PATTY (English) Short form of Patricia. *Notables:* Actress Patty Duke; singer Patty Loveless. *Variations:* Patti, Pattie.

PAULA (Latin) Small. Feminine version of Paul. *Notables:* Singer Paula Abdul. *Variations:* Paola, Paolina, Paule, Pauleen, Paulene, Pauletta, Paulette, Paulie, Paulina, Pauline,
Paulita, Pauly, Paulyn, Pavla, Pavlina, Pavlinka, Pawlina, Pola, Polcia, Pollie, Polly.

PAULETTE (French) Form of Paula.

PAULINE (French) Form of Paula. *Notables:* Film critic Pauline Kael. *Variations:* Pauleen, Paulina.

PAUSHA (Hindu) Month in the Hindu year.

PAVANA (Hindu) Wind. *Variations:* Pavani.

PAXTON (Latin) Peaceful town.

PAZ (Spanish) Peace.

PAZIA (Hebrew) Golden. *Variations:* Paza, Paziah, Pazice, Pazit, Paziya, Pazya.

PEACE (English) Peace.

PEACHES (American) Peach fruit. Term of endearment.

PEARL (Latin) Pearl. *Notables:* Writer Pearl S. Buck; singer Pearl Bailey. *Variations:* Pearla, Pearle, Pearleen, Pearlena, Pearlette, Pearley, Pearline, Pearly, Perl, Perla, Perle, Perlette, Perley, Perlie, Perly.

PEG (English) Short form of Peggy. *Notables:* TV character Peg Bundy.

PEGGY (English) Form of Margaret. *Notables:* Singer Peggy Lee; ice-skating champion Peggy Fleming.

PELAGIA (Greek) The ocean; (Polish) Seadweller. *Variations:* Pelage, Pelageia, Pelagie, Pelegia, Pelgia, Pellagia.

PELEKA (Hawaiian) Bright. *Variations:* Beke, Bereta.

PENDA (African) Beloved.

PENELOPE (Greek) Weaver. *Notables:* Actresses Penelope Ann Miller and Penelope Cruz. *Variations:* Lopa, Pela, Pelcia, Pen, Penelopa, Penina, Penine, Penna, Pennelope, Penni, Penny, Pinelopi, Piptisa, Popi.

PENINAH (Hebrew) Precious stone. *Variations:* Peni, Penie, Penina, Penini, Peninit.

PENNY (Greek) Short form of Penelope. *Notables:* Actress/director Penny Marshall. *Variations:* Penni, Pennie.

PEONY (English) Flower. *Variations:* Peoni, Peonie.

PEPITA (Spanish) God will add. Diminutive feminine form of Pepe (Joseph). *Variations:* Pepa, Peta.

PEPPER (Latin) Pepper plant.

PERACH (Hebrew) Blossom. *Variations:* Perah, Pericha, Pircha, Pirchia, Pirchit, Pirchiya, Pirha.

PERDITA (Latin) Lost.

PERFECTA (Spanish) Perfect.

PERNELLA (Greek) Rock. *Variations:* Parnella.

PERRY (French) Pear tree; (Greek) Nymph of mountains. *Notables:* Actress Peri Gilpin. *Variations:* Peri, Perrey, Perri, Perrie.

PERSIS (Latin) From Persia. *Variations:* Perssis.

PETA (Greek) Rock. Feminine version of Peter. *Notables:* Actress Peta Wilson. *Variations:* Petti.

PETRA (Greek) Rock. *Variations:* Petrice, Petrina, Petrona.

PETRONELLA (Latin) Small rock. *Variations:* Pernel, Pernelle, Peronel, Peronelle, Petrina, Petronelle, Petronia, Petronilla, Pier, Pierette.

PETULA (Latin) Seeker. *Notables:* Singer Petula Clark. *Variations:* Petulah.

PETUNIA (English) Flower. *Variations:* Petunya.

PHEDRA (Greek) Bright. *Variations:* Faydra, Fedra, Phadra, Phaedra, Phedre.

PHEODORA (Greek) Gift from God. Feminine version of Theodore.

PHILADELPHIA (Greek) Brotherly love. *Variations:* Philli, Phillie.

PHILANA (Greek) Lover of people.

PHILANTHA (Greek) Lover of flowers.

PHILBERTA (English) Very bright.

PHILIPPA (Greek) Lover of horses. Feminine version of Philip. *Variations:* Philipa, Philippine, Phillipina, Pippa, Pippy.

PHILOMELA (Greek) Lover of music.

PHILOMENA (Greek) Beloved. *Variations:* Filomena, Philomene, Philomina.

PHOEBE (Greek) Brilliant. *Notables:* Actress Phoebe Cates. *Variations:* Pheabe, Phebe, Pheby, Phobe.

PHYLICIA (Latin) Happy. Form of Felicia. *Notables:* Actress Phylicia Rashad.

PHYLLIS (Greek) Foliage. *Notables:* Comedian Phyllis Diller. *Variations:* Philis, Phillis, Philliss, Phillys, Phylis, Phyllida, Phylliss.

PIA (Latin) Pious. *Notables:* Actress Pia Zadora.

PICABO (American) Town in Idaho. *Notables:* Skier Picabo Street.

PIEDAD (Spanish) Devotion.

PIERRETTE (French) Rock. Feminine form of Pierre. *Variations:* Perett, Perette, Pier, Pierra, Pierette.

PIETY (English) Devoutness.

PILAR (Spanish) Pillar.

PIPER (English) Bagpipe or flute player. *Notables:* Actresses Piper Laurie and Piper Perabo.

PIPPA (Greek) Short form of Philippa. *Variations:* Pip, Pipa, Pippi.

PIXIE (English) Tiny. *Variations:* Pixee, Pixey, Pixi.

PLACIDA (Spanish) Calm. *Variations:* Plasida.

PLEASANCE (English) Pleasure. *Variations:* Pleasant, Pleasants, Pleasence.

POCAHONTAS (Native American) Capricious.

POLETE (Hawaiian) Small. *Variations:* Poleke, Polina.

POLLY (English) Form of Paula or Molly. *Notables:* Actresses Polly Bergen and Polly Walker. *Variations:* Pauleigh, Pollee, Polley, Polli, Pollie, Pollyann, Pollyanna, Pollyanne.

POMONA (Latin) Apple.

POPPY (Latin) Flower. *Variations:* Popi, Poppi, Poppie.

PORTIA (Latin) Offering. *Notables:* Actress Portia de Rossi. *Variations:* Porcha, Porscha, Porsche, Porschia, Porsha.

POSY (Latin) Flower. *Variations:* Posey, Posie.

PRECIOUS (Latin) Precious. *Variations:* Precia, Preciosa.

PREMA (Hindu) Love.

PREMLATA (Hindu) Vine.

PRIELA (Hebrew) Fruit of God.

PRIMA (Latin) First. *Variations:* Primalia, Primetta, Primina, Priminia, Primula.

PRIMAVERA (Italian) Spring.

PRIMROSE (English) First rose.

PRINCESS (English) Royal title. *Variations:* Prin, Princesa, Princessa.

PRISCILLA (Latin) Old. *Notables:* Actress Priscilla Presley. *Variations:* Precilla, Prescilla, Pricilla, Pris, Priscila, Prissie, Prissilla, Prysilla.

PRISMA (Greek) Cut glass. *Variations:* Prusma.

PRISSY (Latin) Short form of Priscilla.

PRIYA (Hindu) Beloved. *Variations:* Priyal, Priyam, Priyanka, Priyasha, Priyata, Priyati.

PROMISE (Latin) Pledge.

PRU (Latin) Short form of Prudence.

PRUDENCE (Latin) Cautiousness. *Variations:* Pru, Prudencia, Prudie, Prudu, Prudy, Prue.

PRUNELLA (Latin) Small plum.

PSYCHE (Greek) The soul.

PUA (Hawaiian) Flowering tree.

PUALANI (Hawaiian) Flower. *Variations:* Puni.

PUANANI (Hawaiian) Beautiful flower.

PULUPAKI (Polynesian) Flower wreath.

PURITY (English) Pure.

PURNIMA (Hindu) Full moon.

PYRALIS (Greek) Fire.

PYRRHA (Greek) Red.

QADIRA (Arabic) Powerful.

QAMRA (Arabic) Moon woman. *Variations:* Camra, Kamra.

QUARTILLA (Latin) Fourth.

QUBILAH (Arabic) Agreement.

QUEEN (English) Queen. *Variations:* Queena, Queenation, Queeneste, Queenette, Queenie, Queeny.

QUERIDA (Spanish) Beloved.

QUESTA (French) Hunter.

QUETA (Spanish) Home ruler.

QUIANA (American) Grace. *Variations:* Quianna.

QUINBY (Scandinavian) Estate of the queen. *Variations:* Quenby.

QUINCY (English) Fifth. *Variations:* Quincey, Quincie.

QUINN (Gaelic) Adviser. *Variations:* Quincy.

QUINTELLA (Latin) Fifth. *Variations:* Quinta.

QUINTESSA (Latin) Essense.

QUINTINA (English) Fifth. *Variations:* Quin, Quinella, Quinetta, Quinette, Quintana, Quintessa, Quintona, Quintonice.

QUITERIE (French) Peaceful.

RABIAH (Arabic) Breeze. *Variations:* Rabi, Rabia.

RACHAV (Hebrew) Large. *Variations:* Rahab.

RACHEL (Hebrew) Lamb. *Notables:* Model Rachel Hunter; actress Rachel Griffiths. *Variations:* Rachael, Racheal, Rachele, Rachelle, Rae, Raelene, Raquel, Raquela, Raquelle.

RADCLYFFE (English) Red cliff. *Notables:* Writer Radclyffe Hall. *Variations:* Radcliffe.

RADHA (Hindu) Prosperity; success.

RADINKA (Czech) Lively.

RADKA (Czech) Happy.

RAE (Hebrew) Lamb. *Notables:* Actress Rae Dawn Chong. *Variations:* Raeann, Raelene, Raelyn, Ray, Raye, Rayette.

RAFA (Arabic) Well-being. *Variations:* Rafah.

RAFAELA (Spanish) God heals. Feminine version of Raphael. *Variations:* Rafa, Rafaelia, Rafaella, Rafella, Rafelle, Raffaela, Raffaele, Raphaella, Raphaelle, Refaela, Rephaela.

RAGNBORG (Scandinavian) Counsel. *Variations:* Ragna, Ramborg.

RAGNILD (German) Power. *Variations:* Ragnhild, Ragnhilda, Ragnhilde, Ragnilda, Renilda, Ranillda, Renilde.

RAHIMA (Hindu) Loving and compassionate. *Variations:* Raheema.

RAI (Japanese) Next. *Variations:* Raiko.

RAIN (English) Rain. *Notables:* Actress Rain Pryor.

RAINA (German) Powerful. *Variations:* Raine, Rainey.

RAINBOW (English) Rainbow.

RAISA (Yiddish/Russian) Rose. *Variations:* Raise, Raisel, Raissa, Raisse, Raizel, Rayzil, Razil.

RAJA (Arabic) Anticipation. *Variations:* Raga, Ragya, Rajya.

RAJANI (Hindu) Night. *Variations:* Rajana, Rajni.

RAKU (Japanese) Pleasure.

RALPHINA (English) Wolf-counselor. Feminine version of Ralph. *Variations:* Ralphine.

RAMONA (Spanish) Wise protector. Feminine version of Raymond. *Notables:* Children's book character Ramona Quimby.

RAN (Japanese) Water lily.

RANDA (English) Short form of Miranda.

RANDI (English) Feminine form of Randy or short form of Miranda. *Variations:* Rande, Randee, Randey, Randie.

RANI (Hindu) Queen. *Variations:* Rania, Ranique, Ranita.

RANITA (Hebrew) Song of joy. *Variations:* Ranice, Ranit, Ranite, Ranitra, Ranitta.

RANYA (Hindu) To gaze.

RAQUEL (Spanish) Lamb. Form of Rachel. *Notables:* Actress Raquel Welch.

---

seeing the forest for the trees

If you're an outdoorsy type who loves nature, these names will evoke the majesty of forests and trees.

Boys	Girls
Ashton	Acacia
Birch	Ashley
Ellery	Hazel
Heath	Ilana
Kirkwood	Juniper
Lyndon	Laurel
Oakley	Lindsay
Oren	Magnolia
Perry	Olivia
Shaw	Ornella
Walden	Rowan
Waverly	Willow

RASHA (Arabic) Gazelle.

RASHEDA (Turkish) Righteous. Feminine version of Rashid. *Variations:* Rasheeda, Rasheedah, Rasheida, Rashida, Rashidah.

RAVEN (English) Blackbird. *Variations:* Ravenna, Ravenne.

RAYLENE (American) Combination of first name "Ray" and suffix "lene." *Variations:* Rayleen, Rayline.

RAYNA (Hebrew) Song of the Lord. *Variations:* Raina, Rana, Rane, Rania, Renana, Renanit, Renatia, Renatya, Renina, Rinatia, Rinatya.

REBA (English) Short form of Rebecca. *Notables:* Singer Reba McEntire.

REBECCA (Hebrew) Joined together. *Notables:* Model/actress Rebecca Romijn; basketball player Rebecca Lobo. *Variations:* Becca, Becky, Reba, Rebbecca, Rebbie, Rebeca, Rebeccah, Rebecka, Rebeckah, Rebeka, Rebekah, Rebekka, Rebekke, Rebeque, Rebi, Reby, Reyba, Rheba.

REESE (Welsh) Fiery. *Notables:* Actress Reese Witherspoon. *Variations:* Reece, Rhys.

REGAN (Irish) Descendent of the little king. *Variations:* Reagan.

REGINA (Latin) Queen. *Notables:* Actress Regina King. *Variations:* Raenah, Raina, Raine, Rainy, Rana, Rane, Rayna, Regena, Reggi, Reggie, Reggy, Regi, Regie, Regiena, Regine, Reginia, Reginna, Reinette, Reyna.

REHEMA (African) Compassion.

REI (Japanese) Appreciation.

REIKO (Japanese) Very pleasant child. *Variations:* Rei.

REKHA (Hindu) Line.

REMY (French) From Rheims in France. *Variations:* Remi, Remie.

REN (Japanese) Lotus.

RENA (Hebrew) Melody. *Variations:* Reena.

RENATA (Italian/Spanish/German) Reborn.

RENEE (French) Reborn. *Notables:* Actresses Renee Zellweger and Rene Russo. *Variations:* Renata, Renay, Rene, Renelle, Reney, Reni, Renia, Renie, Renni, Rennie, Renny.

RESEDA (Latin) Flower.

RETHA (Greek) Virtue. *Variations:* Reatha.

REUBENA (English) Behold the child. Feminine version of Reuben. *Variations:* Reubina, Rubena, Rubenia, Rubina, Rubine, Rubyna.

REVA (Hindu) Sacred river. Form of Rebecca. *Variations:* Reeva.

REXANA (Latin) King and grace. Combination of Rex and Anna. *Variations:* Rexann, Rexanna, Rexanne.

REYNALDA (German) Wise adviser.

REZA (Czech/Hungarian) Harvest. Variation of Teresa. *Variations:* Rezi, Rezka.

RHEA (Greek) Flowing stream. *Notables:* Actress Rhea Perlman. *Variations:* Rhia, Ria.

RHETA (Greek) Eloquent.

RHIANNON (Welsh) Goddess. *Variations:* Rheanna, Rheanne, Rhiana, Rhiann, Rhianna, Rhiannan, Rhianon, Rhuan, Riana, Riane, Rianna, Rianne, Riannon, Rianon, Riona.

RHODA (Greek) Rose; from Rhodes. *Notables:* character from TV's *Mary Tyler Moore Show* and *Rhoda,* Rhoda Morgenstern. *Variations:* Rhodante, Rhodanthe, Rhodia, Rhodie, Rhody, Roda.

RHONA (Scottish) Rough island.

RHONDA (Welsh) Grand; good spear, or noisy. *Notables:* Actress Rhonda Shear. *Variations:* Rhonnda, Ronda.

RHONWEN (Welsh) Fair-haired. *Variations:* Ronwen, Roweena, Roweina, Rowena, Rowina.

RIANE (Irish) Feminine version of Ryan or short form of Briana. *Variations:* Riana, Reanne.

RICARDA (Italian) Powerful ruler. Feminine version of Richard. *Variations:* Rica, Ricca, Richarda, Richel, Richela, Richele, Richella, Richelle, Richenda, Richenza, Ricki, Rickie, Ricky, Riki, Rikki, Rikky.

RICKI (English) Short form of Frederica or feminine form of Ricky or Richard. *Notables:* Actress/TV host Ricki Lake; singer Rickie Lee Jones. *Variations:* Rickie, Rikki.

RIHANA (Arabic) Sweet basil.

RILLA (German) Stream. *Variations:* Rilletta, Rillette.

RIMA (Arabic) Antelope.

RIMONA (Hebrew) Pomegranate.

RIN (Japanese) Park.

RINA (Hebrew) Joy.

RINDA (Scandinavian) Ancient mythological figure. *Variations:* Rind.

RIONA (Irish) Queen. *Variations:* Rioghnach, Rionach, Rionagh, Rionna.

RISA (Latin) Laughter. *Variations:* Reesa, Rise, Risha, Riza.

RISHONA (Hebrew) Initial.

RISSA (Greek) Nickname for Nerissa, a sea nymph.

RITA (Spanish) Pearl. Short form of Margarita. *Notables:* Actresses Rita Hayworth and Rita Moreno; singer Rita Coolidge. *Variations:* Reeta, Reta, Rheta, Rhetta.

RIVA (Hebrew) Joined. Form of Rebecca. *Variations:* Reva, Rivah.

RIVKA (Hebrew) Noose. *Variations:* Rifka, Rifke, Riki, Rivai, Rivca, Rivcka, Rivi, Rivvy.

ROANNA (American) Form of Rosanna. *Variations:* Roanne.

ROBERTA (English) Bright fame. Feminine version of Robert. *Notables:* Singer Roberta Flack. *Variations:* Bobbet, Bobbett, Bobbi, Bobbie, Bobby, Robbi, Robbie, Robby, Robena, Robertena, Robertha, Robertina, Robin, Robina, Robine, Robinette, Robinia, Robyn, Robyna, Rogan, Roynne.

ROBIN (English) Robin. *Notables:* Actress Robin Wright Penn; radio personality Robin

Quivers. *Variations:* Robbin, Robbyn, Robina, Robyn.

ROCHELLE (French) Little rock. *Variations:* Rochele, Rochell, Rochella, Roshele, Roshelle, Shelley, Shelly.

RODERICA (German) Famous ruler. Feminine version of Roderick. *Variations:* Rica, Roderiqua, Roderique.

ROHANA (Hindu) Sandalwood. *Variations:* Rohan, Rohanna.

ROLANDA (German) Famous land. Feminine version of Roland. *Notables:* TV host Rolanda Watts. *Variations:* Rolande, Rollande, Rolonda, Rolonde.

ROMA (Italian) Rome. *Notables:* Actress Roma Downey. *Variations:* Romaine, Romana, Romella, Romelle, Romola, Romolla, Romula.

ROMY (German) Short form of Rosemary. *Notables:* Actress Romy Schneider.

RONA (Scandinavian) Rough isle. *Notables:* Gossip columnist Rona Barrett. *Variations:* Rhona, Roana, Ronella, Ronelle, Ronna.

RONNI (English) Strong counsel. Feminine version of Ronald and short form of Veronica. *Notables:* Singer Ronnie Spector. *Variations:* Roni, Ronnette, Ronney, Ronnica, Ronnie, Ronny.

ROSABEL (French) Beautiful rose. *Variations:* Rosabella, Rosabelle.

ROSALBA (Latin) White rose.

ROSALIE (English) Form of Rosalind. *Variations:* Rosalia.

ROSALIND (Spanish) Pretty rose. *Notables:* Actress Rosalind Russell. *Variations:* Rosalina, Rosalinda, Rosalinde, Rosaline, Rosalyn, Rosalynd, Rosalyne, Rosalynn, Roselind, Roselynn, Roslyn.

ROSAMOND (German) Horse protector; (English) Pure rose. *Variations:* Rosamund.

ROSANNA (English) Combination of Rose and Anna. *Notables:* Actress Rosanna Arquette. *Variations:* Rosana, Rosannah, Rosanne, Roseana, Roseanna, Roseannah, Rosehannah, Rozanna, Rozanne.

ROSE (Latin) Rose. *Notables:* Actress Rose McGowan. *Variations:* Rosabel, Rosabell, Rosabella, Rosabelle, Rosalee, Rosaley, Rosalia, Rosalie, Rosalin, Rosella, Roselle, Rosetta, Rosette, Rosey, Rosi, Rosie, Rosita, Rosy, Ruza, Ruzena, Ruzenka, Ruzsa.

ROSEANNE (English) Rose and Anne. *Notables:* Comedian Roseanne Barr.

ROSELANI (Hawaiian) Heavenly rose.

ROSELLE (French) Form of Rose.

ROSEMARY (Latin) Dew of the sea. *Notables:* Singer Rosemary Clooney. *Variations:* Rosemaree, Rosemarey, Rosemaria, Rosemarie.

ROSIE (English) Familiar form of Rosalind, Roseanne, or Rose. *Notables:* Comedian Rosie O'Donnell. *Variations:* Rosey, Rosy.

ROULA (Greek) Defiant. *Variations:* Rula.

ROWAN (Welsh) Tree with red berries. *Variations:* Rowanne.

ROWENA (Welsh) White-haired. *Variations:* Roweena, Rowina.

ROXANNE (Persian) Dawn. *Variations:* Roxana, Roxane, Roxann, Roxanna, Roxianne, Roxie, Roxy.

ROXY (Persian) Dawn. Short form of Roxanne. *Variations:* Roxi, Roxie.

ROYALE (French) Royal. *Variations:* Royalene, Royall, Royalle.

ROZ (English) Short form of Rosalind or Rosamund. *Variations:* Ros, Rozzy.

RUBY (English) Red jewel. *Notables:* Actress Ruby Dee. *Variations:* Rube, Rubey, Rubie, Rubye.

RUE (French) Street. *Notables:* Actress Rue McClanahan.

RUFFINA (Italian) Red-haired. Feminine version of Rufus.

RUKAN (Arabic) Confident.

RUKIYA (African) To arise.

RUNA (Scandinavian) Secret lore. *Variations:* Rula.

RUPLI (Hindu) Beautiful. *Variations:* Rupala, Rupali, Rupinder.

RUTA (Hawaiian) Friend.

RUTH (Hebrew) Companion. *Notables:* Sex therapist Dr. Ruth Westheimer. *Variations:* Ruthe, Ruthella, Ruthelle, Ruthetta, Ruthi, Ruthie, Ruthina, Ruthine, Ruthy.

RUTHANN (American) Combination of Ruth and Ann.

RUWAYDAH (Arabic) Graceful walk.

RYAN (Irish) Little king. *Variations:* Ryana, Ryann.

RYBA (Czech) Fish.

SABA (Arabic) Morning. *Variations:* Sabah, Sabbah, Sheba.

SABELLA (Spanish) Form of Isabella. *Variations:* Sabela, Sabell, Sabelle.

SABINA (Latin) Sabine, a tribe in central Italy in ancient Roman era. *Variations:* Sabeena, Sabienne, Sabine, Savina, Sebina.

SABLE (English) Black. *Variations:* Sabelle.

SABRA (Hebrew) Rest. *Variations:* Sabrah, Sabre, Sebra.

SABRINA (Welsh) Severn River in Wales. *Variations:* Sabreen, Sabrena, Sabreena, Sabrinah, Sabrinna, Sabryna.

SACHI (Japanese) Blessed. *Variations:* Sachiko.

SADHANA (Hindu) Devotion.

SADIE (Hebrew) Princess. Form of Sarah. *Notables:* Actress Sadie Frost. *Variations:* Sadee, Sadey, Sadi, Sady, Saide, Saidi, Saidie, Sayde, Saydi, Saydia, Saydie, Saydy.

SADIRA (Persian) Lotus tree.

SAFFRON (English) Flower. *Notables:* Actress Saffron Burrows. *Variations:* Saffren, Saffronia, Saphron.

SAFI (Hindu) Friend.

SAGE (Latin) Wise. *Variations:* Saige, Sayge.

SAHARA (Arabic) Desert. *Variations:* Saharah, Sahari, Sahira.

SAKARI (Hindu) Sweet one.

SAKURA (Japanese) Cherry blossom.

SALAMA (Arabic) Peaceful.

SALIMA (Arabic) Of good health. *Variations:* Saleema, Salema.

SALINA (French) Solemn. *Variations:* Saleena, Salena, Salene, Salinda, Saline.

SALLY (English) Princess. Form of Sarah. *Notables:* Astronaut Sally Ride. *Variations:* Sal, Sallee, Salley, Salli, Sallie.

SALMA (Hindu) Safe. *Notables:* Actress Salma Hayek. *Variations:* Salima.

SALOME (Hebrew) Peaceful. *Variations:* Saloma, Salomi.

SALVADORA (Spanish) Savior.

SALVIA (Latin) Healthy. *Variations:* Salviana, Salvina.

SAMALA (Hebrew) Requested of God. *Variations:* Samale, Sammala.

SAMANTHA (Hebrew) Told by God. *Notables:* Actresses Samantha Mathis and Samantha Eggar. *Variations:* Sam, Samana, Samanta, Samatha, Samella, Samentha, Sammantha, Sammee, Sammey, Sammi, Sammie, Sammy, Semanntha, Semantha, Simantha, Symantha.

SAMARA (Hebrew) Protected by God. *Variations:* Samaria, Sammara.

SAMEH (Arabic) One who forgives.

SAMIA (Arabic) Understanding. *Variations:* Samihah, Samira, Samirah.

SAMINA (Hindu) Happy. *Variations:* Sameena, Sameenah.

SAMIRA (Hebrew) Evening talk.

SAMUELA (Hebrew) God has heard. Feminine version of Samuel. *Variations:* Samelle, Samuella, Samuelle.

SANCIA (Latin/Spanish) Holy. *Variations:* Sancha, Sanchia, Santsia, Sanzia.

SANDEEP (Punjabi) Enlightened. *Variations:* Sandip.

SANDRA (Greek) Protector of mankind. Short form of Alexandra. *Notables:* U.S. Supreme Court Justice Sandra Day O'Connor; actresses Sandra Bullock and Sandra Dee. *Variations:* Sandee, Sandi, Sandie, Sandrea, Sandria, Sandrina, Sandrine, Sandy, Saundra, Sondra, Zana, Zandra, Zanna.

SANDRINE (French) Form of Sandra. *Notables:* Actress Sandrine Bonnaire. *Variations:* Sandreen, Sandrene.

SANDY (English) Short form of Sandra. *Notables:* Actress Sandy Duncan. *Variations:* Sandee, Sandi, Sandie, Sandye.

SANNA (Scandinavian/Dutch) Lily. *Variations:* Sana, Sanne.

SANTANA (Spanish) Saint. *Variations:* Santa, Santena, Santina.

SANYA (Hindu) Born on a Saturday; (Arabic) Radiant.

SAPPHIRE (Greek) Blue jewel. *Variations:* Safira, Saphira, Sapir, Sapira, Sapirit, Sapphira, Sephira.

SAPPHO (Greek) Sapphire. *Notables:* Greek poet Sappho.

SARAH (Hebrew) Princess. *Notables:* Actresses Sarah Jessica Parker and Sara Gilbert. *Variations:* Sadee, Sadie, Sadye, Saidee, Saleena, Salena, Salina, Sallee, Salley, Sallianne, Sallie, Sally, Sallyann, Sara, Sarai, Sareen, Saretta, Sarette, Sari, Sarina, Sarine, Sarita, Saritia, Sarotte, Sarra, Sarrah.

SARI (Hebrew) Form of Sarah. *Variations:* Sarai, Saray, Saree, Sariah, Sarri.

SASHA (Russian) Protector of men. Short form of Alexandra or Alexander. *Variations:* Sacha, Sasa, Sascha.

SATIN (French) Satin.

SATO (Japanese) Sugar.

SAVANNAH (Spanish) Treeless. *Variations:* Savana, Savanah, Savanna, Savonna, Sevanna.

SCARLETT (English) Red. *Notables: Gone with the Wind* heroine Scarlett O'Hara; actress Scarlett Johannsen. *Variations:* Scarlet, Scarlette.

SCHYLER (Dutch) Sheltered. *Variations:* Schuyler.

SCOTIA (Latin) Scotland.

SCOUT (English) A scout.

SEAMA (Hebrew) Treasure. *Variations:* Seema, Sima.

SEANA (Irish) Form of Shawna.

SEASON (Latin) Season.

SEBASTIANE (Latin) One from an ancient Roman city. Feminine version of Sebastian. *Variations:* Sebastiana, Sebastienne.

SEDONA Name of a town in Arizona.

SEFARINA (Spanish) Gentle wind. Form of Zephyr.

SELA (Polynesian) Princess. *Notables:* Actress Sela Ward.

SELENA (Spanish) Goddess of the moon. *Notables:* Tejano singer Selena Quintanilla Perez. *Variations:* Celena, Celina, Celinda, Celine, Celyna, Salena, Salina, Salinah, Sela, Selene, Selina, Selinda, Seline, Sena.

SELIMA (Hebrew) Peace. *Variations:* Selimah.

SELMA (German) God helmet. *Notables:* Actress Selma Blair. *Variations:* Anselma, Selmah, Zelma.

SENALDA (Spanish) Sign.

SENECA (Native American) Tribal name.

SEPTEMBER (English) Month.

SEPTIMA (Latin) Seventh.

SEQUOIA (Native American) Redwood tree.

SERACH (Hebrew) Plenty.

SERAPHINA (Hebrew) Fiery one. *Variations:* Sarafina, Serafina, Serafine, Seraphine, Serofina.

SERENA (Latin) Serene. *Notables:* Tennis pro Serena Williams. *Variations:* Sareen, Sarena, Sarene, Sarina, Sarine, Sereena, Serenah, Serenna, Serina.

SERENITY (Latin) Peaceful.

SEVILLA (Spanish) From Seville, Spain.

SHAINA (Yiddish) Beautiful. *Variations:* Shaine, Shanie, Shayna, Shayndel, Sheina.

SHAKIRA (Arabic) Thankful. *Notables:* Singer Shakira. *Variations:* Shakera, Shaketa, Shakirah, Shakirra.

SHALENA (African-American) Newly created.

SHALIMAR (Pakistani) Of the Shalimar Gardens.

SHALOM (Hebrew) Peace. *Notables:* Actress/model Shalom Harlow.

SHALONDA (African-American) Newly created.

SHAMICA (African-American) Newly created. *Variations:* Shameeka, Shameka, Shamika, Shamikah.

SHAMIRA (Hebrew) Guardian.

SHANA (Hebrew) God is gracious. *Notables:* TV news journalist Shana Alexander. *Variations:* Shane, Shania, Shanna.

SHANDRA (African-American) Variation of Sandra.

SHANELLE (African-American) Newly created.

SHANIA (Native American) On my way. *Notables:* Singer Shania Twain.

SHANICE (African-American) Newly created. *Variations:* Shaneice, Shanese, Shaniece, Shanise, Shannice.

SHANIKA (African-American) Newly created. *Variations:* Shaneeka, Shaneeke, Shanicka, Shanikah, Shaniqua, Shanique.

SHANNON (Irish) Ancient. *Notables:* Actress Shannon Dougherty. *Variations:* Shanan, Shann, Shanna, Shannah, Shannan, Shannen, Shannie, Shanon.

SHARI (English) A plain. Form of Sharon. *Notables:* Puppeteer Shari Lewis.

SHARLENE (English) Woman. Feminine version of Charles. *Variations:* Sharleen, Sharleyne, Sharlina, Sharline, Sharlyne.

SHARMAINE (Latin) Roman clan name. *Variations:* Sharma, Sharmain, Sharman, Sharmane, Sharmayne, Sharmian, Sharmine, Sharmyn.

SHARON (Hebrew) A plain. *Notables:* Actress Sharon Stone. *Variations:* Sharan, Sharen, Sharin, Sharona, Sharonda, Sharone, Sharran, Sharren, Sharron, Sharronda, Sharronne, Sharyn, Sheren, Sheron, Sherryn.

SHASTA (American) Mountain in Oregon.

SHAUNA (Hebrew) God is good. Feminine variation of John. *Variations:* Seana, Shaunda, Shaune, Shauneen, Shaunna, Shawna, Shawnda, Shawnna.

SHAVONNE (Hebrew) God is good; (Irish) Form of Siobhan (feminine for John). *Variations:* Shavon, Shavone, Shevon, Shevonne, Shivonne, Shyvon, Shyvonne.

SHAWN (Hebrew) God is good. Another feminine variation of Shawn (John). *Notables:* Singer Shawn Colvin; actress Sean Young. *Variations:* Sean, Shawnee, Shawni.

SHAYLA (Irish) Form of Shea. *Variations:* Shaela, Shaylyn, Sheyla.

SHAYLEEN (African-American) Unknown definition.

SHEA (Irish) Fairy castle. *Variations:* Shae, Shay, Shaye, Shayla, Shaylee.

SHEBA (Hebrew) Pledged daughter. Short for Bathsheba.

SHEENA (Irish) Form of Jane. *Notables:* Singer Sheena Easton. *Variations:* Shena.

SHEILA (Latin) Blind. *Notables:* Singer Sheila E.; actress Sheila Kelly. *Variations:* Selia, Sheela, Shelagh, Shelia, Shila.

SHELBY (English) Estate on a ledge. *Notables:* Singer Shelby Lynne. *Variations:* Shelbee, Shelbey, Shellby.

SHELLEY (English) Meadow on a ledge. *Notables:* Actresses Shelley Winters and Shelley Fabares. *Variations:* Shellee, Shelli, Shellie, Shelly.

SHENANDOAH (Native American) Beautiful girl from the stars.

SHERA (Aramaic) Light. *Variations:* Sheera, Sherah.

SHERIDAN (Irish) Wild. *Variations:* Sherida, Sheriden, Sheridon.

SHERRY (French) Dearest. *Notables:* Film producer Sherry Lansing. *Variations:* Cheri, Cherie, Sheree, Sheri, Sherissa, Sherita, Sherri, Sherrie.

SHERYL (French) Dearest. *Notables:* Singer Sheryl Crow. *Variations:* Cheryl, Cheril, Sheril, Sherill, Sherilyn.

SHEVONNE (Irish) God is gracious. Form of Siobhan. *Variations:* Shevon.

SHIFRA (Hebrew) Beautiful. *Variations:* Shifrah, Shiphrah.

SHILOH (Hebrew) God's gift. *Variations:* Shilo.

SHIRA (Hebrew) Song. *Variations:* Shiri.

SHIRLEY (English) Bright meadow. *Notables:* Child star Shirley Temple; actresses Shirley Jones, Shirley Jackson, and Shirley MacLaine. *Variations:* Shirl, Shirlean, Shirlee, Shirleen, Shirlene, Shirly, Shirlynn, Shurly.

SHIVANI (Hindu) Life and death. *Variations:* Shiva, Shivana, Shivanie.

SHONA (Scottish) God is good. Feminine variation of John. *Variations:* Shonah, Shonda, Shondi, Shone.

SHOSHANA (Hebrew) Lily. Form of Susan. *Variations:* Shosha, Shoshanah, Shoshanna.

SHU (Chinese) Tender.

SHULA (Arabic) Flaming.

SHYLA (Hindu) The goddess Parvati.

SIBYL (Greek) Seer, oracle. *Variations:* Sibbell, Sibel, Sibella, Sibelle, Sibilla, Sibyll, Sibylla, Sybel, Sybella, Sybelle, Sybil, Sybilla, Sybille.

SIDONIE (French) From Sidon, a town in the ancient Middle East. *Variations:* Sidaine, Sidonia, Sidony, Sydonia, Syndonia.

SIDRA (Latin) Stars. *Variations:* Cidra, Cydra, Sidri, Sidria, Sydra.

begins with "sha"

Taking a girls' name and adding the prefix "Sha" will create a whole new and interesting name. Here are popular variations to consider.

Shadrika	Shanida
Shajuana	Shaniqua
Shakayla	Shanisa
Shakera	Shantina
Shaleah	Shantora
Shaleisha	Shantrice
Shalena	Shaquila
Shalonda	Sharissa
Shamika	Sharonda
Shaneisha	Shatoya
Shaneka	Shavonne
Shanice	Shawanna

popular names in japan

Boys	Girls
Shun	Misaki
Takumi	Aoi
Shou	Nanami
Ren	Miu
Shouta	Riko
Souta	Miyu
Kaito	Moe
Kenta	Mitsuki
Daiki	Yuuka
Yuu	Rin

SIENA (Italian) Town of Siena, Italy. *Notables:* Actress Sienna Miller. *Variations:* Sienna.

SIERRA (Spanish) Mountain range. *Variations:* Siera.

SIGNE (Scandinavian) New victory. *Variations:* Signa, Signi, Signild, Signilda, Signilde.

SIGOURNEY (English) Conquerer. *Notables:* Actress Sigourney Weaver.

SIGRID (Scandinavian) Beautiful victory. *Notables:* Clothing designer Sigrid Olsen. *Variations:* Siegrid, Siegrida, Sigred.

SIGRUN (Scandinavian) Secret victory.

SILENCE (English) Quiet.

SILVER (English) Silver. *Variations:* Silva, Sylva, Sylver.

SIVESTRA (English) Of the forest.

SIMCHA (Hebrew) Joyful.

SIMONE (French) God listens. Feminine version of Simon. *Notables:* Actress Simone Signoret; writer Simone de Beauvoir. *Variations:* Simona, Simonetta, Simonette, Simonia, Simonina, Symona, Symone.

SINEAD (Irish) Form of Janet or Joan. *Notables:* Singer Sinead O'Connor.

SIOBHAN (Irish) Form of Jane or Joan. *Variations:* Chavonne, Chevonne, Chivon, Shiban, Shibani, Shivahn, Shivaun, Sioban.

SIRENA (Greek) Enchantress. *Variations:* Sirene, Syrena.

SISSY (American) Short form of Cecilia. *Notables:* Actress Sissy Spacek.

SKYE (Scottish) Scottish place name. *Variations:* Sky.

SKYLER (Dutch) Shelter; scholar. *Variations:* Schuyler, Skye, Skylar.

SLOANE (Irish) Raider. *Variations:* Sloan.

SOCORRO (Spanish) Help.

SOLANA (Spanish) Sunshine. *Variations:* Solenne, Solina, Soline, Souline, Soulle, Zelena, Zelene, Zelia, Zelie, Zelina, Zeline.

SOLANGE (French) Dignified. *Variations:* Solance.

SOLEDAD (Spanish) Solitude. *Notables:* TV newscaster Soledad O'Brien.

SOLEIL (French) Sun. *Notables:* Actress Soleil Moon Frye.

SOLVEIG (Scandinavian) Strong house. *Variations:* Solvag.

SONDRA (Greek) Defender of man. Form of Sandra. *Notables:* Actress Sondra Locke.

SONIA (Slavic) Wisdom. Variation of Sophia. *Notables:* Brazilian actress Sonia Braga. *Variations:* Sonja, Sonya.

SONOMA (Spanish) Place name in northern California.

SONORA (Spanish) Place name in northern Mexico.

SOPHIA (Greek) Wisdom. *Notables:* Actress Sophia Loren; singer Sophie B. Hawkins. *Variations:* Sofi, Sofia, Soficita, Sofka, Sofya, Sophey, Sophie, Sophy, Zofe, Zofia, Zofie, Zofka, Zosha, Zosia.

SPENCER (English) Dispenser. *Variations:* Spenser.

SPRING (English) Springtime.

STACY (Greek) Resurrection. Diminutive of Anastasia. *Variations:* Stace, Stacee, Stacey, Staci, Stacia, Stacie, Stasee, Stasia.

STANISLAVA (Czech) Glorious government. *Variations:* Stana, Stanuska, Stinicka.

STAR (English) Star. *Notables:* Talk-show host Star Jones. *Variations:* Starla, Starlene, Starr.

STARLING (English) Bird.

STELLA (Latin) Star. *Notables:* Fashion designer Stella McCartney. *Variations:* Estelle, Estella, Estrella, Stelle, Stellina.

STEPHANIE (Greek) Crown. Feminine version of Stephen. *Notables:* Princess Stephanie of Monaco; actresses Stephanie Zimbalist and Stefanie Powers. *Variations:* Stefania, Stefanie, Steffi, Stepania, Stepanie, Stephana, Stephannie, Stephena, Stephene, Stepheney, Stephenie, Stephine, Stephne, Stephney, Stevana, Stevena, Stevey, Stevi, Stevie.

STERLING (English) Valuable.

STEVIE (Greek) Short form of Stephanie. *Notables:* Singer Stevie Nicks. *Variations:* Stevee, Stevi.

STINA (German) Short form of Christina. *Variations:* Steena.

STOCKARD (English) Stockyard. *Notables:* Actress Stockard Channing.

STORM (English) Storm. *Variations:* Stormi, Stormie, Stormy.

SUE (Hebrew) Lily. Form of Susan or Susanna. *Notables:* Writer Sue Grafton.

SUELLEN (American) Combination of Sue and Ellen. *Variations:* SueEllen.

SUGAR (American) Sugar.

SUKEY (English) Form of Susan. *Variations:* Sokie, Sookie, Sooky, Suki, Sukie, Suky.

SUMMER (English) The season. *Variations:* Somer, Sommer.

SUNNY (English) Sunny and bright. *Variations:* Sunni.

SUNSHINE (English) Sun. *Variations:* Sunita, Sunni, Sunnie, Sunny.

SURYA (Sanskrit) Sun god.

SUSAN (Hebrew) Lily. *Notables:* Actresses Susan Sarandon and Susan Lucci. *Variations:* Susann, Susanna, Susannah, Susanne, Susetta, Susette, Susi, Susie, Susy, Suzane, Suzanna, Suzannah, Suzanne, Suzetta, Suzette, Suzi, Suzie, Zsa Zsa, Zusa, Zuza.

SUSANNA (Hebrew) Form of Susan. *Notables:* Singer Susanna Hoff; actress Susannah York. *Variations:* Susana, Susannah, Suzanna.

SUSIE (American) Nickname for Susan and Susanna. *Notables:* Financial guru Suze Orman; comedian Susie Essman. *Variations:* Susi, Susy, Suze, Suzey, Suzi, Suzie.

SUZANNE (French) Form of Susan. *Notables:* Actresses Suzanne Somers and Suzanne Pleshette. *Variations:* Susanne.

SUZETTE (French) Form of Susan.

SVETLANA (Czech) Star. *Variations:* Svetla, Svetlanka, Svetluse, Svetluvska.

SWANHILD (English) Battle swan. *Variations:* Swanhilda.

SYBIL (Greek) Prophet. *Variations:* Sibyl, Sybill, Sybille, Sybyl.

SYDNEY (French) St. Denis. Feminine version of Sidney. *Variations:* Sidney, Syd, Sydnie, Sydny.

SYLVAN (Latin) Forest. *Variations:* Silvaine, Silvana, Silvania, Silvanna, Silvia, Silviana.

SYLVIA (Latin) From the forest. *Notables:* Writer Sylvia Plath; psychic Sylvia Browne. *Variations:* Silvana, Silvia, Silvianne, Silvie, Sylva, Sylvana, Sylvanna, Sylvee, Sylvie.

SYMPHONY (Greek) Symphony.

SYREETA (Arabic) Companion. *Variations:* Sireeta, Sirita, Syrita.

TABIA (African) Talented.

TABINA (Arabic) Follower of Mohammed.

TABITHA (Aramaic) Gazelle. *Notables:* TV reporter Tabitha Soren. *Variations:* Tabatha, Tabbitha, Tabby, Tabetha, Tabotha, Tabytha.

TACEY (English) Quiet. *Variations:* Tace, Taci, Tacie, Tacita, Tacy.

TACITA (Latin) Silent.

TAFFY (Welsh) Beloved. *Variations:* Taffee, Taffey, Taffi.

TAHIRA (Arabic) Pure. *Variations:* Tahera, Tahere, Taheria, Tahirah.

TAKARA (Japanese) Treasure.

TALA (Native American) Stalking wolf.

TALIA (Hebrew) Dew; (Greek) Blossoming. *Notables:* Actress Talia Shire. *Variations:* Talie, Talley, Tallie, Tally, Talora, Talya, Thalie, Thalya.

TALINA (American) Combination of Talia and Lina. *Variations:* Talin, Talinda, Taline, Talyn.

TALISA (African-American/Hebrew) Devoted to God. *Notables:* Actress Talisa Soto. *Variations:* Talisha, Talisia, Talissa, Talyssa, Telisa.

TALISE (Native American) Beautiful water.

TALITHA (English) Girl. *Variations:* Taleetha, Taletha, Talicia, Talisha, Talita.

TALLIS (English) Forest. *Variations:* Talice, Talisa, Talise, Tallys.

TALLULAH (Native American) Leaping water. *Notables:* Actress Tallulah Bankhead. *Variations:* Tallula, Talula, Talulah, Talulla.

TALLY (English) Short form of Talia. *Variations:* Tallee, Talley, Talli, Tallie.

TALMA (Hebrew) Hill.

TAM (Vietnamese) Heart.

TAMA (Japanese) Jewel. *Notables:* Writer Tama Janowitz.

TAMARA (Hebrew) Palm tree. *Variations:* Tama, Tamah, Tamar, Tamarah, Tamarra, Tamera, Tami, Tamma, Tammara, Tammee, Tammera, Tammey, Tammie, Tammy, Tamor, Tamour, Tamra, Thamar, Thamara, Thamarra.

TAMASINE (English) Twin. Feminine version of Thomas. *Variations:* Tamasin, Tamsin, Tamsyn, Tamzen, Tamzin.

TAMMY (English) Twin; (Hebrew) Familiar form of Tamara. *Notables:* Singer Tammy Wynette. *Variations:* Tami, Tammi, Tammie.

TAMRA (Hebrew) Short form of Tamara. *Variations:* Tamrah.

TANDY (English) Team. *Variations:* Tanda, Tandi, Tandie, Tandra.

TANEISHA (African-American) Newly created. *Variations:* Taneesha, Tanesha, Taneshea, Tanicha, Taniesha, Tanisha, Tanitia, Tannicia, Tannisha, Tenecia, Teneesha, Teneisha, Tenesha, Teniesha, Tenisha, Tinecia, Tiniesha, Tynisha.

TANIA (Russian) Fairy queen. *Variations:* Taniah, Taniya, Tannia, Tanya, Tonya.

TANNER (English) Leather worker.

TANSY (Greek) Immortality. *Variations:* Tanzi.

TANYA (Russian) Fairy queen. *Notables:* Actress Tanya Roberts; singer Tanya Tucker. *Variations:* Tonya.

TARA (Irish) Hill. *Notables:* Actress Tara Reid; ice-skater Tara Lipinski. *Variations:* Tarah, Taran, Tareena, Tarena, Tarin, Tarina, Tarra, Tarrah, Tarren, Tarryn, Taryn, Taryna, Teryn.

TARYN (Irish) Form of Tara. *Variations:* Taran, Taren, Tarin, Tarina, Tarren, Tarrin.

TASHA (Russian) Christmas. Diminutive of Natasha. *Variations:* Tashina, Tashka, Tasia.

TASMINE (English) Twin. Feminine version of Thomas. *Variations:* Tasmin.

TATE (Scandinavian) Bubbly. *Variations:* Tatum.

TATIANA (Russian) Fairy queen. *Notables:* Actress/singer Tatyana Ali. Feminine version of Tatius, ancient Slavic king. *Variations:* Latonya, Tahnya, Tana, Tania, Tanis, Tanka, Tannia, Tannis, Tarnia, Tarny, Tata, Tatianna, Tatyana, Tatyanna, Tonia, Tonya, Tonyah.

TATUM (English) Cheerful. *Notables:* Actress Tatum O'Neal.

TAURA (Latin) Bull. *Variations:* Taure, Taury.

TAVIA (Latin) Short form of Octavia. *Variations:* Tava, Tavya.

TAVIE (Scottish) Twin.

TAWANNA (American) Combination of prefix "Ta" and "Wanda." *Variations:* Tawanda, Tawanne.

TAWNY (English) Golden brown. *Notables:* Actress Tawny Kitaen. *Variations:* Tawnee, Tawney, Tawni.

TAYLOR (English) Tailor. *Notables:* Singer Taylor Dayne. *Variations:* Tailor, Talor, Tayla, Tayler.

TEAGAN (Welsh) Poet. *Variations:* Teagen, Teaghan, Teaghen, Teague, Tegan, Teige.

TEAL (English) River duck. *Variations:* Teale.

TEDDI (Greek) Short form of Theodora. *Variations:* Teddie, Teddy, Tedi, Tedia.

TEMPERANCE (Latin) Moderation.

TEMPEST (French) Storm. *Notables:* Actress Tempestt Bledsoe. *Variations:* Tempestt.

TENNILLE (French) Last name. *Variations:* Tenneal, Tenille.

TEQUILA (Spanish) Liquor. *Variations:* Takila, Taquila, Tequela, Tequilla.

TERALYN (American) Combination of Terry and Lynn.

TERENA (Latin) Roman clan name. Feminine version of Terence. *Variations:* Tereena, Terenia, Terina, Terrena, Terrina, Teryna.

TERESA (Greek) Harvest. *Notables:* Humanitarian Mother Teresa. *Variations:* Terasa, Teree, Terese, Teresia, Teresina, Teresita, Teressa, Teri, Terie, Terise, Terrasa, Terresa, Terresia, Terri, Terrie, Terrise, Terry, Terrya, Tersa, Terza, Tess, Tessa, Tessie, Tessy, Theresa, Therese, Theressa, Thereza, Thersa, Thersea.

TERRELLE (Greek) Form of Teresa. *Variations:* Tarrell, Terall, Terel, Terell, Terriel, Terrill, Terryl, Teryl, Tyrell.

TERRY (English) Short form of Teresa or Theresa. *Notables:* Actresses Teri Hatcher and Teri Garr. *Variations:* Teri, Terie, Terree, Terri, Terrie.

begins with "ta"

Adding "Ta" to the beginning of or combining it with an existing girls' name creates a whole new name. Here are some popular girls' names that begin with "Ta."

Takeisha	Taneisha
Takenya	Tanielle
Takira	Tanissa
Taleisha	Tanita
Talena	Tashara
Tamesha	Tashauna
Tamila	Tasheena
Tamira	Tashelle

fairest in the land

If your child is blond, fair-haired, or fair-skinned, you might consider these names.

Boys	Girls
Adil	Alina
Alan	Alva
Albion	Anwen
Banning	Aubrey
Bowie	Bianca
Boyd	Blanche
Dewitt	Blondie
Dwight	Candace
Elgin	Cloris
Fairchild	Elvira
Fairfax	Fiona
Finian	Fulvia
Finlay	Guinevere
Finnegan	Gwendolyn
Flavion	Jennifer
Kenyon	Rowena
Whitman	Zanthe

TESS (Greek) Reaper. Short form of Teresa. *Notables:* Actress Tess Harper. *Variations:* Tessia, Tessie.

THADDEA (Greek) Brave. Feminine version of Thaddeus. *Variations:* Thada, Thadda.

THALASSA (Greek) Ocean. *Variations:* Talassa, Thalasse.

THALIA (Greek) To bloom. *Notables:* Singer Thalia. *Variations:* Thaleia, Thalya.

THANA (Arabic) Thanksgiving; happy occasion.

THEA (Greek) Goddess.

THEDA (Greek) Short form of Theodosia. *Notables:* Silent-film actress Theda Bara.

THELMA (Greek) Willful. *Notables:* Singer Thelma Houston. *Variations:* Telma.

THEODORA (Greek) Gift of God. Feminine version of Theodore. *Variations:* Teddy, Teodora, Theadora, Theda, Theodosia.

THEONE (Greek) Godly. *Variations:* Theona, Theoni, Theonie.

THERESA (Greek) Harvest. *Notables:* St. Theresa of Avila. *Variations:* Teresa, Terese, Teresia.

THETA (Greek) Greek letter. *Variations:* Thetis.

THOMASINA (English) Twin. Feminine version of Thomas. *Variations:* Thomasa,

Thomasena, Thomasine, Toma, Tomasina, Tomasine, Tommi.

THORA (Scandinavian) Thor's battle. *Notables:* Actress Thora Birch. *Variations:* Thordia, Thordis, Thyra, Tyra.

TIA (Spanish) Aunt. *Variations:* Teia, Tiana.

TIARA (Latin) Crown. *Variations:* Tiera.

TIBERIA (Latin) Tiber River. *Variations:* Tibbie, Tibby.

TIERNEY (Irish) Noble; lord. *Variations:* Tiernan.

TIFFANY (Greek) God's appearance; (Latin) Trinity. *Notables:* Pop singer Tiffany; actress Tiffani Amber Thiesson. *Variations:* Tifani, Tiffaney, Tiffani, Tiffanie, Tiffiney, Tiffini, Tiffney.

TIGRIS (Irish) Tiger.

TILDA (German) Short form of Matilda. *Variations:* Tildie, Tylda.

TILLIE (German) Short form of Matilda. *Variations:* Tilli, Tilley, Tilly.

TIMOTHEA (Greek) Honoring God. Feminine version of Timothy. *Variations:* Timaula, Timi, Timie, Timmi, Timmie.

TINA (Spanish/American) Short form of Christina. *Notables:* Singer Tina Turner; comedian Tina Fey. *Variations:* Teena.

TIPPER (Irish) Water bearer. *Notables:* U.S. vice presidential wife Tipper Gore; actress Tippi Hendren. *Variations:* Tippy.

TIRION (Welsh) Gentle.

TIRZA (Hebrew) Kind. *Variations:* Thirza, Tirzah.

TISA (African) Ninth child.

TISH (English) Happiness. Variation of Letitia. *Variations:* Tisha.

TITANIA (Greek) Giant. *Variations:* Tita.

TIVONA (Hebrew) Nature lover.

TOBY (Hebrew) God is good. Feminine version of Tobias. *Variations:* Tobe, Tobee, Tobey, Tobi, Tobie.

TOINETTE (French) Short form of Antoinette.

TOKI (Japanese) Chance; hopeful.

TONI (Latin) Praiseworthy. Short form of Antoinette. *Notables:* Writer Toni Morrison; singer Toni Braxton. *Variations:* Tonee, Tonie.

TOPAZ (Latin) Jewel.

TOPSY (English) The topsail; on top; crazy. *Variations:* Toppsy, Topsey, Topsie.

TORA (Japanese) Tiger; (Scandinavian) Thunder.

TORI (English) Short form of Victoria. *Notables:* Actress Tori Spelling. *Variations:* Toree, Tori, Torri, Torry.

TOTTIE (English) Short form of Charlotte. *Variations:* Totie, Totti, Totty.

TOVAH (Hebrew) Good. *Notables:* Actress Tovah Feldshuh. *Variations:* Tova.

TOYA (Spanish) Form of Tory. *Variations:* Toia.

TRACY (English) Summer. Variation of Teresa. *Notables:* Singer Tracy Chapman; comedian Tracey Ullman; tennis pro Tracy Austin. *Variations:* Trace, Tracee, Tracey, Traci, Tracie, Trasey, Treacy, Treesy.

TREASURE (Latin) Treasure.

TRESSA (Greek) Short form of Teresa. *Variations:* Tresa, Trisa.

TREVA (Welsh) Homestead. Feminine form of Trevor. *Variations:* Trevia.

TREVINA (Irish) Prudent. *Variations:* Trevanna, Trevinia, Trevona.

TRICIA (English) Noble. Short for Patricia, feminine version of Patrick. *Notables:* Singer Tricia Yearwood. *Variations:* Treasha, Trichia, Trish, Trisha.

TRILBY (English) Literary name that dates from the Victorian era. *Variations:* Trilbie, Trillby.

TRINA (Greek) Pure. *Variations:* Treena, Triana, Trini, Trinia, Tryna, Trynna.

TRINITY (Latin) Triad. *Variations:* Trinita, Triniti.

TRISTA (Latin) Sad. *Variations:* Tresta, Tristan, Tristen, Tristin, Tristina, Tristyn, Trysta.

TRIXIE (English) She brings happiness. *Variations:* Trix, Trixi, Trixy.

TRUDY (German) Spear of strength. Short form of Gertrude. *Variations:* Trudee, Trudi, Trudie.

TRYPHENA (Greek) Delicacy. *Variations:* Triphena, Tryphana, Tryphene, Tryphenia, Tryphina.

TUESDAY (English) Tuesday. *Notables:* Actress Tuesday Weld.

TURQUOISE (French) Blue-green gem. *Variations:* Turkoise.

TWYLA (English) Twilight; woven. *Notables:* Choreographer Twyla Tharp. *Variations:* Twila, Twylla.

TYANA (African-American) Combination of prefix "Ty" and first name "Anna." *Variations:* Tyanna, Tyanne.

TYESHA (African-American) Combination of prefix "Ty" and first name "Aisha." *Variations:* Tyisha.

TYLER (English) Tiler.

TYNE (English) River. *Notables:* Actress Tyne Daly. *Variations:* Tine, Tyna, Tynia.

TYRA (Scandinavian) Thor's battle. *Notables:* Supermodel Tyra Banks. *Variations:* Tyrah, Tyran, Tyree, Tyria.

TZIPPORAH (Hebrew) Bird. *Variations:* Tzipora, Tzippora, Tzippi, Zippora, Zipporah.

UBERTA (Italian) Bright intellect. Form of Huberta.

UCHENNA (African: Nigerian) God's will.

UDELE (English) Wealthy. *Variations:* Uda, Udella, Udelle.

UDIYA (Hebrew) Fire of God. *Variations:* Udia, Uriela, Uriella.

ULA (Irish) Jewel from the ocean.

ULANI (Hawaiian) Cheerful.

ULIANA (Russian) Form of Juliana.

ULIMA (Arabic) Wise. *Variations:* Ullima.

ULLA (Swedish) Willful.

ULRICA (German) Wolf ruler. *Variations:* Ulrika.

ULRIKA (Scandinavian) Noble ruler. *Variations:* Ulla.

ULTIMA (Latin) The end. *Variations:* Ultimah.

ULVA (German) Wolf.

ULYSSA (Greek) Wrathful. Feminine form of Ulysses.

UMA (Sanskrit) Flax. *Notables:* Actress Uma Thurman.

UMALI (Hindu) Generous.

UME (Japanese) Plum blossom. *Variations:* Umeki, Umeko.

UNA (Irish) Lamb.

UNDINE (Latin) Wave. *Variations:* Ondine.

UNICE (English) Victorious. Form of Eunice.

UNIQUE (Latin) One of a kind.

UNITY (English) Oneness. *Variations:* Unita.

UNN (Scandinavian) Loved.

UPALA (Hindu) Beach.

URANIA (Greek) Heavenly. *Variations:* Urainia, Uraniya, Uranya.

URBANA (Latin) Of the city. *Variations:* Urbanna.

URIELA (Hebrew) Light of God.

URIT (Hebrew) Brightness. *Variations:* Urith.

URSA (Latin) Short form of Ursula.

URSULA (Latin) Little female bear. *Notables:* Actress Ursula Andress. *Variations:* Ursala, Ursella, Ursola, Ursule, Ursulina, Ursuline.

USHA (Hindu) Dawn. *Variations:* Ushas.

USHI (Chinese) Ox.

USHMIL (Hindu) Warm. *Variations:* Ushmila.

USHRIYA (Hebrew) God's blessing. *Variations:* Ushria.

UTA (German) Fortunate in battle. *Notables:* Actress Uta Hagen.

VACHYA (Hindu) To speak.

VACLAVA (Czech) More glory.

VAIL (English) Valley.

VAL (Latin) Short for Valentina or Valerie.

VALA (German) Chosen.

VALDA (Norse) Ruler. *Variations:* Valida, Velda, Vellda.

VALENTINE (Latin) Strong. *Variations:* Valence, Valencia, Valene, Valentia, Valentina, Valenzia.

VALERIE (Latin) Strong. *Notables:* Actresses Valerie Harper, Valerie Bertinelli, and Valerie Perrine. *Variations:* Val, Valaree, Valarey, Valaria, Valarie, Vale, Valeree, Valeria, Valeriana, Valery, Vallarie, Valleree, Vallerie, Valli, Vallie, Vally.

VALESKA (Slavic) Glorious ruler.

VALMA (Finnish) Loyal defender.

VALONIA (Latin) Shallow valley.

VANDA (German) Form of Wanda. *Variations:* Vandah.

VANDANI (Hindu) Honor. *Variations:* Vandana.

VANESSA (Greek) Butterfly. *Notables:* Actresses Vanessa Redgrave and Vanessa L. Williams. *Variations:* Vanesa, Vanesse, Vania, Vanna, Vannessa, Venesa, Venessa.

VANETTA (English) Newly created.

VANIA (Russian) Form of Anna. *Variations:* Vanya.

VANNA (Cambodian) Golden; (Greek) Short form of Vanessa. *Notables: Wheel of Fortune* letter turner Vanna White. *Variations:* Vana.

VANORA (Welsh) White wave. *Variations:* Vannora.

VARANA (Hindu) River.

VARDA (Hebrew) Rose. *Variations:* Vardia, Vardice, Vardina, Vardis, Vardit.

VARSHA (Hindu) Rain shower. *Variations:* Varisha.

VARVARA (Greek) Stranger. Form of Barbara.

VASHTI (Persian) Beautiful.

VASILIA (Greek) Royal. Feminine form of Basil.

VEDA (Hindu) Knowledge, wisdom. *Variations:* Veeda.

VEDETTE (Italian) Sentry. *Variations:* Vedetta.

VEGA (Arabic) Falling star; (Scandinavian) Star.

VELDA (German) Form of Valda.

VELESLAVA (Czech) Great glory. *Variations:* Vela, Velina, Velinka, Velka, Veluska.

VELIKA (Slavic) Great.

VELINDA (American) Variation of Melinda. *Variations:* Valinda.

VELMA (English) Form of Thelma; (German) Form of Wilhelmina. *Notables:* Velma Dinkley from *Scoobie Doo. Variations:* Vellma.

VELVET (English) Velvety.

VENECIA (Italian) From Venice, Italy. *Variations:* Vanecia, Vanetia, Venetia, Venezia.

VENUS (Latin) Love. *Notables:* Tennis pro Venus Williams. *Variations:* Venise, Vennice, Venusa, Venusina.

VERA (Latin) True; (Slavic) Faith. *Notables:* Fashion designer Vera Wang. *Variations:* Veera, Veira, Verasha, Viera.

VERBENA (Latin) Holy plants. *Variations:* Verbeena, Verbina.

VERDA (Latin) Young.

VERDAD (Spanish) Truth.

VERENA (Latin) True. *Variations:* Varena, Varina, Vereena, Verene, Verina, Verine, Veruchka, Veruschka, Verushka, Veryna.

VERITY (Latin) Truth. *Variations:* Verita, Veriti, Veritie.

VERNA (Latin) Springtime. *Variations:* Vernetta, Vernie, Vernita, Virna.

VERONA (Italian) From Verona, Italy.

VERONICA (Latin) True image. *Notables:* Actress Veronica Lake; *Archie* comics femme fatale Veronica Lodge. *Variations:* Veranique, Vernice, Veron, Verona, Verone, Veronice, Veronika, Veronike, Veroniqua, Veronique.

VESPERA (Latin) Evening star. *Variations:* Vespa.

VESTA (Latin) Goddess of the home. *Variations:* Vessy, Vest.

VEVINA (Irish) Kind woman.

VI (Latin) Short form of Viola or Violet.

VIANNA (American) Combination of first names "Vi" and "Anna." *Variations:* Viana, Vianne.

VICKY (Latin) Short form of Victoria. *Notables:* Comedian Vicki Lawrence. *Variations:* Vicki, Vickie, Vikki, Vikky.

VICTORIA (Latin) Victorious. *Notables:* Britain's Queen Victoria; Posh Spice, Victoria Beckham. *Variations:* Torey, Tori, Toria, Torie, Torri, Torrie, Vicki, Vickie, Vicky, Victoriana, Victorina, Victorine, Victory, Vikki, Vitoria.

VIDA (Hebrew) Beloved; (Spanish) Life. *Variations:* Veda, Veida, Vidette, Vieda, Vita, Vitia.

VIDONIA (Portuguese) Vine branch. *Variations:* Veedonia, Vidonya.

VIDYA (Hindu) Instruction.

VIENNA (Latin) Capital of Austria. *Variations:* Viena.

VIGDIS (Scandinavian) War goddess. *Variations:* Vigdess.

VIGILIA (Latin) Alert.

VIKA (Polynesian) Victory. *Variations:* Vikaheilala.

VILHELMINA (German) Will helmet. Form of Wilhelmina.

VILLETTE (French) Small town.

VILMA (Russian) Variation of Wilma.

VIMALA (Hindu) Lovely.

VINA (Spanish) Vineyard. *Variations:* Veina, Venia, Vinia.

VINCENTIA (Latin) To conquer. Feminine version of Vincent. *Variations:* Vincenta, Vincentena, Vincentina, Vincentine, Vincetta.

VIOLA (Latin) Violet.

VIOLANTE (Greek/Latin) Purple flower. *Variations:* Violanta, Violanth.

VIOLET (Latin) Violet. *Variations:* Viola, Violetta, Violette.

VIRGILIA (Latin) Bearing a rod.

VIRGINIA (Latin) Virgin. *Notables:* Actress Virginia Madsen. *Variations:* Vegenia, Vergie, Virginie, Virginai, Virgena, Virgene, Virgy.

VIRIDIS (Latin) Green. *Variations:* Virdis, Virida, Viridia, Viridiana.

VIRTUE (Latin) Virtue.

VITA (Latin) Life. *Variations:* Veeta, Vitel, Vitella.

VITALIA (Latin) Lively.

VIV (Latin) Short form of Vivian.

VIVA (Latin) Alive. *Notables:* Writer Vita Sackwell-West.

VIVECA (Scandinavian) Form of Vivian. *Notables:* Actress Viveca Fox. *Variations:* Vivecka.

VIVIAN (Latin) Full of life. *Notables:* Actress Vivien Leigh. *Variations:* Viv, Viva, Vivia, Viviana, Viviane, Vivie, Vivien, Vivienne.

VLADIMIRA (Czech) Great ruler.

VLADISLAVA (Czech) Glorious ruler. *Variations:* Ladislava, Valeska.

VONDA (English) Form of Wanda.

VONDRA (Czech) A woman's love.

VONNA (French) Form of Yvonne. *Variations:* Vona, Vonne, Vonni.

VORSILA (Czech) Little she-bear. Form of Ursula.

VYOMA (Hindu) Sky. *Variations:* Vyomika.

WAFA (Arabic) Faithful. *Variations:* Wafah, Wafiyya, Wafiyyah.

WAHEEDA (Arabic) One and only.

WAINANI (Hawaiian) Beautiful water.

WAJA (Arabic) Noble. *Variations:* Wagiha, Wagihah, Wajiha, Wajihah.

WAKANDA (Native American) Magical. *Variations:* Wakenda.

WALANIKA (Hawaiian) True image. Hawaiian version of Veronica. *Variations:* Walonika, Welonika.

WALBURGA (German) Strong protection. *Variations:* Walberga, Wallburga.

WALDA (German) Ruler. Feminine version of Waldo. *Variations:* Waldena, Welda.

WALENTYA (Polish) Healthy.

WALIDA (Arabic) Newborn.

WALKER (English) Cloth-walker.

WALLIS (English) One from Wales. Feminine version of Wallace. *Notables:* Wallis Simpson, former Duchess of Windsor. *Variations:* Wallie, Walliss, Wally, Wallys.

WALTRINA (German) Powerful people. Feminine version of Walter. *Variations:* Waltina.

WANAKA (Hawaiian) Hawaiian version of Wanda.

WANDA (German) Wanderer. *Notables:* Comedian Wanda Sykes. *Variations:* Wandi, Wandie, Wandis, Wonda, Wonnda.

WANETA (Native American) One who moves forward; (English) Pale-skinned. *Variations:* Wanetta, Wanette, Wanita, Wannette.

WANIKA (Hawaiian) God is good.

WARDA (German) Protector. Feminine version of Ward. *Variations:* Wardia, Wardine.

WARNA (German) Defender. Feminine form of Warner.

WAVERLY (English) Meadow of aspen trees. *Variations:* Waverley.

WAYNETTE (English) Wagon maker. Feminine form of Wayne. *Variations:* Waynelle.

WELENA (Hawaiian) Springtime. Hawaiian version of Verna.

WEN (Chinese) Cultured.

WENDELLE (English) Wanderer.

WENDY (English) Character in *Peter Pan*. *Notables:* Playwright Wendy Wasserstein. *Variations:* Wenda, Wendee, Wendey, Wendi, Wendie, Wendye, Windy.

WESLEY (English) Western meadow. *Variations:* Weslea, Weslee, Wesleigh.

WHITLEY (English) White field. *Variations:* Whitlea, Whitleigh.

WHITNEY (English) White island. *Notables:* Singer Whitney Houston. *Variations:* Whitnee, Whitnie, Whitny, Whittney.

WHOOPI (English) Excited. *Notables:* Actress Whoopi Goldberg.

WIKOLIA (Hawaiian) Victorious. *Variations:* Wiktoria.

WILDA (English) Willow. *Variations:* Wylda.

WILEEN (English) Form of Wilhelmina. *Variations:* Wilene, Wiline, Willeen.

WILFREDA (English) Peaceful will. Feminine version of Wilfred. *Variations:* Wilfrieda.

WILHELMINA (German) Will helmet. Feminine version of William. *Notables:* Queen Wilhelmina of The Netherlands. *Variations:* Wiletta, Wilette, Wilhelmine, Willa, Willamina.

WILLA (German) Short form of Wilhelmina. *Notables:* Writer Willa Cather.

WILLOW (English) Tree. *Notables:* TV newscaster Willow Bay. *Variations:* Willough.

WILMA (German) Short form of Wilhelmina. *Notables:* Olympic track-and-field champion Wilma Rudolph. *Variations:* Wilmette, Wilmina, Wylma.

WILONA (English) To desire. *Variations:* Wilone.

WIN (English) Short form of Winifred or Edwina. *Variations:* Wyn, Wynn, Wynne.

WINDA (African) Hunt.

WINDY (English) Breezy. *Variations:* Windee, Windi, Wyndi, Wyndy.

WINEMA (Native American) Female chief.

WINIFRED (Welsh) Holy peace. *Variations:* Win, Winifrede, Winifride, Winifryde, Winne, Winni, Winnie, Winny, Wyn, Wynn.

WINNIE (English) Short form of Edwina, Guinevere, Winifred, and Winona. *Variations:* Wini, Winni, Wynni.

WINOLA (German) Enchanting friend.

WINONA (Native American) Firstborn daughter. *Notables:* Singer Wynonna Judd. *Variations:* Wenona, Winnona, Wynona.

WINTER (English) Winter. *Variations:* Wynter.

WISDOM (English) Wisdom.

WISIA (Polish) Victorious.

WISTERIA (German) Wisteria flower. *Variations:* Wistaria, Wysteria.

WREN (English) Bird.

WYANET (Native American) Beautiful.

WYETTA (French) Small fighter. Feminine version of Wyatt. *Variations:* Wyette.

WYNELLE (American) *Variations:* Wynette.

WYNNE (Welsh) Fair, white. *Variations:* Winne, Wynne.

WYOMING (Native American) Big field. *Variations:* Wy, Wyoma, Wyome, Wyomia.

popular names in australia

Boys	Girls
Jack	Emily
Joshua	Chloe
Lachan	Olivia
Thomas	Sophie
William	Jessica
James	Charlotte
Ethan	Ella
Samuel	Isabella
Daniel	Sarah
Ryan	Emma

XANDRA (Spanish) Protector. Short form of Alexandra. *Variations:* Xan, Xandria.

XANTHE (Greek) Yellow. *Variations:* Xantha, Xanthia.

XANTHIPPE (Greek) Form of Xanthe. *Notables:* Xanthippe was the wife of Socrates.

XARA Form of Zara.

XAVIERA (Basque) New house. Feminine version of Xavier. *Notables:* Writer Xaviera Hollander. *Variations:* Xavia, Xavier, Xavyera.

XENA (Greek) Hospitable. *Notables:* Character Xena of TV's *Xena, Warrior Princess*. *Variations:* Zena.

XENIA (Greek) Hospitable. *Variations:* Xeenia.

XIANG (Chinese) Fragrant.

XIMENA (Spanish) Feminine form of Simon. *Variations:* Ximenia.

XIN (Chinese) Elegant, beautiful.

XOANA (Spanish) Variation of Joanna.

XOCHITL (Native American) Flower.

XUAN (Vietnamese) Spring.

XUE (Chinese) Snow.

XUXA (Portuguese) Form of Susanna. *Notables:* Brazilian children's TV star Xuxa Meneghel.

XYLIA (Greek) Forest dweller. *Variations:* Xyla, Xylene, Xylina, Xylona.

YADIRA (Hebrew) Friend.

YAEL (Hebrew) Mountain goat. *Variations:* Jael, Yaala, Yaalat, Yaela, Yaella.

YAFFA (Hebrew) Beautiful. *Variations:* Yafa, Yaffah, Yapha.

YALENA (Russian) Light. Form of Helen.

YALIKA (Native American) Spring flowers.

YAMINA (Arabic) Ethical. *Variations:* Yaminah, Yemina.

YAMINI (Hindu) Night.

YANA (Slavic) Gracious. *Variations:* Yanni.

YARDENA (Hebrew) To descend. *Variations:* Jardena.

YARINA (Russian) Peace. *Variations:* Yarine, Yaryna.

YARKONA (Hebrew) Green.

YARMILLA (Slavic) Market seller.

YARON (Hebrew) To sing.

YAROSLAVA (Russian) Springtime.

YASHIRA (Arabic) Wealthy.

YASMINE (Arabic) Flower. Form of Jasmine. *Notables:* Actress Yasmine Bleeth. *Variations:* Yasmeen, Yasmeena, Yasmena, Yasmene, Yasmin, Yasmina.

YASU (Japanese) Calm. *Variations:* Yasuko, Yasuyo.

YEARDLEY (English) In the meadow. *Variations:* Yardley, Yardleigh, Yeardlee, Yeardly.

YEHUDIT (Hebrew) Praise. Form of Judith. *Variations:* Yudi, Yudit, Yudita, Yuta, Yutke.

YEKATERINA (Russian) Pure. Form of Katherine.

YELENA (Russian) Light. Variation of Helen. *Variations:* Yalena.

YELIZAVETA (Russian) Consecrated by God. Form of Elizabeth.

YEMINA (Hebrew) Strong. *Variations:* Yemena.

YENENE (Native American) Sorceress.

YENTA (Hebrew) Gossiper. *Variations:* Yente, Yentele.

YENTL (Hebrew) Kind.

YESENIA (Spanish) Flower. *Variations:* Yecenia, Yesnia, Yessenia.

YESHARA (Hebrew) Direct.

YETTA (English) Ruler of the house. Form of Henrietta. *Variations:* Yette.

YEVA (Russian) Life. *Variations:* Yevka.

YIESHA (Arabic) Woman.

YIN (Chinese) Silver.

YNEZ (Spanish) Form of Agnes. *Variations:* Inez.

YOANA (Hebrew) God is gracious. Form of Joanna. *Variations:* Yoanna, Yona.

YOCANDA (Spanish) Delightful.

YOKI (Native American) Bluebird.

YOKO (Japanese) Good child. *Notables:* Artist Yoko Ono.

YOLANDA (Greek) Purple flower. *Notables:* Singer Yolanda Adams. *Variations:* Eolanda, Eolande, Iolanda, Iolande, Yalanda, Yalinda, Yalonda, Yola, Yoland, Yolande, Yolane, Yolette, Yoli, Yolonda, Yulanda.

YOLOTA (Native American) Farewell to spring.

YON (Burmese) Rabbit.

YONINA (Hebrew) Dove. *Variations:* Yona, Yonah, Yoninah, Yonit, Yonita.

YORDAN (Hebrew) Descend. Form of Jordan. *Variations:* Yordyn.

YORI (Japanese) Honest.

YOYELA (Hebrew) Rejoicing.

YSABEL (Spanish) Form of Isabel. *Variations:* Ysabella, Ysabelle.

YSEULT (French) Beautiful. *Variations:* Yseulte.

YU (Chinese) Jade.

YUKI (Japanese) Snow. *Variations:* Yukie, Yukiko.

YULA (Russian) Young. Variation of Julia. *Variations:* Yulenka, Yuliana, Yuliya, Yulya.

YURIKO (Japanese) Lily child.

YUSRA (Arabic) Rich. *Variations:* Yusrivva, Yusrivvah.

YUSTINA (Russian) Justice. Form of Justine.

YVETTE (French) Form of Yvonne. *Notables:* Actress Yvette Mimieux.

YVONNE (French) Yew wood. *Notables:* Actress Yvonne De Carlo. *Variations:* Yvetta, Yvette, Yvone.

ZABRINA (American) River in Wales. Form of Sabrina.

ZACHARI (Hebrew) God remembers.

ZADA (Arabic) Fortunate. *Variations:* Zaida.

ZAFINA (Arabic) Triumphant.

ZAHAVA (Hebrew) Golden.

ZAHIRA (Arabic) Bright. *Variations:* Zaheera.

ZAIRA (Arabic) Blossom. *Variations:* Zahara, Zahirah, Zahrah, Zara, Zaria, Zuhra.

ZAKIAH (Hebrew) Pure. *Variations:* Zaka, Zakah, Zaki, Zakia, Zakiah, Zakiya, Zakiyya.

ZALIKA (African) Well born.

ZALTANA (Native American) Tall mountain.

ZAN (Chinese) Support; favor; praise.

ZANDRA (Greek) Defender of man. Form of Sandra or Alexandra. *Notables:* Fashion designer Zandra Rhodes. *Variations:* Zondra.

ZANNA (English) Short form of Susanna. *Variations:* Zanella, Zanelle, Zanette, Zannia.

ZANTHE (Greek) Blonde. Form of Xanthe.

ZARA (Hebrew) Dawn. *Variations:* Zahra, Zarah, Zaria.

ZARIFA (Arabic) Graceful.

ZARINA (Hindu) Golden.

ZARITA (Spanish) Princess. Variation of Sarah.

ZASHA (Russian) Form of Sasha. *Variations:* Zascha, Zashka.

ZAVIERA (Spanish) New house. Form of Xaviera. *Variations:* Zavia.

ZAYIT (Hebrew) Olive.

ZAZA (Hebrew) Action. *Notables:* Classic film/TV actress Zasu Ptit. *Variations:* Zasu.

ZEA (Latin) Grain. *Variations:* Zia.

ZEFFA (Portuguese) Rose.

ZEFIRA (Hebrew) Morning.

ZEFIRYN (Polish) Goddess of the west wind.

ZEHARA (Hebrew) Light. *Variations:* Zehorit.

ZEHAVA (Hebrew) Gold. *Variations:* Zahava, Zehovit, Zehuva, Zehuvit.

ZEHIRA (Hebrew) Careful.

ZELDA (German) Woman warrior. *Notables:* Zelda, princess from popular video game.

ZELENIA (Greek) Moon goddess.

ZELENKA (Czech) Fresh.

ZELFA (African-American) Unknown definition.

ZELLA (German) Hostile one.

ZELMA (German) Divine helmet.

ZEMIRA (Hebrew) Song.

ZEMORAH (Hebrew) Tree branch. *Variations:* Zemora.

ZENA (Greek) Welcoming.

ZENAIDA (Greek) Wild dove.

ZENANA (Hebrew) Woman. *Variations:* Zena, Zenia.

ZENDA (Hebrew) Holy.

ZENOBIA (Greek) Strength of Zeus.

ZEPHYRA (Greek) Wind from the west. *Variations:* Zefir, Zephira, Zephyr.

ZEPPELINA (English) Definition unknown.

ZERA (Hebrew) Seeds.

ZERALDINA (Polish) Spear ruler.

ZERLINDA (Hebrew) Beautiful dawn. *Variations:* Zerlina.

ZERREN (English) Flower.

ZETTA (Hebrew) Olive. *Variations:* Zeta, Zetana.

ZEVIDA (Hebrew) Present. *Variations:* Zevuda.

ZHEN (Chinese) Pure.

ZHO (Chinese) Character.

ZHONG (Chinese) Honest.

ZIGANA (Hungarian) Gypsy.

ZILLA (Hebrew) Shadow. *Variations:* Zilah, Zillah, Zylla.

ZILPAH (Hebrew) Dignity. *Variations:* Zillpha, Zilpha, Zulpha, Zylpha.

ZIMRIAH (Hebrew) Songs. *Variations:* Zimria, Zimriya.

ZINA (English) Hospitable. *Variations:* Zena.

ZINNIA (English) Flower. *Variations:* Zinia, Zinnya, Zinya.

ZIPPORA (Hebrew) Little bird. *Variations:* Cipora, Tzipeh, Tzipora, Tzippe, Zipeh, Zipora.

ZIRAH (Hebrew) Coliseum. *Variations:* Zira.

ZITA (Greek) Seeker; (Italian) Little girl. *Variations:* Zitella.

ZITOMIRA (Czech) To live famously. *Variations:* Zitka, Zituse.

ZIVA (Hebrew) Brilliant. *Variations:* Zeeva, Ziv.

ZIVANKA (Czech) Alive. *Variations:* Zivka, Zivuse, Zivuska.

ZIZI (Hungarian) Pledged to God. Short form of Elizabeth.

ZLATA (Czech) Golden. *Variations:* Zlatina, Zlatka, Zlatuna, Zlatunka, Zlatuse, Zlatuska.

ZOCHA (Polish) Wisdom.

ZOE (Greek) Life. *Notables:* Actress Zooey Deschanel. *Variations:* Zoey, Zoie, Zooey.

ZOFIA (Polish) Wisdom. Form of Sophia. *Variations:* Zofie.

ZOHARA (Hebrew) Brilliance. *Variations:* Zohar, Zoharet, Zoheret.

ZONA (Latin) Belt. *Variations:* Zonah, Zonia.

ZORA (Slavic) Dawn. *Variations:* Zara.

ZORAIDA (Arabic) Charming woman.

ZORINA (Slavic) Golden. *Variations:* Zorana.

ZOYA (Russian) Form of Zoe.

ZSAZSA (Hungarian) Lily. Form of Susan. *Notables:* Actress Zsa Zsa Gabor.

ZUBAIDA (Arabic) Marigold. *Variations:* Zubaidah, Zubeda.

ZUDORA (Hindu) Laborer.

ZULEIKA (Arabic) Brilliant and beautiful. *Variations:* Zeleka, Zuleyka.

ZULEMA (Hebrew) Peace. *Variations:* Zulima.

ZURI (African) Beautiful.

ZUWENA (African) Good. *Variations:* Zwena.

ZUZANA (Czech) Lily. Form of Susanna.

ZYTKA (Polish) Rose.

the everything® baby names worksheet

girls' names

mom's favorite name picks

....

....

....

....

....

....

dad's favorite name picks

....

....

....

....

....

....

boys' names

mom's favorite name picks

....

....

....

....

....

....

dad's favorite name picks

....

....

....

....

....

....

semi-final name picks

girls' names

....

....

....

....

....

....

boys' names

....

....

....

....

....

....

final name picks

girls' first names

....

....

girls' middle names

....

....

boys' first names

....

....

boys' middle names

....

....

bibliography

Books

Lansky, Bruce. *The Very Best Baby Name Book in the Whole Wide World*. Minnetonka, MN: Meadowbrook Press, 2004.

Stafford, Diane. *50,000 Best Baby Names*. Naperville, IL: Sourcebooks, Inc., 2004.

Wallace, Carol McD. *The Greatest Baby Name Book Ever*. New York, NY: Avon Books, 2004.

Web Sites

BabyNamesWorld.com
www.babynamesworld.com

BehindtheName.com
www.behindthename.com

Chinesenames.org
www.chinesenames.org

Italian Baby Names
italian.about.com/library/weekly/aa052301c.htm

"Most Popular Names," Wikipedia
http://en.wikipedia.org/wiki/Most_popular_names

"Names by Chinaroad," Lowchensaustralia.com
www.lowchensaustralia.com/Names.htm

National Hurricane Center
☞ *www.nhc.noaa.gov/aboutnames.shtml*

"Popular Baby Names, 1880-2004," Social Security Online
☞ *www.ssa.gov/OACT/babynames*

"Popular Baby Names Around the World"
☞ *www.babynamecenter.com*
☞ *www.babycenter.com/refcap/1429674.html*

"Popular Baby Names in the UK," BabyCentre.co.uk
☞ *www.babycentre.co.uk/refcap/554645.html*

20000-Names.com
☞ *www.20000-names.com/index.htm*

THE EVERYTHING SERIES!

BUSINESS & PERSONAL FINANCE

Everything® Budgeting Book
Everything® Business Planning Book
Everything® Coaching and Mentoring Book
Everything® Fundraising Book
Everything® Get Out of Debt Book
Everything® Grant Writing Book
Everything® Home-Based Business Book, 2nd Ed.
Everything® Homebuying Book, 2nd Ed.
Everything® Homeselling Book, 2nd Ed.
Everything® Investing Book, 2nd Ed.
Everything® Landlording Book
Everything® Leadership Book
Everything® Managing People Book
Everything® Negotiating Book
Everything® Online Business Book
Everything® Personal Finance Book
Everything® Personal Finance in Your 20s and 30s Book
Everything® Project Management Book
Everything® Real Estate Investing Book
Everything® Robert's Rules Book, $7.95
Everything® Selling Book
Everything® Start Your Own Business Book
Everything® Wills & Estate Planning Book

COMPUTERS

Everything® Online Auctions Book
Everything® Blogging Book

COOKING

Everything® Barbecue Cookbook
Everything® Bartender's Book, $9.95
Everything® Chinese Cookbook
Everything® Cocktail Parties and Drinks Book
Everything® College Cookbook
Everything® Cookbook
Everything® Cooking for Two Cookbook
Everything® Diabetes Cookbook
Everything® Easy Gourmet Cookbook
Everything® Fondue Cookbook
Everything® Gluten-Free Cookbook
Everything® Glycemic Index Cookbook
Everything® Grilling Cookbook

Everything® Healthy Meals in Minutes Cookbook
Everything® Holiday Cookbook
Everything® Indian Cookbook
Everything® Italian Cookbook
Everything® Low-Carb Cookbook
Everything® Low-Fat High-Flavor Cookbook
Everything® Low-Salt Cookbook
Everything® Meals for a Month Cookbook
Everything® Mediterranean Cookbook
Everything® Mexican Cookbook
Everything® One-Pot Cookbook
Everything® Pasta Cookbook
Everything® Quick Meals Cookbook
Everything® Slow Cooker Cookbook
Everything® Slow Cooking for a Crowd Cookbook
Everything® Soup Cookbook
Everything® Tex-Mex Cookbook
Everything® Thai Cookbook
Everything® Vegetarian Cookbook
Everything® Wild Game Cookbook
Everything® Wine Book, 2nd Ed.

CRAFT SERIES

Everything® Crafts—Baby Scrapbooking
Everything® Crafts—Bead Your Own Jewelry
Everything® Crafts—Create Your Own Greeting Cards
Everything® Crafts—Easy Projects
Everything® Crafts—Polymer Clay for Beginners
Everything® Crafts—Rubber Stamping Made Easy
Everything® Crafts—Wedding Decorations and Keepsakes

HEALTH

Everything® Alzheimer's Book
Everything® Diabetes Book
Everything® Health Guide to Adult Bipolar Disorder
Everything® Health Guide to Controlling Anxiety
Everything® Health Guide to Fibromyalgia
Everything® Hypnosis Book

Everything® Low Cholesterol Book
Everything® Massage Book
Everything® Menopause Book
Everything® Nutrition Book
Everything® Reflexology Book
Everything® Stress Management Book

HISTORY

Everything® American Government Book
Everything® American History Book
Everything® Civil War Book
Everything® Irish History & Heritage Book
Everything® Middle East Book

GAMES

Everything® 15-Minute Sudoku Book, $9.95
Everything® 30-Minute Sudoku Book, $9.95
Everything® Blackjack Strategy Book
Everything® Brain Strain Book, $9.95
Everything® Bridge Book
Everything® Card Games Book
Everything® Card Tricks Book, $9.95
Everything® Casino Gambling Book, 2nd Ed.
Everything® Chess Basics Book
Everything® Craps Strategy Book
Everything® Crossword and Puzzle Book
Everything® Crossword Challenge Book
Everything® Cryptograms Book, $9.95
Everything® Easy Crosswords Book
Everything® Easy Kakuro Book, $9.95
Everything® Games Book, 2nd Ed.
Everything® Giant Sudoku Book, $9.95
Everything® Kakuro Challenge Book, $9.95
Everything® Large-Print Crosswords Book
Everything® Lateral Thinking Puzzles Book, $9.95
Everything® Pencil Puzzles Book, $9.95
Everything® Poker Strategy Book
Everything® Pool & Billiards Book
Everything® Test Your IQ Book, $9.95
Everything® Texas Hold 'Em Book, $9.95
Everything® Travel Crosswords Book, $9.95
Everything® Word Games Challenge Book
Everything® Word Search Book

Bolded titles are new additions to the series.
All Everything® books are priced at $12.95 or $14.95, unless otherwise stated. Prices subject to change without notice.

HOBBIES

Everything® Candlemaking Book
Everything® Cartooning Book
Everything® Drawing Book
Everything® Family Tree Book, 2nd Ed.
Everything® Knitting Book
Everything® Knots Book
Everything® Photography Book
Everything® Quilting Book
Everything® Scrapbooking Book
Everything® Sewing Book
Everything® Woodworking Book

HOME IMPROVEMENT

Everything® Feng Shui Book
Everything® Feng Shui Decluttering Book, $9.95
Everything® Fix-It Book
Everything® Home Decorating Book
Everything® Homebuilding Book
Everything® Lawn Care Book
Everything® Organize Your Home Book

KIDS' BOOKS

All titles are $7.95

Everything® Kids' Animal Puzzle &
    Activity Book
Everything® Kids' Baseball Book, 4th Ed.
Everything® Kids' Bible Trivia Book
Everything® Kids' Bugs Book
Everything® Kids' Christmas Puzzle
    & Activity Book
Everything® Kids' Cookbook
Everything® Kids' Crazy Puzzles Book
Everything® Kids' Dinosaurs Book
**Everything® Kids' Gross Hidden Pictures
    Book**
Everything® Kids' Gross Jokes Book
Everything® Kids' Gross Mazes Book
Everything® Kids' Gross Puzzle and
    Activity Book
Everything® Kids' Halloween Puzzle
    & Activity Book
Everything® Kids' Hidden Pictures Book
Everything® Kids' Horses Book
Everything® Kids' Joke Book
Everything® Kids' Knock Knock Book
Everything® Kids' Math Puzzles Book
Everything® Kids' Mazes Book
Everything® Kids' Money Book
Everything® Kids' Nature Book

**Everything® Kids' Pirates Puzzle and
    Activity Book**
Everything® Kids' Puzzle Book
Everything® Kids' Riddles & Brain Teasers Book
Everything® Kids' Science Experiments Book
Everything® Kids' Sharks Book
Everything® Kids' Soccer Book
Everything® Kids' Travel Activity Book

KIDS' STORY BOOKS

Everything® Fairy Tales Book

LANGUAGE

Everything® Conversational Japanese Book
    (with CD), $19.95
Everything® French Grammar Book
Everything® French Phrase Book, $9.95
Everything® French Verb Book, $9.95
**Everything® German Practice Book with
    CD, $19.95**
Everything® Inglés Book
Everything® Learning French Book
Everything® Learning German Book
Everything® Learning Italian Book
Everything® Learning Latin Book
Everything® Learning Spanish Book
Everything® Sign Language Book
Everything® Spanish Grammar Book
Everything® Spanish Phrase Book, $9.95
Everything® Spanish Practice Book
    (with CD), $19.95
Everything® Spanish Verb Book, $9.95

MUSIC

Everything® Drums Book (with CD), $19.95
Everything® Guitar Book
**Everything® Guitar Chords Book with CD,
    $19.95**
Everything® Home Recording Book
Everything® Playing Piano and Keyboards
    Book
Everything® Reading Music Book (with CD),
    $19.95
Everything® Rock & Blues Guitar Book
    (with CD), $19.95
Everything® Songwriting Book

NEW AGE

Everything® Astrology Book, 2nd Ed.
Everything® Dreams Book, 2nd Ed.
Everything® Love Signs Book, $9.95

Everything® Numerology Book
Everything® Paganism Book
Everything® Palmistry Book
Everything® Psychic Book
Everything® Reiki Book
Everything® Tarot Book
Everything® Wicca and Witchcraft Book

PARENTING

Everything® Baby Names Book, 2nd Ed.
Everything® Baby Shower Book
Everything® Baby's First Food Book
Everything® Baby's First Year Book
Everything® Birthing Book
Everything® Breastfeeding Book
Everything® Father-to-Be Book
Everything® Father's First Year Book
Everything® Get Ready for Baby Book
Everything® Get Your Baby to Sleep Book,
    $9.95
Everything® Getting Pregnant Book
Everything® Homeschooling Book
Everything® Mother's First Year Book
Everything® Parent's Guide to Children
    and Divorce
Everything® Parent's Guide to Children
    with ADD/ADHD
Everything® Parent's Guide to Children
    with Asperger's Syndrome
Everything® Parent's Guide to Children
    with Autism
Everything® Parent's Guide to Children with
    Bipolar Disorder
Everything® Parent's Guide to Children
    with Dyslexia
Everything® Parent's Guide to Positive
    Discipline
Everything® Parent's Guide to Raising a
    Successful Child
**Everything® Parent's Guide to Raising
    Boys**
**Everything® Parent's Guide to Raising
    Siblings**
Everything® Parent's Guide to Tantrums
Everything® Parent's Guide to the Overweight
    Child
Everything® Parent's Guide to the Strong-
    Willed Child
Everything® Parenting a Teenager Book
Everything® Potty Training Book, $9.95
Everything® Pregnancy Book, 2nd Ed.

Bolded titles are new additions to the series.
All Everything® books are priced at $12.95 or $14.95, unless otherwise stated. Prices subject to change without notice.

Everything® Pregnancy Fitness Book
Everything® Pregnancy Nutrition Book
Everything® Pregnancy Organizer, $15.00
Everything® Toddler Book
Everything® Toddler Activities Book
Everything® Tween Book
Everything® Twins, Triplets, and More Book

PETS

Everything® Boxer Book
Everything® Cat Book, 2nd Ed.
Everything® Chihuahua Book
Everything® Dachshund Book
Everything® Dog Book
Everything® Dog Health Book
Everything® Dog Training and Tricks Book
Everything® German Shepherd Book
Everything® Golden Retriever Book
Everything® Horse Book
Everything® Horse Care Book
Everything® Horseback Riding Book
Everything® Labrador Retriever Book
Everything® Poodle Book
Everything® Pug Book
Everything® Puppy Book
Everything® Rottweiler Book
Everything® Small Dogs Book
Everything® Tropical Fish Book
Everything® Yorkshire Terrier Book

REFERENCE

Everything® Car Care Book
Everything® Classical Mythology Book
Everything® Computer Book
Everything® Divorce Book
Everything® Einstein Book
Everything® Etiquette Book, 2nd Ed.
Everything® Inventions and Patents Book
Everything® Mafia Book
Everything® Mary Magdalene Book
Everything® Philosophy Book
Everything® Psychology Book
Everything® Shakespeare Book

RELIGION

Everything® Angels Book
Everything® Bible Book
Everything® Buddhism Book
Everything® Catholicism Book

Everything® Christianity Book
Everything® Freemasons Book
Everything® History of the Bible Book
Everything® Jewish History & Heritage Book
Everything® Judaism Book
Everything® Kabbalah Book
Everything® Koran Book
Everything® Prayer Book
Everything® Saints Book
Everything® Torah Book
Everything® Understanding Islam Book
Everything® World's Religions Book
Everything® Zen Book

SCHOOL & CAREERS

Everything® Alternative Careers Book
Everything® College Major Test Book
Everything® College Survival Book, 2nd Ed.
Everything® Cover Letter Book, 2nd Ed.
Everything® Get-a-Job Book
Everything® Guide to Being a Paralegal
Everything® Guide to Being a Real Estate Agent
Everything® Guide to Starting and Running a Restaurant
Everything® Job Interview Book
Everything® New Nurse Book
Everything® New Teacher Book
Everything® Paying for College Book
Everything® Practice Interview Book
Everything® Resume Book, 2nd Ed.
Everything® Study Book
Everything® Teacher's Organizer, $16.95

SELF-HELP

Everything® Dating Book, 2nd Ed.
Everything® Great Sex Book
Everything® Kama Sutra Book
Everything® Self-Esteem Book

SPORTS & FITNESS

Everything® Fishing Book
Everything® Golf Instruction Book
Everything® Pilates Book
Everything® Running Book
Everything® Total Fitness Book
Everything® Weight Training Book
Everything® Yoga Book

TRAVEL

Everything® Family Guide to Hawaii
Everything® Family Guide to Las Vegas, 2nd Ed.
Everything® Family Guide to New York City, 2nd Ed.
Everything® Family Guide to RV Travel & Campgrounds
Everything® Family Guide to the Walt Disney World Resort®, Universal Studios®, and Greater Orlando, 4th Ed.
Everything® Family Guide to Cruise Vacations
Everything® Family Guide to the Caribbean
Everything® Family Guide to Washington D.C., 2nd Ed.
Everything® Guide to New England
Everything® Travel Guide to the Disneyland Resort®, California Adventure®, Universal Studios®, and the Anaheim Area

WEDDINGS

Everything® Bachelorette Party Book, $9.95
Everything® Bridesmaid Book, $9.95
Everything® Elopement Book, $9.95
Everything® Father of the Bride Book, $9.95
Everything® Groom Book, $9.95
Everything® Mother of the Bride Book, $9.95
Everything® Outdoor Wedding Book
Everything® Wedding Book, 3rd Ed.
Everything® Wedding Checklist, $9.95
Everything® Wedding Etiquette Book, $9.95
Everything® Wedding Organizer, $15.00
Everything® Wedding Shower Book, $9.95
Everything® Wedding Vows Book, $9.95
Everything® Weddings on a Budget Book, $9.95

WRITING

Everything® Creative Writing Book
Everything® Get Published Book, 2nd Ed.
Everything® Grammar and Style Book
Everything® Guide to Writing a Book Proposal
Everything® Guide to Writing a Novel
Everything® Guide to Writing Children's Books
Everything® Guide to Writing Research Papers
Everything® Screenwriting Book
Everything® Writing Poetry Book
Everything® Writing Well Book